Public Relations on the Net

Winning Strategies to Inform
and Influence the Media,
the Investment Community,
the Government, the Public, and More!

Second Edition

Shel Holtz

AMACOM
American Management Association

New York • Atlanta • Brussels • Buenos Aires • Chicago • London • Mexico City
San Francisco • Shanghai • Tokyo • Toronto • Washington, D.C.

This publication is designed to provide accurate and authoritative information in regard to the subject matter covered. It is sold with the understanding that the publisher is not engaged in rendering legal, accounting, or other professional service. If legal advice or other expert assistance is required, the services of a competent professional person should be sought.

Various names used by companies to distinguish their software and other products can be claimed as trademarks. AMACOM uses such names throughout this book for editorial purposes only, with no intention of trademark violation. All such software or product names are in initial capital letters or ALL CAPITAL letters. Individual companies should be contacted for complete information regarding trademarks and registration.

Library of Congress Cataloging-in-Publication Data

Holtz, Shel.
        Public relations on the Net: winning strategies to inform and influence the media, the investment community, the government, the public, and more! / Shel Holtz.—2nd ed.
        p.   cm.
    Includes bibliographical references and index.
    ISBN 0-8144-7152-8 (pbk.)
    1. Internet in public relations.   I. Title.
HD59 .H596   2002
659.2'0285'4678—dc21

2002001993

Printing number

10   9   8   7   6   5   4   3   2   1

To my children, Benjamin and Rachel,
who still don't understand what I do for a living beyond
spending an inordinate amount of time online.
Their amusement always helps keep things in the proper perspective.

CONTENTS

"THE COMMUNICATIONS PROFESSION lags woefully behind much of the Internet community."

I wrote those words in the first chapter of the first edition of this book back in 1998. Only four years have passed since *Public Relations on the Net* first appeared; in "Web years," however, four years is an eternity. (The rule of thumb suggests that one calendar year equals ten Web years; consequently, forty virtual years have passed.) Four years or forty, that is plenty of time for the communications profession to get its act together and to begin using the Internet as a strategic communications tool.

Sadly, the profession hasn't progressed much since then. The only significant change is that research now corroborates my belief. The Council of Public Relations Firms (CPRF) commissioned a study in the summer of 2000 that was released in the first quarter of 2001. The study, titled *The New Economy Initiative: The Future Impact of the Internet on the Public Relations Industry* (which I cite frequently in the early parts of this book), notes that professionals who communicate for a living have a long way to go before they are meeting client needs and fully tapping into the new channels the Internet provides for delivering messages.

There continues, therefore, to be a need for this book. However, since four years is a long time on the Internet, there was also a need to update the book. Reading back through the pages I wrote in the late 1990s, I realized several elements could stand change.

First of all, the first edition of *Public Relations on the Net* used a fair number of pages to explain the fundamentals. What is e-mail? What is a discussion group? What is the Web? When I wrote the first edition, I was still running into a frightening number of professionals who did not have a firm grasp on the basics of these new media. It was important, therefore, to explain to practitioners new to the Net exactly what they were dealing with. I tried to draft these sections so that they were meaningful to communicators, and not merely a carbon copy of what you could find in any Internet-for-beginners book. But today, four years later, I no longer find that to be an issue. Those elementary explanations have nearly been excised, and have been relegated to an appendix.

Second, research has revealed more about the dynamics of online communication. Hundreds of research projects and studies have been completed and volumes have been written. The discussion of the many-to-many nature of communications—one of the centerpieces of the first edition—has been greatly expanded to cover new conclusions about how to communicate on behalf of institutions in a networked environment.

Finally, the case studies in the first edition were, frankly, ancient. Not that they were *bad* case studies. For the late 1990s, when the examples used were implemented, they were shining examples of public relations professionals who had figured out how to use the Internet to achieve strategic objectives. They are still good examples, but as an increasing number of practitioners integrate the Internet into their efforts, the number of sophisticated examples has increased. Virtually all of the case studies in this edition are new.

There are other changes throughout the book—new models, new ideas, and enhanced explorations of certain concepts (such as the integration of online and offline communication). In the appendixes, new books are in the bibliography and the listing of useful Web sites has been updated. In other words, almost the entire book has been revised—from cover to cover.

As always, your comments and other input are appreciated. You can e-mail me at shel@holtz.com, or send your remarks through my Web site at *http://www.holtz.com*.

Enjoy the read!

M Y APPRECIATION FOR the Internet's capabilities as a tool for achieving two-way symmetrical public relations outcomes is the result of years of contact with others who share my passion for the Net's capabilities and potential. My continued admiration goes out to all of them, including:

> My fellow members of NetGain, the first virtual consortium of electronic communications professionals: Peter Shinbach of The Birmingham Group and Tudor Williams of Tudor Williams Inc. Then there is the rest of the group that certain members of the International Association of Business Communicators (IABC) refer to as the Technology Mafia: Craig Jolley, and Charles Pizzo of P.R. Public Relations.

Others who have been influential and deserve recognition include:

> Dan Janal, author of *Dan Janal's Guide to Internet Marketing,* good friend, and regularly available conversationalist.
>
> Jeffrey Hallett, now retired, whose insight into the synchronizing of the electronic media with the transformation of the business economy has been a revelation.
>
> Don Middleberg, whose recognition of the Internet as a necessary component of communications planning has led the industry.
>
> Katherine Paine, CEO of The Delahaye Group, and Angela Sinickas, principal with William M. Mercer Inc., have raised the measurement of Internet effectiveness to an art.
>
> Carol Kinsey Goman, who never lets me forget to consider the human side of high tech.

For their continued willingness to share ideas online and off, and in no particular order: Jerry Stevenson, John Gerstner, Sheri

Rosen, David Sussman, Mike Vincenty, Matisse Enzer, Tim Hicks, Brian Kilgore, Steve Crescenzo, Sharon McIntosh, David Murray, Dan Oswald, David Skwarczek, and Peter Dean.

No listing of acknowledgments would be complete without recognizing the importance of IABC in my life. This professional association is, without question, the single most significant contributor to any success I may have achieved in my career. To the members and the tireless staff go my undying gratitude.

And, of course, my wife Michele, who claims she isn't an Internet professional, but uses it in her daily activities. That makes her a model of the Net's potential. And I also have to recognize her increasing tolerance for the amount of time I spend online, writing about being online, and talking about being online.

THE INTERNET REPRESENTS one of the most significant tools ever employed in the practice of public relations (PR). Using it to its best advantage, however, requires strategic thinking about how to apply the Net to communication efforts. Communication professionals need to understand what the medium does best and what it doesn't do as well. They need to understand the nature of audiences online, the impact of a network environment, the expectation of interactivity, and the desire to speak in and hear a human voice. Then, PR counselors need to integrate these factors into comprehensive, strategic efforts that leverage the spectrum of possibilities the Net presents.

Even as we approach the end of the first decade of the Internet as a significant factor on the media landscape, most of the communication efforts we see coming out of organizations are little more than alternatives to print. Cost savings have motivated much of the move from print to online, despite the fact that conducting an online communication effectively—to produce a measurable return on investment—is often an expensive undertaking.

A number of conditions affect the Internet's viability as a dominant communication tool, including:

⮑ *Reach*. About half the households in the United States are wired, with an even larger number of people going online at their workplaces. Critical mass of the online population has been reached.

⮑ *Ease of use*. Although some Web designers are still more interested in producing sites that impress their peers than they are in helping audiences use the site easily, it has nevertheless become easier to use the Internet. Search engines have improved. Common navigation techniques have found their way onto many sites. And, after nearly ten years of using the Net, people are more accustomed to the way it works than they were only a few years ago.

⮑ *Speed*. Telephone companies are competing with cable television companies for a share of the high-speed (or "broadband") market. Given the rapidly expanding availability of DSL and cable access, an increasing part of the population is taking advantage of broadband connections to the Internet. As for the rest, although a modem is painfully slow, it is nevertheless faster than modems were only a few short years ago.

↪ *Convergence*. Studies suggest that, within the next few years, the majority of Internet traffic will not occur over computers. Rather, it will happen on so-called Internet appliances, such as cell phones, handheld personal digital assistants (PDAs), televisions, and even kitchen appliances. (Okay, so you don't need a Web browser on your microwave, but you *would* like your microwave to be able to detect a malfunction and download the fix directly from the manufacturer, wouldn't you?)

↪ *Compression and streaming*. Watching Internet video used to be a great deal more painful than it is today. You had to download the video file (which could take hours) before launching a separate application on which to view it. Compression and streaming technologies have made it much easier to use, bringing the Web closer to a true multimedia platform.

It wasn't too long ago that these factors sounded like science fiction. In fact, in the first edition of this book, I noted that they were in development. Here we are, four scant years later, and all of them are in place.

Defining Public Relations

This book is designed to help communicators and their organizations figure out how to achieve measurable business results by using the Internet to communicate. Taking advantage of the principles and tactics outlined in these pages requires a fundamental, up-front understanding of what the term *public relations* means—at least in the context of how it can be applied effectively online. If your view of public relations is wrapped in notions of spin-doctoring and covering up problems, you won't find nifty new ways to accomplish these ignoble objectives here. Similarly, public relations (in my view) is not a synonym for *marketing*: This book is *not* about how to generate publicity for products or services, or how to brand. There are plenty of books that already adequately cover Internet marketing and publicity.

So in order to be absolutely clear, let's establish a working definition of public relations right up front:

> *Public relations is the strategic management of relations between an organization or institution and its various constituent audiences to affect business outcomes.*

Every organization has a number of strategic audiences, those constituents that can influence the company's ability to stay in business and succeed. Organizations only do business with the consent of these audiences. If these audiences revoke their consent, the company faces often insurmountable obstacles to continued operation. These audiences include:

- Customers
- Consumers at large
- Employees
- The financial community
- The media
- Communities in which organizations do business
- Government (local, regional, and national)
- Activist groups
- Academia

Each one of these audiences can be divided into subaudiences. Included in the financial community, for example, are shareholders, investment analysts, and brokers. Subaudiences can be further broken down. Among shareholders, there are institutional owners (such as mutual funds and pension funds), large individual shareholders, and mom-and-pop owners. Each audience and subaudience has different interests and issues—and consequently, different informational needs and different reasons for engaging in a dialogue and interacting with the organization. The same subdivisions can be applied to any audience. Within the media segment, there are print and electronic media; consumer and trade media; daily, weekly, monthly, and quarterly publications; large and small outlets; general and niche vehicles (for example, the difference between the *Los Angeles Times* and *The Wall Street Journal*).

Companies are organized into discrete functions that facilitate the day-to-day and long-term issues associated with getting the job done. Without an effective, strategic public relations function, these companies would encounter no end of trouble in managing all these varied and complex relationships. The representative of one department could say one thing to a regulatory agency while somebody from another department could offer a contradictory point of view to a newspaper reporter. When the inconsistency becomes a public issue, the company's credibility suffers. Furthermore, few individuals in the company, no matter how admirable their motives, would present a view that balances *all* of the organization's interests with a thorough understanding of the implications of adopting a certain position.

The professional practice of public relations, then, is the effective management of relations with all of the audiences in a manner consistent with the best interests of the organization. Of course, some PR challenges focus on specific target audiences. Later in this book, we'll look at a case study showing how the Internet was used to target "tweens" (youths who are 10, 11, and 12 years old) and teenagers with an antidrug message. But the principle is the same— ensuring a consistent message across all media to achieve the desired result.

Under this definition, where do press kits come in? Press conferences? Press releases? These are some of the *tactics* employed in a communication effort that has been developed to achieve specific measurable objectives. Campaigns that are limited to the distribution of materials and messages to audiences often do not work well. These efforts are top-down, one-way communication endeavors that do not address an audience's need to engage in an evolutionary discussion with the organization. There are even *two-way* communication processes that are ineffective, because the company holds all the cards. Sure, you may offer audiences an opportunity to submit input, but is it a real dialogue? The best public relations efforts are not only two-way but also *symmetrical*—that is, they afford both the company and the strategic audience equal opportunities to participate in the discussion and—even more important—equal opportunities to achieve their objectives. This notion is the essence of the second overarching principle of public relations necessary to take advantage of the material in this book:

> *Effective public relations efforts are designed to result in a win-win situation for both the organization and the audience with which it is communicating.*

For many, this approach to public relations may be unfamiliar. After all, the very concept of public relations has been besmirched in recent years by a minority of practitioners who embody the worst tactics associated with the profession. These practices have led many in the public to associate public relations with redefining issues, twisting facts, diverting focus, and even outright lying. Of course, the unethical and unprincipled practitioners are the ones who grab the headlines. However, the majority of people engaged in public relations go about their work quietly and rarely draw any attention.

Defining Strategic Public Relations

Now that we've defined public relations, we need to ask: What does it mean to be strategic? Simple. It means that the public relations efforts undertaken are designed to affect business outcomes consistent with the goals of the organization. For example, let's say that a company is seeking to build a new manufacturing facility. The company has taken great pains to ensure that the facility will be safe and environmentally sound. Still, residents near the proposed site may want to derail the effort. A proactive public relations campaign could be undertaken with the local community to prove the feasibility of the plan and communicate its advantages to the community, to hear concerns, and to negotiate changes that satisfy the majority of the members of the audience. By influencing the audience's opinion about the proposed site, little or no opposition surfaces—and the company is able to build its plant. The outcome is affected by influencing the audience. The influence is not wielded through misdirection, confusion, hypnosis, bribes, or any other unethical means, but rather through active engagement, honest and compelling communication, and open negotiation. These are the true skills of a public relations practitioner.

Thus, in order for a communication plan to be strategic, it cannot start with tactics. Too many online efforts begin with "We gotta have a Web site," when this actually is part of the *final* step in communication planning.

There are many communication-planning models available, including seven-step and ten-step plans. For the sake of simplicity, though, we'll narrow the steps required to develop a strategic communication plan down to the following four:

↪ *Step One:* The Goal. What are you trying to achieve? What does success look like if you achieve it? In the example cited previously, the goal would be, "Build a new manufacturing facility on the site of our choice." The goal is the outcome you are trying to attain. In a strategic communication plan, it is not a communication goal, but rather the outcome that the organization is looking for.

↪ *Step Two:* Strategies. How will you go about achieving the goal? In this example, the overriding strategy is to move public opinion so that most of the members of the local community—including influencers and opinion leaders—support the construction.

↪ *Step Three:* Objectives. Each strategy needs to have measurable objectives, or steps that must be taken to complete the strategy. In this case, one objective would be to thoroughly and candidly communicate information about the project, including everything being done to minimize environmental impact and the benefits of the project to the community. Another might be to actively engage community representatives in discussions about the project to negotiate the issues that present a concern.

↪ *Step Four:* Tactics. It is only after the goal, strategies, and objectives have been established that you can finally talk about how to go about it. How to communicate? Meetings? Newspaper articles? Advertising? E-mail? Web? Billboards? Or some combination of all of these? How to identify the opinion leaders? How to conduct the negotiations? If you start with "Let's build a Web site," you won't know how that Web site is supposed to affect the outcome!

Enter the Internet

Even the best, most altruistic efforts to communicate strategically with core audiences have been hampered by the triple limitations of time, money, and resources. There isn't enough money to staff a department to develop and implement comprehensive communication strategies with *every* audience whose activities could possibly have an impact on the organization—and no organization could afford the fees an agency would charge to handle such communications on its behalf. It is nearly impossible to identify every one of those audiences, much less establish and maintain channels of communication with them and meet their needs and address their continually evolving issues.

I remember the first time I was responsible for producing an annual report. I grabbed a piece of paper and a pen and began jotting down the audiences for the annual report. My list wound up looking like this:

- Institutional shareholders
- Individual shareholders
- Financial analysts
- Brokers
- Reporters and editors
- Employees at large
- Employees who are also shareholders
- Prospective employees
- Customers
- Prospective customers
- Strategic partners, allies, and suppliers
- Prospective partners, allies, and suppliers

Each of these audiences had separate issues, separate information needs, and unique perspectives on the company. Yet, we could only produce *one* annual report. It had to be all things to all people!

The Internet and many of its associated technologies offer a solution to these challenges. When integrated into a strategic communications effort based on solid, business-oriented objectives, the Net can make it easier to achieve those most effective win-win scenarios. That is what this book is designed to help companies, agencies, and other institutions do—apply the Internet to communication strategies that result in the achievement of measurable, bottom-line outcomes.

About This Book

In *Public Relations on the Net*, I've taken an approach to the subject that is both strategic *and* tactical. That is, the material addresses the means by which you can establish a return on investment for your online efforts *and* it suggests the various tactical tools to use as you implement your strategy.

A word of caution: Don't become giddy at the range of options available to you. By no means am I suggesting that every communicator needs to employ every tactic listed here. That is the idea behind the strategic planning process outlined earlier. You'll only apply those tactics that lead to achieving the objectives that support the strategies that affect your outcome.

Here is how *Public Relations on the Net* is structured:

Structure

Before we can understand where public relations is going on the Internet, we need to step back for a few minutes and assess where it has been and what its current state is.

Part One: Communications on the Internet

Part One begins with a report card on public relations efforts on the Internet, then covers in detail the considerations that must be integrated into any online communications activity. It looks at the ways in which electronic communications tools have changed the way audiences expect to receive and use information.

A full understanding of the Internet and its components—such as e-mail, the World Wide Web, and discussion groups—is necessary, and that is presented here as well. Part One also discusses the principles of influencing audiences online and how to monitor online activity.

Part Two: Audiences

Part Two, the heart of the book, dissects each of the key strategic audiences with which public relations professionals work. These include:

- ⇝ The media
- ⇝ Financial and investment communities
- ⇝ Employees
- ⇝ Government
- ⇝ Communities
- ⇝ Cause- and issues-oriented audiences
- ⇝ Activist groups
- ⇝ Audiences affected by organizational crises

Your company may have audiences that are not covered in specific chapters. Customers and consumers are generally targets of marketing efforts as opposed to public relations campaigns, although they certainly become a strategic audience during a crisis or when an activist makes an unanswered claim that garners significant attention. In a larger sense, though, this book will cover *all* audiences in the context of the various types of issues covered.

Part Two wraps up with a review of the various ways your organization can use the Internet to take its message directly to its smallest defined audience without relying on other media, as well as methods you can use to measure the effectiveness of your online efforts.

Appendixes and Glossary

No Internet-based book would be complete without a set of Web sites and other online resources, so the Appendixes include this information. There is also a list of recommended readings—printed materials that can supplement the information presented in these chapters. The appendixes also cover how to establish a beneficial working relationship with your Information Technology (IT) department, how to promote your online efforts, and writing for the computer screen. The book concludes with a Glossary of online terms.

Audience

This book is aimed primarily at public relations and organizational communication professionals—whether they work for corporations, in big or small agencies, or as independent practitioners—who are trying to make sense of the Internet and to figure out how to use it effectively on behalf of their companies and clients. The reach of the material in these pages, however, goes well beyond the limits of the profession. In the information economy, after all, *everyone* is a communicator! I can think of two reasons why nonpractitioners would want to understand how to communicate and wield influence on the Internet:

1. Every organization and institution has audiences with which it must communicate, but not every organization is large enough to retain a communications staff or pay a public relations agency to handle its efforts. In these cases, senior management—often the CEO—is responsible for coordinating communication efforts. Those individuals need to learn to use the online tools to achieve their objectives in the absence of a communication professional to do it for them.

2. Sadly, there are public relations practitioners out there who are not interested in learning new tools. (Worse, there are those who prefer propaganda and "spin" rather than effective, strategic public relations.) Frankly, CEOs don't care who manages the relations with constituent audiences, as long as the communication gets done. In many organizations facing this dilemma, strategic communication falls to other departments, running the gamut from human resources to investor relations to legal. The individuals in these jobs, facing the added responsibility of managing communication processes, can learn a lot from this book.

In short, every organization has audiences on which it relies to varying degrees to exist and thrive. If you are responsible in any way for managing your organization's relationship with one of these audiences, you'll find value in these pages.

PART ONE

Communications on the Internet

CHAPTER 1

A Report Card on PR
Use of the Internet

SOME PUBLIC RELATIONS practitioners have figured out what the Internet has done to communication models and channels, and have crafted innovative efforts to tap into the Internet to achieve measurable communication results.

Sadly, these are the exceptions and not the rule. For the most part, the communications profession hasn't progressed in its understanding or application of the Internet since the first edition of this book hit bookstores in 1999. At that time, I offered an excuse: The Internet is so new, I suggested, that businesses, unsure of what to do with it, are applying old uses to it. That is not uncommon, since the initial uses of any new technology are, in fact, the same things that were done with the old technology. Consider television, for example. In its infancy, television was mostly used to do what was already being done with other, older technologies. Situation comedies (such as *The Jack Benny Show* and *The Burns and Allen Show*), dramas (such as *The Shadow, Inner Sanctum,* and *Playhouse 90*), and live television broadcasts (including presidential speeches and boxing from the Los Angeles Olympic Auditorium) made the switch from radio to television. It took some time for the technology to become common enough for outside-the-box thinkers such as Rod Serling and Paddy Chayefsky to expand the scope of television's uses. Only after the technology was integrated into our culture were they able to apply new uses to television that had never been possible before.

Personal computers (PCs) followed the same path. Most of us who were around back in the mid-1980s when computers hit the workplace used our first computers for their word-processing capabilities. We replaced perfectly good typewriters with far more expensive

PCs and went to training classes to learn how to use them. Later, desktop publishing replaced the tools of publication production: X-ACTO knives, waxers, artboards, and typesetting machines. Once the PC had been around for a while, we were more likely to take advantage of new applications that could never have existed without the computer, such as relational databases and brainstorming assistants.

Finally, along came the Internet (which, although it had been around since 1969, only became part of the general landscape around late 1993). The Internet turned the computer into a communication device. That led communicators to adopt the same model: They used the computer's communication capabilities to do what they were already doing with other media. I would love to meet the individual who decided to call what we see on a Web screen "pages." For as long as there has been a public relations profession, communicators have been using print tools to create pages for distribution to audiences. Thus, the association between print pages and Web "pages" led many in the profession (not to mention cost-conscious management) to view the Web as a perfectly logical (and cheaper) alternative for distributing brochures, magazines, newsletters, handbooks, and other print-based material.

Unfortunately, what we see on the Web is not a page; it is nothing remotely like a page. And now, public relations professionals don't have the excuse of the newness of the Internet to explain away the continued use of the medium as a simple replacement for traditional one-way, top-down communication. In fact, the adoption rate of the Internet has eclipsed others. It took thirty years for radio to become a popular medium; television took thirteen years. From the time the first graphical Web browser was introduced,[1] it took only three years for the Web to penetrate as many U.S. homes.

Evidence of Lagging PR Adoption of the Net

Some practitioners will argue that they are doing a perfectly good job of integrating the Net into their public relations efforts. Most of these efforts, however, are tactical rather than strategic. A client says, "We need a Web site," and the counselor responds, "We have a unit in our agency that builds Web sites." And soon, a Web site is launched.

In fact, in a study conducted by IMT Research for the Council of Public Relations Firms (CPRF), public relations agencies characterized the impact of the Internet on the profession as an obstacle rather than an opportunity. Sixty percent of respondents cited shorter cycle times as the Internet's greatest impact on communication. Few practitioners spoke of such opportunities as tapping into online communities, shifting to network information flows, or virtual communication strategies.

The research also showed that agencies placed lower priorities on most of the opportunities afforded by new technology, compared with the authors and consultants interviewed as part of the research. Among those items getting short shrift from the agency world are:

- Wireless communication
- Data mining
- Content syndication
- Search engine optimization
- Custom Web programming
- Chat rooms
- Instant messaging
- Online bulletin boards

The only categories in which agencies showed *greater* interest were automated clip tracking, extranets (for management of relationships between the agency and its clients), and public relations campaign automation. Clearly, the tools that make it easier for the agency to do a traditional job were viewed favorably. Those that required a new way to view public relations were not.

Another part of the study revealed that agencies are less interested than their clients and the media in adopting new sets of skills required to embrace online communication. Among these are:

- Online events
- E-business strategies
- E-newsletter development
- Digital press rooms and journalist opt-in e-mail

The fact is—and this is an important point—the public does a better job of online public relations than the professionals tasked with influencing them! Consider merely a few examples:

↝ Activists opposed to the corporate takeover of a chain of small, independent radio stations identify an attorney who is on the board of the corporation, and develop a Web-based toolkit for organizing local protests against the corporation and the board member.

↝ A member of a health plan believes that the merger of his plan with another local health care provider will result in inferior patient care. He uses online discussion groups to launch a movement to oppose the merger.

↝ A tireless believer that aspartame (the active ingredient in the artificial sweetener NutraSweet) poses a health risk has spearheaded an online campaign that has spanned several years. Posts to health-related newsgroups direct concerned individuals to dozens of Web sites, an effort that has led to the proliferation of this belief. No amount of scientific information or endorsements from reputable groups (such as the American Diabetes Association) has slowed down the activist effort that has influenced countless people.

What all these efforts—and thousands more like them—have in common is that the people behind them sufficiently understand the Internet's networked nature to use it to their advantage. They are influencing audiences through active engagement and participation, not through traditional top-down, one-way communication. They are not simply building cool Web sites.

Why the Profession Is Behind

So why *is* the profession so far behind? I'd like to suggest these reasons:

↝ The industry is doing just fine without the Net, thank you very much.
↝ Practitioners do not live part of their lives online.
↝ The industry doesn't have much of a technology infrastructure.

Feeling No Pain

People everywhere, in every walk of life, are change-averse. Change is brought about only when circumstances demand it, or when the consequences of failing to change exceed the pain of change. Public relations practitioners—and, in particular, the larger agencies, which are encumbered by the same bureaucracies that hinder change in other large organizations—are no exception. And until recently, the conditions necessary to spark dramatic change had not surfaced.

In fact, the public relations industry has been doing quite well, from a profit standpoint, employing the same type of efforts it has been offering clients for years. From 1998 to 1999, industry billings increased 32 percent, according to the CPRF. With those kinds of earnings, there isn't much incentive for the leaders of these organizations to mandate a massive shift in the approach taken to public relations.

The Internet boom years added to the euphoria the agencies enjoyed. Many agencies reported turning down companies seeking public relations representation, opting to deal only with those organizations that offered the best deals; some agencies even demanded stock options in addition to hourly fees! There was so much demand for public relations activities as company after company vied for the public's attention—and the need for imaging and branding grew when companies decided it was time to issue an Initial Public Offering (IPO) of its stock. Agencies resorted to hiring warm bodies to fill positions required to handle the increasing amount of work. The result was, in many instances, truly awful public relations efforts. Magazines covering the Internet business world reported on some of the most embarrassing instances, and one publication ran a weekly column dedicated to the worst public relations effort of the last seven days. But as long as the clients kept knocking and billings kept rising, it was one big party for the industry.

Detachment

The remoteness of many public relations professionals from the Internet is another reason the industry has fallen behind in its ability to embrace the Internet as a true public relations tool.

That is not to suggest that professional communicators do not use the Internet. E-mail is a popular tool, and many agencies rely on the Web as a means of conducting client-based research. But the Web and e-mail, for all their focus, are the superficial manifestations of what the Internet is really all about: community!

E-mail mailing lists, Web-based bulletin boards, Usenet news-groups, and even Web sites themselves are places where like-minded people gather to exchange information, ideas, and opinions. This many-to-many exchange drives the Internet; it is the basis for many of the models and concepts we will explore throughout this book. But it is not the part of the Internet in which many practitioners are engaged.

Why is the public relations industry able to do such a good job of placing articles in publications? Because counselors routinely read publications and understand the nature of the content those publications seek. They understand the audience of each publication, the editorial policies, and the needs of the editors and writers. The same holds true for television: PR counselors watch television, they study the demographics of the audiences that watch certain shows during particular times of the day, and they research the requirements that producers have established for their shows.

But most counselors are not regular participants in online communities. Whenever I speak to audiences of communicators (which I do frequently), I always ask for a show of hands of those in the audience who have ever participated in any kind of an online discussion. Usually, fewer than 5 percent raise their hands. To be sure, there are reasons why these professionals are not spending their free time in virtual communities, not the least of which is billable hour pressure, which leads to most practitioners working long hours. When they go home, the last thing they probably want to do is sit at a computer!

But it still raises the question: How can communicators effectively employ a medium as part of a communication strategy when they are not intimately familiar with the medium? In my opinion, they cannot. Whenever I am asked what communicators can do to become better at online public relations, I offer this simple answer:

> Spend time online. Find a community that resonates with you. It doesn't have to be about public relations. It can be about your favorite rock band, your hobby, movies, cars—it doesn't matter. Find an online home that includes a discussion area where you can engage with others who share your interest. Spend at least two hours a day engaged in these activities. It won't be too long before you integrate

the unique many-to-many nature of the Internet into your consciousness.

No Technology Focus

Corporations have Information Technology departments, but few public relations agencies have more than a few network administrators at their disposal. Big companies, with their large marketing budgets, have been able to leverage their IT resources. The agencies, with their scant resources, have had nothing to leverage. Getting up to speed on the Internet—and, in particular, building the internal resources to serve clients strategically through Internet-driven initiatives—requires starting from scratch. Even in the boom times, that kind of money wasn't easy to come by. Billings may have grown by 32 percent from 1998 to 1999, but the industry's total revenues of about $4 billion (according to CPRF) doesn't leave much room for significant investment.

How Did We Get Here?

We can view the rapid evolution of the Internet as a component of business through four stages. Many organizations—including specialty and boutique communication shops—have made it into the fourth stage, where online public relations become strategic, focusing on results rather than tactics. Many traditional agencies and corporate PR departments, however, are mired in the third stage. Let's look at these four stages.

Stage 1: Nerds in Charge

The Internet's history is well documented in a variety of books, articles, and online resources, so I won't spend a lot of time recounting it here. It is sufficient to say that the Internet had its beginnings as a tool that allowed university-based scientists working in various government-funded programs to exchange information with one another despite their use of incompatible computer systems. The Net's popularity grew among the scientific, academic, and computer-science community, notably as a means of exchanging e-mail and participating in discussion groups.

The Internet did not appeal to audiences outside this limited group (popularly referred to as "nerds") for a variety of reasons. At first, computers were not widely available or widely used. Even after the introduction of the PC in the early 1980s, modems were seen as exotic tools for hackers, with no practical business application. The growth of the bulletin board system (BBS) community initially did little to change that perception. BBSs were seen as the archaic, chaotic provinces of bedroom and garage hobbyists; there was little if anything of value to businesspeople online. It was still a difficult environment to learn to navigate even after larger commercial online services (such as CompuServe) began providing businesspeople with useful resources online. Configuring a modem was complicated, the speed at which a modem worked was pitifully slow, and the text-based commands that users had to employ were far from intuitive. Only the most intrepid individuals from outside the scientific, academic, or computer-science community made the effort.

Not even the development of the World Wide Web changed the Internet's enthusiasts-only nature. The Web that was introduced in 1989 by Tim Berners-Lee was a far cry from the Web with which we are familiar today. My first experience with the Web required me to log on through a remote server; therefore, my computer became a dumb terminal (which you'll be able to relate to if you ever worked on a Wang workstation). The interface was purely ASCII. (ASCII stands for American Standard Code for Information Interchange, which is the formal name for plain text.) The hyperlinks were reversed out of black and you had to tab from one hyperlink to another, hitting the "enter" key to link to the next site, which was also entirely plain text.

But the idea behind Berners-Lee's Web was a compelling one. Why go through the inconsistent and complex routines required to telnet into each network that made up the Internet before you could find the document in which you were interested, when it would be so much easier to create a link between a word or phrase and a related document?

Hyperlinking was not a new concept. Visionary Ted Nelson popularized the idea with his never-completed Xanadu system, initially conceptualized in 1960. Berners-Lee turned the idea into a reality by developing a new protocol called the Hypertext Transfer Protocol, or HTTP. (A *protocol* is a rule that governs how various elements of the

Internet work.) The early users of this "web" of online information were the same people who embraced the early Internet. Scientists, academics, and computer professionals used the system to more easily find documents related to their work (and, often, their recreation). After all, in those days the only documents you were likely to find online were those posted by the people already using the Net.

Back in those days, the idea of business and commerce on the Internet was a trigger for confrontation. Michael Strangelove, a Canadian computer enthusiast who saw the potential for business online, launched a print publication called *The Internet Business Journal* around 1990—and received death threats. The upshot of the messages he got was: "How dare you threaten to sully our collegial online community with something so base and depraved as business?" The mantra among the early Internet crowd, "Information should be free," was repeated endlessly. How could the Internet ever be used to charge anybody for anything?

The introduction of the Mosaic browser represented the real turning point for the Net. This graphical "front end" to the Web ushered in several advances over the text-driven version, such as:

- ⇝ Rather than tab to a hyperlink, users simply moved their mouse to the link and clicked.
- ⇝ Document formatting made what users saw on the Web more appealing, with headlines, bullet lists, italics, and a host of other treatments.
- ⇝ Graphics could be added.
- ⇝ The software resided on the user's computer rather than on a remote server, making it faster and easier to use.

Suddenly, the Web became a graphics-rich, easy-to-use environment. And the code that drove the Internet—the Hypertext Markup Language (HTML)—was so easy to learn that building a site on the Web was practically child's play. Still, since it was mostly the existing Internet community that was familiar with the Web, it was the members of this community that built the first Web sites.

These folks weren't trying to sell anything or influence anybody. They were simply trying to see what the Web could do, tinkering with code so that they could show off their creations to their peers. The Web, at this primitive stage, was a global show-and-tell free-for-all. It was fun, it was weird, it had attitude. But it wasn't anywhere near commercial.

Stage 2: The Nerds Go Commercial

By now, the pool of systems professionals who were using the Internet had expanded beyond those based in universities and research centers and into the business world. Employees in company IT departments hooked their company systems into the Internet so that employees could send and receive e-mail, and found themselves linked to the Web. Being technically minded people, many of whom were already using the Internet as hobbyists, these corporate employees began building rudimentary pages for their companies. Why not? They had already established domains for their organizations so employees could be identified by their e-mail addresses (for example, john.smith@acme.com). Web server software was free for the download. It was easy to scan the company's logo and product images and build a simple site.

These first business sites—still not engaged in e-commerce—joined a network of other sites that were built as an increasing number of people began experimenting with HTML. Sites were dedicated to favorite movies, sports, singers, conspiracy theories, and political and social points of view. At this point, the vast majority of sites—and especially those dedicated to businesses—were little more than brochureware, or billboards in cyberspace that had no specific business or communication objectives. They simply screamed, "Hey! Here we are!"

Any IT professional reading this book should take note: I'm definitely not slamming those early efforts. If it hadn't been for people like you, the business world would have been even later to the game. But just as communicators don't, as a rule, learn how to write software code, network administrators don't learn the principles of audience influence. Granted, the Web won't work without programmers—but magazines and brochures are not printed without professional printers, either. How many organizations turn the content of their annual reports and sales materials over to their printers? The printers ensure that the document looks the way that it should—that the ink doesn't smear, the pages are in the right order, and the pictures are right side up. However, professional communicators establish the content and professional designers prepare the pages that the printers will print.

As it turns out, the Web was no different from print in that regard. It would take people who knew how to use communication to achieve organizational objectives to turn the Web into a measurable advantage.

Stage 3: Communicators Elbow In

Inevitably, communicators were among those who succumbed to growing media hype about the Internet. They found ways to get online—through their companies' networks, through local Internet Service Providers (ISPs), through proprietary online services like CompuServe, Prodigy, and America Online. They logged on and began to explore the contents of the Net. Many of them found that their companies had sites they didn't even know about. Wait a minute, they thought. How come somebody is communicating about our company and it is not being coordinated by the communications department?

Of course, communicators were not the only people who discovered the existence of so-called official company material on the Internet. The organization's legal staff discovered unauthorized use of copyrighted and trademarked material. And surprised executives were often informed of their company's online presence by their children. ("Hey, Dad! I didn't know your company used four-letter words in its advertising.")

The discovery of the company's Web site led communicators to knock on the IT department's door. (In some cases, it was the lack of a company site—the fact that a competitor had a site but they did not—that led communicators to approach IT about building a site.) The goal was the same: to apply fundamental communications principles to the company's online presence. "If we're going to have a Web site," the communicators figured, "we may as well make sure it sings out of the same hymnal as all our other communications."

In some cases, the two departments worked together smoothly. In others, turf wars erupted between IT and communications. Communicators believed that the systems-based Webmaster was misusing the Web—since it was a communications medium, it belonged in the jurisdiction of the communications department. The IT group felt that the communicators, who had heretofore expressed absolutely no interest in the Web, suddenly wanted to wrest it away from the department that had built it from scratch—in their spare time, using scrounged resources and blood, sweat, and tears—only because it had suddenly become popular. (Unbelievably, these turf battles continue. How communicators can deal with this problem is addressed in Appendix A.)

Stage 4: The Net as a Business Tool

The fact that many organizations have entered the fourth stage doesn't mean they necessarily have created effective online tools. Rather, it simply means they have figured out that the Net is more than a toy for hobbyists—it is an efficient tool for communication and transaction, which means it can be used for all the business activities associated with communication and transaction such as marketing, advertising, sales, and, of course, public relations.

The Internet has fostered a *Field of Dreams* mentality among many businesspeople: "If we build it, they will come." This fallacy has been the downfall of hundreds of dot-com companies that tried making it on the Web, from eToys to Pets.com. Many traditional companies that tried selling on the Web also experienced disappointment, from Barnes & Noble Booksellers to Wal-Mart. The issues that led to these failures and near-failures include lack of customer service, complicated structures, unfathomable purchase procedures, and a host of other problems. (This book will not go into the principles of creating a good business-oriented Web site. There are many other resources that offer that kind of advice. Some of my favorites are listed in the Recommended Reading section at the back of the book.)

Successful or not, these businesses recognized that there is something to the idea of the Net as a business resource, and they built the first efforts at applying their conviction that profits could be made by going where the customers were—that is, online.

Today, there are still many organizations that think publishing a few pages (or tens of thousands of text-heavy, hard-to-navigate pages) equals a good business model. Then there are those that have done their homework and figured out how to leverage the Internet as a component of a larger customer-satisfaction strategy. Consider Circuit City, the electronics retailer. The company learned that customers like to use the Internet for research, but often like to buy directly from a brick-and-mortar store. As a result, the site has been reconfigured as a research tool, helping customers find just the right stereo or big-screen television, then giving them the option of buying online or picking it up at the local store. Customers can even pay online and pick up the system that same day, if they choose.

Business and institutional use of the Internet is continuing to evolve as companies figure out how to apply this new medium and its users to their business strategies.

Grading Public Relations on the Internet

Unfortunately, as indicated earlier, most of the public relations profession is stuck in stage three—brochureware, or billboards in cyberspace. Their efforts are not strategic (that is, they are not aligned with the company's or the client's bottom-line goals). They are not measurable (that is, there is no mechanism for assessing their effectiveness). They are not targeted toward specific audiences or constituencies.

For the most part, the online public relations effort of most companies is limited to a small component of a larger, catchall company site on the World Wide Web. Most companies establish their outpost on the Web using the company name: *www.acme.com*. The home page is static—it never changes. On the page, the company proudly displays its logo and links to the various sections of the site. As a result, the one site must accommodate all possible audiences, from customers and consumers to the media (public and trade) and the financial community. One link points to product information, another to job opportunities. Click here for the latest annual report, or here for a listing of dealerships (or sales offices or medical networks, and so on).

The public relations department often deals with the less pleasant aspects of business. Product recalls, lawsuits, labor actions, boycotts, accidents, and crises—these are the province of PR. If the marketing department owns the company's presence on the Web, how inclined will the marketers be to allow negative news and information to appear on their site, which is designed to convey a rosy view of the organization and its products and services? As a result, many public relations (or corporate communications, or public affairs, or whatever it is called from organization to organization) sites are nothing more than an afterthought, an archive of press releases, accessible by clicking on a link typically called something like, "In the News." Some organizations include speeches. There is virtually nothing on the site that would draw a member of a specific defined constituency to a particular release, speech, or other document. And there is even less that helps a representative of a constituent audience meet a specific need. As a result, it is impossible to assess the impact of this kind of online effort on the objectives that have been established for that audience.

Fortunately, since the release of the first edition of *Public Relations on the Net,* many organizations have begun to adopt next-generation approaches to the Internet. As a result, nearly all the case studies in this book are new, spotlighting some of the best, most innovative applications of public relations to the online world. Although the individuals, corporate departments, and agencies practicing this next-generation form of public relations continue to represent the minority, it is a minority that is definitely growing.

Next-generation online public relations, to my way of thinking, incorporates four overarching characteristics. They are:

1. *Strategic.* They are designed to affect business outcomes.
2. *Integrated.* They use the Internet as an element of a broader communication plan.
3. *Targeted.* They use the Internet based on its advantages over other forms of communication to reach specific targeted audiences.
4. *Measurable.* Plans include the means by which the effectiveness of the effort can be assessed.

Incorporating measurement into a communication plan ensures that the return on the organization's investment in the campaign can be assessed. It also provides the means by which communicators can show that the effort succeeded on a strategic level, proving the value of public relations to the organization. Communication efforts— online and off—could stand more measurement than is currently being undertaken. As a frequent judge in communication competitions, I am routinely amazed that communicators develop plans with solid, measurable objectives, but then claim success based on a nice letter from the chairperson's spouse, the number of column inches obtained in newspapers that printed a press release, or a reader-response survey that indicated most readers "liked" the publication.

Who cares if readers liked it? Who cares how much ink the press release got? All that matters is that readers were influenced by what they read, and reacted accordingly.

The Internet has led to a new class of tactical measurement that does not reflect the true effectiveness of the communication effort. I frequently hear communicators proudly proclaim that their Web site obtained some impressive number of hits, which (they assert) is a sign of the site's success. Katherine Paine, former CEO of Delahaye Medialink, a public relations research firm, suggests that the term *hits* is an acronym for How Idiots Track Success. She is correct. Hits don't tell us much of anything, beyond how busy the server is. (More on this in Chapter 15, when measurement and evaluation is addressed in detail.) A hit is a record of each file transferred by the server to the browser; thus, if a Web page features three graphics and a Java applet, five hits will be recorded—one for the Web page file, one for each of the graphics, and one for the applet.

Software is available to record individual unique visits to Web sites, but even this is of limited value. Claiming a communication effort was successful simply because the site received a large number of visits is like declaring a publication was successful because it was mailed to a large number of people. The questions still remain: Who were they? Were they part of the targeted audience? Did they read it? Did they believe it? Was it relevant to them? Did they act based on what they read?

Still, hits and visits represent most of the measurement going on in the public relations industry—among those practitioners who are measuring anything at all. So, despite the increased number of solid, strategic, integrated, targeted, measurable online public relations, we are still seeing mostly:

- ⇨ Useless media relations pages on business Web sites
- ⇨ Standalone Web sites with no clear link to a business strategy, as though somebody simply said, "Let's build a Web site for this campaign"
- ⇨ Lack of solid measurement

Thus, despite impressive advances from some corners of the public relations world, the industry still rates a low grade on its overall understanding and application of the Internet.

The Need for Change

I noted earlier that the lack of pain was one factor in the PR industry's failure to adapt to the changes the Internet has wrought. I suspect many agencies are feeling pain now. When the first edition of *Public Relations on the Net* was published, we were in the middle of the Internet boom years. Since then, the bubble has burst. Hundreds of companies that were desperate for public relations representation no longer exist, while others are struggling to survive and have slashed their communication budgets. Billings are down from the boom years.

(Incidentally, much has been made of the Internet bust; pundits claim that the failure of the dot-coms is symbolic of the failure of the Internet as a whole. Nothing could be further from the truth. The Internet did not fail. Rather, businesses with poor models and bad management failed. During the Internet gold rush, venture capitalists and other investors threw money at any company that had an "e" at the beginning of its name or a ".com" at the end. It didn't matter that there was no plan to become profitable, or that the company's leaders had no experience or ability to run a business. Their failure was inevitable. But audiences continue to use the Internet, and those companies that were around long before the Internet became popular have discovered that they must become Internet companies as part of their larger business operations. The Internet isn't going anywhere. It will continue to grow, and businesses will continue to explore ways to leverage it in order to be more customer-focused, more efficient, and more profitable.)

Add to the decline in overall billable time the fact that the client base is looking for help using the Internet to reach its varied constituent audiences. The CPRF study asked clients, "What are the value propositions that will drive your business for the PR industry in the next three years?" The top two answers reflected traditional communication roles: old-fashioned media relations and senior management strategic consulting. Clients rated online media relations the third most important driver of PR value, and ranked overall Internet communication strategy fourth. Clients are, without question, looking to the public relations world to provide leadership in the development of online strategies.

Since the PR industry—particularly at the agency level—isn't currently providing that level of leadership (with the exception of those pockets referenced earlier), clients are beginning to look elsewhere, including boutique specialty agencies, marketing agencies (which have gotten a better grip on the Internet than the PR industry, by understanding how to establish or enhance a brand using online tools), Web development agencies, advertising agencies, and even management consulting firms.

Given time, the industry—and those noncommunication professionals who still have responsibility to communicate on behalf of their institutions—will embrace the Internet strategically. The current pressures—reduced billings, greater client demand, and the threat of client defections—are the type that can kick-start change, so I am optimistic that improved online public relations will happen sooner rather than later.

Not that we have much choice. The Net is already an integrated part of our culture, a routine element of the landscape, and it will continue to be threaded into the fabric of our day-to-day lives.

I often define technology as stuff that doesn't work right yet. We don't think of our telephones or televisions as technology; they're more like furniture. We think of the Internet as technology because our connections drop, the servers go down, the browser files become corrupted, and viruses strike. That, too, will change. As the Net becomes more stable and easier to use, as it finds its way onto more noncomputer devices (such as cars, video games, cell phones, and kitchen appliances), society will take it more for granted.

The pressure the industry is under is a good thing, because we don't have time to wait for the Net's evolution to sweep us up. Our audiences are already online, and demographics indicate the audience (in the United States and Canada, at least) is a mirror of society. I recently saw a study that indicated laborers and factory workers are the fastest growing online demographic group, followed by administrative assistants and homemakers. The fastest growing income group is under $30,000 per year.

We also have moved beyond the ability to dismiss the online population as a bunch of perverts downloading pornography and slackers engaged in mindless chat. Plenty of research has been conducted pointing to the fact that most Internet users are conducting research online—developing opinions and molding perceptions.

And, as I've noted before, based on the fact that these audiences spend time online, they have already developed an innate understanding of how to use the Net themselves to communicate and influence. They have cultivated this ability without joining professional associations or earning communication degrees, and without accumulating professional experience. It is simply part of the culture that is unfolding at light speed. This has significant implications for public relations professionals. On the Internet, anybody can become a publisher and customers can—and do—organize campaigns to influence company behaviors. Online protests can achieve previously unheard-of results. Boycotts can be undertaken overnight. Products and services can be disparaged in open forums populated by people who share common interests. Concerned audiences may assume that lies and misrepresentations are accurate, and those lies can spread like the Ebola virus. Crises can be created online, and crises generated elsewhere can be exacerbated. We must learn to use the Internet to identify and address these issues on behalf of our organizations.

But we must also learn to use it proactively, as a means of reaching our audiences with the most effective tools, of engaging them, and of listening to them. And if we wait? Then we deserve our fate. We put our organizations at risk and we leave communication to people who do not fully comprehend the process of managing institutional relationships in support of the organization's key strategies.

Conclusion

Excellent communications and public relations are those that serve to facilitate the relationship between an organization and its strategic public. The Internet can play a significant role in this type of public relations, but the industry has been slow to embrace it to that end. The balance of this book focuses on exactly how to begin applying the Internet to strategic communications.

Notes

1. Mosaic was built by a group of students at the National Center for Supercomputing Applications (NCSA) at the University of Illinois; it eventually evolved into Netscape Navigator.

CHAPTER 2

How Communication Has Been Forever Changed

IF YOU'RE ANYTHING like me, you're sick to death of hearing people gush, "The Internet has changed everything."

The truth is, it hasn't. It hasn't, for instance, changed customer service. People still expect to be treated like individuals. They expect questions to be answered and problems to be solved. They expect to be taken care of. The Internet also hasn't changed the need people have to interact one-on-one with other people—especially when they're making contact with an organization. Far too many companies thought that building a Web site would take care of customer service and eliminate the need for one-to-one contact. Many of those companies are no longer around. Either their Web sites were not a substitute for what the customers really needed, or the Web site wasn't designed to meet the customers' needs.

But communication is one category where we can say that the Internet has changed everything . . . forever.

Many public relations professionals who started out as newspaper reporters (like me) and are firmly grounded in the principles of one-to-many, top-down communication still don't want to hear it, but there is no hiding from it: The principles that once guided the process of communication no longer work, thanks to the Net. They have been replaced and augmented by a new set of principles that must be clearly understood before we can begin to take advantage of the best tool for communicating in the information economy.

Communicating in the Information Economy

Is it merely hyperbole, or have we indeed entered a new age? While some may scoff at the idea that things have really changed all that much, the evidence suggests that one of those rare, historic changes has occurred, leaving us in a new world where many of the old rules no longer apply—and we must learn the new rules if we are to thrive and succeed.

What does it mean to be in an information economy? After all, General Motors still assembles cars, General Electric still makes toasters, and Exxon-Mobil still produces gasoline. It is not difficult for big-iron companies like these—firmly rooted in industrial-economy processes—to dismiss the information economy as a phenomenon that affects only businesses that deal in information for a living.

That is a dangerous mistake. When defining an economy, one of the key factors to consider is the primary element of production. Human history's first economy of significance was agricultural; land and labor were the key elements of production. When machines began replacing the work of humans a few hundred years ago, the industrial economy was born and capital was added to land and labor to create the triumvirate of primary production elements.

(Another key factor to consider when defining an economy is the currency used. What has value in any economy is that which is scarce. In an industrial economy, raw materials are scarce. In an information economy, it is the attention of the marketplace—that is, your attention is the currency of the information economy. In a sea of information, how do you get your target audience to pay attention to your message? This issue is addressed elsewhere throughout this book.)

Today, however, all three primary elements of production—land, labor, and capital—have been supplanted by information. That is not to say that land, labor, and capital no longer play a part in the production process. Without them, how could Levi Strauss & Company stitch together pants to sell in retail outlets? However, information today has become more important. It is information that helps determine the markets for the company's various products, establish the fashion trends to pursue, and identify the fabric needed by each manufacturing site based on forecasted volumes. Without systems that provide this information—and a host of other data—and open access to it by any Levi Strauss employee, partner, or supplier who needs it, the company would founder. It is no longer sufficient to put high-quality pants on store shelves, buy some advertising, and hope the product will move. The best factories, the most qualified workers, and the strongest capitalization do not matter without the information flows to support the efforts. The days are gone when somebody like Henry Ford could simply introduce a car to the marketplace and everybody would buy it.

Consider retailer Wal-Mart, about whose information systems volumes have been written. Knowing exactly what products are moving at what kind of pace, in practically real time, helps Wal-Mart instruct its suppliers about what types of products to ship and when. Or look at FedEx, which despite the fact that it ships packages, insists it is an Internet company—that is, it relies on the Internet to facilitate its business.

Characteristics of Communication in the Two Economies

The industrial economy was distinguished by a series of characteristics, or protocols for behavior, that governed how industrial organizations were managed. The way organizations managed their formal communications was entirely consistent with those characteristics, which have been turned on their head in the information economy.

INDUSTRIAL ECONOMY	INFORMATION ECONOMY
• Top-down	• Networked
• Based on quantity	• Based on quality
• Batch-processed	• Customized
• Producer-driven	• Customer-driven

Let's explore each of these characteristics and how communicating with constituent audiences is changing as a result of the evolving nature of business at large.

Top-Down vs. Networked

Industrial economy companies were organized around a command-and-control structure, as exemplified by the organization chart (see an example in Figure 2-1).

The typical organization chart had one box at the top, which was occupied by the top dog (whose title might be president, chief

FIGURE 2-1. A TYPICAL ORGANIZATION CHART.

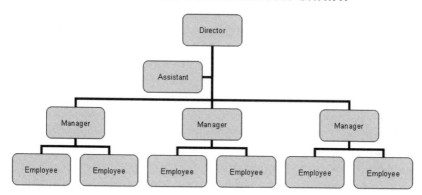

executive officer, chairperson, or principal). Below this person were a few boxes occupied by the top dog's direct reports. Each was responsible for a specific part of the organization's operation, and the cascading set of boxes beneath each of those direct reports worked to produce results associated with their specific aspects of the business. The idea of a department is based on the idea that a small team, given all the resources it needs to accomplish its tasks, can operate independently of other departments, reducing the need for complex information flows and employees with great depth of knowledge about the entire operation. The function of the organization chart is to control the flow of information to the departments that need it to complete their discrete tasks. (That is not surprising when you consider that the organization chart has its genesis in the military command-and-control structure, also designed to control information. The commander in chief, in the solitary box at the top of the chart, possesses all the information, while the foot soldier at the bottom of the chart—the most likely to be captured—possesses only what he needs to know to accomplish his tasks for the day.)

In the environment depicted in the organization chart, decisions are made at the levels where authority has been assigned. The more important the decision, the higher up the chart you must go, since that is where the information required to make an informed decision resides. In many organizations, even decisions that could be made farther down the chart are kicked up to higher levels of authority, since many employees don't want to run the risk of making the wrong decision. That fear is based on a lack of information needed to make the correct decision. (Although the notion of employee empowerment has been overused and become a laughable cliché, the original notion is still a sound one: Give employees the information they need to make decisions at the level where the work is done.)

The work performed by professional communicators in this environment mirrored the organization chart process. As communicators, we occupied boxes near the top of the chart. (In the box at the top resided the top dog, whether a CEO or a client, whose strategies we were working to support.) From this lofty position, we set objectives. We identified audiences, segmenting them based on the research and demographics at our disposal. We picked the issues to communicate based on our objectives. We selected the tools to use, such as press releases, video news releases, story placements, or press conferences. We selected the channels to use. Audiences had little to say, despite their needs. Of course, we might have used focus groups and other techniques to obtain audience feedback, but those still were on our terms. We selected the focus group participants, the venue, the facilitator, and the subject matter.

The information economy has rendered this traditional communication model fundamentally useless.

> *The introduction of online networks is the single most significant change to the environment in which communicators do their work.*

In the information economy, where people are networked—making time and distance meaningless—control of information gives way to open access to information. The hierarchical organization chart, which was an effective tool in the industrial economy, is now a liability in an environment where success depends on moving quickly and being flexible and adaptive. In place of the organization chart, successful companies are developing networks of people and information, all accessible by any party who needs to make an informed decision, solve a problem, or capitalize on an opportunity.

Similarly, the way we communicate with our audiences needs to become more networked. How do we get a message out to targeted audience members when those individuals no longer accept a top-down message?

This network was not significant a few years ago, because not enough people were part of it. However, as with any network, the more people who join it, the more valuable it is. As an example, look at the network of fax machines. When only a few people owned the first high-priced fax machines, the network wasn't very valuable. Now that virtually everybody has a fax machine, the network has become indispensable. That type of exponential growth has happened over the Internet, not only creating a vast community of networked individuals but also altering their information and communication habits. We'll talk more about networks and the implications for communicators in the section titled "Four New Communication Models."

Based on Quantity vs. Based on Quality

Companies earned wealth in the industrial economy by selling as many units of their products as they could. The front office cried "More, more, more!" and it reverberated through the marketing department (which created the need) to the sales department (which filled the orders) to the factory floor (where output had to keep up with demand). All efforts were geared toward producing and selling as many widgets as possible.

Public relations efforts mimicked the quantity imperative. If we had a press release to distribute, it had to go to as many media outlets as possible, so that we could rack up as many column inches of print and minutes of airtime as we could. If we identified a spokesperson to represent a product, we worked our tails off to make sure that as many writers and reporters interviewed her as we could scare up. If she appeared on *Good Morning New York,* she also had to be on *Good Morning Detroit, AM Toronto,* and *Regis.* When we published an annual report, we crammed it with all the messages we wanted our audiences to absorb, and we printed scores of them. The prevailing belief was that the more opportunity there was for our target audiences to see the message, the more likely it was that they *would* see it. We measured effectiveness primarily by the number of pairs of eyeballs that had potentially seen the message.

The information economy turns the quantity imperative on its head. The number of items an organization sells depends entirely on the quality of the item. People pay for quality, but they won't pay even a deeply discounted price for something that falls below their quality standards. Ever since the Japanese began to beat U.S. businesses by offering better products, thousands of companies in the United States have made quality a focus. It has been years since quality improvement programs were trendy add-ons to company training efforts; today, producing quality goods and services is merely the price of admission to the marketplace. Raising the bar on its ability to meet requirements gives a company a competitive edge; hence, the push to continually improve quality—that is, to come closer to achieving the Holy Grail of zero defects.

The same concept holds true of communication in the information economy. Successfully placing a billion impressions is counterproductive, to say the least, if the quality of the message is substandard. Quality communications are those that meet the requirements—the needs and expectations—of the audience for which they were intended. Public relations practitioners can achieve quality with a single well-placed message in an Internet discussion group, an invitation to join a mailing list, a powerful dialogue in an online community, or a meticulously researched position statement on a targeted Web site.

Batch-Processed vs. Customized

If quantity was an imperative of the industrial economy, then economics demanded that each of the widgets produced be exactly like all the others. Making a widget that was different would mean increased costs, even though a customer or two would have benefited from a revised configuration. Henry Ford, when introducing the Model A to the public, wryly noted that the car was available in any color the customer might want—as long as it was black! If a customer wanted a Model A, black was the only option.

No longer. Now, a driver expects to be able to order a customized car that meets his or her specific and unique desires. The customer can specify not only the color but also the type of stereo, power equipment, moon roof, spoiler, wood paneling, and transmission. Customization is the key to market share in the information economy, based on knowing what various classes or categories of customers want. Just try to tell a homemaker that she can obtain a product one way and one way only. She doesn't have to acquiesce: Competitors are ready to satisfy her needs with different sizes, strengths, scents, ingredients, and packaging that are designed to address different situations. (If you think that there is only one way to buy Tide laundry detergent, for example, it has been a long time since you've moseyed up and down the aisles of a grocery store.)

Still, public relations efforts generally result in the production of one kind of information to accommodate all members of an audience—and these communications are sometimes meant to accommodate all audiences. A press release is blasted out over the wire to every publication, whether it's a trade publication, a metropolitan daily newspaper, a weekly throwaway newspaper, or a radio talk show. Why is there only one for all these different audiences, each with unique information needs? Because the cost of producing multiple versions of one release can be staggering. It has been our job to keep the per-unit cost of press releases (or annual reports or special-event press kits) as low as possible. Crafting documents that suit each target audience makes it impossible to achieve that cost target.

Today, however, people—including those who populate our target audiences—expect customization. Watts Wacker, a futurist and author of *The Visionary's Handbook,* said,

> The PR industry has to recognize that the world is that different and let go the way it is used to doing things and apply a beginner's mind. In a life of complete media-centricity—beyond media saturation—everyone feels they could and should be marketed to as an individual. If I can customize my computer online, or my blue jeans or my loafers, I certainly expect I should receive custom-made messages.[1]

The one-size-fits-all approach no longer cuts it. Since each individual expects to get exactly the information he needs, information that answers the question he has right now, it becomes a role of the communicator to provide that information.

Producer-Driven vs. Customer-Driven

Industrial economy companies made their decisions at the top of the organization chart, determined by what those at the top believed would provide a return on investment. How did they arrive at the conclusion that this or that product or service would be a success? Some of them relied on market research. Others looked to internal research and development departments. Some took cues from their spouses (and not always unsuccessfully: Lillian Disney suggested to Walt that Mickey was a better name for his new animated mouse than Mortimer, his first choice). A number of executives pursued new technologies developed in-house, regardless of how useful the public might find them. (And many of the dot-com companies that pursued this approach are not around to reflect on their mistakes.) The point is that the decisions were made by a core group of high-ranking executives acting in virtual autonomy.

But customers call the shots in the information economy. Improved customer satisfaction is the new rallying cry at many organizations, and consultants are garnering high prices teaching companies how to be more customer-driven. In most cases, the answer is simple: Listen to what customers say they want, and make sure you provide it. Companies such as Matrix Marketing, Inc., are earning big returns providing telephone-based customer service on behalf of clients, by listening and cataloging the information customers provide in sophisticated databases. They feed that information back to their clients, who use it to make product and service decisions. Other companies find other ways to tap into the collective network consciousness. Ford Motor Company, for example, analyzed online discussions about its Lincoln LS sedan and determined that car buyers most often cross-shop the LS against the Chrysler 300M; the analysis also revealed that LS drivers like the ride but wish the car had more interior storage. Be assured that this kind of information is being incorporated into the company's plans for the LS, ranging from design to marketing and advertising.

Companies engage in communication with strategic audiences by counting on their public relations departments and counselors to establish key messages and push them down to their audiences. Generally, the company dictates the theme of these discussions. In the information economy, the dialogue must be multidirectional, with the company engaging in discussions in which the agenda can be set easily by either the audience or the company.

Four New Communication Models

The shift from an industrial to an information economy would not have been possible without the introduction of the technologies that facilitate the flow of information that is the economy's engine. The Internet—along with proprietary online communication services, ranging from hobbyists' bulletin board systems to America Online—has hastened the changing expectations of audiences about how they get and use information. Four models of communication that public relations practitioners have taken for granted since the inception of the profession have undergone irrevocable changes as a result of the introduction and rapid assimilation of online technology—changes entirely consistent with (and, in fact, partly driven by) the shifting characteristics of successful information-age businesses. Let's analyze the four models.

Network-Driven: From Few-to-Many to Many-to-Many

If the four communication models we're discussing have a hierarchy, this one—the network-driven model—is at the pinnacle, miles above the others. If communicators understand nothing else about the Internet and its impact on the practice of public relations, they must understand this: Everybody is a publisher, and everybody is connected to everybody else.

Media critic A.J. Leibling suggested that freedom of the press belongs to those who own one. Since the advent of modern mass communications (heralded by the invention of the printing press), most formal communication has been a one-way, top-down affair. A media elite, made up of the limited number of organizations, institutions, and individuals with the wherewithal to publish and distribute to the masses, communicates to audiences. The audiences are simply consumers of information, with little or no ability to communicate themselves, either back to the company that originated the message or to other members of the audience. For the vast majority of people, the ability to publish our thoughts, opinions, or positions is beyond the realm of possibility. The cost of a page in *The Wall Street Journal* or a minute of advertising time on *Friends* is simply more than the average person—and even some institutions—can afford.

In the old, traditional, one-to-many communication model, the organization sets the agenda and exercises control over the nature of the information to be published. The objective of the communication is in the hands of the organization that pays for it. The audience can be targeted through tried-and-true demographic segmenting. Once identified, the organization then selects the publications the target audience reads, places billboards in the neighborhood the target audience populates, and buys airtime on the television and radio shows to which the target audience tunes in.

Once the members of the audience receive the information, their opportunities to engage the publishing organization in any kind of substantive dialogue are limited. They can write letters to the editor or call the organization's offices. The organization has no compelling reason to respond (although they often aggregate the results of feedback to assess the effectiveness of the communication). In fact, organizations, even those with the budgets and staff resources to engage in the initial communication, do not have the ability to respond to individuals—at least, not outside the scope of day-to-day customer service activities (and even those are being outsourced more and more).

Furthermore, audience members have limited opportunities to engage other audience members in a discussion of the company's message. How would you go about finding somebody who viewed the same material you read and is sympathetic to your point of view?

The introduction of computer-mediated communication has turned the one-to-many communication model on its head. The Internet provides a platform for publication that anyone can afford, and helps individuals target their audiences. The exclusive ability to publish that organizations once held has been redistributed to the masses, representing a fundamental redistribution of power (which, by the way, is one of the dictionary definitions of the word *revolution*); the consequences are staggering. No matter how much money an organization spends on its communication efforts in the wired world, they now are merely one voice among many.

Institutions accustomed to simply blasting their messages out to audiences should consider some of the following long-term repercussions the networked environment has had on traditional business models:

↪ Manufacturers used to work behind closed doors to produce the latest model or version, and then launch it on a public susceptible to marketing techniques. The network, however, allows customers to engage in discussions with one another about what they want in a product, leading them to reject anything that does not comply with their collectively developed standards. In some instances, the customers have even been able to create the product they want themselves. The open source movement in the world of computer software grew out of dissatisfaction with the closed world of Microsoft's Windows PC operating system. Before the Internet, these individuals would have been unable to do much more than complain in small, local user groups. Thanks to the network that connects them all together, however, individuals have been able to generate code, which they then make available to all the other members of the network who improve it and send it back out to the network for even more tweaking. The most ambitious open source project has been Linux, a Unix-based operating system that has become popular on Internet servers and a host of other devices, eating into Microsoft's Windows market share. By August 2000, Linux—the programming effort undertaken by scores of online volunteers—had amassed a 24 percent share of the server market.

↝ Napster represents perhaps the most notorious example of the power of the network. Music fans wanting to listen to a particular song whenever they wanted took for granted that they had to buy a CD. The introduction of the MP3 data compression format—a compression scheme developed specifically for music files—made it possible for music fans to store their copies of their favorite songs on their computer hard drives (copied from other sources, including copyright-protected CDs, using readily available multimedia software). Shawn Fanning, then a nineteen-year-old college student, created a simple tool that would allow music fans to search for a song on the hard drives of others willing to share their files. This "peer-to-peer" system—which ultimately became a full-fledged company called Napster—enabled millions of people to download any song they wanted without paying a nickel, fundamentally disintermediating the music industry from the process and leading to legal wrangles that have all but shut down the music-sharing service. But consumers have not gone back to spending money for CDs. Instead, they have simply found alternative services, such as Gnutella, to satisfy their hunger for free music available whenever they want it. We can argue the ethical pros and cons associated with MP3 music sharing, but the fundamental point is indisputable: The network has forced the powerful music industry to face a new world in which the old models no longer apply.

↝ Trust communities and trust intermediaries have replaced authoritative sources of information among consumers seeking information to help them make decisions. A trust community is an online destination populated by people who share a common interest and discuss that topic with one another—such as epinions.com, a Web site where consumers can publish their reviews, praise, and complaints about products and services. Anybody thinking of buying, say, Nintendo's new GameBoy Advance, can find that 107 epinions members have rated the handheld game, giving it a cumulative four-star rating out of five. One message gushes about the device, extolling its virtues, while another gives it only three stars, asking, "If it's so advanced, why can't I see anything?" These opinions of real people speaking in their real voices trump the top-down reviews that appear in consumer publications such as *PC Gamer*. These publications continue to attract subscribers, but the reviews of the so-called authorities writing for the publications have less credibility and validity than those written by people who are just like you and me. Trust aggregators are online destinations where an individual collects and publishes the information produced by members of the community. Many investors, for example, would rather visit Motley Fool (*http:// www.fool.com*) than trust their investments to a traditional broker working on commission for a brokerage. The Gardner brothers, Tom and Dave, own Motley Fool, but their information comes from the tens of thousands of people who contribute. In their book, *The Motley Fool Investment Guide*, the Gardners tell this story about Iomega Corporation's Zip drive:

> In metropolitan centers east to west across the union, private investors starting polling their local computer stores, inquiring about their current stock of Zip drives and their backlogged orders for this product . . . Using computers outfitted with modems, they then signed online to publish this information in a public discussion of Iomega available to anyone (who would) listen. Concurrently, an anonymous engineer took a simple tour of the plant in Roy, Utah, and observed the Zip manufacturing process. From fifteen minutes of observation, he contributed his own numerical estimates of Iomega's production . . . Further, another fellow on the East Coast had his parents, who lived an hour away from the factory in Utah, drive to the company's headquarters on a Sunday afternoon in order to report how many cars appeared in the company parking lot . . . What

resulted from the collection and online publication of these seemingly inconsequential details was a national public conversation of a kind that had never taken place before, that had never been *possible* before . . . How well the company was doing—a subject of so much speculation among benighted *offline* investors—had a sure answer among enlightened online investors.[2]

That information was aggregated on the Gardners' Motley Fool Web site. (Of course, investors also use trust communities, such as the finance discussion boards at Yahoo.)

↪ Activists in the old economy organized protests through marketing techniques that don't differ much from those used by any organization. If an animal rights group, for example, wanted to launch a protest, they had to print literature and distribute it to target audiences. With the Internet, though, we have seen the introduction of what the Rand Corporation in a study from the early 1990s called "Net warriors." These are the individuals who plan protests in discussion areas on the Internet—which is precisely what happened in Seattle in 1999 when the World Trade Organization (WTO) convened there. Both Seattle city officials and WTO were caught unawares because they saw no overt organizing efforts. However, in only one discussion community populated by opponents to genetically engineered foods, more than two thousand messages were distributed over a ninety-day period to other like-minded participants of the group. Undoubtedly, only a fraction of the individuals receiving those messages decided to act by protesting in Seattle (or alternate protest sites). But that was only *one* group. Multiply those individuals by members of other groups who received similar messages and it becomes easy to understand how quickly Seattle wound up with more than twenty thousand protestors on its streets. Authorities claimed the protest was organized covertly because the discussion communities were beneath their radar. But there was nothing covert about it—communicating in communities has become the norm for the people who participate in such communities. (The tactic was refined for the April 2000 spring meetings of the International Monetary Fund and World Bank in Washington, D.C. In addition to postings in discussion groups, a Web site was established to serve as a clearinghouse for information about the protests. The site, *http://*

www.a16.org, has expanded to address protests related to a variety of socioeconomic causes.)

⮑ When U.S. Desert Storm forces landed in the Gulf to repel Iraqi forces that had invaded Kuwait, news-hungry audiences tuned in to CNN and other news outlets to find out what was going on. Journalists from the authoritative, top-down news services were the only source of information upon which we could rely. However, when military activity escalated in Kosovo a few years later, the same news-hungry audiences tapped into chat rooms and discussion boards on the Internet, where they could get unfiltered, first-hand accounts of the fighting from real people reporting from the locations of the actions. The difference between getting news from CNN and from individuals who are there is the difference between looking at a map and being on the landscape.

In each of the previous examples, the Internet served as an agent of change in the way people get and use information. The implications of these changes are as profound as any change through which civilization has gone before. These implications relate not only to major categories of change but also to simple individual transactions.

In the Internet's formative years, the many-to-many communication model did not involve business, but did spotlight the power of the networked community to diminish the power of—and the need for—traditional, institution-driven communication. My son, Benjamin, who was 10 years old at the time, had fixated on an animated Japanese movie called *Lensman.* The name of the movie rang a bell; I had several friends who read science-fiction novels when I was in high school, and I thought one of them had mentioned a book by the same name. Since my wife and I were trying to entice Ben to read more, I thought finding the book on which his favorite movie was based would motivate him to read it. The local library did not have the book in its card catalogue, and I couldn't find it listed in *Books in Print.* I drove to a science-fiction and fantasy bookstore, but the youngster behind the counter had never heard of it.

At this point, most of us would be inclined to believe we were mistaken; it wasn't *Lensman,* it must have been something like *Cameraman.* But I was a relatively new subscriber to the CompuServe information service, so I spent a few minutes rummaging through the list of discussion forums before finding the Science Fiction and Fantasy Literature group. I posted a message there that explained my plight, then checked back about four hours later to see whether anybody had seen my query.

I found fourteen replies waiting for me. Each one identified E.E. "Doc" Smith as the author. Each one pointed out that Smith had written an entire series of *Lensman* books, not just one. Several of the replies listed the titles of all the books in the series. A few of the messages offered synopses of each book's plot. Two reviewed each book in the series. My favorite reply came from a U.S. serviceman stationed in Germany who explained that he was a big fan of the books, and he knew they were out of print in the United States. However, he said, they were in print in English in Germany, and if I failed to find the books at home, I could send him a check and he would ship the books to me from Europe.

Let me reiterate: It took only four hours to learn from ordinary, run-of-the-mill people who shared a common interest in science fiction what I was unable to learn from the official sources of information.

Since then, I have had hundreds of similar experiences, and I have heard of thousands more. During one workshop I taught, a participant told me the following story: His daughter, who had just given birth to twins, was interested in finding a network of parents of twins. She found one on the World Wide Web that featured, among other things, a database of other members. If you could find a participant whose twins were six months older than your own, you could arrange to have that participant send you her hand-me-downs. Searching the database, she found an ideal candidate—two blocks away from where she lived. Or this story, from another member of an audience where I was giving a speech: A woman was diagnosed with a fatal disease. Her husband was chief of staff at a major medical center, and querying his colleagues at the hospital confirmed their worst fears—there was no cure for his wife's illness. Not willing to accept that fate, she took to the Internet and found an experimental program to treat the illness at one university. She was accepted into the program where the radical treatment was performed. At last report, she had outlived her doctor's projection by several years. (Interestingly, statistics indicate that most people who have Internet access will eventually use that access to conduct medical or wellness-related research.)

I encountered another instance of many-to-many communications after I submitted a letter to the editor of *FastCompany* magazine. I was disturbed that a series of articles on change management failed to recognize the importance of a strategic communications effort. My letter appeared in the magazine along with my name and my e-mail address. Within a few days, I received a message from a *FastCompany* reader who thought the entire issue of change management warranted continued discussion. She had sent her message to every author of a letter to the editor that had been printed in the magazine, establishing a de facto Internet mailing list. The discussion among that group of letter writers continued for several weeks.

Some other examples of how the many-to-many model has enabled networks of people to gather and engage in ways that were impossible before include the following:

- Senior citizens, who form communities to engage in social activities in the evening, when many are reluctant to go out. Seniors, in fact, represent the second-fastest growing online audience.
- Medical patients, who uncover treatments about which their doctors were unaware.
- Alzheimer caregivers, chained night and day to their loved ones, who form an online support group.
- Investors, who create an online club to share successes, tips, and advice.
- Employees, who visit a "sound off" discussion group to vent their anger or frustration.

Note that none of these examples have anything to do with computers, computer users, the online world itself, computer games, or anything related to the digital world. Rather, they are real-world subjects; the audience has simply found a forum using the new tool of cyberspace.

Receiver-Driven Communications

Before the Internet, communications were producer-driven (as noted earlier in this chapter) and linear. That is, material was presented in a logical, sequential order. As gatekeepers, the authors and editors gathered the facts and information they would use in the document, then culled from that the elements that would make it into print, making judgments about the importance and relevance of each bit of information. Then they arranged the information in a sequence that begins at the beginning and proceeds through a logical progression. The objective is ultimately to bring the reader along to the publishing organization's point of view (or compel the reader to undertake an action consistent with the company's goals).

The order in which the material is presented is based on the perspective of the author and the institution for which the author works. For example, an insurance company might present its information to prospective and existing customers based on plans: "We have health-and-welfare plans, disability plans, life insurance plans, and property-and-casualty plans. Under health-and-welfare, we offer medical, dental and vision insurance plans. In the category of medical insurance, we offer an indemnity plan, a Health Maintenance Organization, and a Preferred Provider Organization." Within each section, you can find descending levels of information. Also, each section is written in such a way that the reader is taken by the hand and led through the information. Anybody trying to start in the middle will be confounded, because the context of the material was set in the beginning. In the linear environment of communications before the Internet, readers had no choice but to start at the beginning and read from start to finish, the way the author intended.

If a consumer wanted an overview of an insurance company's lines of business, this type of presentation would be fine. When we dive into this type of information, however, we usually already know what we need to know: "I already have a life insurance policy. We are about to have a baby, and I'd like to be a responsible parent. I would like to increase the level of insurance I'm carrying. How many levels of insurance can I increase from my current level before I am required to take a physical and get a doctor's approval?" In a linear document, it can take a fair amount of time to dig up that information, particularly if the way you come at the information is inconsistent with the structure used to present it. Even more frustrating to a consumer might be this scenario: "I carry your medical insurance. My kid just fell off his bike and broke his arm. What do I do?" To flip through a long document designed to provide detailed information on all kinds of plans would simply be too time consuming.

Information Overload

In fact, most people are crushed for time these days. We live in an era that is suffering the consequences of the downsizing/rightsizing/capsizing binge of the 1980s and early 1990s (and companies continue to use layoffs as an economic adjustment tool today). Downsizing rarely is accompanied by a reduction in work requirements. Instead, the tasks performed by those who have been let go shifts to those who remain. Eight-hour workdays are nothing more than a joke in many organizations. We work ten, twelve, fourteen-hour days. We work Saturdays. We bring work home with us.

Part of the blame for the amount of time we spend at work is the amount of information with which we must cope. *Information overload* is the term most often associated with this flood of information that constantly overwhelms us. Through various traditional and emerging media, we are blasted with messages day and night, and from this barrage, we must find those nuggets of information that meet our own individual needs. The amount of time we spend sifting through the irrelevant material to identify that which is relevant is a source of frustration.

Tom Davenport, a specialist in the use of information, suggested in a *Harvard Business Review* article that there is no such thing as information overload. We are an information-hungry society, he suggested, anxious to get our hands on all the information we can—*about the things that interest us*. It's all the *other* stuff that gets in the way, he said.[3]

There are many reasons for the increased volume of information. Publishing technology has allowed publishers to create cost-effective special-interest magazines that target small audiences. Imagine visiting a newsstand twenty years ago and finding magazines like *Ferret World*! Desktop publishing has made it easy for everybody to produce his or her own material. Companies that once produced a single employee publication now distribute dozens of separate departmental newsletters, bulletins, magazines, and other communications. We live in a world where information is delivered through a fire hose, but our individual capacity is about the size of a thimble.

A study conducted by the Institute for the Future (sponsored by Pitney Bowes) reveals that information technology is largely to blame for information overload. The study—an ongoing series titled "Managing Communication in the 21st Century Workplace"—concluded that the average worker sends and receives well over two hundred messages per day—and the increasing number of message-delivery technologies is responsible. New technologies—such as e-mail and groupware—do not replace older, more traditional methods of communication (for example, faxes, telephone, voice mail). Instead, they are additive, making it harder and harder to get the attention of an individual to whom you need to communicate. Individuals with access to multiple communication vehicles use multiple vehicles. People mix and match methods to ensure that their message gets through: "Hi, Mark. I'm leaving this voice mail to confirm you got the e-mail that followed up on the fax to remind you about the overnight delivery that you should have received yesterday."

The information overload that our society experiences has led to a fundamental shift in audience requirements. It is ironic, I suppose, that when I was a child and my father worked an eight-hour day (with considerable time to absorb messages), there were fewer media and less information to absorb. Today, when time is precious, there are vastly more messages that are considerably more complex. It once was perfectly acceptable to adopt the communication attitude that said, "You'll get what we've got when we get it to you." That accommodated delivery of scheduled communications like annual reports, the distribution of press releases, and the production of institutional material. But it does not accommodate the new paradigm, in which the audience demands, "I want what I want when I want it."

(This new requirement is, of course, consistent with the customization characteristic of an information economy.)

Many of those who fear the Internet and its associated technologies (such as corporate intranets) are concerned about key messages getting lost in the tidal wave of material that a many-to-many environment can produce. How does a most important message stand out when it is ultimately just one more drop in the sea?

In accommodating the "I-want-what-I-want-when-I-want-it" model, though, it becomes easier to distinguish between messages that are *pushed* at audiences because of their importance and those that are made available to satisfy the information needs of individual audience members. You can employ strategies that ensure important top-down messages get the attention they deserve, and leave everything else in an environment where individuals only *pull* it if they need it, rather than having it thrust upon them whether or not it is relevant.

Case Study: California Franchise Tax Board

When my accountant called asking for a prior year's California state tax return, I had to laugh. I'm sure the photocopy is in a box in my garage somewhere, but I have a large number of boxes that aren't organized in any particular fashion. When I explained this, my accountant replied that I would have to order a photocopy from the California State Franchise Tax Board.

Nothing sounded like less fun than calling a government agency and proceeding through their interactive voice response system. Instead, I launched my Web browser and entered "California Franchise Tax Board." The appropriate link was the top listing, so one click took me to the agency's home page.

The agency offers a great deal of information, including news headlines they want you to see, information on electronic tax filing, and a host of other resources. Since I wasn't interested in any of this material, I frankly didn't see it. My eyes scanned the page until I saw the link I was looking for: Forms and Publications. I clicked that link and found myself on a page that listed the tax year in which I was interested. I picked 1998 and retrieved a page of forms, manuals, booklets, and instructions. It took only a few seconds to find Form 3516, the form to request a copy of a personal income tax form. I clicked the link and was presented with a PDF (Adobe Acrobat) version of the form, which I printed. Less than five minutes after hanging up the telephone after speaking with my accountant, I was holding the needed form in my hands. I want what I want when I want it!

Planning Template: Web-Based Receiver-Driven Communications

Far too many companies employ the "shovelware" principle, tossing whatever information they already have in other formats onto a Web site and claiming they have established a presence in cyberspace. If you are going to achieve measurable results, you need to carefully plan the kind of material that will satisfy the needs of your audience. Follow these steps to ensure success:

1. *Identify the target*

   Who is the audience?

2. *State your objectives*

   Why is your organization communicating with this audience? What do you want to achieve? How will you know when you have achieved it?

3. *What key messages* must *be pushed to the audience?*

Clarify top-down messages and identify distribution methods for delivering (for example, advertising or direct mail).

4. *What information are audience members likely to want?*

Based on your key messages, and factoring in your knowledge about the audience's interests, list the types of questions individuals may ask or additional information they may want.

5. *How are audience members likely to seek additional information?*

What path will individuals follow to get to the information they want?

6. *Integrate your communications.*

Make sure that your initial top-down communication includes information about how to obtain additional information and how to engage the organization and/or other audience members in providing feedback or discussing the issue.

Access-Driven Communications

If I want what I want when I want it, the institution had better make sure I have access to the vehicle being used to make it available. After all, making the information available through means to which I do not have access won't do me any good!

This is a difficult concept for public relations practitioners to accept, since part of communication training—and one of the most fun elements of doing the job—is selecting media. Of course, the traditional approach to media selection has not been entirely arbitrary, with communicators picking the tool that sounds coolest. Each medium must be appropriate to both the audience and the message. But, when you were pushing the message to the audience, the range of options was greater. You could send a printed brochure, a videotape, or a solar-powered calculator with your message imprinted on it. You could produce billboards, stage a media event that results in television and newspaper coverage, place an article in a magazine, sponsor a promotion, or buy advertising. As long as the audience tuned into the news, opened a morning newspaper, read the magazine the demographics suggest they read, or received their mail, they saw your message.

When individuals *pull* the information they want, however, they are discarding the bulk of the communication tools thrust at them as a means of dispensing with the superfluous data that constitutes overload. You need to make the information available specifically in the media they are most likely to use when they pull information.

Until recently, the telephone has been the best tool to accommodate individuals who pulled information. Interactive Voice Response (IVR) empowered individuals to follow recorded prompts in search of information. While IVR can be a source of tremendous aggravation when it is not well designed, it can, when implemented effectively, facilitate quick retrieval of desired data. Examples of IVR satisfying individual information needs include the following:

↪ *Bank Balances.* When was the last time you waited until a monthly statement arrived in the mail to find out how much money you had in your account? Even the most technophobic among us will pick up the telephone and punch one or two keys in order to obtain our balance as of yesterday's bank closing time.

↪ *Movies.* 777-FILM has become a huge success in major motion picture markets by helping people get information on the films they want to see and when those movies are playing. They can even purchase advance tickets using the system.

↪ *Technical Support.* Most computer problems have been experienced by others, and these problems have been resolved. Why wait half an hour for a live tech-support staff member when you can use a series of prompts to get the answer yourself? Usually, these prompts work by starting with some broad questions, the answers to which help narrow the field of problems to yours, then providing the answer.

Fax-on-demand is another tool that meets the need for information on demand. These systems provide users with a menu of documents. When you dial into the fax-on-demand IVR system, the voice prompt asks you to enter the number of the document you want and your fax number. The document is then automatically faxed to you. Fax-on-demand has been a success in some quarters because of the predominance of fax machines. Once an expensive toy for the rich, fax machines now have places in private homes. Computers come equipped with the ability to send and receive faxes. Services allow

you to retrieve faxes from anywhere in the world without being where
your fax machine is.

In the cases of both telephone IVR and fax-on-demand, the
dominance of the tool among the general public—and, by extension,
within targeted audiences—has made them desirable pull communication tools. Today, the World Wide Web is fast becoming the tool of
choice for individuals seeking to retrieve specific information. Acces-
sibility is becoming less of a problem as Web and e-mail kiosks pop
up in airport terminals and hotel lobbies, and the popularity of Internet cafes continues to grow. Additionally, the Web is a resource
common to both businesses (which provide access to the World Wide
Web, as well as intranets, which take advantage of the same interface) and the public at large (in homes, schools, housing projects,
nursing homes, and other residences). People are getting Web-based
information from their computers, from their network PCs, even
from television sets and telephones.

As the number of people who routinely use the Web skyrockets,
the case for making information available on the Web grows stronger.

TIP:
Be Redundant . . . and Repetitive . . . and Redundant
Although many members of your target audience may be
on the Web, it is highly unlikely that *all* of them are. It pays
to send your message through multiple media to increase
the odds that as many members of your audience see it as
possible. Offer the information on the Web *and* via fax-on-
demand or IVR. Go ahead and get the media placements,
and hold the special events. It always has been a rule of
communication that redundancy is a good thing, and the
existence of the Web doesn't change that!

Attracting a Market Sample of One

Under traditional communication models—those that evolved
while the industrial economy was in full swing—we learned to target
our audiences by using demographics. Whole businesses prospered
by establishing those demographic groups, identifying that people
who voted one way were likely to be in a certain income category,

with certain academic credentials, and certain buying patterns. The ability to cross-reference trends and patterns against demographic niches was vital. How else would we know which newspapers to target with our press releases? Which magazines to seek article placements in? Which cities to hold special events in?

In the information economy, however, demographics mean less and less—particularly when pushing information in media you have no guarantee your audience will see. The environment that encourages individuals to pull the information they want requires a new approach, one in which you need to ensure that information is waiting where individuals are likely to go looking for it.

Demographics still play a part in this approach, known as a "market sample of one." If you are promoting a wine-tasting event, you need to know the types of sites the high-income members of the target audience you are trying to attract are likely to visit. You may want to buy banner advertisements on, say, travel and gourmet sites. If you are seeking support for a new initiative to ease export regulations, you may want to lure people from appropriate trade publications, business journals, and sites that address international trade.

In any event, your goal is not to distribute the material to every possible member of the target audience, but rather to entice each individual, one at a time, to your site. The same principle applies to the use of other online resources to direct individuals to your business, your cause, or your product, *even if you don't have a Web site.*

The audience-targeting role of public relations professionals— and even much of the other work they do—will go through a significant transition as a result of this new model. "We won't need people who churn out press releases or design ads," according to Marian Salzman, corporate director of emerging media for advertising giant Chiat/Day. "The challenge will be to spread branded information so that it gets to the targeted individual. That requires understanding the consumer on a niche level."

Case Study: Hobart Corporation

Hobart Corporation is one of the leading suppliers of equipment and systems for the food service and food retail industries. By the time the Ohio-based manufacturer got onto the Web, somebody else had already snatched up the domain Hobart.com. The company settled for Hobartcorp.com—not exactly intuitive, according to e-business director Dean Landeche. In order to attract attention to the site, the company initially tried banner advertisements, but had limited success.

As a separate venture, the company launched a magazine called *SAGE: Seasoned Advice for the Food Industry Professional,* designed to address food industry issues. The magazine is clearly not designed to sell Hobart products—at least, not directly. Rather, it establishes the company's expertise through content about subjects in which Hobart customers would have a natural interest. An online version of the publication soon followed.

It was about this time that Dorothy Lane Markets contacted Hobart. Dorothy Lane Markets is not a megachain like the better-known supermarkets. In fact, there are only three of them, both in Dayton (Hobart's home town). Still, the three-store chain is recognized nationally as an innovator in supermarket practices ranging from marketing concepts to safety. For years, executives from large grocery chains visited Dorothy Lane to get ideas based on their current best practices. When Dorothy Lane Markets launched a Web site, many supermarket professionals began making regular visits to the online destination; it was cheaper than flying to Ohio, and even if executives did make the trip to Dayton, the Web site was a way to stay current without having to make frequent trips.

It was Dorothy Lane Markets that approached Hobart about adding content to the grocery store's Web site. Landeche's team created pages on the site dedicated to food safety. Each article included the Hobart logo linked to Hobart Corporation's Web site. The link drew an unexpected volume of visitors to Hobart's site, leading Landeche to explore the idea of sponsoring content on other sites where his target audience was likely to spend time. "We collected a list of Web sites that were used regularly by people in a position to buy or recommend our products," he said. For example, one of the top sites identified was the online version of the trade magazine, *Foodservice Equipment and Supplies.* Landeche developed the "Hobart Pavilion" on the site, featuring Hobart products along with original articles on topics such as governmental food service regulations. Again, Hobart hit pay dirt with increased visits to its site from just the right audience.

Hobart even undertook total sponsorships of entire sites, such as that of Peter Goode Seminars. The company, which offers training and motivational speaking focused on the hospitality industry, wanted a homestead on the Web but had neither the time nor resources to tackle the logistics. Landeche offered to host the entire site—as long as it included the Hobart logo and a link to Hobartcorp.com. Again, Landeche was rewarded with new visits from his target audience.

Hobart continues to syndicate content and promote sponsorships while the company explores new ways to draw visitors to the site, according to Landeche.

What It Takes to Communicate in the Online World

These four models required public relations practitioners to acquire new skills. But that does not mean communicators should forget the skills they have acquired over the years of performing traditional communication. The importance of other channels has not diminished, even as the importance of the Internet has increased.

Some experts have suggested that public relations can never be practiced the old way again. If that means that the practice of public relations must now integrate these new skills and processes, I agree. If it means we should forsake all non-Internet communications, I couldn't disagree more. Media relations, no matter how much it can be enhanced on the Web, is still primarily based on solid personal relationships with real-world contact. And dealing with the media is not a waste of time just because the Internet provides us with the ability to reach our constituents directly. Any good communication process employs message redundancy through multiple channels; making use of those multiple channels is even more critical when audience attention is at a premium and different members of our audiences give their limited attention to different media.

We need to continue to practice good, solid public relations management and tactics. But we also need to learn the new skills required to incorporate the Internet strategically. These skills were categorized aptly by the CPRF study:

↬ *Online constituent intelligence.* Public relations has served as the mouthpiece of the organization throughout its history. Public relations professionals have routinely turned to other experts to conduct research, including market research and competitive intelligence experts, all of whom are seen as part of different industries. Given the many-to-many nature of the Internet, however, it becomes vital for public relations practitioners to also be the eyes and ears of the organization online, monitoring constituent content, extracting value from that content, and providing intelligence based on that content, which the organization can use to make strategic business decisions.

↬ *Online communication management.* The organizations we represent need to have a clear, common online voice. This voice must be reflected in the company's various Web presences, its e-mail responses to queries, its participation in discussions, its engagement of constituents, and the content it contributes to other online resources (for example, interviews in online publications). To complicate matters, this voice cannot be inconsistent with the image that is projected offline. This voice cannot happen by accident—we need to carefully plan and craft the approach the organization takes online, serving as architects of the company's online communication efforts.

↪ *Community building and participation.* It should be clear by now that no communicator can control online dialogues, but we certainly can—and should—foster such communication and develop it. Communicators must learn to participate in discussions on behalf of their clients and companies, and to create communities targeting constituent audiences that support the institution's objectives.

↪ *Technology skills.* There is no way out of it—we must learn enough of the technology to know which tools to employ and to manage the vendors and suppliers who will create the online resources for us to assure the desired outcomes are achieved. This does not mean we must know how to write code or configure servers—but then again, few public relations professionals know how to produce class-A four-color separations for print. (It has always seemed like wizardry to me! I send a transparency to a service bureau and back come four separate sheets, each containing only one color, but when they are aligned, they present a perfect four-color image. But then again, I don't *have* to know how to produce a four-color separation—I only need to know that I need one and where to send the transparency in order to have one made.) The most important technologies to understand include those used for:

↪ The creation and maintenance of online communities

↪ The review and analysis of information residing on the Net (sometimes referred to as *data mining*), including the use of search utilities

↪ Custom communication development, including understanding of how databases work

Conclusion

Some communicators seem to believe there is a place for those who use the new tools of online communication and a place for those who hold onto the traditional tools. Nothing could be farther from the truth. Communicators will be expected to integrate all of the tools to achieve measurable results. That integration will require a solid understanding of the new communication models, and how to use them in tandem with the traditional tools to achieve the measurable results of the communication effort.

Notes

1. Watts Wacker, speaking at the "eCommunications Conference," IABC, September 25, 2000, Toronto, Ontario, Canada.

2. David and Tom Gardner, *The Motley Fool Investment Guide* (New York: Fireside Press, Simon and Schuster, 1997), 7–9.

3. Tom Davenport, "Saving IT's Soul: Human-Centered Information Management," *Harvard Business Review* 72, no. 2, (March-April 1994).

CHAPTER 3

Public Relations Tools

of the Internet

A DISCUSSION OF the strategies for employing the Internet in your communication efforts must be based on an understanding of the tools available on the Net and the various ways in which they can be applied. The Internet itself features a host of tools, many of which (such as file transfer) are technical in nature and have become inherent parts of other key tools (like the World Wide Web). For the purpose of addressing tools that can be used for public relations purposes, we will limit our discussion to the following three communication-focused applications:

1. E-mail
2. The World Wide Web
3. Virtual communities

E-Mail

E-mail existed—in fact, had become a common business tool—long before the Internet gained popularity. Since the introduction of the graphical Web browser, the World Wide Web has grabbed most of the attention that the Net gets. The media focus on innovative Web sites. And you are far more likely to hear someone recommend a great Web destination than an e-mail service.

Yet e-mail remains the Net's killer application. Far more e-mail is sent than Web pages visited. According to a 2001 study conducted by Gallup, more than half of Internet users spend most of their online time with e-mail. According to the study, the typical e-mail user spends seven to eight hours on the Net weekly, and sending and reading e-mail for them is more common than searching for information, paying bills, or using Instant Messaging. The vast majority of those users note that e-mail has made their lives easier.

In fact, statistics suggest that many people who cannot access the World Wide Web—for reasons ranging from workplace restricted access to inadequate computing resources—are able to receive and send e-mail. For purposes of effectively communicating to many audiences, e-mail must be a primary consideration.

E-mail comes in many flavors, but the following three key categories are worth considering in thinking through the appropriate application of e-mail to a public relations effort:

1. *One-to-one*. The most commonly used e-mail, in which one person sends a private message to somebody else. We'll cover some one-to-one applications of e-mail in various audience-focused chapters, (notably in Chapter 6, on media relations)

2. *One-to-many*. Also very common, one-to-many e-mail covers a variety of subcategories. The use of a "cc" list is the most common, in which several individuals are copied on a message intended primarily for one or more other people. For example, a member of a project team may send an update via e-mail to the other members of the team, and copy ("cc") it to her manager. One-to-many also describes the thousands of e-mail newsletters and bulletins that are distributed to audiences by individuals and organizations. Again, we'll look at the use of the one-to-many model in audience-specific chapters.

3. *Many-to-many*. The software used to manage many one-to-many mailing lists also makes it possible for members of a virtual community to engage in an e-mail-facilitated dialogue.

All of these e-mail categories function, at the most fundamental level, in exactly the same way. That is, the technology that sends an individual message from one person to another also sends the messages distributed to a group of people, whether that group has five members or five thousand.

E-mail was the first Internet tool that allowed anybody with access to become a publisher. As a result, e-mail is the Pandora's box that was opened, releasing the decentralization that has led to the loss of message control with which public relations practitioners must cope. And yet, e-mail has tremendous potential as a public relations tool in this new decentralized world in which practitioners still must influence audiences in order to provide value to clients and employers.

Permission-Driven Communication

Most of the e-mail applications that lend themselves to public relations begin with the World Wide Web. It is on the Web that individual audience members can give you permission to send them e-mail. E-mail you send to audiences without their explicit consent is called *spam,* one of the most unpopular commercial uses of the Internet. Hardly anybody likes getting a pitch they didn't ask for, regardless of whether the pitch is for a product or service they can use.

If research shows that e-mail is the most commonly used online application, it stands to reason that people already get a lot of e-mail. In fact, some studies show that the average employee (who uses e-mail as part of the job) spends about a full workday each week dealing with e-mail . . . and that is only the e-mail received at the office! Add to that the e-mail that employee deals with at home and you're talking about an incredible volume of messages. When you consider that an employee already spends one-plus days sorting, discarding, replying to, and creating original e-mail messages, it is easy to see why spam is so deeply resented.

To be sure, there are arguments in support of spam, the most compelling is that if it didn't work, the people who send it would stop sending it. Enough people respond to those "Make money now" and other mass-distributed e-mail messages—somewhere in the neighborhood of 3 percent—to make it worthwhile to the losers who employ the practice. Since they are making money from the 3 percent, and spam costs a fraction of traditional print-oriented marketing, they couldn't care less that they've alienated the other 97 percent. While suckering a small percentage of recipients may be an acceptable return on investment for spammers, annoying the vast majority of your audience is *not* a reasonable objective for practitioners of public relations. Don't do it.

Instead, get permission to communicate with an individual or to engage him or her via e-mail. Get them to opt in—hence the term *opt-in communication*.

Some argue that opting out is a more sensible approach. To understand the difference in how audiences will perceive opt in versus opt out, consider my e-mail newsletter, *HC + T Update*. At each of my speaking engagements, I invite members of the audience to visit my Web site to subscribe to my monthly e-mail newsletter. Each one of them must take the initiative to visit my Web site, fill out the brief form, and send permission before I will send them my newsletter. That's *opt in*. Another approach would be to send around a sheet asking for each member of the audience to jot down his or her e-mail address. When I get back to my office, I add each of them to my subscription list. The first issue of *Update* they receive would include instructions for unsubscribing from the distribution list. That is, they would receive the newsletter without asking for it, but have the ability to *opt out*.

E-mail opt out has made its way onto the World Wide Web. You have probably seen it if you've ever registered new software on a Web site, or if you have ever signed up for proprietary access to a members-only online service. At some point during the sign-up process, a screen presents you with a question like, "Would you like to receive messages about new products and services?" More often than not, the box is already checked. If you don't deliberately uncheck it, you have given implicit permission for the company to send those messages. (It is not uncommon for a company to include more than one opt-out opportunity—for their own products along with, for instance, those of their business partners.)

Logistically, opt out has many advantages. It is not as difficult to grow a distribution list. Many people won't unsubscribe simply because they do not know how, they can't find the information about how to do it, or because it is simply easier to delete the darn thing than it is to go to the trouble of sending the opt-out request. And some small percentage of the recipients may wind up spending some money. But again, are those small gains worth earning the enmity of so many individuals?

From the public relations perspective, the most important attribute of opt-in communication is that people pay attention to what they've asked for.

In our society, we are overwhelmed by the volume of information that we receive. Anybody who has ever taken an economics class

knows that what has value in any economy is that which is scarce.
We may call the current economy an information economy, but information is hardly scarce! A study from the University of California at
Berkeley determined that, worldwide, we are producing in excess of
1.5 exabytes of information per year. An exabyte is one billion gigabytes—that is the equivalent of 250 megabytes for every man,
woman, and child on Earth. Only .003 percent of that information is
in print; the lion's share is digital—e-mail messages (which in the
year 2000 accounted for 11,285 terabytes of data), Web pages, postings to discussion groups, etc. We are awash in information. Yet the
same study revealed that the average household spent 3,380 hours
consuming information in 2000, compared with 3,324 hours in
1992—a full year before the graphical Web browser was introduced,
heralding public awareness of the Internet. That represents a net
increase of only fifty-six hours per year per household. In other
words, the average person spends about as much time today focused
on information as he did nearly a decade ago. Or, as internal communications expert Roger D'Aprix put it in a mid-1990s issue of the
weekly communications journal, the *Ragan Report*, "It takes just as
much time to read a page of text today as it did during the Reforma-
tion." There is all this information, but no more time to devote to it.

> *What has value in the information economy is the
> audience's attention.*

Marketers and advertisers are hungry for new ways to get our
attention as we begin to tune out messages, which is the inevitable
reaction to message overload. If we hear or see in excess of three
thousand marketing-oriented messages daily, they will eventually
turn into the messaging equivalent of white noise. None will stand
out from the rest.

Consequently, we are seeing marketing messages in places that
used to be blissfully free of such intrusions. Airports are selling advertising space on baggage conveyors; as the leaves on the conveyors
expand, they reveal billboard-like advertisements for everything from
vacation properties to headache medicine. Property owners sell space
in restrooms above urinals and on the inside of toilet stall doors. One
company is installing television monitors in elevators based on the

belief that audiences are captive in an elevator for up to three minutes *and* they are desperate for something to look at besides the other people trapped with them in the elevator. What better place for an Internet-connected system that offers weather, sports scores, and, of course, advertising messages?

As every last vestige of freedom from pitches is appropriated, it gets exponentially harder to get targeted audiences to pay attention to the messages we need to get across to effect the outcomes that serve as the measure of public relations success. But it is a fact that people *will* pay attention to those messages they have asked for.

Opt-In Communication as a Public Relations Tool

Getting someone to say, "Yes, please send me e-mail that is designed to influence me" has to start with value: What's in it for the recipient? Promise value and deliver a steady stream of pitches, and you'll alienate someone who had taken the active step of allowing you to e-mail them. Value isn't something *you* determine. Value is in the eye of the audience.

Consider an investment audience—institutional investors, individual investors, financial analysts, and brokers. A company wants an outcome that these people can deliver, which is long-term investment in the company's stock. None of the members of these audiences will long subscribe to an e-mail bulletin that simply touts the company's strength. If you keep the audience up-to-date on company news that will help them make sound decisions, you will accomplish the following two objectives:

1. Recipients of the e-mail update will want to continue to subscribe because they are getting information of use to them.

2. Their appreciation for the company grows, resulting in a long-term positive perception and actual strengthening of the company's brand.

And, of course, now you can incorporate into the e-mail bulletin any additional messages you want the audience to hear—as long as they continue to get the valuable information they have come to expect.

During the California energy crisis of 2001, several municipalities and energy agencies (such as the Turlock Irrigation District) allowed customers or residents to subscribe to e-mail alerts that would notify them of the potential of a stage-three power alert, which meant that rolling blackouts were likely to occur. Again, the benefits derived from such an effort cover both the immediate value of advance knowledge of potential blackouts *and* improved perception among the target audience (California residents, many of whom are likely to vote in the next election and whose decisions will likely be influenced by the power situation) of what the agency is doing to help people through the crisis. Even a subscriber who gets two hundred e-mail messages a day will spot the energy alert and read it. The fact that she asked for it—that she thought it was an important enough piece of information to have pushed to her in-box—means that it will be more prominent than any of the other messages she has received.

Of course, the kind of e-mail to which you want your audience to opt in depends on the outcome you are trying to achieve, the strategies you are employing, and the objectives established. Let's look at a couple possible approaches to permission-driven e-mail.

Case Study: Edison International

Edison International, the parent company of Southern California Edison (the utility that provides electrical power to much of Southern California), has long made an e-mail update available from its investor relations page. During the California power crisis, the company advised subscribers of online press conferences and announcements, making it easier for the target audience—primarily investors, media, and analysts—to plan to "attend" these online events. Although key members of these audiences were undoubtedly notified directly, the subscription e-mail bulletin enabled the company to reach a larger audience, including some potentially influential groups who, for one reason or another, are not on the company's contact list.

Following is a sample of one of the e-mail messages distributed by Southern California Edison:

April 9, 2001

SCE to Webcast Financial Conference Call

Tomorrow, Southern California Edison (SCE) will hold an "invitation-only" telephone conference call for holders of SCE's 5–7/8% senior unsecured notes and maturing commercial paper. Although two-way participation in the telephone call is limited to holders of SCE 5–7/8% notes and SCE commercial paper only, all other interested parties are invited to participate in a "listen-only mode" through a simultaneous Webcast on the company's Web site.

Subject: "Update on the California Electricity Crisis"

When: Tuesday, April 10

Time: 1:30 p.m. PST

Web site: *www.edisoninvestor.com*

In addition to the "live" simulcast, telephone replays will be available through Tuesday, April 24 at the following numbers:

(877) XXX-XXXX—for callers in the U.S.
(402) XXX-XXXX—for international callers.

Please use pin number XXXX.

Case Study: Federal Express

During negotiations with the pilot's union in 1997, the package shipping company sent a one-time e-mail to all of its customers who maintained accounts advising them of the availability of an e-mail update that would ensure customers would be first to get strike-related information that could affect their shipments. The updates—also available on the company's Web site for those who did not want the information pushed into their in-boxes—let customers know the earliest date a strike might occur, after which date shipments might be affected, and which class of shipment would be affected.

Case Study: Greenville College

Greenville College, a private Illinois-based Christian liberal arts institution, communicates via e-mail to subscribers who represent the college's primary audiences:

- ↪ Prospective students
- ↪ Alumni
- ↪ Parents
- ↪ Current students
- ↪ Faculty and staff

The newsletters are highly specialized, targeting each audience with information of specific interest to them. For example, subscribers to the athletics newsletter get a weekly newsletter containing the preceding week's scores and the following week's schedule. Other audiences—with less timely needs—get their newsletters monthly; some come out on an as-needed basis. In addition to targeted content, each newsletter features links to material on the campus Web site. "Many of our e-mail recipients state their heaviest activity on our [Web] site comes when linking from our e-mail newsletter to specific pages of interest on our site," said Robyn Florian, Web communications manager.

Guidelines for E-Mail Newsletters

Your goal is to make the audience get into the *habit* of reading the newsletter. As soon as it shows up, the reader doesn't even have to think about whether or not she'll read it; of *course*, she'll read it. After all, she *asked* you to send it to her, she knows it always (or, at least, sometimes) has valuable information, and it's so *easy* to get through. Here are some tips on turning your e-mail newsletter into a habit:

↪ E-mail newsletters are best when they're short. Those that are long will take more time to read, and people short on time—especially when they're retrieving several e-mail messages—are more likely to print the newsletter to read later (maybe), move it to a separate folder, or leave it in the in-box with the intent of coming back to it later (yeah, right).

↪ Since most e-mail newsletters are designed to lure visitors back to the company's Web site, this should be easy: Offer only a headline and a short paragraph that provides readers with a capsule version of the information, along with a link to the complete item on the Web. Make sure your paragraph provides enough information—the good, old-fashioned who, what, when, where, and why—so that readers aren't *forced* to visit the Web merely to figure out what you're talking about. The link is for people who want *more* information.

↪ If your newsletter is *not* meant to draw readers to your Web site, you should still strive for brevity. Try to keep stories to four or five short paragraphs (see the example of my e-mail newsletter below).

↪ On the first screen that the reader sees, include an index of all the stories in the newsletter. Index items should mirror the head-lines that appear over the stories word-for-word, and should appear in the order in which the stories appear. Readers will scan the head-lines to see whether there is anything they want to read, then scroll to find the stories they've identified as interesting. As they scroll, they look for the exact headline they saw in the index, not something similar.

↝ Make your headlines explicit. Subscribers who scan won't react to a headline that is meant to be intriguing or clever. Rather, the headlines should be written so that they are direct and unambiguous.

↝ Include information on how to unsubscribe from the newsletter *and* on how to subscribe. Since you'll encourage subscribers to send the e-mail to others who may benefit from it, they'll need to know how to get onto the subscriber list if they want to.

↝ If you are sending an HTML-based newsletter, take advantage of hyperlinking to make it easy for readers to move from article to article. Limit each article to no more than a full screen of text.

The following is an example of an e-mail newsletter—specifically, mine! (You may feel free to subscribe at *www.holtz.com/subscribe.htm*):

```
From:      Holtz Communication + Technology
Subject:   HC + T Update

July 2001

<><><><><><><><><><><><><><><><><><><><><><>
In This Issue:
1. Not Enough Bandwidth to Stream Intranet Video?
   Here's an Alternative
2. Adapting Viral Marketing to Public Relations
3. E-mail: It's Still the Killer App
4. Net Warriors Flex Their Muscles:
   Another Lesson in Online Organizing
5. Increased Use of Internet from the Office
   Argues for More Open Access
6. HTML vs. ASCII for E-mail Newsletters:
   Wireless Explosion Settles the Issue
7. HC + T Update
8. Boilerplate and Subscription Information
<><><><><><><><><><><><><><><><><><><><><><>

*********************************************************
1. NOT ENOUGH BANDWIDTH TO STREAM INTRANET VIDEO?
   HERE'S AN ALTERNATIVE
*********************************************************
```

There's hardly an intranet communicator around who doesn't want to stream video to employees. When the IT department nixes the idea—not enough bandwidth, they assert—the communicators shake their heads and lament the fact that the intranet is still not taking full advantage of the Web's increasingly multimedia capabilities.

There is a middle ground between streaming video and no video at all, and General Mills has found it. On the venerable food products company's intranet, employees can tap into Champions TV, a site that broadcasts a steady flow of video to employees who want to watch.

The difference between streaming and Webcasting is technical. With streaming media, the user decides what to watch and when to watch it. Upon clicking the link, the video begins to stream. Ten employees viewing ten different videos simultaneously take up a significant amount of the network's resources. A Webcast, on the other hand, is the push of a single video to anybody who wants to watch it. (Webcasts can be live, such as a press conference or a Victoria's Secret fashion show, or a recording.) The single Webcast feed is much easier on network resources.

Anybody visiting the General Mills Webcast page can find a virtual "TV Guide"—a listing of the videos scheduled for Webcasting. These routinely include the new-hire orientation video, along with various speeches, meetings, and other events of interest. A new employee can check to see that the new-hire orientation will be on at 3 p.m., and be sure he's at his computer when it starts to play.

No, Webcasting is not as sophisticated as streaming, and streaming has more potential uses. But your system may more easily accommodate a Webcast, and General Mills has realized significant return on Champions TV, one of the more popular destinations on the intranet.

****
2. ADAPTING VIRAL MARKETING TO PUBLIC RELATIONS
****

The number of resources audiences have at their disposal from which they can obtain information and opinions has not only exploded—thanks to the Internet—but also the very nature of those resources has undergone a fundamental change. Centralized, authoritative sources such as *Forbes* or *Fortune* used to serve audiences seeking information about businesses. Today, it's decentralized, user-fed destinations like The Vault and finance discussion boards on Yahoo! that are fulfilling the public's information needs.

For communicators, this presents a serious conundrum. The channels for message distribution—magazines, newspapers, television, radio, etc.—were easy to tap into. A well-placed press release here, a solid media contact there, and the message reached the masses. How, in this new world of decentralized and uncontrolled channels, do we get the message out?

One of the channels, according to research conducted last year by the Council of Public Relations Firms, includes viral communication. Take viral marketing and apply it to the practice of public relations. A message is viral when the person who receives it is inspired to pass it along. Potentially, such messages can spread exponentially. However, organizations don't seem willing to give the viral approach a try. Research conducted recently by Jupiter concluded that most companies define customer loyalty too narrowly, overlooking important behavioral characteristics. Jupiter's Consumer Survey determined that word-of-mouth recommendations result in a choice of e-commerce sites among 45 percent of online shoppers, but that only 7 percent of companies are measuring how viral their messages are.

While viral marketers struggle to get companies to track customers' viral behaviors, those of us who work in the non-marketing side of communication may be able to leapfrog the trend and track how those messages crafted to take advantage of the viral model are influencing audiences.

Not that I've seen a lot of viral technique applied to the non-marketing world. But there are huge opportunities, particularly in the use of e-mail newsletters and bulletins. Consider the investor relations department that offers an e-mail bulletin to subscribers from the IR site on the company Website. All it takes is for one investor to forward an interesting update to a friend; that message has become viral. Now, add a line at the top of the update "encouraging" subscribers to pass the email along, and the viral approach has become strategic. The same concept works on Website articles that offer the ability to e-mail the article to a friend.

By the way, feel free to e-mail this newsletter to anyone you like.

****
3. E-MAIL: IT'S STILL THE KILLER APP
****

Speaking of e-mail as the key to viral communication, one reason it may not be taking off is that most communicators are more focused on the sexier, cooler Web. While the Web, with all its bells and whistles, may indeed be a more compelling medium in which to work, it's not the online medium most used. That would be e-mail.

The Gallup Organization surveyed Internet users and found e-mail continues to dominate online endeavors, with more than half the respondents noting that e-mail is their most common online activity. According to the study, the typical e-mail user spends seven to eight hours on the Net weekly, and sending and reading e-mail for them is more common than searching for information, paying bills, or using Instant Messaging. The vast majority of those users note that e-mail has made their lives easier.

How can communicators make better use of e-mail? Viral communication has already been discussed (in the article above). Other ideas:

* Permission-driven (or "opt-in") newsletters aimed at our target audiences.
* Opt-in "tips" services. Targeting people who do their own housework? Give them laundry tip-of-the-week.

* Mailing lists that allow a targeted audience to engage in a many-directional conversation about a topic or issue.

How are you using e-mail as an audience-focused communication tool? Pass along your applications, and I'll list them here next month.

Read more about the study results at:
http://www.gallup.com/poll/releases/pr010723.asp

****
4. NET WARRIORS FLEX THEIR MUSCLES:
   ANOTHER LESSON IN ONLINE ORGANIZING
****

When I'm asked why public relations practitioners don't really understand how to use the Internet as a communication tool, I usually answer like this: "We know how to use press releases and media placement because we read newspapers and magazines. We know how to use public service announcements because we watch TV. But we don't understand how to use the Internet because we don't regularly hang out online." By this I don't mean that PR professionals don't visit Web sites. I mean that we don't participate actively in online communities.

Once again, those who do live part of their lives in virtual communities have shown the rest of us how communicating in this medium can affect outcomes in incredibly short order.

On July 17, a Russian programmer named Dmitry Sklyarov was arrested by the FBI while attending the DefCon conference in Las Vegas. Sklyarov works for a Russian software company called Elcomsoft, which distributed an application that allows users to convert documents from Adobe's secure eBook format into the Portable Document Format (PDF). Sklyarov was one of the employees who worked on the program, which was not designed to circumvent copyright. In fact, in Russia a document must be copyable at least once in order to comply with Russian law. The program works only with eBooks purchased legitimately, and is used (for example) by blind people who can't access the works they've bought in eBook format.

But Adobe didn't like the program, and worked with the FBI to ensure Sklyarov was picked up as soon as he was in the United States. As of this writing, the programmer continues to sit without bail in a Las Vegas jail.

The online community of programmers and others responded by sitting down—at their keyboards. A number of protest sites cropped up almost immediately, including Boycott Adobe (at http://www.boycottadobe.org) and Free Sklyarov (at http://www.freesklyarov.org). The sites were referenced in countless e-mails and discussion groups, prompting strong media coverage. In the meantime, the same people building Web sites were also organizing real-world protests across the United States, including one set for Adobe's California headquarters. One prominent programmer resigned—very publicly—from a group that met in the United States, noting that, "With the arrest of Dimitry Sklyarov it has become apparent that it is not safe for non-U.S. software engineers to visit the United States." The Electronic Frontier Foundation got into the act, issuing communiques online and insisting on meetings with Adobe.

The pressure is, after only a few weeks, having an impact. Adobe has recommended Sklyarov's release, and has stated that it is withdrawing its support for the criminal complaint filed against the programmer.

Whether you support Sklyarov or Adobe in this matter, the instructive element is how quickly the Net was used to mobilize an activist group that did not exist before July 17. Look beyond the issue to the use of special-purpose Web sites, discussion groups, e-mail lists, and other tools brought to bear in virtually no time at all in support of a specific, measurable goal. We, the public relations profession, can do this, too. All we need to do is spend enough time online for it to become as natural as sending out a press release.

****
5. INCREASED USE OF THE INTERNET FROM THE OFFICE
   ARGUES FOR MORE OPEN ACCESS
****

Statistics released recently by Nielsen//NetRatings reveal a steady increase in employees' use of the Internet from work. In June 2001, employees accessed the Net from the office 43 times, a 10 percent increased from the same period in 2000. That increase means that workers are online about 22.5 hours each month, during which they visit some 35 Web sites.

If that sounds like ammunition for the forces that would restrict and monitor employee Internet use, guess again. While the study noted an increase in traffic on virtually every category of Web site (including, yes, the dreaded XXX sites), corporate information sites have grown faster than any other category, showing a 49 percent increase from 2000. In other words, most of the Web use by employees is work-related. "Office workers are moving beyond e-mail and integrating more use of the Internet to complete their tasks," according to Sean Kaldor, vice president of analytical services at NetRatings. "From accessing internal corporate Web sites to planning business trips online, workers are conducting many different business-related functions on the Web as part of their daily work routine." Similar statistics are being logged in Europe, where the most common online activity from the office is booking business travel.

****
6. HTML VS. ASCII FOR E-MAIL NEWSLETTERS:
WIRELESS EXPLOSION SETTLES THE ISSUE
****

I recently got a Blackberry e-mail pager. This is my second foray into wireless e-mail; the first was a wireless modem that connected to my personal digital assistant (PDA). In both cases, e-mail is displayed only in ASCII (also known as "plain text"). When I get an e-mail coded in HTML, I have to wade through all the coding to get to the substance, which is hard to read because it, too, is loaded with intrusive tags.

Based on the number of people I see in airports accessing their e-mail from their handhelds, this mode of staying in touch is gaining in popularity faster than the latest computer virus can infect your system. I read recently in one of the publications addressing online communication that communicators should lean toward HTML e-mail newsletters. I say, "Nonsense."

Sure, HTML looks better, gives you more control over appearance, and makes it easier to embed links. But they're worthless on wireless devices ranging from PDAs to WAP-enabled cell phones. Some might argue that you can use technology to determine the user's e-mail client and send the right version. But keep in mind how the Blackberry and wireless PDAs work: The e-mail still goes to my regular account, but I have set up a forwarding rule so that a copy goes to my handheld. By the time I've discarded an unreadable newsletter from my handheld, I've already determined that I won't pay attention to it a second time when I retrieve it at my desk.

Like so many issues online, this one is best resolved by leaning toward simplicity, and nothing is simpler than ASCII.

****
7. HC + T Update
****

>>>Shel will work with a major high-technology company to apply online and offline techniques to a culture and organization change effort.

>>>Shel will speak about internal communication audits at a meeting of PRSA in Oakland on August 13.

>>>Shel will present a telephone-based session on writing for the Web to communicators from General Electric on August 28.

>>>Shel presents workshops and consults with pharmaceutical companies in Denmark in September, with a stop in Slovenia to speak at the Slovenian Government PR office and to the Slovenian IABC chapter.

>>>Shel wraps up writing the second edition of his book, *Public Relations on the Net,* in August. The second edition is due out from AMACOM in spring 2002.

****
8. BOILERPLATE AND SUBSCRIPTION INFORMATION
****

You received this newsletter either because you asked for it or somebody who likes you forwarded it to you. Please feel free to forward it to someone you like!

HC + T Update is published monthly by Holtz Communication + Technology. You can subscribe by visiting the HC + T site on the World Wide Web at http://www.holtz.com and selecting the FREE E-MAIL NEWSLETTER page. Or, send e-mail to subscribe-HoltzUpdate@Holtz.unitymail.net.

Holtz Communication + Technology helps organizations apply online technology to strategic communication efforts.

For help with this newsletter, send e-mail to
hctupdate-help@topica-emailpublisher.com
To submit an item for this newsletter, send e-mail to
Submit-HoltzUpdate@HOLTZ.COM
To comment on this newsletter, send e-mail to
Comment-HoltzUpdate@HOLTZ.COM
To unsubscribe from this newsletter, send e-mail to
hctupdate-unsubscribe@topica-emailpublisher.com

Visit Holtz Communication + Technology on the World
Wide Web at http://www.holtz.com.

Note in the example that I keep the column-width constrained.
The recommended width for e-mail newsletters produced in ASCII
is sixty-five characters—most people won't have their e-mail software
open to a width narrower than would accommodate sixty-five characters, so you won't run the risk of irritating line breaks that are common in so many e-mail messages.

E-Mail Communities

A more thorough discussion of communities—their importance and
how to leverage them in a public relations context—occurs elsewhere
throughout this book. Here, we'll limit ourselves to a review of the
use of e-mail as the basis for a community.

E-mail communities are, by their very nature, permission-based.
Very rarely, and usually only by mistake, are individuals subscribed to
community-oriented mailing lists. As a rule, individuals only become
members of such lists when they deliberately join.

Most of the communities you'll find on the Net are asynchronous (that is, they do not take place in real time). Usenet newsgroups
and Web-based discussion groups are typical of these communities.
E-mail is yet another way to facilitate an asynchronous community.

E-Mail vs. Other Communities

Why would anybody want to engage in community by e-mail?
Let's look at some of the differences between e-mail and other types
of communities:

E-MAIL COMMUNITIES	WEB/USENET COMMUNITIES
Participants must subscribe or be invited	Usually, anybody can drop in
Messages are pushed to participants	Participants must visit the community to view recently added messages
Participants can select various options as to how to receive messages, including individual e-mail and daily digest	The host usually determines the method of viewing the group's contents

Based on these differences, it becomes easier to understand when an e-mail discussion may be preferable to a Web-based community. The ability to limit participation to those who take the trouble to subscribe—those who are willing to add to the volume of e-mail they receive—is the key benefit. Participants in e-mail discussions tend to be serious about the topic under discussion, while Web-based communities can also include casual visitors.

E-mail communities also tend to be smaller than the easier-to-join Web communities.

Establishing an E-Mail Community

Once you have determined that an e-mail community will better help you achieve your objectives, it is time to launch one. (Attracting and inviting participants is addressed later in this chapter in the section "Setting Up an E-Mail Mailing List"—this process is similar for both one-to-many and many-to-many lists.) Here are some guidelines for setting up an e-mail community:

↪ *Establish a charter for the community to ensure that the discussion stays on topic.* For the classic car community hosted by the motor oil company, the charter might be something like, "This mailing list is for the open discussion by classic car owners of issues of maintenance and operation of classic cars."

↪ *Get a moderator.* As with Web-based discussion groups, the moderator should be a member of the community, an individual who is passionate about the topic and thrilled to have the opportunity to take a lead role in the growth of the community. Under no circumstances should a public relations or company representative serve as the moderator, but the moderator is accountable to the organization; that is, he agrees to moderate the group based on the rules and guidelines the company has established.

↬ *Seed the list.* Individuals who subscribe to a list and get only sporadic messages won't remain members for long. This doesn't mean you should create bogus messages or hire people to pretend to be enthusiasts. Rather, you should identify some likely members of your audience and offer them incentives for conducting their conversations over the list.

↬ *Don't pitch products or services to the group.* Most group members (except for those who choose to receive an index or digest version) receive each contribution as an individual e-mail. If their in-boxes start getting flooded with advertisements as a consequence of having joined the community, they will quickly unsubscribe.

↬ *Monitor the group discussion.* If anybody poses a question or raises an issue that is pertinent to the products or services you represent, offer an answer, but only if one of the other participants doesn't do it for you first.

↬ *Make an archive of the group's messages available on the Web.*

↬ *Send a monthly message to group participants.* In the message, remind them of list basics (such as unsubscribing, changing their subscription options, or the list charter). Include a prominent reminder that your organization (or the one your agency represents) sponsors the list, and provide a link to the company's Web site. This is also the place where you can add any marketing message that you may want to push to subscribers.

Hybrids

We've talked about e-mail bulletins and updates you can send to a list of subscribers. We've looked at community-based discussions that take place by using e-mail. There is no reason you cannot have both concepts integrated into a single e-mail list. The notion is simple: You send out the periodical newsletter and encourage recipients to engage in discussions about the contents you distributed. If participants decide to conduct discussions outside of the scope of your newsletter, so much the better—it only means that your collection of disparate subscribers has evolved into a community, with all the enhanced power and potential a community brings with it.

Your e-mail lists—one-to-many, many-to-many, or hybrid—are not limited to large organizations or large distribution lists. In fact, an e-mail list is ideally suited to small groups. Here are two examples:

Case Study: Sister to Sister

Sister to Sister is a hybrid of a weekly e-mail update and a community conversation for the members of the Sisterhood of Temple Isaiah, a Reform Jewish congregation in Lafayette, California. (I'm intimately familiar with Sister to Sister; my wife, Michele, manages it!)

Although Sister-to-Sister is a small, local effort, it was developed using the following basic communications strategic planning process:

⮑ *Goal.* Affect the recruiting and retention of Women of Isaiah members.

⮑ *Strategy.* Enhance the value of membership by increasing participation in events (members who participate in events are more likely to retain their membership so that they can take part in more events); increase the sense of community among the members (as opposed to a collection of individuals who do not relate to one another as members of a community).

⮑ *Objective.* Develop an inexpensive means of keeping members updated about upcoming opportunities for participation that also allows members to engage one another in community-like discussions.

⮑ *Tactic.* Establish an e-mail newsletter (one-to-many) that allows recipients to discuss the contents of the newsletter and other Women of Isaiah issues.

Michele started Sister to Sister as an opt-out effort. All current Women of Isaiah members whose e-mail addresses were recorded in the database received the first issue with instructions about how to unsubscribe if they did not want to participate. Since that initial distribution, it has been an opt-in device. Each year, membership materials mailed to all prospective members (all women members of the 800-family synagogue) include an invitation to subscribe to Sister to Sister. They can subscribe either by sending e-mail to the list address or by completing a brief form on the Women of Isaiah section of the Temple Isaiah Web site.

Each issue begins with a brief listing of upcoming events that would be of particular interest to the audience (as opposed to a listing of all upcoming Temple events, which is distributed through other means), along with volunteer opportunities. Following this news update, Michele writes a brief column about an issue of interest to Jewish women, and includes links to Web sites where more information can be found. For those issues where discussion is likely to be lively, Michele also invites comments. List subscribers have engaged in spirited discussions about everything from political issues to vacation travel.

Sister to Sister is distributed to subscribers every Monday morning. If Michele is ever late, she gets e-mail and telephone calls asking where it is. Recipients have begun to perceive Sister to Sister as a valuable benefit of their Women of Isaiah membership.

Case Study: Job of the Week

Job of the Week—also known as JOTW—started as part of Edward "Ned" Lundquist's own job search. Recently retired from the U.S. Navy, where he served as a communications officer, Ned was seeking employment as a communications manager in the civilian world. His online search routinely turned up a number of communication jobs from a variety of sources. Ned consolidated those jobs into a bulletin he sent to a few select friends. In true viral fashion, recipients forwarded the e-mail to other job seekers, who wrote to Ned asking to be added to the list. As the list grew, Ned transferred JOTW to a service that handles distribution and maintenance for him.

He also added a variety of features that transformed JOTW from a top-down one-to-many venture to a community of people who have been getting to know one another. Ned often will editorialize on various communication-related issues, and then publish replies from his readers. He also invites readers to submit a one-paragraph pitch about their strengths and experience; Ned publishes one per issue. (JOTW is supposed to come out weekly, but as Ned gathers more jobs—people have started sending jobs to him for inclusion in upcoming issues—he sends out as many as three supplements each week.)

Setting Up an E-Mail Mailing List

E-mail mailing lists—both top-down and many-to-many—can be managed in one of the following three ways:

1. Set up a distribution list in your e-mail client and simply send a message to the list. This will work only for one-to-many communications, and is the least efficient means of managing a list. Don't do it.

2. Set up the mailing list software to manage the community on a server you (or your company or client) own. The programs available for maintaining mailing lists range from the free (such as Listserv and Majordomo) to the costly (such as UnityMail, a product of MessageMedia).

3. Use an outside service to handle the e-mail, taking advantage of simple Web interfaces to manage the account. As with software you install yourself, the options range from the free (one such service is available from Topica at *http://www.topica.com*, another is offered by Yahoo at *http://groups.yahoo.com*) to the more sophisticated and costly (MessageMedia, for example, will host your UnityMail account if you don't want to run the program from your own server).

There are no simple rules to help you determine which option is best for you. For instance, a large mailing list does not automatically mean you should consider a more costly service. The rock-and-roll band The Grateful Dead maintains a huge mailing list for its fans on a Yahoo Groups list.

Inviting People to Join a List

The first question to ask is: How do you attract your target audience to join the community? There are several approaches you can take, depending on the nature of your audience:

➽ If the members of your audience are already receptive to receiving e-mail from you, you can send them a personal invitation to join the group.

➽ You can employ the "market sample of one" approach, posting invitations in places where your audience is already likely to be hanging out. Let's say you represent a motor oil company and you want to start an e-mail community of classic car owners. You can post messages in classic car discussion groups inviting participants to join your exclusive new mailing list. You can even buy banner advertising at classic car Web sites.

If you want your list to be open to anybody who is interested in joining, you can register your list with various services, such as Topica (*http://www.topica.com*), a kind of search engine for mailing lists. If you use Topica or Yahoo Groups as your mailing list service, you can include your list in a directory of lists the services maintain on their sites.

Viral E-Mail

Online, *viral* refers to anything that spreads by word of mouth (or, as some put it, "word of mouse"). As noted elsewhere in this book, viral techniques are critical to public relations consultants who need to spread messages through a network that won't support a traditional top-down push approach. While viral communication takes many forms (some of which are addressed elsewhere in this book), e-mail is the most prevalent—and most successful—because it also is the easiest for users to spread. Simply click the "forward" button, type in an e-mail address or two, and then send.

In fact, some of the earliest viral marketing efforts involved e-mail—e-mail services, that is. Hotmail (now owned by Microsoft) is a Web-based e-mail service that grew large enough to attract Microsoft ownership by including a brief tagline on each e-mail a subscriber sent, noting that Hotmail was free. Recipients of e-mail sent by a friend, family member, or work colleague were one click away from signing up for the service themselves (as many did). Unintentional viral communication happens frequently as well. If a friend or colleague has ever sent you a computer virus alert that you forwarded on to others, you were part of a viral e-mail (in more ways than one!). Urban myths—those stories that make the rounds on the Internet—also are viral.

Any e-mail–based communication tool can be made viral simply by encouraging recipients to forward the message to others who might find it useful, and including information about how to subscribe. Such efforts work best, of course, when the newsletters, updates, and other e-mail–based tools target a particular audience that already is something of a community. Engineers, for instance, are likely to forward valuable engineering tips to their fellow engineers (ones they work with, ones they've met through professional associations, ones with whom they went to engineering school). Doctors will forward to doctors, travel agents to travel agents, landscape architects to landscape architects. Let's return to our newsletter for classic car owners, the one aimed at creating a strong motor oil brand. Classic car owners meet at weekend rallies. They participate in online discussion groups and chats. They belong to clubs. It is easy to see how one subscriber to a concise, useful e-mail newsletter would be inclined to forward it to a friend, or even mention it in a discussion group.

Getting Audiences to Send E-Mail

E-mail has one other compelling use for practitioners seeking to wield influence. You can compel members of one audience to send e-mail to members of another audience, the digital equivalent of a letter-writing campaign.

Under this model, you encourage individuals who have a vested interest in an issue to express their point of view via e-mail to someone in a position to influence an outcome consistent with the individual's viewpoint. If the campaign is effective, enough people will send e-mail letters voicing the same position so that the target of the e-mails is influenced by the onslaught.

(Although this approach may seem viral, it is not. One person sends an e-mail to a specific recipient, who does *not* send it along to others. The effort could be made viral, however, if a utility is added that allows interested individuals to encourage friends and colleagues also to send e-mail, adding to the deluge.)

Case Study: American Civil Liberties Union

The American Civil Liberties Union (ACLU) was one of the early adopters of an integrated Web–e-mail approach to activism, leading to tens of thousands of faxes and e-mails sent to legislators by individuals endorsing the ACLU's position, often influencing legislators to change their votes on related legislation.

The ACLU Web site invites visitors to subscribe to Action Alerts, e-mail notification of a pending vote. The following e-mail is an example of an Action Alert on Carnivore, the proposed FBI online wiretapping system:

TO: ACLU Action Network
FR: Jared Feuer, Internet Organizer
DT: August 9, 2001

Ignoring the privacy protections of the Fourth Amendment, the Federal Bureau of Investigations (FBI) is conducting searches on the Internet through an online wiretapping system called "Carnivore." This system forces Internet Service Providers (ISPs) to attach a black box to their networks—essentially a powerful computer running specialized software—through which all of their subscribers' communications flow.

In traditional wiretaps, the government is required to minimize its interception of nonincriminating—or innocent—communications. But Carnivore does just the opposite by scanning through tens of millions of e-mails and other communications from innocent Internet users as well as the targeted suspect.

Take Action! Rep. Richard Armey (R-TX) has recently said that he is considering seeking budget cuts to stop the use of Carnivore. You can help keep the pressure up by asking your Representative to join in the efforts to cage Carnivore from our action alert at:

http://www.aclu.org/action/carnivore107.html

The link at the bottom of the message in the above case study takes visitors to a page on the ACLU Web site where concerned individuals enter their zip codes. The zip code submission extracts the individual's representatives in the Senate and the House of Representatives, and provides the option of sending a message via e-mail or fax, or through the traditional mail. Part of the message is hard-coded; the first paragraph cannot be changed. The sender can modify or completely rewrite the balance of the message, however, or opt to send the default text prepared by the ACLU. (The effort is further viral through a link at the end of the page that invites users to "Let your friends know of the need to defend civil liberties.")

To HTML or Not to HTML?

Web-like e-mail has become increasingly popular. Most of the current pack of e-mail clients (including Microsoft Outlook and Qualcomm's Eudora) are able to parse HTML so that e-mail messages look exactly like Web pages. They can even display graphics—photos, illustrations, or banner advertisements—that are drawn from a server. Several organizations have moved toward offering *only* HTML e-mail because of its visual appeal. I have even read some professionals advise that all e-mail newsletters move to HTML.

My advice: Stick with text-only e-mail. At the very least (and it's not an inexpensive option), create two versions—one in plain text and one in HTML—and let your subscribers choose the method by which they would prefer to receive your newsletter.

The explosion of noncomputer Internet devices is exploding. Most of the handheld personal digital assistants (PDAs) such as the Palm Pilot, Handspring Visor, and the entire line of Microsoft Windows CE-enabled devices offer hardware attachments that allow users to retrieve e-mail. Some handle HTML, others do not, but whether they can display Web-like pages is not the issue. Those that do display HTML (Windows CE devices, for instance) still do not provide enough viewing space to display the message the way the designer intended it to be seen. And those that do not display HTML will offer readers a message garbled with scripting tags that make it impossible to read.

(Even on my desktop computer, with an e-mail client that parses HTML, I receive many e-mail messages where the HTML code is displayed rather than the Web-like appearance I was meant to see. Doing HTML e-mail badly will leave the recipient with a bad experience and a negative impression of your company or client.)

Today, a new device—the Research in Motion (RIM) Blackberry handheld—is gaining popularity at an astonishing rate. You can hardly spend time in a place where businesspeople congregate (hotel lobbies, airports, and convention centers) without seeing several in use. These devices get e-mail in real time—that is, the e-mail is delivered as soon as the sender sends it; the user does not have to request a download. The Blackberry displays only plain text, and while most users still get a copy of the e-mail on their desktop computers (where it will be displayed in all its HTML glory), their first contact with it will include all those intrusive HTML tags, rendering it unreadable.

I'll admit that I usually subscribe to e-mail newsletters in HTML format. I *like* the way those well-designed publications look. But I inevitably unsubscribe and then resubscribe to the plain text version. (If a plain text version is not available, I simply don't resubscribe.) In addition to wanting to be able to read the message on my Blackberry device, I have the following reasons:

☞ I don't like waiting for graphics that reside on the same servers as Web pages to download into my e-mail. My expectation for e-mail is that it is fast, and banner advertisements, logos, and other artwork only inhibit the download time.

➢ I often grab e-mail on my laptop so that I can read it on the airplane while I'm offline. All those images that must be obtained from a server result in broken graphic icons all over the message when the laptop isn't on the network.

➢ Those HTML e-mail messages employ a lot of color. After all, just like the Web, color in e-mail doesn't cost any more than black-and-white. Sadly, most people (particularly those in offices, which accounts for a substantial amount of online access) have laser jet printers that produce only black and white. That rich color just turns to mud when it comes out in a gray blob at 600 dots per inch!

If your strategy does lead you to an HTML-based e-mail newsletter, try to follow these guidelines:

➢ Keep articles to a single screen. If the reader cannot tell how many screens of scrolling will be required before she gets to the end, she'll probably just give up.

➢ List all of the article headlines at the beginning of the message, just as you would with a plain-text message. Nobody wants to scroll through the entire newsletter to find there is nothing interesting in the current issue.

➢ Take advantage of the hyperlink capabilities of HTML so the reader can follow a headline directly to the story she wants to read.

General E-Mail Guidelines

Clearly, e-mail can be a powerful tool. It also can get you into trouble if you don't use it correctly. As with any other form of communication, standards have emerged for the proper construction of e-mail messages. Ignoring any of these guidelines can result in the perception that you are an incompetent online communicator, or that you simply don't care how you are perceived. Both consequences ultimately affect your credibility. Here are some basic e-mail rules, which you can apply to newsletters, lists, and one-to-one messages:

1. Write in complete sentences.

2. Use appropriate capitalization and punctuation.

3. Avoid excessive use of abbreviations.

4. Sign your message. Consider using the signature feature available in most current e-mail software packages, which allows you to create a default signature block. Whether you use this feature or type in your information from scratch with each message, be sure to include your name, organization, and pertinent contact information. Some people also use the signature block as one last opportunity to communicate a key message.

5. Use a short, descriptive subject line. For e-mail newsletters, make sure it is the *same* subject line for each issue (except for the date, which obviously will change). My e-mail newsletter always uses this subject line:
   HC + T Update: August 2001

6. Don't attach *anything* to your e-mail unless individual recipients know the attachment is coming. In addition to the frustration of waiting for multiple-megabyte downloads, many people are now wary of opening *any* attachment for fear that it contains a virus.

7. Answer replies to your e-mails promptly.

8. For one-to-one e-mail messages, quote the part of the previous message to which you are responding so that readers know what you're talking about. However, *never* quote the entire message to which you are responding. If your e-mail software automatically inserts the entire message, be sure to edit it down to only the part you want to include to make your response more meaningful—or delete it altogether.

The World Wide Web

The worst thing to happen to the World Wide Web, as noted earlier, is the designation assigned to what you see on your monitor when a page loads onto your browser. Somebody (and I'd love to know who) decided to call them *pages*.

The page label has led to egregious misuse of the Web. It has been used by cost-cutting executives as an excuse to do away with print. "We can print our pages on the Web for a fraction of the cost!" they exclaim. It has encouraged graphic designers to apply print design principles to the Web. ("I've been designing *pages* for years; don't tell me I don't know how.") It has motivated legions of amateurs to create some of the most awful sites imaginable under the belief that they can produce online pages using Web-authoring tools that are as easy to use as the desktop publishing tools they use to create newsletters (which are equally as awful).

Let's be clear. Despite the vernacular (and I won't wage a losing battle to change the lingo), what you see on a Web browser is not a page. It is nothing remotely *like* a page. And our audiences do not use them like pages. Applying the Web effectively as a public relations tool requires recognizing some fundamental concepts.

We already covered a few of those concepts in Chapter 2, notably the *receiver-driven* model in which audiences pull only what they're interested in and skip the rest. You can't push anything to anybody on the Web. Print is all about push.

Understanding the key differences between print and the Web is the price of admission to engage in successful Internet-based communications. The same proposition exists in the print world: If they can't (or won't) glean your message, you've wasted your money. So let's explore the key differences between reading text on paper and on a monitor, and how these differences can influence your communication effort.

Nonlinear

Paper is linear. When you get a memo, you automatically begin reading it in the upper left-hand corner, word by word. If it is a multipage memo, you *still* start at the beginning, on page one. Books begin at the beginning, as well. Generally, you cannot open a book to a random page and begin reading. It won't make sense. The art of writing has been one of taking readers by the hand, starting them at the beginning and walking them through the information we have to present, in an order that makes sense.

Information housed on an Internet server is nonlinear. There is no telling how somebody got to a particular chunk of information, where they started out, or what they already know. The whole notion of hyperlinking suggests that I can create a link that anyone can follow from my page to one of yours. The context of your page will change from what you intended based on the nature of the page where the link was provided. And all of the pages you crafted to set the stage of the information on that page will have gone unseen by your reader.

When writing material that will appear on the screen, then, you need to trust that the reader will take away from your site what he needs. That is quite a change from the traditional approach of giving them the information you want. You must write for the reader who has dropped in from parts unknown. You must anticipate why that individual is visiting your site, and make sure that what he sees has an established context, appropriate navigation to related information, and ultimately satisfies the reader.

Two-Dimensional

What you see on a computer screen is not three-dimensional. Of course, computer applications can render objects in three dimensions, but it is an illusion. The image twists and turns on a flat screen. Print, on the other hand, is *three*-dimensional. You can pick up a book and hold it in your hands. You can thumb through the book, getting a sense of how many pages it has, how small the type is, whether there are any pictures, how the material is structured. And you can do all that in a matter of mere *seconds*.

Online, what you see is what you get. If it is not on the screen *right now*, you cannot see it. As a result, browsing the structure is not an option, short of laboriously clicking through each page of text. And that defeats the purpose of putting material online in the first place!

When a visitor comes to your site, she needs to be able to understand immediately where she is and where she can go from there. Her options and the means by which she will navigate through them need to be clear.

Interactive

Reading is passive. About the most we interact with text is the physical act of holding it and turning pages. We interact even less with television screens. From the computer screen, however, we *ex-*

pect to interact—and to interact well beyond the action required to scroll through text that appears below the bottom of the screen.

In fact, interactivity now has a minimum standard, just as video productions must meet the minimum standards set by local nightly news broadcasts. The substandard quality of videos that do not meet this standard is distracting, which limits the comprehension of the key messages about which the videos were produced. Similarly, on-line content—particularly Web content—that does not provide the minimum standard of interactivity will be of less use to the reader, inhibiting comprehension of the message.

On the Web, interactivity takes many forms. It could be access to a database in order to assemble information in a meaningful way; it could be a calculation, such as a financial planning tool. Many Web sites feature surveys or the ability to provide feedback to the owners of the site. Almost all Web sites provide choices about what to look at next, about which path to follow.

Discussion forums have their own built-in interactivity. The idea behind a discussion group (also known as a bulletin board) is the interaction among the participants of a group narrowly focused on its topic of interest. Even e-mail can incorporate interactivity. You can encourage replies, build your e-mail so that it looks and acts like a Web page, even generate discussions among a list of people receiving the e-mail.

There also are levels of interactivity over which we have no control. Once somebody has reviewed information we make available, they can visit a discussion group and initiate a conversation about what we have written. Suddenly, large groups of people who share a common interest in our work can discuss it together—and perhaps choose to take action. (All companies should monitor online discussions about them; how to monitor is the focus of Chapter 5.) Furthermore, readers can respond directly to the author. This happened not too long ago when readers of a public relations journal took umbrage with an article that portrayed communicators in a less-than-favorable light. The discussion about the article erupted in the Public Relations and Marketing Forum on CompuServe. The anger displayed by some of the participants prompted others to read the article. As the conversation intensified, the author joined the discussion by attempting to defend his approach to the article. Ultimately, the discussion degenerated into some name-calling and heated disputes. In the interactive world of the Internet, people who communicate on behalf of companies are going to need to learn how to engage directly with their audiences. It is the nature of the medium.

Multimedia

In print, you are limited to words and pictures. Online, the options available to you expand to include audio, video, animation, user-controlled three-dimensional environments, and all forms of interactivity. Communicators need to explore these new tools to determine which will best meet the objectives of the communication plan and the needs of the audience.

Physiology

Reading light affects the human body differently than reading paper. One of the most obvious ways our body reacts to reading light is for our eyes to blink less. Try it sometime. Count the number of times you blink normally. Then spend a few minutes reading a computer screen. Without averting your eyes, count how many times you are blinking now. That is the impact light has on us. The reduced blink rate leads to a higher incidence of eyestrain and headaches.

The size of type on the screen doesn't help. When you read paper, you unconsciously move the book or magazine closer or further away, depending on your eyesight, to get the proper distance between you and the print. Computer monitors are fairly well fixed, however, as is the distance from the monitor to your chair. You don't often see people hoisting their monitors and moving them back and forth to better see a new document with a slightly different approach to typography than the last page. Instead, your eyes are forced to adjust to the type, rather than the other way around.

As if that isn't enough, scrolling text induces nausea. It's the same phenomenon as carsickness. Your eyes capture images in frames, not unlike the individual frames of 35-millimeter film. Your brain assembles the images and creates the sense of fluid motion. A car speeding around curves or going over bumps causes your eye to snap more frames than the brain can assimilate. The overload of visual information is the cause of the nausea. Rapidly scrolling text through a window on a computer screen is no different.

So What?

Okay. So information on a computer screen is a nonlinear, two-dimensional, interactive, multimedia-laden source of eyestrain that can make you feel like you want to throw up. What does all this mean to you, someone who is trying to get a message across to an audience using the Internet?

First of all, it means that you can be fairly certain that people don't read what they see on a computer screen.

> *People scan text on computer screens; they do not read it word for word.*

Their eyes bounce all over the screen, looking here, looking there, in no particular order, trying to find the information they came for. In fact, a study conducted in 1997 by Sun Microsystems revealed 79 percent of people who visit Web sites scan them instead of read them! As a result, if you want to get your message across to people online, you need to make sure they can find the message during the process of scanning.

We also can surmise that when people do read online, they read more slowly. The Sun Microsystems study bears that out: People read 25 percent slower on a computer screen. By necessity, then, copy prepared for the screen needs to be about 50 percent shorter than copy written for paper.

(Many people find this observation to be a blinding flash of the obvious. Of *course* people scan Web pages; we know that! Yet, the sites they create still demand word-by-word reading to glean meaning or deliver a message.)

The fact is, we can ensure that our online messages are absorbed by recognizing how differently people approach and use the medium. To treat the computer screen as a newfangled magazine page or television screen is to make a tactical error that could result in your messages getting lost, or never being read at all. (Tips on how to write for the computer screen are covered in Appendix C.)

Intuitive Pathways

Establishing intuitive pathways on the World Wide Web requires an intimate understanding of your audience.

> *Your audiences do not think about the information they*
> *want the same way you do.*

Many Web sites are organized based on the company's organization chart: Click here for products, click here for customer service, click here for media relations, click here for investor relations, click here for . . .

Other sites provide access to content based on what the company makes (or the service it provides).

Both approaches depend on an internal view of the company. Does your audience come at the information based on a perspective that is uniquely internal? Probably not. Knowing your audience will allow you to understand the way *they* think about your information.

Hewlett-Packard's Web site provides an intriguing example of knowing your audience's predilection for site navigation. The most dominant pathways on the home page are to Products and Services, Support, HP Store (where you can buy products directly from the company), and Drivers.

Drivers? These are the software files that allow the Windows operating systems to recognize and interact with the printers, scanners, and other devices Hewlett-Packard makes. The company knows that a significant proportion of the visitors to its site have come *specifically* seeking to download drivers. The same is probably true of the sites of Hewlett-Packard competitors, but these sites do not offer one-click access to drivers. Instead, users of their products must figure out whether the people who built the Web site thought drivers belonged under a *products* listing or a *support* listing, or somewhere else.

The second most dominant navigation tool on the Hewlett-Packard site offers resources for Home and Home Office, Small and Medium Businesses, Large and Corporate Businesses, Government, Educators, and Developers and Software Partners. In other words, if you know the product you are looking for, you can opt to click the "Products and Services" button, but you also have the option of selecting a path that directs you to information based on *who you are* rather than *what the company makes*. Selecting Large and Corporate Businesses links you to a subsite dedicated to the solutions the company offers that are aimed at that particular target audience. The feature stories are relevant to a corporate audience, as are the services covered on the page.

Who Owns Your Web Site?

The question of Web-site ownership continues to cause consternation in many organizations. Sometimes it is a matter of a turf war—different departments want ownership of the Web site for the prestige or to push an agenda. Other times it is a matter of entitlement—IT wants to own it because it's a technology-based tool while Marketing wants to own it because its primary function is marketing-driven. Just as often, it is simply a matter of confusion—where *does* it belong?

Although this is only a philosophical answer, it can still go a long way toward minimizing conflict in your organization *and* leading to a more effective Web site:

> *The audience you are targeting with your Web site owns it.*

Obviously, this is not meant to be a tactical solution. Your audience won't maintain the servers on their premises, manage content revisions, or come to the rescue when something goes wrong. But in terms of what should go on the Web site, how it should be organized, what it should look like, and how it works—your target audience is in the ideal position to "own" the site.

You can turn ownership of the site over to your audience by establishing audience advisory panels. These panels are made up of individuals who represent the profile you have created of the typical (or ideal) member of the audience. These profiles should be extremely detailed, covering demographics, geography, and a host of other criteria. (What those criteria are will depend on the nature of the audience. A media audience will have a different type of profile than a consumer audience.)

You'll need to offer incentives to the individuals you select. After all, they are going to be spending a fair amount of time working on your Web site. For many, however, the idea that their efforts will result in a Web site they can actually use will be all the incentive they need. Reporters who routinely cover your company, for example, are frequently happy to volunteer to help create or revise your media relations Web site, because the end result will be a media site that helps them to get their work done more efficiently.

These panels are not focus groups, because the same participants will serve on the panel for the long haul. The more familiar they become with the site, the better their input will be. Because the site is designed to serve them, they know better than anyone else (including you) what it should contain and how they would go about looking for it. They can also tell you what content works, what doesn't, and what needs tweaking. Allow them to contact you by e-mail or telephone. Give them a private discussion area so you can benefit from the synergies created by their dialogue. Bring them to your offices once a year for a face-to-face discussion about what the site can do, how well it is doing what it is supposed to do, and what is not working. Give them password access to parts of the site that are under development so they can offer you feedback before you launch the pages to a larger audience.

Virtual Communities

The successful practice of public relations depends on knowing which publics—which strategic audiences—can have an impact on the organization's ability to meet its objectives, and what kind of dialogue will bring the organization and the audience closer together. The idea is to manage the relationship so that, ultimately, the organization's objectives are not inconsistent with those of the strategic audience.

Traditionally, audiences come in all types of configurations. Local communities are bound by a common geography, and can be easily identified. Journalists with an interest in your organization can be harder to peg. Some might cover your industry; others might cover a beat that is tangentially related to one of your company's products; still others may report on business in a broader sense, and will be interested in your company only when you engage in a certain type of activity, such as a merger, a proxy battle, or a recall. Activist groups can present a special challenge, particularly if they are not members of an organized group such as People for the Ethical Treatment of Animals, Greenpeace, or Mothers Against Drunk Driving.

Online, however, it can be much easier to find these audiences, since they tend to congregate in virtual communities that have emerged as an online center for people who share a common interest. Knowing how to find and tap into the power of these virtual communities can be a powerful public relations tool.

Until recently, virtual communities were limited to discussion groups (also known as newsgroups and forums), where the concept originated. It was in these discussion groups that people with common interests—but who were located in diverse geographic locations—were able to congregate to share their ideas, ask questions, seek solutions, and engage in debate. Initially developed so that research scientists and academics from distant universities could take advantage of the intellectual capacity of the entire community, discussion group subject matter soon expanded to address all manner of issues and themes. On Usenet alone, you can find discussion groups on *Star Trek,* dolphins, Appalachian literature, Toyotas, bass fishing, glamour photography, multilevel business, evangelical Christianity, conspiracy theories, nuclear engineering, Jodie Foster, tiddlywinks, ham radio, the Titanic, journalism, big band music, hamsters, New Orleans, baking, gardening, Bolivia, and genealogy.

Certainly, all of the individuals who possessed an interest in or a passion for these topics existed before online newsgroups were introduced. How, though, did they find other people to share their interests? Their sphere of peers often was limited to a few friends or members of a local club. With the introduction of discussion groups, however, it became possible to expand the realm of peers to hundreds or thousands of others just like them regardless of where they lived or what time zone they were in.

Suddenly, the members of these discussion groups became influential communities in their own right, and worthy of the attention of organizations. Consider, for example, the following excerpt from an actual posting to the Usenet newsgroup *alt.consumers.experiences.* The message is in response to a complaint posted by another newsgroup participant:

> I returned my Computer Model 8888 because the technician (that was promised) never showed up. I called Acme on December 21st—and the technician must have gotten

lost. I haven't even received a call from Acme . . . I will
NEVER buy another Acme computer.[1]

Thousands of people who participate in the *alt.consumers.expe-
riences* discussion group read that post, and it unquestionably influenced their opinion about the computer manufacturer. Each of them
can express that opinion to dozens of other potential computer buyers, including many who are not online participants. (Information on
how to monitor discussion groups, along with more details about how
newsgroups influence public opinion, appears in Chapter 5.) The
computer company—which, based on its lack of participation in the
discussion, does not monitor these forums—could exercise its own
influence by participating in the discussion, or by contacting the dis-
satisfied customers directly.

As more people populate discussion groups, they get to know
one another and rely on each other for information based on their
areas of expertise. Certain participants obtain varied levels of status
based on the value of their contributions. The informal groups grow
into full-blown communities, with all the properties that are inherent
in community structures. There are cultural norms, standards of behavior, internal disputes, struggles for control, cooperative community-
building efforts, and, in times of crisis, a coming together of community members to protect their common interests. As these community
structures grow, so does the community's influence.

The growing power of this actualization of the many-to-many
environment discussed in Chapter 2 opened new possibilities for organizations beyond monitoring discussions to identify issues and
looming crises.

SPSS

"There are several newsgroups that are dedicated to our products, and others address related areas," says Mark Battaglia, vice president of corporate marketing for
the Chicago-based company SPSS. "Monitoring the discussion in these groups is not
only a way to take the pulse of our customers; it also serves as two-way communication." Most of the SPSS executive team members monitor several newsgroups every
day.

The focus of most of the discussion in the product-specific newsgroups is on
how-to issues, according to SPSS President Jack Noonan. "The communication goes

on between multiple people in the group. What I look for is anything that seems to be broken when people ask how to do something. Is there something wrong in the implementation of the user interface? Is something wrong in the documentation?" These kinds of issues provide Noonan and his team with pointers to problems that can be addressed before they become major issues.

Battaglia notes that the newsgroups also help the company identify changes in the marketplace. "People ask about the ability to get a certain kind of file format exported from our products. That kind of feedback allows us to stay on top of product planning; it's a place to identify new opportunities."

There are additional benefits to monitoring the newsgroups, each of which generates about twenty to thirty messages per day, according to Noonan. "They can be a leading indicator of customer sentiment," he says, pointing to a recent example. The company had released an upgrade to one of its products, distributing a notice by mail that the upgrade would be available at a discount for a limited time. On a Usenet newsgroup, one customer noted the deadline was too soon; he didn't have enough time to process the paperwork. Others said they needed more time to evaluate their need for the upgrade. "We could hear these concerns, and as a result we extended the deadline, making it possible for people to have a smooth transition." For several days, Noonan says, he received e-mail directly from customers who thanked him for listening to their concerns. "That kind of response goes a long way toward improving customer satisfaction," he says. It also establishes the company's reputation as one that listens and responds—a reputation it couldn't buy with the most bloated publicity budget. The end result was probably better than if the company had offered a longer deadline in the first place.

Participating in the discussion groups also builds customer loyalty. Once, a competitor joined an SPSS-specific newsgroup and began bad-mouthing the company, violating newsgroup netiquette. The regular participants took offense, noting that they used the newsgroup for specific reasons, and didn't want to be distracted by commercial issues.

Although the SPSS executives mostly lurk in newsgroups, they do participate several times a week, "Particularly when the participants are talking about our policies or asking about the status of various products," Battaglia says. "I'll jump in and let them know what we're thinking, or point them to a part of our Web site where they can get some answers." Often, the messages to which SPSS executives respond begin with words like, "Is anyone from SPSS aware of . . ."

Which means the participants in the newsgroups *know* the SPSS staff is listening in. "They'll even advise us when there's a discussion in another newsgroup that we ought to be aware of," Noonan says. Often, SPSS executives will meet the Usenet newsgroup participants face-to-face at a conference or other gathering. "The relationship we've established online can be very beneficial," Noonan says. "You never know; he could turn into a beta tester for us."

Web-Based Communities

The greatest obstacle to an explosion in online communities was the fact that participants had to learn how to use special software or pay proprietary services to participate. Participating in CompuServe's highly lauded business-oriented forums, for example, requires paying CompuServe's monthly membership fee.

For most people to take advantage of Usenet, they had to learn how to operate a piece of software called a news "reader." (Free-Agent, from Forte, is one of the better commercial readers. A freeware version, called FreeAgent, is available from the Forte Web site at *www.forteinc.com*. Both Microsoft Outlook Express and Netscape Navigator come with news readers built into them, but they still function as utilities separate from the Web browser. Google manages the best of the Web interfaces to Usenet at *groups.google.com*.) Those who made the effort were those who liked learning new software and those who were serious enough about the field in which they were interested to make the effort. Those with modest interests tended to stay away.

As the World Wide Web continued its evolution, enterprising software developers crafted the means by which discussion groups could be facilitated directly on a Web page. Now, people can participate in discussion groups without ever leaving the simple point-and-click Web interface. Web authoring programs like Microsoft Front-Page have taken the Web-based discussion group to another level, in which anybody can create a discussion forum with no programming and no special software that needs to be installed on the Web server. Suddenly, anybody can develop a newsgroup on any subject without having to go through the bureaucratic rigmarole required to establish a new Usenet, CompuServe, or America Online discussion forum.

As a result, the kinds of communities that have flourished in the text-only environments of Usenet are now emerging on the World Wide Web. By making these discussion groups integrated elements of the sites, the site owners are building loyalty to the site based on their sense of belonging to a community. Consider, for example, *Intranet Journal* (at *www.intranetjournal.com*), a biweekly online publication that includes eXchange, a Web-based discussion group. Participants in eXchange include several knowledgeable experts who have been regulars, and upon whom other community members rely for ideas and the benefit of their experience. Given a limited amount of time to read online publications, the audience for *Intranet Journal* would be unlikely to begin reading a new competing magazine because they would not be able to take advantage of those community members upon whom they have come to rely.

The same concept applies to nearly any type of venture, even professional associations. The International Association of Business Communicators, for example, includes a member messaging section as part of its Web site at *www.iabc.com*. Here, members and others can discuss whatever public relations or communications issues are on their minds. A recent review of the site revealed discussions on how to communicate employee compensation programs, what to pay for freelance editors, banking public relations, and event planning.

The Future of Commerce

The convergence of Web sites and discussion groups is likely to herald in a new forum for commerce. This new electronic marketplace already exists in some online outposts, such as Agriculture Online (at *www.agriculture.com*). Here, farmers and others involved in the agriculture business can get up-to-the-minute information on such issues as the markets, weather, and farming trends. They can interact with one another in discussion forums, such as one on livestock, or another on the farm business. Finally, the site includes a transaction section, which features a marketplace, a listing of companies that pay to appear on the site. A classifieds section also appears (visitors pay $4.95 for their advertisements to appear for thirty days); advertisements read like one that offers a 1991 John Deere front-fold planter: "Well maintained and stored inside." A telephone number and e-mail address is included. There is even an online auction center.

The site effectively establishes a community of people *and* vendors, creating the potential for synergies that cannot exist in any other type of environment. A farmer having problems with a particular crop can get advice from an experienced community member about increasing yield by using a particular brand of fertilizer, which can be obtained directly from the vendor who maintains a link in the site's marketplace.

According to John Hagel and Arthur Armstrong, online commerce specialists with the management consulting firm, McKinsey & Company, this convergence ultimately will lead to a seminal shift in power from vendors to consumers. The owners of the communities, with their databases of members and the ability to target information to those participants who would genuinely be interested in it, will be able to command significant prices from vendors. Vendors would then bid on opportunities to sell to community members seeking certain products or services. (In the Agriculture Online example, a farmer requiring fertilizer with certain characteristics would announce his intent to buy ten thousand pounds of a product that meets his requirements. Suppliers who carry products that match those requirements would offer it to the farmer, who would be able to select the product offered at the lowest price.) The site owner would profit by taking a fee for each transaction completed on the site.

The Public Relations Role

Each of the virtual communities out there in cyberspace—on Usenet, proprietary services like CompuServe, or on Web sites—represents a potential strategic constituency for your organization. These audiences can be customers or prospective customers, critics, members of activist groups (such as animal rights or environmentalist groups), representatives of the media, or members of just about any other strategic audience.

Thus, the principles of public relations apply to these new communities, as well. Each needs to be assessed in terms of its potential impact on the organization, and a strategy mapped out that directs the company's relationship with the group. Once the nature of the organization's level of participation in the group has been defined, the individuals within the organization who will be responsible for that relationship need to learn the nuances of participating in discussion groups. (Refer to "Netiquette Guidelines for Discussion Forums" in Chapter 4.)

Conclusion

The Internet has provided communicators with an entire new toolbox loaded with tools that can be applied to communication challenges. Knowing which tool to use, and when, is a strategic matter, however. The willy-nilly application of tools just because they are cool, or you're interested in trying them out, will rarely achieve measurable results. Remember, "the right tool for the right job" is a maxim that applies to public relations as much as it does to home repair!

Notes

1. The name of the computer company and its product have been altered.

CHAPTER 4

The Principles of Influencing
Audiences Online

PUBLIC RELATIONS, AS I have already suggested, is all about influence. Why would a company or client pay good money to communicate if they didn't expect to obtain some sort of return on the investment? Organizations are not like the public media; they cannot communicate out of a sense of altruism, and profit by selling space in their communication vehicles to advertisers who want to reach the same audience. Organizations communicate because they want something from the audience. What they want depends on the audience. They want consumers to buy their products. They want activists groups to leave them alone. They want voters to elect candidates who endorse the company's point of view. They want community members to support the construction of a new plant in the backyard. It all comes down to the same thing: Organizations want to influence the opinions, attitudes, or behaviors of their audiences.

(I want to reiterate that influence does not mean tricking, conniving, bullying, lying, spinning, twisting, or distorting. The best public relations practitioners exercise influence through a thoughtful, candid, accurate, and honest engagement in a two-way dialogue with audiences designed to result in an outcome in which the organization *and* the audience both win. Often, the influence comes in by convincing the audience to alter a viewpoint in which the company would come out a loser.)

The Internet represents a new approach to wielding that influence. As we already have discussed, the Internet is not paper on a screen or television on a computer. It is a new medium, and requires a new mind-set about how to approach it as a public relations tool.

In this chapter, we'll explore the following critical communications elements of the Internet:

- ↝ Understanding your audiences
- ↝ Wielding influence in the many-to-many world
- ↝ Narrowcasting
- ↝ Integration
- ↝ Netiquette
- ↝ Push versus pull

Understanding Your Audiences

People *drive* business Web sites rather than surf them. The concept of *surfing* (which has nothing to do with waxing up your surfboard and hitting the waves at Malibu) comes from *channel-surfing* with your television remote control. The metaphor is a bad one. You click your TV remote because you're no longer interested in what you're watching, and what you get on the next channel has absolutely no relationship to what you were watching on the channel you clicked away from. On a Web site, people click because they *are* interested, and the link invariably takes them to content that is *directly* related to the content on the page they clicked from.

Our job in providing access to information is to recognize that our audiences demand the ability to pull the content they want, and to provide easy, intuitive access to that content.

Wielding Influence in the Many-to-Many World

By now, the implications on formal organizational communications should be clear. Let's review some of the specific issues the network creates for communicators, and some of the ways in which communicators can apply new skills to leverage these new conditions.

Self-Regulated Quality and Authenticity

Organizations no longer have the luxury of assuming their words will be accepted at face value. Formerly, it was sufficient to get cover-

age of a company issue or event in a major daily newspaper or network newscast, which had built-in credibility. Today, the Internet has
lured away a substantial part of the audience for these media, while
many of those who continue to read newspapers and watch television
news are nevertheless more skeptical of what they read and watch.
Thanks to the volume of information available on the Net, audiences
have been able to determine for themselves which resources are most
useful, believable, and authentic. (This is not meant to suggest that
people will believe anything they read just because it appeared on a
Web site. To the contrary, audiences are increasingly discriminatory,
settling on only those resources that seem to resonate with them.)

If fewer people rely on traditional channels of information—and
if those that do are less likely to automatically believe the material
presented in those channels—it becomes incumbent upon communicators to tap into the channels people *do* trust. The sites people visit,
the individuals whose postings they read, these are the influencers of
online opinion and behavior. Thus, part of the communication job
revolves around identifying those channels for each communication
assignment, and then finding ways to influence the influencers.
(Again, I am not promoting unethical behavior such as incentives,
but rather ethical communication endeavors such as active discussion and negotiation with the influencers.)

Some of the categories of influencers online include:

☞ *Discussion communities.* Usenet newsgroups, Web-based
bulletin boards, forums on America Online and CompuServe all
serve as examples of open communities where everybody participates
on equal footing. Here, you can find the individuals who seem to
sway opinion and open a dialogue with them, or you could engage in
the discussion yourself on behalf of your organization.

☞ *Complaint sites.* Sites like epinions.com and PlanetFeed-
back.com, as noted earlier, aggregate comments from contributors.
While it is never appropriate to "shill"—that is, offer bogus good reviews of your company's products and services—you can respond to
individuals who post negative reviews, fix their problems, and take
other actions to influence the people who read and contribute to
these sites.

☞ *Trust intermediaries.* These are the sites in which an individual or organization collects material for publication. Harry J.
Knowles, for example, gathers information about upcoming movie

releases for his site, Ain't It Cool News. Editors are in charge of the content posted on health sites such as WebMD. The Gardner brothers, as noted earlier, handle content published to Motley Fool. Public relations counselors should identify relevant sources such as these and determine how to convey messages through these channels.

↝ *Open-source sites.* When I need technical support for my Adobe Systems Incorporated products (such as Adobe Acrobat or Pagemaker), I don't call tech support. I visit the Adobe User-to-User Forum, where I post my question, then check back in a couple hours to check whether somebody has posted a reply. The replies *never* come from Adobe tech support staff, but instead are published by other users who populate the forum. This is an example of an open-source site, where people exchange their knowledge on a particular topic. (Adobe, by the way, has employed an effective online communication technique. Freelancers who are qualified to address customer and technical support issues troll discussion groups and open-source sites where Adobe products may be discussed, and offer help when it is appropriate.) Another open-source site is the Internet Movie Database, where movie fans can vote on their favorite movies and contribute their own reviews. (In case you're interested, *The Godfather* ranks as the all-time top movie, netting over 38,000 votes; 329 people wrote reviews.) Amazon.com's book reviews are another example of open-source contributions, with anybody who has read a book encouraged to contribute a review. At Vault.com, employees can contribute anonymous messages about what it's like to work at their company so that prospective employees can make decisions about where to hunt for jobs.

↝ *First-tier influencers.* Some individuals have gained reputations on the Web, leading readers to trust them (whether they deserve that trust or not). These individuals include Matt Drudge, the self-proclaimed journalist who publishes rumors on his site (*http://www.drudgereport.com*), including the report of former U.S. President Bill Clinton's involvement with White House intern Monica Lewinsky. There is also Jesse Berst, a technology analyst and commentator whose site draws visitors interested in hearing what Berst has to say about the latest software and hardware (*http://www.jesseberst.com*).

Increased Information Flow

Material available for our audiences to read no longer comes primarily from communicators like us. In a world in which everyone is a publisher, the volume of information to which everybody has access has exploded. With more messages created by our audiences than we in the communications profession could ever dream of generating, it becomes an added element of our work to not only create messages but also to study those that other people are creating.

Earlier, I referred to an analysis of content in automotive-related discussion groups that revealed drivers likened the Lincoln LS sedan to the Chrysler 300, and that although they liked the way the car drove, they thought it could use more interior space. This kind of market research, drawn from the collaborative discussions of auto enthusiasts, was invaluable to Ford (invaluable enough that Ford Ventures bought a stake in the company that provided the access to the discussion groups). Yet conducting market research by analyzing what people are saying in online communities is only one benefit of monitoring what other people publish online.

You can also extract value from online content by:

↪ *Identifying trends.* Trends that emerge online almost always spill over into the rest of the world. Monitoring the right online information may help you identify what the people in your markets are thinking, what they will think, and how they will react to your organization's moves.

↪ *Crisis detection.* You may be able to detect a looming crisis by monitoring what people are saying and publishing about your company and its products and services. In the early days of the modern Internet, chipmaker Intel failed to identify a crisis in the making on a bulletin board where a flaw in its latest chip was under discussion. Intel waited until the discussion had spread beyond the Internet's boundaries before taking action, leading to one of the worst public relations disasters in business history.

Expansion of Media Channels

With the Web, we have seen scores of new media channels that never existed before. In order to convey the messages that influence behaviors, the public relations profession must develop new models to cover those media. These coverage models will not compare well with the top-down push communications PR counselors are accustomed to producing. For example, we will need to employ:

↝ *Opt-in (or "permission") communications.* Interested members of our target audience subscribe to our newsletters, enter our contests, or otherwise give their explicit permission for us to send our messages to them. (We covered this concept in detail in Chapter 3, in our discussion of e-mail as a public relations tool.)

↝ *Self-service offerings.* The more we can allow audience members to do things for themselves online, the more they like it. Downloading a printer driver from the Hewlett-Packard Web site is more satisfying than calling a customer service representative and having the driver file mailed to you on a diskette. It is exciting to manage your own investment portfolio on a service like E*Trade. These same kinds of self-service offerings translate well into the realm of public relations. Consider a self-service media relations site, where journalists can get the information and resources they need without having to leave a call-back voice-mail message for an otherwise-occupied media relations representative. (Self-service media relations Web sites are covered extensively in Chapter 6.)

↝ *Reference sites.* Providing a useful online place where our target audiences can get answers to questions creates a natural draw to the content we want people to see. These resources can range from a simple encyclopedia-like resource to a panel of subject matter experts who respond to ask-the-expert inquiries. We can gain credibility among our audiences simply by providing links to resources we have identified (and qualified as credible and reputable) elsewhere on the Web.

Diminished Centralized Control

If we cannot push our messages at readers through traditional channels, we must find new channels that *will* compel our target audiences to pay attention. These new channels will often be outside of our direct control; still, we must leverage them, since they are the places our audiences are looking for information and resources. Communicators have traditionally seen themselves as so-called gatekeepers of information, controlling the flow of information—who gets what information in what format at what time. Online, we must start to see ourselves not as gatekeepers, but rather as the *gateway*, providing direction to the information our audiences want. Some of the ways we can engage audiences and make them more receptive to our organization's and clients' messages include:

↪ Hosting bulletin boards on Web sites and e-mail–based discussion forums on topics of interest to our target audience. (We'll explore communities and the role PR can play in online communities in Chapter 9.)

↪ Participating in existing discussions—as Adobe does through its network of freelance support professionals.

↪ We can host special online events that attract attention. Probably the most successful—and notorious—online event was the first Webcast of a Victoria's Secret fashion show. Although the Webcast was a technical failure (the servers could not handle the unexpected volume of people logging in), it was a public relations coup, raising awareness of the company's online catalog and e-commerce offerings well beyond what any traditional communication would have been able to accomplish. (Subsequent fashion-show Webcasts went much better, the technical issues having been resolved.)

↪ Viral communication (which we analyzed in Chapter 3) will be equally important to our communication efforts. Now taken for granted by marketing professionals, viral communication takes advantage of individual enthusiasm to spread the message; it is sometimes referred to as "word of mouse."

Speed of the Internet

In reacting to the impact of the Internet, many communicators have been intimidated by the medium's speed. The velocity of information online is, indeed, one of the Net's characteristics. In fact, the Internet is likely to render the notion of a periodical meaningless. One of my colleagues, Dr. Don Ranley (who teaches journalism at the University of Missouri), claims one of his favorite oxymorons is "quarterly newsletter," as though the news happens only once every quarter. News happens all the time, moment by moment; those publishing quarterly newsletters only get around to *reporting* on the news once a quarter.

Now, with the immediacy of the Net, even the idea of a *daily* newspaper can be incongruous. When news breaks, sites like CNN.com publish it online as soon as a writer can crank out the copy. Companies with Web sites recognize the same thing: When the organization is in the news—particularly in a crisis situation—interested individuals will swarm to the company's Web site. It becomes critical to ensure that information is waiting when they arrive. (We'll talk more about this in Chapter 13.)

But it doesn't take a crisis to appreciate the need for speed. If you offer an "Ask the Experts" page on your Web site, individuals submitting questions expect answers quickly. They also expect answers when they submit questions through a "Contact Us" link. Failure to respond in a timely manner (as close to instantly as possible) reflects poorly on the organization. (Interestingly, few companies have made a dedicated effort to respond quickly to online queries. Although more than half of retail companies respond to customer queries within six hours, organizations in nonretail lines of business are failing to meet customer expectations. A 2001 study by Jupiter Media Metrix reveals that customers want their queries answered within six hours, but only 38 percent of companies meet that expectation, with 33 percent of companies taking three days or longer to reply to online inquiries. As the number of non- and slow-responding sites increases, the study concludes, customer confidence in e-mail as a service channel will also diminish.)

When the organization's reputation is at stake, it falls to the PR professional to implement new processes and employ new technologies that accommodate the audience's expectations. Developing the systems that allow companies to respond to e-mail inquiries and other queries from the organization's Web site (such as requests for interviews generated from the media relations page) should be a primary task. Practitioners also need to focus on establishing processes that ensure news and information is posted as soon as it is available, not only to the company's site but also through distribution channels (including formal relationships with other sites and general content syndication) to news outlets and other online sources where the message will be sought by target audiences.

The Internet's Collaborative Nature

People in communities are not passive. Rather, they are interactive, talking to one another, helping one another, arguing with one another, and always collaborating in one way or another. These collaborative efforts take place in close to real time, and they adopt the tone of a genuine human voice, not the typical "corporatese" that communicators churn out on behalf of their companies and clients. The one-way, top-down push of information over the Internet simply will not work (as we'll see in the next section of this chapter, when we discuss receiver-driven communications). To appeal to online audiences, it is necessary to engage them as real people (not as corporate flacks). Counselors can host discussion forums targeting constituent audiences. We can participate in existing discussions, whether they are on the Web or in e-mail mailing lists. We must integrate feedback components into our strategies, encouraging a dialogue upon distribution of our messages. (This can be as easy as including an e-mail address for comments—as long as you include in your plan the means by which e-mail questions will be answered within six hours!)

We also need to incorporate strategies that enable a dialogue even when individuals pull the information from a site that has the information or resources for which they were searching. A media relations Web site provides one example. The site contains resources to help journalists prepare their stories, but also features invitations to participate in online press conferences, to submit questions, or to schedule an interview with an executive. The reporter went to the site expecting to retrieve needed information but winds up engaged in a dialogue with the organization.

Narrowcasting

Most business sites on the World Wide Web represent the greatest mistake that companies make on the Internet. "It's called the *World Wide* Web," comes the cry from the corporate boardroom. "Therefore, it has to accommodate everybody in the whole wide world!" These sites try to be all things to all people. In an environment in which individuals *pull* information based on their unique information needs, the World Wide Web represents the greatest opportunity in the history of media to target audiences without the need for mailing lists or demographic breakouts.

Heretofore, narrowcasting required you to know that your target market comprises mostly, for example, affluent women, age 18 to 32. Then you had to know details about the habits of that audience, such as which publications they read. Armed with that knowledge, you would then buy advertisements in those magazines and place articles in those newspapers. On the World Wide Web, conversely, all you need to do is make sure your site contains material that would interest your target market. *They* will now be able to find *you*. (Of course, you will need to promote your site appropriately, a subject covered in Appendix B. Even if you did not undertake a comprehensive promotion, however, if your site contained worthwhile material, the word would get around among members of your target audience.)

Knowing your target market, and establishing objectives for that market, means your site can be configured to address their needs. Most sites on the Internet, however, are designed to serve a one-site-fits-all function. The home page proudly displays the company logo and links to material that is so broad in nature that it doesn't really meet the specific needs of any one group. Companies that recognize the Internet's narrowcasting capabilities can establish any number of independent sites, each addressing a specific audience with a specific set of objectives.

When you consider unique, discrete sites for different audiences, it becomes easy to move away from some of the more parochial considerations of Web development, such as having a common look and feel. Maintaining consistent *branding* across a site is critical, but does not preclude a unique look and feel for each of the narrowcast-focused sites. Why would anybody assume that the design of a site meant to appeal to a consumer audience would appeal equally to an investor? These dramatically different audiences react to different visual cues, meaning that you should focus your design efforts on the audience, *not* on the site!

Let's consider a number of narrowcast sites and how they meet specific needs of target audiences:

The most obvious kind of narrowcast sites are those designed for a clearly defined audience. Many corporate sites offer a subsite for the media with content that meets the unique needs of the media. Many of these sites are small archives of press releases, entirely similar in look and feel to the rest of the site. The Verizon News Center, however, offers a look that is substantially different from the rest of the Verizon site—although on first glance, you may disagree. The initial impression that the look and feel is consistent from the consumer-oriented part of the site to the News Center, which is aimed at journalists, is driven by the navigation bar (which spans the top of the page) and the positioning of the contents menu (along the left-hand side of the page). Beyond these elements and the page title, though, the page has a starkly plain appearance. Hardly any graphics must download, and links along the lower left-hand side of the page (to press kits, an e-mail subscription service, and other features) are not mirrored on other parts of Verizon's site. The lack of graphics (crucial on the consumer pages that act as advertising and are designed to compete with other glitzy telephone companies) recognizes that journalists, generally using slower dial-up connections from their newsrooms while they are on deadline, don't *want* to watch graphics resolve on the screen.

Similar concepts apply to investor relations sites (very serious for the conservative financial community) and job sites (edgy and youth-oriented, if that is your market for new hires).

Issues sites represent another type of narrowcast site. Unocal, the oil company, offers a link to a special subsite addressing Myanmar (the country also known as Burma), where Unocal does business. Activists seeking improvements to human rights in Myanmar have criticized Unocal; the subsite explains the company's position. It is a minisite (featuring links to pages that assert Unocal is improving lives in the country, pages that cover the various lawsuits filed by activists, pages that list shareholder resolutions, and others) that is dedicated entirely to this issue—and thus does not take on the appearance of the more dominant part of the site designed to promote Unocal's products and its value as an investment. Nike maintains similar subsites on issues the athletic shoe company faces, primarily regarding working conditions in its international facilities. Like Unocal, Nike has given these pages a look and feel that is appropriate to the content and the audiences.

Product-specific Web pages constitute another category of narrowcast sites. While a visit to Mattel Toys's home page provides access to corporate information, links also take visitors to sites like Barbie.com, a separate site that bears absolutely no resemblance to the corporate page. The audience is little girls of the age at which they would play with Barbie dolls. The site is a so-called brand portal, designed to reinforce the Barbie brand to girls of doll-playing age with fashions, music, games, and other features. Levi Strauss takes the same approach, providing a corporate site for corporate issues, along with independent product sites like Dockers.com, which target the demographic audience that buys clothes like Dockers (as opposed to the different demographic group that buys Levi's 501 jeans).

Microsoft offers a comprehensive look at the idea of narrowcasting. Visitors to any part of Microsoft's vast online presence never have any doubt—not even for a second—that they are on the Microsoft site. The top navigation banner, which appears only on the right-hand side of the page, includes the Microsoft logo and key navigation links. On the upper-left, you'll find the theme of the subsite you are on—PressPass, the media relations site, for instance, or Office XP, the office productivity suite. Everything below this narrow band at the top of the page, however, is unique to the audience; the look and feel of the pages are completely different. Because of the consistency of the navigation banner, logo, and page name on every page, users are never confused; they know they are on a Microsoft page. But the design of the media page is completely different from the design of the investor relations page, in recognition of the fact that the two audiences are different. In fact, even within the Windows family of operating systems, the design varies between Windows ME (created for home use and sporting a design that would appeal to individual consumers) and Windows 2000 (created for corporate office environments with a Web site designed to appeal to chief information officers or others involved in the operating system decision-making process).

Case Study: Hear-It AISBL

Hear-it AISBL is a not-for-profit organization dedicated to heightening public awareness of hearing impairment. According to Soeren Petersen, public relations consultant with the Denmark-based agency Xylofer A/S, putting the organization online involved creating five targeted global Web sites. Cumulatively, Petersen said, the sites were designed to address hearing loss and hearing issues "with the aim of increasing the general awareness about hearing impairments and their personal and socio-economic consequences among different stakeholders.

"One of the main problems on the Internet," Petersen asserts, "is that far too few home pages are not made—and targeted—toward specific target groups. Instead, they often—and with little success—try to communicate with different stakeholders at the same time."

The sites developed for Hear-it include:

↪ A comprehensive site at *http://www.hear-it.org*, aimed at the hearing-impaired and their families

↪ A site for young people, dealing particularly with tinnitus and noise, and which also serves as a resource for educators in primary and secondary schools (located at *http:// www.youth.hear-it.org*)

↪ A site for the media, where journalists working with health and hearing-related issues can get information (at *http://www.press.hear-it.org*)

↪ A site for doctors, with information on counseling, identifying hard-of-hearing patients, and hearing diseases (at *http://www.medical.hear-it.org*)

↪ A site with information aimed at politicians and civil servants who work with related issues (at *http://www.political.hear-it.org*) that addresses the social cost of hearing impairment, and offers information about hearing health regulations in different countries

"The information we write and publish appears on the Web sites where the information might be relevant," Petersen said. "By doing this, we only publish information that is relevant to specific stakeholders on the individual stakeholder sites— and cut off irrelevant information."

The Microsoft sites depicted in Figures 4-1 to 4-4 all contain common branding and navigation across the top of the page. Yet, the balance of each page—which occupies most of the available real estate—presents a unique design targeting a different audience. Figure 4-3 and Figure 4-4 are both pages promoting Microsoft's Windows operating system, but Figure 4-3 targets corporate audiences for the Windows 2000 operating system while Figure 4-4 is aimed at home users of its Windows ME operating system.

Integration

I have been making the point tacitly throughout the book to this point; it is time to be explicit:

> ### The World Wide Web is not the Internet!

The Web is, in fact, only one facet of the Net. E-mail, file transfer, network news—these also are facets of the Internet. A strategic

FIGURE 4-1. USING PRESSPASS FOR TOP NEWS STORIES.

public relations effort on the Net is not restricted to the use of only the Web; it integrates all of the elements of the Net that can help achieve the objectives established for the campaign.

At a higher level, the Internet is merely one channel among all the traditional media we have been using for years. A strategic public relations effort on the Net integrates the Internet into a broader effort; it does not involve two separate and independent campaigns—one that occurs online and one that occurs in the rest of the world.

Let's use a hypothetical example. Amalgamated Magnets is trying to convince an offshore government to continue providing us with a tax break for the two manufacturing facilities we have located in their country (which we can define as the goal). The public relations strategy objective might read like this:

> Communicate the benefits Amalgamated has brought to the country directly to the tax authority, as well as to legislators, the media, and the public at large, and clarify the company's plans for future enhancements.

The idea would be to make clear that the company is bringing the country far more than the measly tax dollars it might collect if

FIGURE 4-2. TARGETING SHAREHOLDERS.

the special status were to be revoked, and that more such advantages are on the way. (And, of course, we also would be willing to negotiate additional actions to retain our current tax status.)

Once the strategy is in place, it is time to outline objectives. One objective, for example, might be to channel information to the general public through the media to inspire citizens to voice their support of the company to their legislative representatives. With objectives for each of our audiences, we now can begin to outline public relations tactics to employ in support of the goal. A traditional approach might include:

- Meetings between the plant management (well briefed by the public relations department) and representatives of the tax authority.

FIGURE 4-3. TARGETING CORPORATE AUDIENCES.

↪ Meetings between government relations representatives (equally well briefed) and key influential legislators.

↪ An open house at one (or both) of the plants highlighting the programs the company has undertaken to educate local employees in high-tech skills (rather than bringing U.S. expatriates into the plant); the open house also highlights new investment in equipment and facilities. The open house will result in a video news release for local television news broadcasts, press releases, and copies of executive speeches.

↪ Press releases on the company's total investment in the local community, and its indirect impact on the local economy.

↪ Institutional advertisements in the local business press announcing the company's latest investment plans.

The Internet should be applied to this campaign in an integrated manner; that is, it should be treated as one of the media employed to achieve the advantages to which it is best suited. Some of the elements of the Internet to take into account include:

FIGURE 4-4. TARGETING HOME USERS.

⇨ Announcement of open house activities on the company's home page.

⇨ Establishment of a site dedicated to the company's positive image within the country, in both English and the native language of the country. The site would feature an archive of all press releases and speeches, photographs from the open house, and data about the company's investment and impact in the local economy. It could include testimonials from employees who have received the kind of training and opportunities that allowed them to dramatically improve their overall prospects. Details about the various plants and operations, including interactive maps of the plant floors and details about products made there, also could be part of the site. A survey could query locals about the value of the company's participation in the local economy and the most appealing enhancements to Amalgamated's current operations. Finally, the site would invite visitors to send an e-mail, fax, or letter to their legislator in support of the company's efforts in the country. (The site, of course, would be included in all press releases, and media interviews would include a request to print the URL of the site in all stories about the company.)

↪ Banner ads promoting the special-purpose site on selected World Wide Web sites that deal with the culture of the country.

↪ Participation in selected discussion groups dedicated to conversations about the country.

↪ Further integration can be achieved by including the address of the special-purpose Web site on all printed material, and by issuing a press release that introduces the site. Any graphic identities, such as a logo, should be used on all materials, including the Web site.

Ultimately, this integrated approach establishes a consistent impression, a *brand identity*. Each element of the campaign reinforces the others, with each taking advantage of the strength of the medium that it employs:

↪ *Press releases* establish a record and inform key media of the primary messages we want to convey.

↪ *One-on-one meetings* allow us to position our messages based on the interests of each influential government representative. They also give government representatives an opportunity to voice their concerns and issues, which we can assimilate and address in subsequent stages of the campaign.

↪ *The open house* is a visible display of our commitment, and an opportunity for our senior management to be seen.

↪ The *video news release* means that members of the public at large have an opportunity to hear key messages and see what Amalgamated is doing inside the walls of an otherwise anonymous manufacturing facility.

↪ *Institutional advertisements* seek the support of the local business community.

↪ *Discussion groups* provide us with direct feedback from interested members of the general population, which we can incorporate into our thinking. We also can try out various suggestions for compromise before broaching them with decision makers.

↪ The *Web site* in general provides interested parties with an archive of all materials, including levels of detail that could not realistically be incorporated into press releases and other print vehicles; interested parties would *pull* those elements in which they are interested.

⇨ The *Web-based survey* can be used as proof that the population believes the company is contributing to the local economy. It also can generate relevant ideas for new efforts that would further stimulate the economy or otherwise offer advantages to the local population.

This approach represents only one type of integration. Another approach might, for example, be sequential. Amalgamated Magnets advertises its magnets in a full-page display advertisement in *Magnets Today*, and invites readers to visit the company's product-oriented Web site to get more information than would reasonably fit in a typical advertisement. Visitors to the site get the information they need to make a purchase decision, then type their zip code into an interactive locator program to find the closest independent dealer who has the right magnet in stock. The program produces not only the name of the dealer but also an address, a map showing how to get to the dealer's location, and a telephone number. The dealer has been instructed to ask customers who buy an Amalgamated magnet, "How did you hear about us?" and make a hash mark on a special form for each customer who answers, "I found you on Amalgamated's Web site." Now Amalgamated can measure how many magnets it sells thanks to its Web site.

TIP:
Build the Internet into Your Plans

Too often, the people who are responsible for crafting the Web site are not part of the same group generating the total public relations campaign strategy. Build the elements of the Internet you will use into the overall strategy, then work with the Web design team the same way you would work with a printer, a video producer, or any other vendor—as part of the team working toward the same set of objectives.

The integration of the Internet into a public relations effort produces far greater results than isolated online campaigns that are unrelated to the company's other communication efforts. Take Ragu, for example. The site is unquestionably great, featuring good information, interactivity, entertainment value, everything that makes a site compelling. But the brand that is promoted on the site is the fictitious Mama Ragu. Mama's personality infuses the site; you can even opt to receive an occasional e-mail from Mama, alerting you to coupon offers or advising you of a new product introduction. But Mama is an element *only* of the Web site; she appears in no other aspect of Ragu's advertising or communication effort. If you went to the grocery store after visiting the site, you might be inclined to look for Mama on the shelf, but you would be disappointed; she's not there. Ragu's Internet public relations effort is *not* integrated with its other communications; it is isolated, and therefore, misses its potential for significant influence.

Levels of Integration

Integrating the Internet into a broader communications effort can be easy with limited benefits, or it can be complex with far-reaching impact. Let's consider nine levels of integration of the Net with broader communication efforts:

Use Print to Drive Readers Online

Your print publications can include pointers to relevant material on the Web or intranet. Your intranet can feature reminders to review information included in print. Both concepts allow you to use the medium the reader is currently using to heighten the visibility of the other.

Print-to-Web is perhaps the most useful of these models. An article can include links to a variety of supplemental elements for which there was no room in the magazine, including:

⇝ The complete text of the interview
⇝ Links to related resources
⇝ Additional photos
⇝ A forum where readers can engage in discussions about the article

In one company, traffic to the intranet increased dramatically after the president, during an all-hands meeting, noted that the intranet was the source of valuable information he had referenced during a question-and-answer session. At Sears, former Communications Technologies Manager Sharon McIntosh produces a simple monthly bulletin that advises employees about new additions and features available on the intranet. The result—traffic to the intranet increases following the distribution of each issue.

You are by no means limited to the print-to-Web model. Many Web sites are successful in their efforts to get visitors to order print or other traditional communication tools. Investor relations sites commonly invite visitors to order a printed copy of the annual report, while other sites offer to deliver catalogs, videotapes, audio CD samplers, and other offline media.

Integration rating: Low. The most basic form of integration simply uses one medium to create awareness of another.

Publish Material of Marginal Value Online, Freeing Up Space in Print

How much time do you spend producing lists of service anniversaries for print? Or birthdays? Promotions? Transfers? New-hires? Do you include employee classifieds in your print mix? These standards of internal communication unquestionably have value; but how important are they compared with material that explains organizational strategy, connects employees with the marketplace, or facilitates interaction? With an intranet, communicators have new space they can use for these listings, freeing up the limited print budget for material that lends itself more effectively to the print medium. The anniversaries, company picnic photographs, bowling league standings, and baby pictures are available to anybody who wants to see them—online—saving the "push" print for the truly important information.

Integration rating: Low. Audiences accustomed to getting their information from one source make the move to an alternate source.

Link Current Copy to Archival Material

Hard disk space is cheap. Paper is expensive. Use your digital archives of your print material to add value to the content you have deemed important enough to put into print.

That is the approach taken by *Network World*, a trade magazine aimed at computer network professionals. Many publications offer online archives of their print content, but they do little to help users take advantage of them beyond providing fundamental search capabilities. *Network World*, on the other hand, bundles archival content (along with some other links) to current content through its Doc-Finder system.

DocFinder is an alternative search capability of the magazine's Web site, Network World Fusion *(www.nww.com)*. Readers of the magazine who find a DocFinder logo accompanying an article can type the associated DocFinder number into the Web site's search field, and retrieve related material from the archives. Here is an example:

A mid-2001 issue of *Network World* featured an article about unified messaging systems. Typing the associated DocFinder number—5626—into the text field on the *Network World* home page took readers to the Web version of the article, along with a series of links to related articles. These included other articles from past issues of *Network World*, a piece from a news service, and a link to a primer on unified messaging from a completely unrelated Web site. Also featured were any items on the *Network World* site that matched the search term *unified messaging*, along with a reprint request form and a short questionnaire about the value of the article. Through its careful integration, the magazine makes it easy for people interested in a topic to extract related information from the archives. (The page also included information on how to contact the author, and the ability to offer feedback about the article.)

Integration rating: Low. While simple archiving is hardly integration at all, this method adds value by preselecting relevant archived material and making it instantly available. The DocFinder number prevents users from having to resort to using clumsy search engines.

Let Readers Engage with Subjects and Authors of Print Articles

Reading is a passive, one-way experience. If the subject of an article expresses a viewpoint that is contrary to the reader's, the reader can only sit in exasperated silence, imagining how a confrontation might proceed. If the subject raises questions in the reader's mind, the reader has no immediate means of seeking answers.

Internet technology makes it possible for publication editors to expand the scope of printed material by offering subsequent online interaction. The San Jose *Mercury News* was one of the first publications to capitalize on the technology, inviting readers to participate in live chats with the subjects of articles, such as then-California Governor Pete Wilson. *Wired* magazine has made similar offers, promoting in print the availability of authors of articles and their subjects on specific dates for interaction with readers.

Integration rating: Medium. Audiences take advantage of both media to enhance the value of the information.

Expand Existing Offerings in Ways That Wouldn't Be Possible Without the Net

EDS, the high-tech consulting company based in Plano, Texas, has had an effective face-to-face program for years. Dubbed "Straight Talk," it ensures that traveling executives make time to meet in person with employees at the location they are visiting. The company's communicators had already found an intranet application for Straight Talk: Questions and answers recorded at each session were posted on the Straight Talk intranet site.

But Jerry Stevenson, who managed EDS's intranet, found the face-to-face nature of Straight Talk limiting. Yes, it was critical for executives to be seen, and for employees to have the opportunity to ask them questions. But only employees at the site where an executive was physically situated could participate. Wouldn't it be great, he wondered, if any employee, anywhere, could ask an executive a question during a Straight Talk session?

Stevenson adopted chat-room technology so that an executive could conduct a virtual, online Straight Talk. These interactive sessions have not replaced the traditional face-to-face Straight Talk sessions; they have supplemented them. (The transcripts of these sessions are archived on the Straight Talk intranet site, along with the questions and answers recorded at the face-to-face sessions.) The key to the integration effort was to make the chat a new feature of the existing program, rather than launching it as an entirely new technology-driven program. (Many companies have done exactly that, promoting their all-new, high-tech Online Executive Chat Series or what-have-you.) Hence, the focus is on the substance of the executive-employee engagements, and not on the technology that makes it possible.

Integration rating: Medium to High. The media employed in the program are seamless, each used based on the benefits it brings.

Build Media Convergence into Your Site

More tools are under development that can technically integrate your site with other media. One customer service-technical support site was built to help customers solve their own problems with the company's products. Expecting that some customers still would be unable to resolve their issues, however, the company provided an intriguing feature. A customer can type in his telephone number, then click a "Call Me" button. A heartbeat after clicking the button on the Web site, the customer's telephone rings. As soon as he answers the phone, he is connected with a live customer support representative.

Opportunities to merge tools such as this onto a Web site are expanding as rapidly as the technologies are developed. Webcams are one of the older means of converging long-standing media—that is, video—onto a Web site. Although most Webcams offer questionable value, Toronto provides its citizens with a site where clicking on any of several hot spots on a freeway map instantly produces a live video stream of traffic on that freeway at that precise moment.

In both instances—the telephone connection and the traffic-cam—the Web simply becomes the intermediary connecting the user with a non-Web medium.

Integration rating: Medium to high. In the examples, the Web is used merely as a delivery mechanism for viewing video or access to a live human being, blurring the line between the Web and the content it delivers.

Build the Web into Your Value Chain

Rather than expect your Web site to serve as an all-inclusive alternative to other media, you can use elements of your Web site to serve as a step in a sequential process you would like your audience to follow. Consider, for example, a company that manufactures a line of digital cameras. In order to attract a large audience to its cameras, this company advertises in a variety of magazines, including the numerous photography magazines on the market.

These advertisements, however, offer limited real estate where images captured on one of the company's digital cameras can be displayed. To expand the range of images available for review, the print advertisement directs readers to a Web site where many more images can be stored. Customers could conceivably view the images based on the camera model, the lighting conditions, indoor or outdoor photography, portraits or landscapes, and a variety of other criteria.

Kodak takes this approach, although its digital picture gallery limits viewing to the camera model with which the picture was taken. The same images are available, of course, to consumers visiting the Web site to study digital cameras.

Integration rating: Medium to high. Each medium is used to its advantage in a linear, sequential communication process. The value of the print component is diminished if the user does not take a cue from the advertisement to visit the Web site.

Expand the Definition of a Communication Vehicle

Remember the old commercials for Certs breath mints? "It's two, two, two mints in one!" It's a philosophy that could apply today to Web sites and their relation to other communication tools.

By way of example, let's look at a book. Many books introduced for sale in bookstores and through online retailers have associated Web sites. Almost without exception, however, these sites are designed to promote the sale of the book. A recent book that promotes the idea of corporate journalism over strategic employee communication, titled *Beyond Spin*, is promoted at *www.beyondspin.com*. Visitors find author biographies, the book's table of contents and bibliography, a listing of the case studies included in the printed book, and information on buying the book.

Seth Godin's book, *Permission Marketing*, is promoted with only a single-page Web site at *www.permission.com*. You will find a few quotes from positive reviews along with a form to submit your e-mail address in exchange for which you will receive the first four chapters of the book free in your in-box. It's clever marketing, consistent with the theories articulated in the book, but it's still marketing.

Compare these sites to *www.blursite.com*, the site developed in conjunction with the book, *Blur: The Speed of Change in the Connected Economy.* In the book, the authors claim that successful competition in the Internet age will require organizations to create products that are indistinguishable from services, and vice versa—that is, that the line between a product and a service will by necessity be blurred. Their Web site (no longer online) served as a case study of what they mean. The site's welcome message proclaimed that the site was "our means of transforming a simple product, a book, into an online, interactive, customized, learning and upgradeable offer."[1]

The site allowed the authors to offer updates to the material in the book, provided readers with quick overviews of the book's contents, and offered checklists for readers to use when implementing the book's ideas in their own organizations. Another section allowed readers to submit examples of how they blurred their businesses—with prizes for the best examples (many of which will, undoubtedly, appear in the next printing of the book). Prize-winning entries were published on the site. Discussion groups enabled readers and the authors to engage in dialogue about the contents of the book. The authors added a section on health care, providing insight into how health care is (and should be) blurring its businesses. Separate discussions and case studies were featured in the health care discussion.

Was it a book, or was it a Web site? The answer is, of course, yes. The distinction between the two was blurred, to the benefit of the reader.

Integration rating: High. This represents one of the most complete examples of integration available, in which the boundaries between the Web and the printed book all but evaporate.

Build Tools to Make Offline Life Easier

How can a tool on the Internet or an intranet make life easier than the tools that facilitated the same activities before the introduction of the Net? Any number of organizations—outside of the communication function—have started to develop innovative answers to these questions. On the World Wide Web, you can book an airline, hotel, or rental car reservation and get a confirmation without having to make a long-distance telephone call or listen to annoying music while waiting on hold. You can order everything from computers and software to books, furniture, music, chain saws, apparel, and artwork. You can pay bills and obtain customer support.

The intranet has seen the development of an equally impressive list of tools. Using the company's network, employees can enroll in a health care plan, manage a retirement account, order office supplies, conduct a performance appraisal, requisition a new staff member, and order logoware from the company store.

These may seem quite different from the kind of work in which communicators are engaged. There are, however, several reasons communicators should consider getting involved with such projects, such as the following:

➯ Even a simple form communicates a message to the individual viewing it. Principles of communication should be applied to the execution of the form.

➯ These tools can enhance an overall communication. The benefits enrollment form and the online version of the enrollment booklet are inseparable in the mind of the user. Thus, the form becomes a part of the total communication effort.

➯ Tools such as these help a Web site achieve the critical mass it requires to become a genuinely valuable resource to the user. Consider BizTravel at *www.biztravel.com.* The content of the site is the equivalent of any print-based travel magazine. But it is the integration of the magazine with an online travel service that builds the critical mass necessary for users to find a full spectrum of value on the site.

Integration rating: High. When visitors use online tools to engage in day-to-day activities, integration is complete.

Netiquette

It is dangerous to think of the Internet as a technology. True, technology enables the Internet, and a certain amount of technological expertise is required to take advantage of it. But all that technology without people using it would represent a huge global network of nothing. The Internet is people connecting with people. Each member of the growing community of Internet users is an individual who, to varying degrees, has accepted the cultural standards that have emerged as part of the Net's social fabric.

The *Jargon Dictionary* defines the term *netiquette* as "the conventions of politeness used on Usenet, such as avoidance of cross-posting to inappropriate groups and refraining from commercial pluggery outside the biz groups."[2] The *Webopedia* offers this explanation: "Contraction of *Internet etiquette,* the etiquette guidelines for posting messages to online services, and particularly Internet newsgroups. Netiquette covers not only rules to maintain civility in discussions (i.e., avoiding flames), but also special guidelines unique to the electronic nature of forum messages. For example, netiquette advises users to use simple formats because complex formatting may not appear correctly for all readers. In most cases, netiquette is enforced by fellow users who will vociferously object if you break a rule of netiquette."[3] One more definition comes from WhatIs.com: "Netiquette is etiquette on the Internet."[4] Since the Internet changes rapidly, its netiquette does too, but it's still usually based on the Golden Rule. The need for a sense of netiquette arises mostly when sending or distributing e-mail, posting on Usenet groups, or chatting. To some extent, the practice of netiquette depends on understanding how e-mail, the Usenet, chatting, or other aspects of the Internet actually work or are practiced—so a little preliminary observation can help. Poor netiquette because you're new is one thing, but such practices as spam and flaming are another matter.

The definition of netiquette has, in fact, expanded beyond newsgroups and discussion forums, because the introduction of Web-based discussion and chat capabilities has blurred the lines between discussion groups and Web sites. Fundamentally, netiquette suggests that you had better behave in a manner consistent with the accepted standards of behavior in any given online locale, or you will suffer the consequences.

For organizations seeking to curry favor with a particular audience, it is particularly important to understand the netiquette that has evolved among the members of that audience in each of the online locales they populate. Committing an online *faux pas* can have dire consequences among members of a strategic constituency already suspicious of your organization's motives and inclined to expect the worst.

Of course, the traditional practice of public relations is one in which those doing the communicating need to mind what they say.

Each year, Fineman Associates, a San Francisco public relations agency lists what it considers to be the worst public relations blunders of the year. For example, the 1997 list was topped by Philip Morris president James Morgan, who compared cigarette addiction to his own fondness for Gummi Bears. "I love Gummi Bears," he said. "And I want Gummi Bears, and I like Gummi Bears, and I eat Gummi Bears, and I don't like it when I don't eat my Gummi Bears, but I'm certainly not addicted to them."[5] Morgan certainly should have known that the comparison would offend many of those who heard it. Whether he had the counsel of a public relations professional when he made the statement is questionable.

Online, however, the situation becomes even more hazardous. It's not only what you say that can hurt you; it is where you say it, how you say it, the format in which you present it, and to whom you say it. Unfortunately, there are no specific, detailed guidelines for engaging in appropriate netiquette, because each online venue has its own set of values. However, there are some steps you can take to ensure your message is not lost as the result of inadvertently offending members of your audience.

Netiquette Guidelines

FOR DISCUSSION FORUMS

- ↪ "Lurk" before you participate. Lurking is a bit of online jargon that means you should read what other people are saying before you make your own contribution to the discussion. Getting the lay of the land will help you develop a sense of what is appropriate and what is not.
- ↪ Read the Frequently Asked Questions (FAQs). Most Usenet newsgroups have developed FAQs based on the questions most newcomers to the groups have routinely asked. Discussion group regulars get so tired of repeatedly answering the same questions that they collect the questions and answers into FAQs, which new participants are encouraged to read to avoid asking questions that have already been addressed. Many other discussion venues have adopted the same concept.
- ↪ Behave as an equal participant in the discussions, a member of the community, rather than as an authoritative figure.

Nothing will turn off an online audience faster than somebody invading their turf to set them straight on an issue.

↪ Be honest about who you are—a representative of your client or your organization. Make it clear that you are there to make positive contributions. For instance, you can tell other forum participants that you are looking for feedback, or that you would like to offer solutions to their problems.

↪ When you reply to something somebody else has posted, quote the relevant part of the post to which you are responding so that readers know what you're talking about. However, you should never post the entire previous message, which takes up too much space and makes your message difficult to read.

FOR E-MAIL

↪ Do not send mass e-mail messages to people who have not given you specific permission to contact them. Mass e-mail solicitations are known as *spam* (much to the chagrin of the Minnesota-based Hormel company, makers of the meat product of the same name). Little that occurs on the Internet raises the ire of the online community as much as unsolicited e-mail.

↪ Make sure the subject line of your e-mail clearly articulates what the message is about.

↪ If you are responding to a message, do not include the entire original message. Instead, only quote the specific part of the message to which you are responding.

↪ Don't send an e-mail if you have nothing substantive to say. People become frustrated receiving messages in their inboxes that simply say, "Thanks for your message," or "I agree!"

FOR E-MAIL MAILING LISTS

↪ All the rules of discussion forums apply.

↪ All the rules of e-mail apply.

↪ Do not attach files to your e-mail. Since the message will go to multiple recipients, including people you do not know, you cannot be sure that they all have software that is compatible with the file you are sending. Also, people subscribe to e-mail mailing lists to engage in discussions, and could resent receiving a large file attached to a message.

FOR WEB SITES

↪ Know your target audience. A site that is designed to encourage institutional investment in an organization's stock should not adopt the flip, sarcastic tone of many noncommercial sites aimed at younger audiences. A site aimed at children should not make blatant sales pitches.

↪ If your site features a feedback button (for example, "Contact Us"), you must set up a mechanism to ensure a response will be sent to anybody who takes advantage of the offer.

↪ Do not provide links to other Web sites to which your audience might take offense. For example, if your site supports a point of view about a controversial political issue, such as gun control, avoid linking to sites that address other unrelated issues, such as abortion. Your target audience came to the site based on a common interest in gun control, and may well not share your organization's point of view on other topics. In fact, some people may be so incensed by your position on the unrelated issue that you could lose their support for your primary issue.

By following the rules of netiquette, you ensure that your communication efforts will not be undermined by an inadvertent slip of the key!

Push vs. Pull

In Chapter 2, we examined the receiver-driven model of communication that has become pervasive online. The allure of the World Wide Web is based on its accommodation of the receiver-driven model. People don't sit staring at their computer monitors waiting to receive whatever information you have to deliver. The Web allows them to engage in the new activity of "pulling" the information they want based on what they need, when they need it.

The Web is such a media phenomenon that the need for a Web site has become standard for many organizations. And many organizations are looking at the Web's potential for cost savings as a means of assessing its return on investment. "Our catalog is online," the thinking goes, "so we don't have to print it anymore. That'll save us a bundle!"

The problem with this thinking is that not every message or every component of a public relations effort is best suited to a pull environment—notably those that you want to be sure people see, regardless of whether they think they are interested in what you have to say. You cannot influence an individual or an audience if they never see your message.

The simple answer to this dilemma is to assess the effectiveness of each element of your communication effort in both a push and pull environment. The Web will not suffice for those messages that simply must be seen by the target audience. However, once a member of the audience has seen the key message, she can visit a referenced Web site for additional levels of information.

A host of companies have emerged in the last couple of years promoting the ability of their proprietary technologies to push content over the World Wide Web. The first and most successful of these was PointCast (now called Infogate). People who downloaded and installed the PointCast software received a regular stream of news and information, which they viewed on their Web browsers or the PointCast interface. When their computers were idle for a set amount of time, PointCast headlines automatically appeared as screen savers on their monitors. Clicking on an interesting headline launched that particular item. Most of the other entries in the push marketplace are spins on the same idea.

These technologies do not represent a solution for the communicator intent on getting his message to a targeted audience. No single push technology has become pervasive enough that it can be relied upon as a channel for distributing your message. More important, few of these mechanisms truly represent a pure push to the audience. Instead, the user configures the tool to receive only material in categories that are of interest. On PointCast, for instance, you can receive winning lottery numbers only for the state of California, a horoscope only for Sagittarius, and sports items only about the

Washington Redskins. Distributing your message over such a channel no more guarantees that your audience will see it than storing it on a Web site.

Rather than actually pushing messages, these technologies allow audiences to engage in what might be called "intelligent pull." Most people know where their interests lie, and once they have found a site on the World Wide Web that suits their needs, they return frequently to see whether new information has been added to the site. Programs that incorporate intelligent pull notify users when the site has been updated so that the user no longer has to pull the page in order to check. Different programs take different approaches to this notification, but the end result is the same: Users learn automatically that a chosen site has new material and is worth checking.

Still, intelligent pull does not assure you that those who are unaware of your site's existence will ever get your message. You need to be able to push information at those audiences, even if the information is nothing more than a compelling reference to the location of your Web site. You can push using traditional communications tools, such as print or video, depending on who and how sophisticated your audience is. If you are going to use electronic tools as the cornerstone of your plan, however, there is only one true push technology available: e-mail.

E-mail has been the most effective form of push on the Internet since its inception, and there are a number of strategies you can employ to take advantage of e-mail's push nature in a manner consistent with proper netiquette. Some of these approaches include:

- Enabling visitors to your Web site to sign up to receive various categories of e-mail that interest them
- Inviting members of an audience to subscribe to a mailing list, through which you will distribute messages consistent with the theme of the list
- Giving visitors to your online publication the option of receiving an e-mail digest of each issue's table of contents; they can click on individual headlines to go directly to that story, bypassing the rest of the content that may be of less interest

Your e-mail messages should be short and succinct. Most people have little time to spend reading e-mail; they want to glean from the messages that have arrived in their in-boxes the information they need to know, then move on. Your e-mail should state only the facts, then provide links to Web sites where they can select the information they want. It can also point them to other non-Internet resources, such as 800 telephone numbers, publications, television programming, upcoming meetings, or other sources.

E-mail messages distributed to lists of people who have given you tacit permission to send messages to them should contain common elements.

COMMON ELEMENTS OF MASS-DISTRIBUTED E-MAIL MESSAGES:

- ⤷ The name of the individual or institution that sent the message
- ⤷ The date the message was distributed
- ⤷ A listing of the contents of the message in the same order in which the items appear
- ⤷ Information on how to contact the author of the message
- ⤷ Information on how to unsubscribe from the mailing list

Conclusion

You can toss Web pages up, engage in discussions, and blast hundreds of thousands of e-mail messages across the Internet. It all will be for naught if it does not conform to the principles of how audiences and individuals use the Internet, and how the Net is affecting the building blocks of communication. One of the best ways to assess how well your organization is perceived online is to monitor references to the company. How to engage in such monitoring is the focus of Chapter 5.

Notes

1. *www.blursite.com, Blur: The Speed of Change in the Connected Economy.*

2. *www.hasc.com/jargon, The Hacker's Lexicon,* a jargon dictionary from Hutchison Avenue Software, 1995.

3. *www.webopedia.com, Webopedia,* an online dictionary from Internet.com, 2001.

4. *whatis.techtarget.com,* Whatis.com, a glossary of Internet jargon from Tech Target, 2000-2001.

5. Sworn deposition, April 1997.

CHAPTER 5

How to Be the Eyes and Ears of Your Organization or Client

EARLIER, I NOTED that public relations has traditionally served as the mouthpiece of an organization, but that in the Internet age, the function must also serve as the organization's eyes and ears. Online research has become a critical component of any public relations strategy. Understanding what people think, what they are saying, and how they are reacting to company initiatives will drive the approach you take to communicating both online and offline.

In this chapter, we'll consider two approaches to online research:

1. Monitoring what people are saying about you online
2. Conducting audience research using the Internet as your research tool

Monitoring the Global Conversation

Even if, for some reason, your proactive communication effort does not require research, you need to know what people are saying that can affect your company by influencing others. False or inaccurate postings in places like Yahoo's finance discussion groups have caused stock prices to plunge. The consequences can be even longer term. The fashion designer Tommy Hilfiger still represents the classic example of what can happen when online rumors and misinformation go unchecked.

In 1997, somebody posted a message to several Usenet newsgroups that criticized fashion designer Tommy Hilfiger. The post claimed that Hilfiger had appeared on the Oprah Winfrey show, where he used racially charged language while noting that, had he known members of those racial groups would like his clothing so much, he would not have made them so nice. The message went on to report that Winfrey subsequently threw Hilfiger off the show.

Outraged participants in those discussion groups copied the message, cross-posting it to other groups, and e-mailing it to lists of friends. In short order, the story became accepted as fact. (A message that spreads through cyberspace and becomes accepted as truth is known as a *meme*, borrowing the term from the biological phenomenon.) The only problem was that it was not true. Not only had Hilfiger not used the offensive words, he had never even appeared on the Oprah Winfrey show.

But it was too late; the damage was done as soon as the story became part of the lore of the Net. Months after Hilfiger's organization undertook efforts to disabuse the public of the story, you could find Web sites extolling visitors to boycott Hilfiger products.

This story illustrates the power of the Internet and the need to incorporate monitoring activities into your online public relations plan. (We'll talk about how to respond to a crisis on the Internet in Chapter 13.) It is not enough to proactively use the Internet as a component of your coordinated communication efforts. You need to monitor activity initiated by others that could have an impact on your company, your markets, or your ability to do business. If the Internet is a digital, modern-day equivalent of the telephone party line, it is important to listen to *all* the conversations, not only those in which you are engaged.

The material that can be posted to the Internet about your organization comes in several varieties:

- That which is a direct response to your communication efforts
- That which is posted by individuals or institutions with their own agendas
- Messages posted by employees

There are two fundamental means by which the global Internet audience can create material to influence others about your institution and its activities:

⇨ By posting so-called rogue or attack sites to the World Wide Web

⇨ By engaging in discussions in Web-based discussion groups, Usenet newsgroups, or mailing lists

Monitoring these discussions can play an important role in how online audiences—and, ultimately, all audiences—perceive your company. You will be able to respond to accusations, reinforce positive messages, and correct misconceptions. More important, though, is the ability to identify looming crises and develop plans to address them before they transcend the Internet and begin making headlines in traditional media. Most companies become aware of the significance of the Internet as a communication medium when an issue that began online finds its way into the newspapers and onto television news.

What to Monitor

The idea of monitoring the Internet for references to a company, an issue, a market, or some other topic makes many public relations people nervous. The volume of material is daunting, and trying to find relevant information often appears like the proverbial search for a needle in a haystack. By using some of the tools available, and by making such monitoring part of your institution's routine environmental scanning process, the task of finding important or substantive material becomes much easier.

Presumably, your organization already is making some effort to detect what is being said in public. The most common means of making this type of assessment is through a clipping service that scans newspapers and magazines for reference to your organization, and then sends you the clippings on a regular basis. You (or someone in your company) then reads each clip to find those that meet the criteria for your attention. To this and any other scanning methods you employ, you need to add the two primary sources of information on the Internet.

As noted previously, those two sources are many-to-many discussions and pages posted to the World Wide Web.

The Global Conversation

USENET newsgroups are discussion forums that individuals access using the Internet based on key areas of interest. About thirty thousand USENET newsgroups are currently available, although not all newsgroups are available to all Internet users. Each Internet Service Provider (ISP) decides which newsgroups will be offered to its users. However, a core group of about eighteen thousand newsgroups (this number ebbs and flows, and varies depending on which newsgroups an ISP chooses to offer) tends to be available to all users. People use USENET newsgroups by posting "articles" to the groups, which can be read by anybody else visiting the newsgroup at a later time. Individuals reading an article can respond either directly to the author of the original article, to the author of a follow-up article, or by creating a follow-up article that is, in turn, posted to the newsgroup.

Newsgroups are identified using a hierarchy of words. The top-level hierarchy designates the broadest nature of the newsgroup. For example, "rec" signifies a recreation-oriented topic, "talk" suggests a debate, "sci" is scientific. Subsequent levels narrow the discussion. For example, *talk.politics.animals* suggests that the newsgroup is a forum for a political debate over animal rights; *rec.music.beatles.lyrics* would be a place where Beatles fans could gather to discuss the lyrics of the band's songs.

In Figure 5-1, a "thread" on the *alt.autos.gm* Usenet newsgroup is dedicated to the discussion of General Motors cars. The thread begins with one participant asking a question about a problem he has had with a car; three other participants then offered their thoughts. (Presumably, GM is aware of the newsgroup and monitors it regularly.)

The conversational nature of the discussion is critical for public relations practitioners to understand. Given access to the Net and all the other people who populate it, people who are online have come to prefer getting help and advice from real people instead of companies. That is, they would rather visit a newsgroup, a Web discussion group, or a mailing list to get an answer to a question than call the company. There are a number of reasons for this preference. The answers you get from the alternate sources are not colored by a company trying to get you to buy a new doodad or to pay for a new service. You are able to weigh several answers to decide which is best for you (or most accurate). But what people truly appreciate about getting their information from other people is the sense that they are, indeed, engaged with a real person and not an institution. As the authors of *The Cluetrain Manifesto* (*www.cluetrain.org*) put it, "Markets are

FIGURE 5-1. THREAD FOR DISCUSSION OF *GM* CARS.

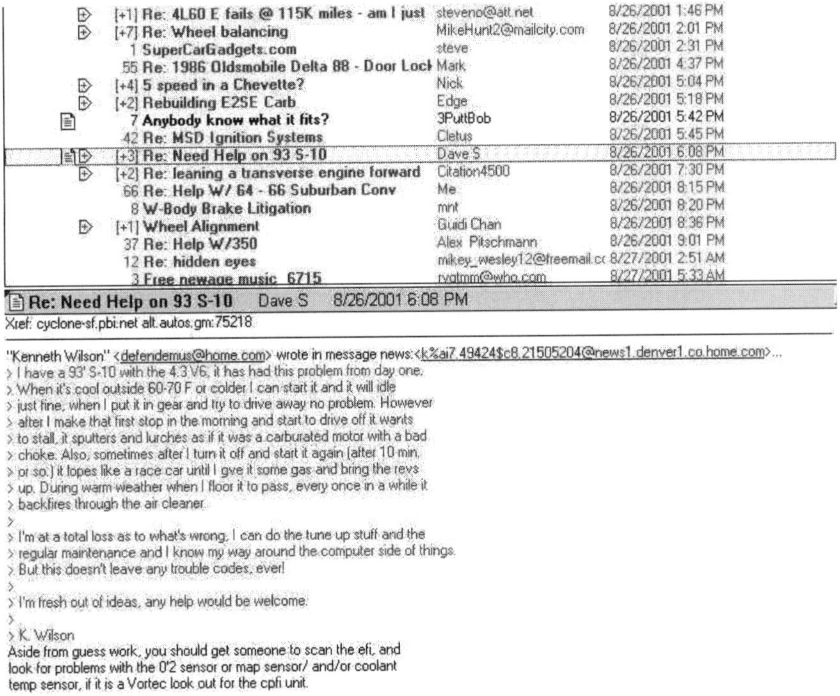

conversations." (For a more detailed discussion of the global conversation, refer to the discussion of the many-to-many model in Chapter 3.)

Online Discussions and Their Impact

Discussions online—whether in Usenet newsgroups, Web discussion areas, or mailing lists—can be devastating, enlightening, troublesome, annoying, or beneficial. Because they transcend geographic barriers, newsgroups provide a forum for people who share a common interest to engage in discussion and debate. When something hot appears in an online discussion, it can be addressed quickly, and the participants can elect to take some kind of action based on the results of the discussion. These actions can be taken individually, or the group can band together in an activist mode.

Let's look at both uses of newsgroup monitoring, beginning with the consequences of negative or false information posted on the Internet. The most famous case involves the Intel Pentium chip, the math flaws of which were first discussed online among mathematicians using computers with the chip. Intel probably could have defused the situation by participating in the discussion and listening to the concerns of those few customers who actually needed that particular math function to work correctly. Instead, the debate spilled over the newsgroup environment and into the public media, where it became a significant crisis for the company.

What happened to Lexis-Nexis, the online database of articles from newspapers and magazines, along with public records and other information, provides another view of the consequences of ignoring messages posted to newsgroups.

Case Study: Lexis-Nexis

P-TRAK was actually a catch-up product for Lexis-Nexis; several of its competitors already offered access to databases that contained information on individuals. The legal community and private investigators use these databases to track down litigants, heirs, and others being sought in relation to legal cases. The information includes names, addresses, and telephone numbers. Initially, Lexis-Nexis also included Social Security numbers, but that feature was withdrawn (although a user can type in a Social Security number to learn to whom it belongs). Competing databases do offer Social Security numbers.

Concerns over privacy, however, led to the following Usenet newsgroup posting *months* after Lexis-Nexis withdrew Social Security numbers from the dataset:

> LEXIS-NEXIS P-Trax Database WARNING: Your name, social security number, current address, previous addresses, mother's maiden name, birth date, and other personal information are now available to anyone with a credit card through a new Lexis database called P-Trax. As I am sure you are aware, this information could be used to commit credit card fraud or otherwise allow someone else to use your identity. For Lexis response to this post go to: *http://www.lexis-nexis.com/lncc/about/ptrak.html.*
> LEXIS-NEXIS has been swamped with requests to remove personal data from this database (thanks to the wonders of electronic communication, no doubt). It is no longer possible to remove your name from the database simply by calling the LEXIS-NEXIS phone number. To remove your name from the P-Trax database, you must make a request in writing. You can either mail or fax this in: fax: (513) 865-1930, or surface mail to: LEXIS-NEXIS P.O. Box 933 Dayton, Ohio 45401-0933 If you would like to register any additional comment against this product, the product manager is Andrew Bleh (rhymes with "Play"). He can be reached at the LEXIS-NEXIS toll-free number: 800-543-6862. Ask for extension 3385. According to Lexis, the manager responsible is Bill Fister at extension 1364.

The post was copied and reposted in hundreds of newsgroups, from privacy-related discussions to such unlikely venues as a forum for Pakistani culture. The message also was copied into e-mail messages that well-meaning individuals sent to their lists of friends, business colleagues, and acquaintances. Lexis-Nexis public relations officials began to recognize the post as the source of complaints from the misspelling of the service (P-TRAK is the official name of the service; P-TRAX is how it was spelled in the Usenet post).

To this day, four years after the story erupted, Lexis-Nexis still takes heat over the perceived impropriety of providing sensitive information to subscribers, and still receives calls from reporters who, upon reading the post for the first time, believe they are breaking a hot news story.

Had Lexis-Nexis caught the erroneous message early, however, the inaccuracies could have been corrected and the spread of the message through the Internet probably would never have happened.

Clearly, however, you can do far more than stem a crisis by monitoring discussions about your organization. You can, for example, detect trends, such as dissatisfaction with a particular product or service.

If discussion groups provide individuals with a means of engaging others sympathetic to their issues, the World Wide Web establishes a forum for publishing any kind of position about any organization or issue. The Web is rife with sites that attack organizations, praise products, condemn practices, and idolize celebrities. Because the cost of publishing on the Web is so low and the process so simple, anybody with an axe to grind can find an audience of like-minded souls, along with those cruising for whatever information they can find. Some of the organizations that have been attacked online include Nutrasweet, Ford, Microsoft, Allstate, and McDonald's.

Once a page containing damaging information appears on the Web, the allegations can spread through Usenet newsgroups, e-mail, and other vehicles. By monitoring these pages, you can deal with the inaccuracies before they spread; you also can develop a plan to address divergent viewpoints the Web site may take.

Legal action is one way to handle attack sites, but it is a strategy that can backfire on the Internet. There, in discussion groups, individuals can comment *ad nauseum* about your company's strong-arm tactics to remove a page rather than deal with the issues it raised. Legal threats—even successful ones—can lead to worse problems than the page itself created. It is better to use the conventions of the Internet itself to address misinformation.

Case Study: Emulex

The case of a false press release offers an example of exactly how devastating misinformation on the Internet can be. On August 25, 2000, a press release was distributed over Internet Wire, an online press release distribution service. Supposedly coming from Emulex, a California-based supplier of Fibre Channel host bus adapters, the release claimed that the company was under investigation by the Securities and Exchange Commission, the company's chief executive officer was resigning, and that Emulex had revised its recent earnings report to show a loss instead of a profit.

The release was, in fact, issued by a former employee of Internet Wire, a college student who had conceived the scheme as a way to capitalize on the knowledge that the stock price would fall. Indeed, the price plummeted, from more than $110 per share to less than $43 dollars per share—all in less than one hour.

After discovering that the release was a hoax, the NASDAQ stock exchange halted trading in the stock. Emulex issued a genuine release that included a quote from Chairman Paul Folino:

> The negative statements in this fictitious press release are categorically false. Emulex has just completed an audit of our year-end results, which we announced on August 3, and there is no truth to the rumor that our historical results will be restated. We have contacted the appropriate authorities, who are investigating this matter and we intend to launch our own investigation into this fraudulent release. Emulex shareholders should be assured that our business is at record levels and the fundamentals of our business and my commitment to this company have never been stronger.[1]

Although the company recovered most of its share value, the company's stock price did not return to its pre-hoax levels. The company had to commit significant resources to the hoax, and even faced threat of shareholder suits. Despite acting fast, the consequences were significant. The speed of the Internet rendered a rapid response less effective than it once might have been—yet failing to respond quickly would have had even more dire repercussions.

Employees can be another source of concern, particularly in companies where things are not going well. Employees often seek venues to discuss the situation, often with other employees. The online environment provides employees with a place to find like-minded colleagues with greater ease than they would have canvassing the limited world of employees with whom they work day in and day out. Most organizations opt not to allow employees to engage in online discussions within the confines of the intranet. (Intranet-based discussions are housed on many intranets, but far more resist the use of this extremely effective tool. The reasons vary. In some cases, corporate lawyers advise against them as a means of protecting the company from the risk that employee conversations will be made public during a legal discovery phase. In other cases, management views such discussions as non-work-related. And in some cases, management simply doesn't want to hear anything negative employees may have to say.)

This restriction on the intranet does not hinder employees, however; they simply find other places online to engage in such discussions. Companies routinely find employees (or, at least, individuals who talk like they are employees—it's hard to tell when anonymity is a characteristic of these discussions) talking about the company on the Yahoo bulletin boards dedicated to shareholders who want to talk about the companies whose stocks they own. Vault.com is another interesting venue. Vault.com offers insight about companies where job-hunters may want to apply, or from which they have already received a job offer. In addition to editorial content produced by the site owners, bulletin boards invite employees to discuss—anonymously—what it's like to work in the organization. Here's a sample of one Vault.com message about a company (whose name has been changed):

> I left the Acme Service Unit. The management is a joke. Acme corporate had been letting Acme Service run the show on their own for a while, with crappy results. Acme Corporate had no idea which direction they wanted to take Acme Service. It was a mess.

Offering employees an intranet-housed discussion area is the easiest way to keep employees from airing a company's dirty laundry in public discussions. However, companies need to earn employees' trust; employees need to believe they are free to talk about what is on their minds (within the limits of professional conduct, of course) without fear of reprisal. It is also important for management to ensure that employees understand their obligations as employees when it comes to posting in public discussion groups. Although a company should not tell employees they absolutely cannot participate (especially if they are using their own computers and Internet connections at home on their own time), they should understand the consequences for divulging company secrets or violating financial disclosure laws and regulations.

Ford Motor Company's page on Yahoo, as shown in Figure 5-2, includes an open bulletin board where anybody—employees included—can discuss the company.

Figure 5-3 shows the discussion board for Xerox employees on Vault.com.

The rapid development of the World Wide Web and software to facilitate a wide range of functions on the Web has led to the emergence of Web-based discussion groups. There are several reasons why these discussion groups are cropping up everywhere and attracting audiences and participants.

First off, they are easy to create. You can purchase off-the-shelf software that will allow you to manage the establishment of groups.

FIGURE 5-2. YAHOO'S OPEN BULLETIN BOARD FOR DISCUSSION OF FORD MOTOR COMPANY.

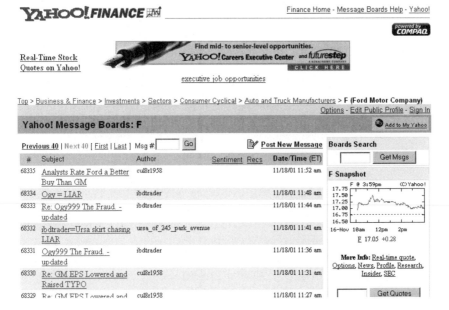

FIGURE 5-3. A DISCUSSION BOARD FOR XEROX EMPLOYEES.

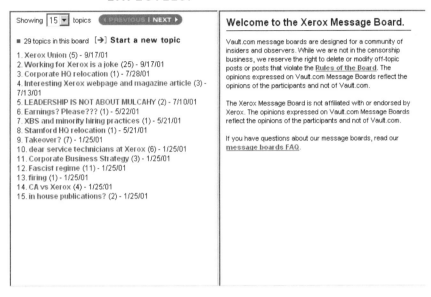

Showing 15 ▾ topics ◄ PREVIOUS | NEXT ►

■ 29 topics in this board [→] **Start a new topic**

1. Xerox Union (5) - 9/17/01
2. Working for Xerox is a joke (25) - 9/17/01
3. Corporate HQ relocation (1) - 7/28/01
4. Interesting Xerox webpage and magazine article (3) - 7/13/01
5. LEADERSHIP IS NOT ABOUT MULCAHY (2) - 7/10/01
6. Earnings? Please??? (1) - 5/22/01
7. XBS and minority hiring practices (1) - 5/21/01
8. Stamford HQ relocation (1) - 5/21/01
9. Takeover? (7) - 1/25/01
10. dear service technicians at Xerox (6) - 1/25/01
11. Corporate Business Strategy (3) - 1/25/01
12. Fascist regime (11) - 1/25/01
13. firing (1) - 1/25/01
14. CA vs Xerox (4) - 1/25/01
15. in house publications? (2) - 1/25/01

Welcome to the Xerox Message Board.

Vault.com message boards are designed for a community of insiders and observers. While we are not in the censorship business, we reserve the right to delete or modify off-topic posts or posts that violate the Rules of the Board. The opinions expressed on Vault.com Message Boards reflect the opinions of the participants and not of Vault.com.

The Xerox Message Board is not affiliated with or endorsed by Xerox. The opinions expressed on Vault.com Message Boards reflect the opinions of the participants and not of Vault.com.

If you have questions about our message boards, read our message boards FAQ.

You can even create them yourself using some of the over-the-counter Web page creation software packages, such as Microsoft FrontPage.

Next, they can be integrated with other material. A Web site that includes a discussion group is more than merely the sum of the discussions; other resources are available from the site. The information on the site can generate discussion, and the discussion can lead the site owners to offer additional information. In fact, not everybody who joins a Web-based discussion came to the site with the intention of engaging other users. Often, a new participant came in search of information and discovered the existence of the discussion group. (For an example of a Web-based community, see "Virtual Communities" in Chapter 3).

Web-based discussion groups are highly targeted. They appeal directly and uniquely to the audience of people who would visit that particular site.

Finally, Web-based discussion groups are easy to use. Before the introduction of Web discussion groups, you needed special software to take advantage of the Internet's global conversations. These news readers, as they are called, do not function the same way the Web does. Web-based discussion groups use the same interface as any other Web page: just point and click.

Individuals—armed as they are with the publishing and information-sharing tools of the Internet—are learning to put the Internet to effective use. Combining online discussion with Web publishing, it becomes simple for anybody to wage a campaign in favor of or in opposition to their particular cause.

How to Monitor

Two options are available for monitoring company-related Internet activity:

1. Outsource the work
2. Do it internally

Outsourcing

Several companies have sprung up to monitor the Internet on your behalf. The prices they charge vary as much as their range of services do. Some report on Internet activity, others provide analysis and recommendations, others apply measurement principles to help you appraise the effectiveness of your efforts.

When you select a service, make sure the services you get are consistent with your organization's information needs.

⇝ Several services are dedicated to providing online intelligence. These include Ewatch, a unit of PR Newswire (*www.ewatch.com*), NetCurrents (*www.netcurrents.com*), and Cyveillance (*www.cyveillance.com*).

⇝ The Delahaye Group (at *www.delahaye.com*) offers an image analysis based on the content of online discussions.

Do It Yourself

There are a number of reasons to consider doing your own monitoring; or, at least, supplementing the work done by the service with which you have contracted. First, nobody understands the issues that face your company the way insiders do. Companies contracted to look for key information could miss something subtle that only an insider would be able to identify. You'll also benefit from the immediacy of doing your own monitoring. If something is brewing online, you won't have to wait to get a report in order to act on it.

The methods of monitoring fall into four basic categories:

1. Reading discussions
2. Search engines and other Web services
3. Software
4. Subscribing to mailing lists

Reading Newsgroups

If online discussions exist that are dedicated to your company, the products your company makes, or the issues your company faces, then you should add those discussions to your regular reading list. Once you get the hang of reading these discussions, you will be able to scan a day's worth of messages in a few minutes. You'll learn the kinds of subject headers that warrant your attention, and to dispense with the remaining headers quickly.

One way to keep from driving yourself crazy is to make sure you limit the newsgroups you read only to those that are directly related to your business. Those that occasionally address the business should not be added to your regular reading list. For example, just because your company's stock is mentioned now and then in one of the investment bulletin boards doesn't mean you want to start scanning all the various messages posted to that newsgroup.

STEP-BY-STEP:
Participating in Discussions

So, a message to a discussion group sends up a red flag. Do you respond? Before jumping in and engaging the audience, follow these steps:

1. Lurk first. *Lurking* is an online term that means retrieving and reading articles posted by others in

the newsgroup without posting one yourself. Unless you post a message, nobody knows you are there. By lurking for a while (several days at least), you can learn the lay of the land.

2. Determine who is posting to the newsgroup. Is it an audience that is worth your time? Are they taken seriously? Are messages from the newsgroup cross-posted elsewhere on the Internet? Who are the players in the newsgroup; that is, who has influence?

3. Learn the culture of the newsgroup. How do people reply to messages? What is the ruling netiquette of the group?

4. Does the group have an FAQ document? If so, read it to see what more you can learn about the group.

5. Assess the current situation. How is the group likely to respond if you jump in? Are you better off dealing with the individual who posted the article in question, or is there value in speaking to the entire community?

6. If you decide to contribute, make sure you participate as a new member of the community rather than preach as a representative of the company.

7. Don't succumb to "flame bait." Some participants in a newsgroup will drop messages deliberately constructed to make you lose your temper or jerk your knee. You're best off ignoring these and engaging in discussion only with those who post substantive messages.

Search Engines and Other Web Services

A host of services make it easy to monitor the ever-increasing volume of discussion taking place online.

Search engines routinely send "spiders"—or agents—to scour the Web, collecting information about what is out there and putting that information into a database. When you type in a search term, the result is a list of items in the database that match your query.

Basic search engines will generally turn up many of the sites that mention your company's name, product names, issues, or markets.

I personally use Google more than any other—it's at *http://www. google.com*; other favorites are HotBot at *http://www.hotbot.com,* and Northern Light (at *http://www.northernlight.com*).

Whichever search engine you use, make sure you know how to get the best results by reading about the advanced search features. Strategy is the key when using a search index. Resist the temptation to fire off a couple words and see what comes up. Instead, take a step back and think about the information you're trying to retrieve. Let's say your company is introducing a new managed care benefits plan, and you want to find out what the negative consequences of a managed-care approach might be so that you can plan a communication effort that proactively addresses the issue. Simply typing "managed care" will produce more results than you can cope with— everything online about managed care, along with every link that contains the words *managed* and *care*. Instead, think about the information you *really* want. This might cover such combinations as:

> *managed care* and *employee*
>
> *managed care* and *communication*
>
> *managed care* and *reaction*
>
> *benefits* and *managed care*

When you are finished, you can combine the queries to come up with a search request that might look like this: (*managed care* or *benefits* or *managed health care* or *health care* or *PPO* or *EPO*) and (*employee* or *employee communication* or *change* or *reaction* or *consequences* or resistance).

Yahoo is not a search engine, but rather an index. Since sites are catalogued on Yahoo, it can be easy to find attack sites, since they appear in attack categories.

With search engines and Yahoo-like catalogues, however, you run the risk of missing important sites and postings that have not been added to the archives in a timely manner because these services do not update automatically.

Another breed of search services has recently taken to the Net specifically with company intelligence in mind. These services do update frequently, and include much of the content on the Web that is hidden from typical search engines. Intelliseek (at *http://www. intelliseek.com*) and Bright Planet (at *http://www.brightplanet.com*) both make a point of archiving not only the pages of the Web that are readily available to any random visitor but also the "deep" or "hidden" Web (depending on whose marketing literature you read). This includes material in databases that is used to create Web pages based on specific queries; Bright Planet estimates the content hidden from view is between 400 and 500 times the size of the conventional Web. Both of these services also claim to produce more targeted results than typical search engines.

Searching the Usenet newsgroups is possible on the Web through Intelliseek and Bright Planet, as well as Google's groups feature (available at *http://groups.google.com*). Google Groups allows you to use key words to search the entire Usenet community, restrict your query to only certain groups, or read all and participate in any group.

Software

Any number of companies produce software you can install either on your own computer or on a network server to conduct searches for you. Bright Planet sells two PC versions of its search software, for example. InfoGist (at *http://www.infogist.com*) offers a search utility geared toward public relations professionals that grades the likelihood that content found matches your needs; it also searches news and company information in addition to basic Web content, but does not search online discussions.

Other Web searching software tends to work as a meta-search, conducting the search across several Web-based search engines and categorizing the results. Some of these include Ferret and Copernic.

As you become more proficient at your searches, you will probably find a favorite search tool that, more often than others, produces results that meet your needs. Don't ignore the others, though. Some tools are better for some searches than others. Get a sense of which tool gets you better answers for different *types* of searches. For instance, if you are looking for a particular product or information outlet, a directory may allow you to drill quickly to that information. If, however, you are trying to find what authorities have posted about a particular issue—with information appearing on sites that could easily be listed in dozens or hundreds of different categories—you may be better off using a search engine.

Subscribing to Mailing Lists

Some of the online surveillance companies include mailing lists among their resources. If you don't use these outside services, opting instead to go it alone, you will need to subscribe to those services most likely to include references to your organization, products, and markets. Of course, any discussion taking place in mailing lists to which you do not subscribe will go undetected—at least until they show up elsewhere on the Net.

Every newsletter has its own requirements for subscribing, so you'll need to know how to go about getting on the list. One way to find lists and subscription information is through a list search utility, such as Publicly Available Mailing Lists (at *http://www.paml.net*), or Tile.net (*http://www.tile.net/lists*).

Many of the software programs that are used to manage mailing lists allow you to receive a digest version of the list (with all the day's messages consolidated in a single message) or an index version (with only the subject headers; you retrieve the messages you want to read separately).

TIP:
Keep Your Welcome Letter!

Virtually every e-mail mailing list will send you a welcome letter as soon as you subscribe. These welcome messages generally provide you with all the information you need to manage your subscription, including how to change to a digest or index version of the list, and how to unsubscribe. Many welcome letters also cover the list's charter and standards of conduct. Don't toss this message! Keep it where you can refer to it.

Conducting Audience Research Online

In our discussion of the Web in Chapter 3, I insisted that your audience owns your Web site, and that you need an audience advisory panel to represent those owners. Developing that panel—or developing an effective Web site *without* a panel—depends on your having an intimate understanding of the audience whose needs you intend to meet with the site. The Web can serve as a boon to your conducting that research.

In fact, since the practice of public relations is based in large part on research, the Web becomes an important tool. Several professionals have raised a skeptical eyebrow at the idea of conducting research online, asserting that the results are not representative of the overall population, that the Net cannot provide statistically valid results, and that the Net fails to offer the type of results you can get from face-to-face focus groups.

These were valid concerns not too long ago, but things have changed. For example, the online population is becoming increasingly reflective of the general population. Recent research from Nielsen/NetRatings indicates the fastest growing segment of the Net is made up of factory workers and laborers, administrative assistants, and homemakers. The Pew Internet Project reveals that people with incomes under $30,000 per year make up 38 percent of the U.S. Internet population, up from 28 percent in 2000. An August 2000 study by the U.S. Department of Commerce determined that some 42 percent of homes are currently connected to the Internet. Most researchers now agree that a representative sample can be obtained by recruiting Internet users. Companies on average dedicate nearly 20 percent of their marketing research budgets to online research efforts.

As a result, the Internet is becoming a more acceptable source for audience research. The research community is starting to agree. Validity tests and case studies are being conducted that add to the credibility of online research, according to Monica Zinchiak, owner of Z Research Services in San Diego and a regular user of the Net to conduct research. "Literature on this topic has grown exponentially," Zinchiak said. "One of my colleagues recently did a search for online focus group-related articles that returned 270 relevant articles." Zinchiak added that conferences dedicated to the advancement of the technology and the industry have begun cropping up, with presenters recognized as pioneers and industry leaders. Furthermore, associations dedicated to online research have sprung up, including the Interactive Marketing Research Organization. The number of Net-based tools for research developed and sold by reputable companies has increased.

Zinchiak finds Internet research capabilities most useful for qualitative research, the kind obtained by focus groups.

Online Focus Groups

Focus groups are part of every communicator's research arsenal. There are drawbacks to focus groups, however. One is the difficulty getting participants to come to a central meeting location. Another is what experienced facilitators refer to as the "herd mentality," in which quieter participants in the group tend to agree with dominant personalities rather than stake out their own positions.

Neither of these are issues when focus groups are conducted online. Of course, when to conduct a focus group online is a call to be made based on the specific research objectives. Online focus groups do not replace face-to-face, which continues to be the best overall approach to focus groups. However, according to Zinchiak, online focus groups are particularly suited to the following types of research:

- Studies with low-incidence respondents where face-to-face groups are not feasible.
- Studies where respondents are widely dispersed, such as those in rural areas. For research with widely dispersed members (or prospective members) of a Web advisory panel, online focus groups may be your best solution.
- Studies where anonymity is required, such as research on sensitive topics.
- Research to evaluate a Web site or other Internet communication component.

Under these circumstances, Zinchiak said, online focus groups can perform as well as—and in some cases even better than—traditional groups. Zinchiak's approach is to use chat room technology to facilitate a real-time group.

Newer chat room software designed for conferences, meetings, and focus group research has enabled focus group moderators to incorporate visuals into the mix. "Any image that can be transferred into a graphic file or Web page can be displayed during an online focus group," Zinchiak said.

Additionally, Zinchiak notes that the environment has grown extremely secure for research based on advances in password protection and firewall technology. She also points out that the software used to facilitate focus group research includes its own security measures to protect graphic images and other multimedia displayed to focus group participants.

Zinchiak asserts that an online moderator needs the same skills as a traditional focus group leader. "Extra thought should be put into writing the discussion guide to eliminate misinterpretation of the questions," she said.

> Probing questions should be phrased to welcome responses from all respondents. Clarification will be even more important in the text environment as you will not be able to use non-verbal clues to determine the meaning of the respondent's answer. And you may find analysis more or less demanding depending on how much you rely on the transcripts. Familiarity with chat room culture and slang, along with competent typing skills, are also helpful.

Most researchers who have used online groups have found that respondents are inclined to be candid. "Respondents compose their answers before reading others' postings," said Zinchiak of her experience.

> As a result, they only express their own opinions, rather than parrot what others have said. Peer pressure sometimes happens in traditional groups. Online, though, it's difficult for a person to dominate a focus group because of the text environment. Everyone is an equal with no body language, facial expressions, or perceived social status.

Respondents also seem to express their opinions without the tempering sometimes seen in traditional groups, Zinchiak added. "For example, respondents feel more comfortable giving you negative or controversial feedback if they are not sitting at a table where people might verbally challenge them."

Most of her online focus group participants are prerecruited, although Zinchiak says she has done some online recruiting from lists of people who have expressed an interest in participating. Although the recruitment process—including invitations and confirmations—is handled by e-mail, diligence in the process is particularly important in an online environment. Certain parts of the process are designed to surface issues that are of no importance in a live, face-to-face environment.

For instance, you need to make sure that the unseen participant at the other end of a keyboard is, in fact, part of the demographic group you were seeking. And qualifying participants requires more than an e-mail message, as far as Zinchiak is concerned. She calls the participants on the telephone. That is how she learned that one participant recruited for a group designed for people over age 50 was, in fact, the target participant's son. "He was Steve Junior," she says. "The list just said 'Steve,' so the son didn't know he wasn't supposed to participate, but if I hadn't called, I would have had a seventeen-year-old kid answering questions instead of the fifty-four-year-old Steve Senior—and I would never have known."

Before the focus group begins, participants receive printed information about the focus group that covers such things as how to express emotions when typing by using *emoticons*. Then, before the focus group begins, participants visit a Web site where they log on for last-minute instructions. Then they move into a Web-based chat room in which Zinchiak and the participants will type to each other in real time. The Web environment in which Zinchiak conducts her focus groups is based on proprietary software. "If Bob has something interesting to say, I can pursue that line of thought with him in a separate window that I'm controlling; the rest of the group never sees it," Zinchiak says.

Still, many of the issues that arise in focus group facilitation are the same online as they are in the real world. Zinchiak needs to keep the conversation focused, deal with rogue participants who get out of line, and handle other nuances. Plus, the online environment presents new challenges. "First of all, you have to use more colorful language, more exciting phrases. You don't want people drifting off because the kids are talking to them, the television is on, or something is distracting them. You have to keep their attention." As a result, online focus groups tend to run shorter than live ones. "Sixty to ninety minutes is about as long as most people can stay focused."

Participants tend to be less inhibited online—there is a detachment that comes from the anonymity of the keyboard, which diminishes the herd mentality issue and tends to make everybody equal. On the other hand, some people can type faster, have a higher-speed modem, or are more adept at getting their responses in quicker. You generally have fewer people in an online focus group than in a face-to-face meeting because too many voices can confuse the discussion.

There are other advantages to online focus groups, Zinchiak said. They are fast; the text is recorded as it is being typed, which makes it easier to jump into analysis and fire off results to the client. And with e-mail as the medium through which recruitment is handled, the entire process can be completed in less time than traditional groups.

In addition to the real-time focus groups Zinchiak facilitates, you can conduct focus groups asynchronously (that is, not in real time) using everything from discussion group software to mailing lists. Bob Novick, of Impulse Research in Los Angeles, has used listserv software to control the subscriber list so that only focus group participants receive list mail. Participants are recruited from Usenet newsgroups and other listserv mailing lists where the target audience tends to congregate. "We pay them the way we normally do in a focus group and pretty much conduct the groups the way you conduct a normal one, except it's not live," Novick says. "It takes longer, but the quality of response is much better. People have more time so, when they write their responses, they are more thoughtful, longer, and they get less carried away by the emotion of the moment."

There are some drawbacks to these e-mail based focus groups that operate asynchronously. "First of all, they take longer," Novick says. "It's more difficult to show visual and other kinds of exhibits if you want the group to evaluate an advertisement or taste a product. And, not every audience is available on the Internet—although we haven't yet had a project where we weren't able to find the people we needed."

Although online focus groups—or, for that matter, live ones—do not provide quantitative results, Novick insists they are wonderful forums for qualitative research. As for more statistical research, he says: "You do need to be aware that it's very difficult, if not impossible, to do statistically accurate surveys on the Internet because of the voluntary nature of the medium." According to Novick, "It's very difficult, if not impossible, to reach everyone, which makes it difficult to sample. People need to agree to participate, and most don't. That makes for low response rates."

But the dynamics of focus groups can't be beat, Novick insists. "We've had several cases where the participants in the focus group asked to keep the listserv going even after the focus group was concluded," he says. "In one case, a focus group about a particular medical condition, the participants kept the discussion going for several weeks, then formed their own support group by establishing a USENET newsgroup."

As shown in Figure 5-4, Itracks' real-time focus group utility allows a moderator to manage a real-time focus group, incorporating Web pages, images, and multimedia to which participants can respond.

Quantitative Research

Qualitative research helps you to get answers to questions, find out what people are thinking or feeling, and assess the "why's" of a situation. Where hard numbers are needed, quantitative research

FIGURE 5-4. A REAL-TIME FOCUS GROUP.

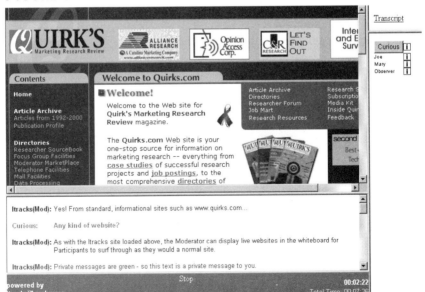

must be undertaken. Surveys and polls are among the most important tools for quantitative research, and an increasing number of organizations are using the Internet as a channel for conducting those surveys.

Novick's CyberPulse, for example, does a comprehensive multi-client survey over the Internet every two weeks, using a new sample of 1,200 men and women over age 18, representing a cross-section of the U.S. population. Clients book space on a survey to obtain measurable answers to questions about their products or services. SPSS, the Chicago-based company that has for years produced statistical analysis software, recently branched into quantitative online research. In addition, several do-it-yourself sites have emerged, such as Zoomerang (*http://www.zoomerang.com*) and Itracks (*http://www.itracks.com*), where you can develop a survey, notify participants, and keep track of the results.

In addition to SPSS, countless companies have entered the business of producing sophisticated online survey software, including Corporate Pulse (*http://www.datadome.com*), Advanced Survey Software (*http://www.advancedsurveysoftware.com*), and SurveyPro (*http://www.apian.net*).

Polls

Polls offer another way to generate feedback, although the results are far from scientific. Polls reside on a Web site and usually consist of a single question or statement. Respondents answer true or false, or select from a multiple-choice set of answers. Most polls also allow the respondent to see immediately the result of the poll to date, including her answer. (Instant gratification goes a long way in inspiring people to click!)

Polls tend to be unscientific because anybody can answer them—you cannot preselect a representative cross-section whose contributions will be statistically valid. Still, in addition to heightening the interactivity of a Web site, polls can reveal trends that may lead you to undertake further research.

Just as with focus group software and survey software, dozens of companies have entered the polling software field, including Poll Pro (*http://www.pollpro.com*), Active Votes (*http://www.activevotes.com*), UpTilt (*http://www.uptilt.com*), and PollCat (*http://www.pollcat.com*). In addition, you can create polls for free using FreePolls (*http://www.freepolls.com*); the service generates script that you simply paste onto your Web page; your page pulls the poll from the FreePolls site, where the tabulations are handled. Poll Pro also offers a free poll option.

Mix It Up

A solid research effort can capitalize on qualitative *and* quantitative research, and even add a poll or two to spice things up. "The objectives of your study will dictate whether or not a quantitative piece is needed before, during, or after qualitative research," Zinchiak suggested. Among the approaches to consider:

- Online focus groups can be used to uncover information you would then measure with an audience using a quantitative survey.
- Surveys can reveal trends that require qualitative analysis, leading to a follow-up focus group.
- Participants in Web-driven surveys can be drawn to participate further by being part of a follow-up focus group.
- Some online focus group software can insert surveys into the discussion. The results of the survey can be shown immediately to the moderator and to participants.
- Polls can uncover trends that can then be measured scientifically using a survey.

Using the Internet to Monitor the Press

The Internet not only gives you resources for monitoring your company's online image, you can use it to monitor the traditional media, as well. You can supplement the information you receive from your clipping service, or transition your existing online database accounts (with companies like Lexis-Nexis or Dow Jones News Retrieval) to a Web-based account.

Web-Based Subscription Services

Several subscription services are available on the World Wide Web that deliver news reports via e-mail, a personalized Web page, or both. News updates and alerts are available from a variety of traditional print-based publications via their Web sites. For example, *The Wall Street Journal* allows you to subscribe to receive news by e-mail as soon as it breaks. You can subscribe in categories such as major business news, markets alert, special reports, and technology alert. CNN's Web site offers a similar service. Specialty magazines and professional publications offer their own e-mail news alert services.

Major Databases

Lexis-Nexis and Dow Jones represent the two biggest databases of articles from newspapers and magazines in the world. Tracking your company name and other key words through these more robust (and proportionally more expensive) services can result in more detail and greater depth. Both services have begun providing access to their databases through a World Wide Web interface.

Dow Jones Interactive allows you to search its entire publications database for free, then charges $2.50 for each article you retrieve. Lexis-Nexis offers telnet access to its databases for existing customers and has opened a Web-based service for Lexis, its legal database; presumably, Web access to its other services will follow soon.

When to Monitor

How often should you check your online resources to identify references to your organization and issues in which you have an interest? That depends on the organization and the issues! In general, try to follow these guidelines:

- *Reading targeted newsgroups.* Check the newsgroups that are directly related to your business once a day.
- *General image monitoring.* Review the articles that match your queries at least once a week.
- *Crisis monitoring.* Maintain separate queries that retrieve articles about key issues (such as boycotts, environmental topics, and other issues that require immediate attention), and review them once a day.

Conclusion

Being vigilant about what is said about you on the Internet is most likely your single most important Internet-based activity. Unfortunately, it also is one of the most time-consuming and—most of the time—dull. Don't let it slide, though; make sure you either undertake the monitoring yourself or contract it out. Although the cost may seem high, it will be a pittance compared with having to deal with a crisis you could have prevented had you been monitoring the Internet. (Just ask Intel!) Once you know what is being said about you and where, it becomes easier to implement strategies to communicate with your various strategic audiences using the Internet. In Chapter 6, we will explore the means by which you can bring the Internet to bear in your communication with your various key publics.

Notes

1. Emulex Corporation press release, August 25, 2000.

PART TWO

Audiences

Media Relations

DIFFERENT ORGANIZATIONS MUST address a wide variety of constituent audiences, but they share the press in common. The press is not only one of the most important groups with which an organization must communicate; it also is one of the easiest groups to apply to the Internet. Most organizations already have this figured out to some extent. You can hardly find an institutional Web site that does not feature a link to material produced by the media relations department.

Contrary to the apparent belief of many observers, the role of an organizational media relations department is not to make the company look good in the press, nor is it to keep the company out of the newspapers. Most reporters who cover business are savvy enough to know when their chains are being yanked and are experienced enough to know how to circumvent a flack-oriented public relations department. Ideally, the job of the media relations department is to help reporters and editors do their jobs. That objective is entirely consistent with the broader goal of public relations, which is to manage the relationship between the organization and its various constituent audiences.

Reporters have a job to do. (I know. I used to be a reporter, years ago before I made the change to the business world.) That job involves covering news and events and reporting on their beats—categories of news and information that some reporters have assigned to them. A beat might be the chemical industry, all companies in Orange County, high tech, or mergers and acquisitions. Every story has a deadline, and news stories have the most unforgiving deadlines.

In the days before the Internet, the media wielded unparalleled influence. Audiences looked to the media as one of the few credible sources of information about unfolding events. Organizations relied on the media to get their messages out. A game ensued as a result of this odd relationship. Reporters needed public relations representatives to provide them with the information they needed to write their stories, but they viewed the PR reps as biased and untrustworthy. The PR reps needed the reporters to convey the organization's messages, even though they would rather go directly to the audience, but knew they had to find a chink in the reporter's armor in order to get the ink.

This relationship continues today, a decade into the Internet's penetration of the media landscape. The Internet has diminished audiences' reliance on traditional media, but the influence continues to be significant. Public relations professionals would be foolish to think they could use the Internet to influence audiences while completely ignoring the press. Instead, an integrated communication strategy would involve a media relations effort coupled with an online effort. And any media relations effort involves providing reporters and editors with the opportunity to engage the company online.

Journalists on the Net

Journalists increasingly rely on the Internet as a source of information to help them cover their stories; as a result, media relations representatives must start to apply the Internet to their jobs of making reporters' lives easier.

Research with reporters has uncovered the following two sets of facts:

1. How much they use the Internet and what they use it for
2. What they expect to find online

Middleberg Euro RSCG, a New York public relations agency, has since 1997 (in conjunction with Dr. Stephen Ross of Columbia University's Graduate School of Journalism) conducted a study, *The Middleberg/Ross Survey of Media in the Wired World,* which seeks to quantify journalists' use of the Internet, "detailing everything from their search patterns and e-mail practices to their views on the credibility of online information." Based on the results of these studies, we can with reasonable certainty determine the prevalence of reporters on the Internet and the ways in which they use it to do their jobs. With that information in hand, it becomes easier to establish online communication processes and programs that meet their specific needs.

The first thing to know about reporters is that they are, in fact, online. Of the four thousand print and broadcast journalists participating in the survey (out of forty-thousand who received the survey), nearly all respondents (98 percent) reported going online at least daily to check e-mail; they spend about fifteen hours each week reading and sending e-mail. Fifty-three percent claimed to be online "continuously" (defined as at least two or three times a day or more), while an additional 29 percent use the Net "frequently"—up to twice a day.[1]

What are they using the Internet for? According to the seventh annual study in 2000, journalists' use of the Net is at an all-time high in every category. Consider the following results:

- Eighty-six percent of journalists use the Net for article research and to retrieve reference material.
- Seventy-two percent obtain press releases online.
- Seventy-one percent use the Net to find new sources and experts to interview and quote.
- Seventy percent read publications online.
- Fifty-four percent accept story ideas and pitches over the Net.
- Forty-six percent download still images or video for use in their work.

Although journalists traditionally don't scour the Web for story ideas (preferring their regular sources and press releases as inspiration for new stories), e-mail is catching up as a source of new story ideas. Seventy-two percent of reporters listed e-mail as a source of new story ideas. Additionally, reliance on mailing lists and bulletin board discussions is up among newspaper respondents, though only slightly and still not a significant resource. Newsgroups, however, are somewhat more important to reporters already researching a story. And while newsgroups don't score high as a general resource, 49 percent of reporters said they would consider using discussion group postings or already have used those postings as either a primary or secondary source.

Seventy percent of reporters noted they would consider reporting information that had its genesis on the Net, and another 21 percent said they might consider doing so sometime in the future.

When news breaks, 21 percent of survey respondents indicated that they go to a company's Web site; it becomes an even more important resource when reporters are unable to get crucial information from a preferred source. Interestingly, most reporters don't find company Web sites to be credible. The sites of branded news agencies, such as CNN or the *New York Times*, rank the highest among reporters, followed by government agency sites, industry information services (such as chambers of commerce), and information provided by nonprofit or public interest groups. On a scale of 1 to 5 (5 being most credible), corporate sites scored a 3.1 (It could be worse: Activist Web sites scored a 2.3.)

The Middleberg/Ross study also queried journalists on the kind of information they find most useful. At the top of the list (84 percent) was contact information—how to get in touch with the appropriate media relations representative. Contact information was followed by using a search engine, press releases, text files, site map, photographs, biographies, financial information, and feedback.

That finding is not inconsistent with the findings of another study conducted by the Nielsen Norman Group, a Web-usability consulting firm based in Fremont, California. In the usability study Nielsen Norman conducted, twenty reporters were asked to visit ten corporate Web sites to gather information they might need for hypothetical story assignments. The reporters indicated that their top-five information needs were:

1. Contact information
2. Basic fact checking (such as correct spelling of an executive's name or the location of a plant)
3. The company's own spin on events
4. Financial information
5. Downloadable images for use as illustrations in the story

The reporters participating in the study indicated they were able to find these nuggets of information only about 60 percent of the time, leading the firm to give corporate Web sites a *D* grade when it comes to meeting the needs of journalists. What are the consequences of *not* meeting those needs? Consider this quote, from one of the Nielsen Norman test participants: "I would be reluctant to go back to the site. If I had a choice to write about something else, then I would write about something else."[2] It certainly defeats the point of providing press-oriented material on your Web site if it inspires the press to give coverage to other companies (including, perhaps, your competitors).

Based on what we know about the public relations role with the press, the needs of reporters, and the way the media use the Internet, we can identify some effective online tools for use in media relations efforts:

- ➫ Media relations Web sites
- ➫ Customized information delivery
- ➫ Positive e-mail relationships

TIP:
Use the Internet as an Enhancement,
Not as a Replacement

As powerful and valuable as Internet-based media relations tools can be, they are not a substitute for personal contact. Reporters are clear that they plan to stick to personal and public relations contacts as the source of their leads, even as e-mail creeps up as a source. And the Web is still hardly a tick on the meter—reporters overwhelmingly stay away from the Web as a new-story source. The Internet is a tool to enhance your relationship with reporters—and, by extension, to obtain better coverage—by providing a valuable service to those reporters who cover you. It will not replace the traditional practice of effective media relations.

Developing Media Relations Web Sites

Your media relations Web site is not a corner of a larger marketing-oriented Web site dedicated to archival of press releases, nor is it a news center where reporters *along with any other visitors* can learn what the company considers news. Make no mistake: Your media Web site is a dedicated source designed to help the targeted audience of reporters do their jobs, and it is available twenty-four hours a day, seven days a week.

Remember the Internet's fundamental pull model. Reporters can get the information they need, at any time of the day or night, often in a format that is ready to use. I can remember from my days as a reporter the frustration of an approaching deadline and needing to speak with sources who were away from their desks. ("Leave a message," their voice mail suggested, "and I'll get back to you as soon as I can." Like two hours after my deadline had passed!) In the years during which I was responsible for company media relations, reporters often waited on hold, their own deadlines approaching, while I spoke with another reporter who had called first. Today, if you provide answers to reporters' questions on the Web, they often do not need to call at all.

Some media relations experts are concerned about reporters retrieving information from a Web site without their knowledge. Often, it is the reporter's call for this or that bit of information that tips the company off to the fact that the reporter is working on a story about the company. But reporters generally will not limit their research to the Web. They will still seek interviews, responses to specific questions, and quotes directly from authoritative live sources. As a result, the media relations site should be loaded with the types of facts and information reporters need, along with the means to request interviews and pose questions.

What Do Reporters Need?

Deciding what to put on a media relations site could be as easy as referring back to the lists from the Middleberg/Ross study or the Nielsen Norman research. However, those are aggregated results from journalists responding to questions about sites in general. Your company has specific issues, and is covered by certain types of reporters working for particular publications. The best way to find out what the reporters covering your organization want to find on a site dedicated to their needs is simply to ask them.

As with any site that targets a public relations audience, you should treat the media site as one that is owned by the journalists who use it. Your job is simply to provide them with the resources they need. In order to identify those resources, you should initially convene a media advisory panel, a group of reporters who are representative of those that cover your organization. It shouldn't be too difficult to obtain volunteers—a built-in incentive for participating is a Web site that genuinely meets the panel member's needs, making it easier to cover the company. Consider including print and broadcast reporters; representatives of public and trade press; and journalists from local, regional, national, and international outlets. If the press that covers your business is typically local trade press, you would naturally emphasize reporters from those outlets on your panel. There is no point inviting a disproportionate number of media representatives who do not work for the kind of media that covers your business! However, you *should* include at least one or two, since these types of reporters *will* cover your business should it become embroiled in crisis or controversy. Make sure your site is set up to make it as easy for them to do their research as it is for the media with which you have daily contact.

Ask the members of your panel the following questions:

- What information about us do you routinely need to do your job?
- What resources would you like to have online access to?
- In what format would you like to have these resources? (For example, would they like images in the TIF or JPEG format?)
- Is e-mail an acceptable means for delivery of content you request?
- Would you be willing to use a site dedicated to the press to set up interviews or submit questions?

The answers you get will help you determine the priorities for your site. In any case, there are certain elements you should ensure are prominent parts of your media site. (Incidentally, it is highly advisable to give the media site a name that makes it clear that the site uniquely targets the media. Press Room, Press Center, News Room, or even Public Relations are names that leave no doubt as to the nature of the content on the site).

In Figure 6-1, Verizon's media relations site contains categories of information reporters need, and its look and feel differ somewhat

FIGURE 6-1. VERIZON'S MEDIA RELATIONS SITE.

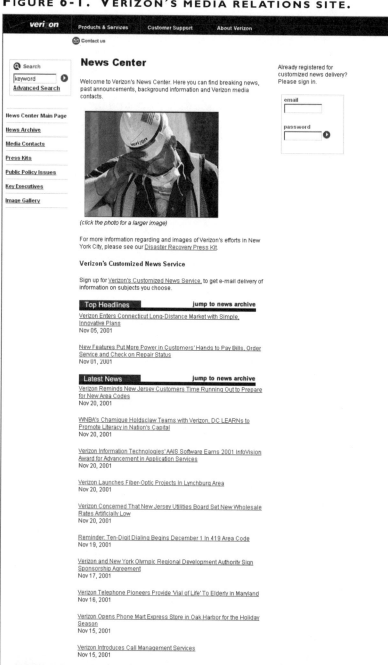

from the rest of the company's site; it is free of large graphic files that would inhibit the page from opening quickly.

Breaking News

The home page for your media site should not be limited to a static presentation of links. Prominently display your most current news. These can be press releases if they have been produced in a timely fashion. They can even be links to other news sources, such as newspaper Web sites, CNN, or any other reputable online news outlet. Microsoft includes links to coverage the company has received in the media as a prominent part of its press site (which is called PressPass, another name that leaves no question about the site's intended audience). Note that links to third-party coverage, while acceptable, are not complete—you still need to offer journalists your company's take on the events being covered.

As shown in Figure 6-2, Microsoft's PressPass site features links to articles written about the company and published by a variety of media outlets (you'll find them on the right-hand side of the page, under the heading, "Of Note").

FIGURE 6-2. MICROSOFT'S PRESSPASS SITE.

In addition to using the home page of the media relations site for breaking news, you should not neglect the overall home page of the institution's Web site. As soon as news about your organization breaks, many people (not only the media) will make a beeline for the home page to see what the company has to say. Finding nothing there can seem uncomfortably similar to a "no comment," ultimately affecting public perception of the organization and its credibility. As for journalists, there are many who may cover the breaking news story without having visited your site before; they don't know about the comprehensive media site. In the absence of information on the home page, journalists (like other interested parties) may scamper off to third-party sites, obtaining their messages from sources over which you have no control. (We'll cover techniques for using the home page as a crisis communication vehicle in Chapter 13.)

Contact List

One of the great failings of many Web sites is the lack of contact information. Scores of companies build Web sites that fail to offer a mailing address or telephone number. (There is no question that many of these companies *deliberately* exclude this information. Their philosophy is: "All our information is on the Web now; let them get it online so they won't bother us anymore.") The problem is that many people visit company Web sites *specifically* to get a mailing address or telephone number.

So it is with journalists. Often, all they want from a media relations site is the name and telephone number of the right person to talk to about the issue they are covering. A prominent link on the media site's home page, then, should take journalists to a comprehensive contact list. Categorize your contacts by their areas of responsibility—what geographical area they are responsible for, which company business units, or which product lines. Verizon offers contacts in the following categories:

- International
- Regulatory/Legislative
- Financial
- Corporate/Human Resources/Legal
- Philanthropy
- U.S. Wireline
- Products

➣ U.S. Wireless

➣ Print Directories and Advertising

A reporter preparing a story on the use of text-messaging services among wireless users would not need to be routed from one contact to another—he could click on the U.S. Wireless link, where he could see a contact for financial issues, another for consumer products, one for data and Internet issues, and one for public policy and regulatory issues—along with the vice president of corporate communications in the wireless division.

Each contact includes:

➣ The contact's name

➣ Title

➣ Telephone number

➣ E-mail address, hyperlinked so clicking the address automatically launches the reporter's e-mail software

➣ Areas of expertise (for example, Verizon's listing notes that the vice president of corporate communications in the wireless division is available to talk about "strategic direction and initiatives, all markets, and all issues")

In addition to including this information in a comprehensive listing, the same information should appear on every press release and every other document on the media relations site. Put yourself in the reporter's shoes: If you have a question after reading a speech, a legal document, a press release, or a white paper, whom do you call? The answer should be at the top of the document.

In Verizon's case, not every contact listed is part of the media relations department, but all have media relations responsibilities. This is a perfectly legitimate approach—reporters actually prefer talking to an expert over a public relations representative. You can be sure, though, that each of these contacts has been fully briefed and prepared to speak with the press.

Some argue against providing complete contact information despite the clear call from reporters for the information to be available. A company's online newsroom, the argument goes, must serve many masters. Sure, it was *designed* to meet the needs of the media, but the media are not the only ones using it. (We'll address the idea of forcing reporters to register for access later in this chapter.) As I have already noted, the Internet has inspired millions of people to bypass the media and find their own sources of information, leading many to corporate Web sites and, from there, to companies' online newsrooms. Your press center could be getting visits from job hunters, suppliers, financial analysts, even competitors. Do you want all of them to have access to your telephone number and e-mail address? Do you want all of them calling and writing to you?

To preclude too many of these irrelevant calls and e-mails, consider the following tactics:

- ➪ Include language at the top of the page that indicates the site is *only* for journalists.
- ➪ Where names and contact information appears, include a disclaimer that reads, "Media contacts only, please."
- ➪ Make sure the media site provides clear links to other parts of the site so that people seeking financial information can easily get to the investor relations site, job seekers can get to the recruiting site, and customers can get to the e-commerce part of the site.

Under no circumstances, however, should you withhold the contact information a reporter on deadline needs. Yes, you may get some unwanted telephone calls and e-mails, but for now, that is just part of the price to pay.

Fact Sheet

No reporter likes to misspell the name of somebody referenced in an article. Every reporter likes to have his facts right—how many employees work in a particular location, under what brand name a product is marketed, and in what territories a service is available. This kind of background information is perfect fodder for the fact sheet on your media Web site. Some categories to consider are:

➪ *Executive bios.* Include complete name, age, place of birth, education, and company history. You can also include downloadable, print-quality image files (print-quality means TIF or EPS, not Web graphic files like GIF or JPEG). These will also be available in the downloadable images section of the site.

↪ *Product/service information.* Include the product name, what it does, who the target market is, where it is available (which countries, for instance), the names of appropriate contacts for information about the product, label information (particularly for pharmaceuticals and other products for which this is important), and package art (also available in your downloadable images section).

↪ *Company structure.* How the company is organized, including a list of key business units, divisions, and departments, along with how many employees work in each unit and where key facilities are located. Provide contact information for queries about specific parts of the organization.

↪ *Markets.* An overview of the markets in which the company operates.

↪ *Company history.* A brief background, including a timeline.

↪ *Financial highlights.* You can provide a link to the investor relations site for detailed information, but here you can offer a snapshot of the company's finances, including your immediate past year's revenues, net earnings, quarterly dividends (if any), a current stock price along with a fifty-two-week high and low, shares outstanding, market capitalization, number of share owners, information on any stock splits, total assets, international revenues, and research and development expenditures. Based on your industry, additional key information may be important to include.

↪ *Honors.* Any recognition or awards the company has received, such as the Malcolm Baldrige quality award, a *Fortune* or *Forbes* 500 ranking, or a listing as a "most admired company" or "best company to work for."

Background Information

If the fact sheet offers at-a-glance information about the company, the background information component of the site offers snapshots of various key aspects of the organization. General Electric's Press Room, for example, offers ten different background briefs, including:

- The company's mission statement
- Environmental, health, and safety
- Executive development
- Leadership and training

As shown in Figure 6-3, General Electric's media relations site offers background briefs.

Key Initiatives

Most organizations operate within the framework of overarching initiatives established by management to move the organization forward. These initiatives range in scope from product-focused to those affecting recruitment and retention of key employees. Each of the initiatives in your organization should be explained on the media site. Looking again at General Electric, the key initiatives listed include globalization, services, "six sigma" quality, and e-business.

Figure 6-4 shows that a growth initiative is covered in some detail on General Electric's media site.

FIGURE 6-3. GENERAL ELECTRIC'S MEDIA RELATIONS SITE.

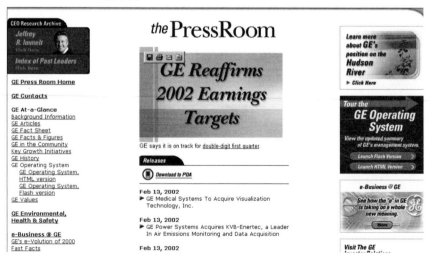

FIGURE 6-4. GE's COVERAGE OF A GROWTH INITIATIVE.

Key GE Growth Initiatives

GE is a diversified services, technology, and manufacturing company with a commitment to achieving worldwide leadership in each of its businesses.

To achieve that leadership, GE's ongoing business strategy revolves around four key Growth Initiatives – <u>Globalization</u>, <u>Services</u>, <u>Six Sigma Quality</u>, and <u>Digitization</u>.

Start ▶

Position Statements

Most organizations take positions on events both internal and external. A company that manufactures cellular phones, or provides cell phone service, is likely to take a position on the issue of driving while talking on the phone. From the external standpoint, consider the following scenarios:

Pharmaceutical companies will have a position on medicine pricing issues. Oil companies take a stand on drilling in protected regions. A nonprofit organization dedicated to combating a particular medical condition will have a position on government funding of research for a cure of that condition.

Internally, a company will take a position on ongoing negotiations with a labor union representing its employees, on a merger it wants to pursue, on the decision to close a facility or lay off employees.

If your organization has any official positions on any issues at all, they should be articulated clearly in a section dedicated to such issues. These statements can be kept short, inspiring journalists to call for more information, but a reporter should not have to dig deep into your site to find out that your organization opposes a particular piece of legislation.

Activity Calendar

Let reporters know about upcoming events, and give all the information they might need, including:

- ⇝ Time, date, and location of the event
- ⇝ The nature of the company's involvement
- ⇝ The media contact (hyperlinked to detailed contact information)

These calendars can include activities you might normally not want to reveal to the general public, such as testimony before government bodies or receptions for lobbying groups. These calendars can help editors make decisions about what to cover and assist reporters assigned to cover the event.

Press Release Archives

Post your press releases on the site, but make certain reporters can easily find the releases they want. Organize them chronologically (starting with the most recent) *and* by other categories that make sense (for example, product line, geographical region, or issue).

Speeches

The text of speeches delivered by your key executives should be archived online. You have the option of including a sound file of the actual speech, or actualities of key segments of the speech. A streaming audio capability will allow you to make sound available to broadcast media, and will let reporters hear the actual speech (allowing them to hear the volume of applause and the degree of commitment and enthusiasm in the speaker's voice). Additionally, a reporter who listens to a twenty-second clip in which the president outlines plans for a stock repurchase may decide that it would be worthwhile to go ahead and read the entire speech. However, reporters are not dazzled by multimedia, and rate simple Web sites as the best. Do not let your multimedia elements get in the way of quick scanning; rather, make them available as options the reporter must choose to see or hear.

Government and Legal Filings

Most of the documents your company files with the federal government, along with those filed in court actions, are public anyway, so you may as well put them on your site and save the reporter the time she would have to spend digging them up somewhere else. Microsoft's comprehensive archive of documents related to its federal antitrust case made the site a popular research source for reporters covering the trial. The company made every effort to ensure impartiality in the archive, presenting documents filed by both the company *and* the government. Napster, the music downloading service, also made every legal document available from its site (related to its fight to continue offering music over the Net).

Napster, the music file-sharing service, has been the focus of considerable legal activity as the Recording Industry Association of America and its various members sought to curtail the company's activities. As shown in Figure 6-5, Napster's media site includes an archive of legal documents pertaining to the case.

Links to Alternative Information Sources

If the Internet is indeed a modern multimedia version of the old party line, reporters have access to everything being published about an issue that is important to your organization. By using the various search engines available on the Net, reporters can root out available information, whether or not it's favorable to your company. Since they are going to find the information anyway, you may as well save them time and provide pointers to it.

Granted, pre-Internet media relations efforts never included guiding reporters to your critics and naysayers. Today, however, you give yourself a distinct advantage when you create these links. A reporter who finds such information on his own may not think about checking its accuracy with you. But if he finds it because you provided a link to it, the link itself can include a disclaimer about the source and an offer to discuss what he reads there. You can even provide bullet points refuting significant misinformation the reporter

**FIGURE 6-5. NAPSTER'S ARCHIVE OF LEGAL
            DOCUMENTS.**

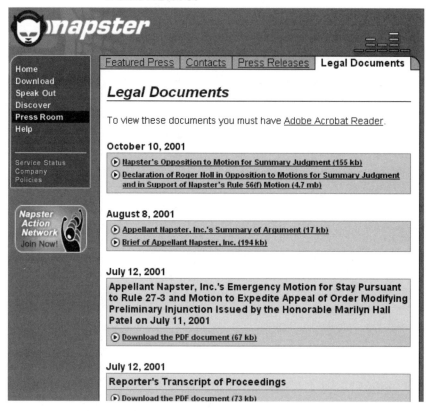

will find on the site to which you are linking. By displaying the link, you imply that the organization is aware of the content of the material; you also earn a reputation as being unbiased and more helpful than usual to reporters conducting research.

Include links to Web sites, mailing lists, and discussions where your company, operations, products, or services are being discussed.

Press Kits

Press kits in the real world can be a pain. You must print several versions of press releases, add fact sheets and data sheets, reproduce photographs, print captions on the backs of the photographs, toss in any appropriate supplemental material (such as brochures), then mail the entire thing out at high postage rates. And then you have no way of knowing how well this one-size-fits-all kit meets the needs of each individual editor.

Online press kits are much easier and more effective. These virtual resources for journalists can include original material as well as links to related resources scattered throughout your Web site. In fact, a virtual press release is nothing more than a collection of links about a common topic.

You can produce press kits about company products, much the way Coca-Cola does. The press kit for Coca-Cola's "Life Tastes Good" advertising campaign, for example, features links to:

- The news release about the campaign
- A white paper
- A fact sheet
- A Q&A
- An image library
- Media contacts
- A timeline of Coca-Cola's advertising history
- Interviews about the campaign with key Coca-Cola executives
- Video clips of television advertisements from around the world

A reporter (covering Coca-Cola or advertising campaigns) could choose the elements of interest to him from among the many options Coca-Cola has made available on this one topic. Based on the theme of your press kit, you can also include downloadable photographs, logos, maps, financial information, reviews, and any other information that a journalist might find useful.

One of Coca-Cola's online press kits is shown in Figure 6-6.

In addition to press kits focusing on products and services, they also can be assembled about short-term issues, such as a merger, a court case, or a labor dispute.

Document Subscription Services

The Web is a great pull service—on a good media site, journalists can find nearly anything they need. However, not a journalist

Figure 6-6. An online Coca-Cola press kit.

alive will check the Web site of every company on their beat every day to see whether new releases or other documents have been posted. In order to be certain the reporters who routinely cover your organization or market segment are getting the information about your organization you want them to have, it is important to offer a subscription service that allows reporters to request materials be pushed to them via e-mail.

Subscription services currently available on the Web cover a broad spectrum from those that simply request an e-mail address and then send every new release, to those that allow tremendous levels of customization. Most journalists do not appreciate the former type of service—they don't *want* every release your company distributes. A release on financial performance will be of little use to a reporter whose beat includes the types of products your company manufactures. It is worth the trouble to allow at least some level of customization.

A minimum level of customization is offered on CIGNA's media relations site. In CIGNA's Newsroom, reporters can choose to receive releases related to the corporation or its various business interests, including health care, employee benefits, retirement services, life insurance, international insurance, and investments.

As shown in Figure 6-7, CIGNA's newsroom offers basic sub-

Figure 6-7. CIGNA's newsroom offering basic subscription capabilities (©2002, CIGNA).

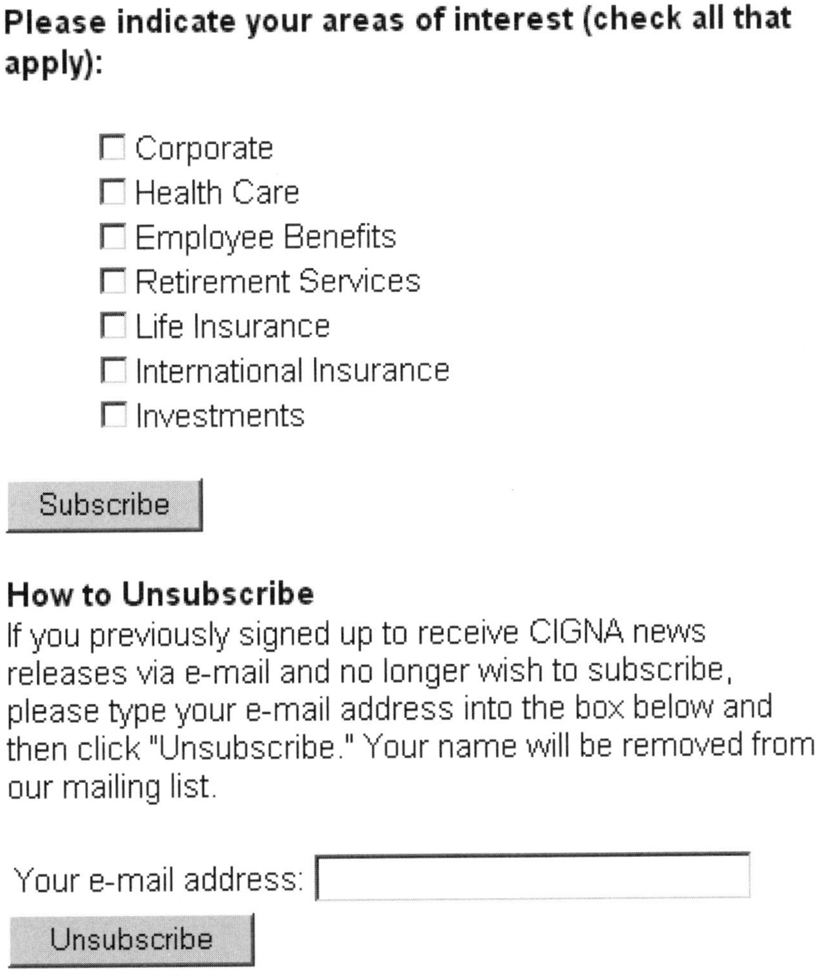

Please indicate your areas of interest (check all that apply):

☐ Corporate
☐ Health Care
☐ Employee Benefits
☐ Retirement Services
☐ Life Insurance
☐ International Insurance
☐ Investments

[Subscribe]

How to Unsubscribe

If you previously signed up to receive CIGNA news releases via e-mail and no longer wish to subscribe, please type your e-mail address into the box below and then click "Unsubscribe." Your name will be removed from our mailing list.

Your e-mail address: [   ]
[Unsubscribe]

scription capabilities. Reporters can choose to receive e-mail press releases based on the company's primary activities.

Verizon offers far more sophisticated customization, one of the most impressive of all the Web-based media sites. Here, a reporter is able to specify the region in which he is interested, the kinds of press releases (with fifty-two choices available), and other types of documents that could be of use (government filings, position statements, and speeches). Consider a reporter for the *Boston Globe* working in the business section who prepares a weekly column on local businesspeople who have been promoted, hired, or transferred. By selecting "Massachusetts" from the regional options and "Executive Staffing" from the press release category, that reporter knows beyond doubt that any press release arriving from Verizon is going to be appropriate material for his column. Consequently, that reporter will *always* open e-mail from Verizon.

As shown in Figure 6-8, Verizon's subscription capabilities are far more sophisticated, tapping a database to establish relationships between journalists' choices. A reporter can choose to receive only news releases from a specific region *and* only newsletters dealing with a particular topic.

Public relations agencies can adopt the same concept. Edelman Public Relations, one of the world's largest public relations agencies, was an early PR adopter of the custom-delivery concept. Edelman represents clients from myriad businesses and institutions, producing thousands of press releases. Edelman allows reporters to subscribe to receive press releases based on the industry categories Edelman represents (medical/health care, corporate/financial, business to business, travel/tourism, consumer, technology, public affairs, event/sports marketing).

Requests for Interviews

As noted earlier, you cannot possibly anticipate everything a reporter may need while researching a story—and no reporter expects your Web site to have every answer to every possible question. In fact, reporters *want* to do interviews, ask follow-up questions, and probe more deeply into an issue. Once they have completed their online research, it should be easy for the reporter to request an interview with you, a key executive, or a subject matter expert. It should

FIGURE 6-8. VERIZON OFFERING SOPHISTICATED SUBSCRIPTION CAPABILITIES.

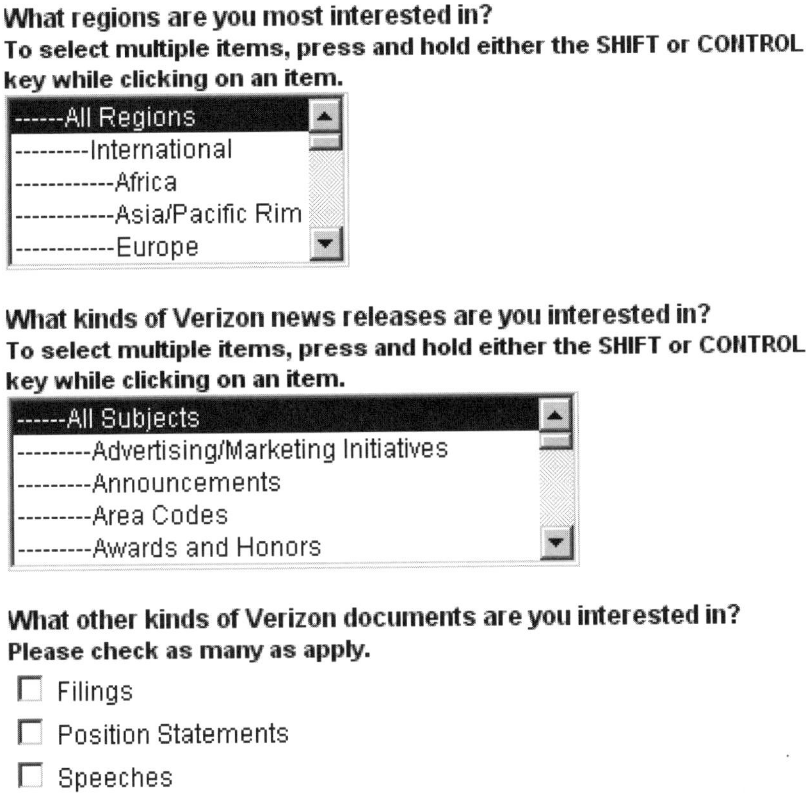

What regions are you most interested in?
To select multiple items, press and hold either the SHIFT or CONTROL key while clicking on an item.

```
------All Regions          ▲
--------International       
------------Africa          
------------Asia/Pacific Rim
------------Europe         ▼
```

What kinds of Verizon news releases are you interested in?
To select multiple items, press and hold either the SHIFT or CONTROL key while clicking on an item.

```
------All Subjects                      ▲
---------Advertising/Marketing Initiatives
---------Announcements
---------Area Codes
---------Awards and Honors              ▼
```

What other kinds of Verizon documents are you interested in?
Please check as many as apply.

☐ Filings

☐ Position Statements

☐ Speeches

be equally easy to submit questions the reporter needs answered. A simple form is sufficient for satisfying this requirement.

Or, you could take it to another level. The Insurance Information Institute (III), an industry group that provides data and documentation about the property-and-casualty insurance industry, provides a simple form on its media site, which reporters can use to submit questions or request interviews. Unbeknownst to the reporter, as soon as he clicks the "Submit" button, the media relations manager is paged. Wherever he is, he knows immediately that a reporter is looking for more information. Based on the reporter submitting the request, the media relations manager can choose to respond later or immediately. (For instance, a monthly insurance trade publication probably has some time to spare and the call can be returned later in the day; *The Wall Street Journal*, on the other hand, probably demands an immediate callback.) Reporters have been surprised to get calls from the III before they have even clicked away from the company's Web site!

Image Archives

Photos of your executives are great—but there probably are many other images reporters could use. When they call, you normally have to find a print, then courier it to the media outlet making the request. A comprehensive online library of images representing those you can be certain editors need can save time for both you and the publication. For example, Verizon offers printable images of maps showing the territories in which their telephone services are available. Some other images to consider offering include:

- Product shots
- Package shots
- Images of customers using your products
- Pictures of your headquarters and other key facilities
- Shots of workers on the factory floor or assembly line
- Diagrams of how key products work
- Diagrams of key corporate processes
- Other diagrams (for example, molecular diagrams or images showing how a medicine works on a part of the human body)

Extra Goodies

Depending on your industry, the business climate, and the media that cover your institution, you can add other services to your media relations Web site. The Vanguard Group, a financial services company, includes a page of story ideas. Reporters covering the financial services industry may be inclined to look at what Vanguard suggests; any of the ideas that become stories would most certainly benefit Vanguard (which would never suggest stories that would make them look bad). "Searching for a story idea or angle?" the page asks. "Here are some timely topics on mutual fund investing and personal financial planning to consider." Some other extra features you might consider on a media relations site include:

↪ *Customer stories.* Many reporters call media relations representatives in search of customers they can interview about your products. Providing some ready-to-go customer stories can save a reporter time.

↪ *The chief executive officer's Web page,* such as the one Bill Gates maintains on the Microsoft site. Gates uses the page as a personal forum for his key messages as well as an archive for his speeches and print columns.

↪ *News clippings.* Provide links to stories other media outlets have written about your company. Microsoft routinely offers a few such links on the home page of PressPass, always about topics favorable to the company. Although this is a good idea, it can also be valuable to offer links to *all* stories about your organization, regardless of whether they painted a positive image of the company. Remember, if the stories are on the Web, reporters conducting research will probably find them anyway.

↪ *Online press briefings.* These live presentations would allow reporters to cover a briefing without leaving their desk.

↪ *List of newsroom participants.* Journalists would be able to see other reporters who are registered to use the site.

↪ *PDA download capability.* Let reporters download material from your site to their Palm Pilot or other handheld device.

TIP:
Decide Whether You Want Visitors to Register or Not

From virtually every corner you will hear admonitions to make your media site available to reporters without making them register. "Do not force journalists to register in order to contact your company's press office or read press information," warned the authors of the Nielsen Norman study. "In fact, do not force them to register for any reason. They don't want to."[3] The same advice comes from Esther Schindler, site editor for the trade publication *Information Week* and author of "The Care and Feeding of the Press" (which we'll come back to later in this chapter): "One of the worst things you can do is require that a press person register for access to the media section of the Web site," Schindler writes. "We know all the reasons that you chose to implement that policy, but we don't care. If we're writing a review, we're apt to access this sort of information at 11:00 P.M. PST on Sunday night when the review is due at 8:00 A.M. EST. If we aren't yet writing about your company, you've presented us with one more barrier to doing business with you."[4] Despite this advice, there can be good reasons to restrict access to at least some of your media-focused content to genuine members of the press. Daimler Chrysler requires registration—and it has not kept reporters covering the automotive industry from registering. There is a good reason for the registration. Editors who need a color photo of a new car will want to download the print-quality file quickly—which probably won't be possible if every car lover in the world is downloading the same file (or some other file on the same server) so they can use it as wallpaper on their desktop computers. The site also includes an event calendar that could, presumably, include events about which the company would not want the general public to know—but *would* want to make accessible to the press. In general, I would agree with the advice to keep your site unrestricted. But if you have material where it does make sense to ensure only real members of the working press can get to it, take the following steps:

- ⮑ Make reporters register *only* for the sensitive material. Fact sheets, press releases, and other material that is public record anyway should be on the first tier of the media site, which requires no registration.
- ⮑ Explain clearly and simply *why* you want reporters to register for this material.
- ⮑ Make the registration process simple and immediate. A reporter registering on Sunday night will not wait until a department representative arrives at 8:00 A.M. the next day to verify her credentials and then issue a password. Issue the password via e-mail automatically; if you need to follow up, do it later.

As shown in Figure 6-9, Chrysler's event calendar could include events about which the company would want journalists to be aware, but would rather not share with the general public.

FIGURE 6-9. CHRYSLER'S EVENT CALENDAR.

EVENT CALENDAR

Jul 31, 2001	**Hightech Report 2001** Your Contact: ▶ **Wolfgang Scheunemann**
Aug 25, 2001 through Sep 02, 2001	**Caravan Salon** Düsseldorf/Germany Your Contact: ▶ **Raimund Grammer**
Sep 11, 2001 through Sep 12, 2001	**Frankfurt Auto Show (IAA) - Press Days** Frankfurt, Germany Your Contact: ▶ **Chrysler Communications**
Sep 13, 2001 through Sep 23, 2001	**IAA Frankfurt** Your Contact: ▶ **Wolfgang Inhester**
Oct 20, 2001 through Nov 07, 2001	**Tokyo Motor Show** Tokyo/Japan Your Contact: ▶ **Wolfgang Inhester**

Organizing Your Media Relations Web Site

The structure of your media relations Web site should accommodate the likely ways reporters will look for information. The hyperlinked nature of the Web allows you to create more than one path to the same information. Consider providing such paths based on elements including:

- ↪ The primary resources reporters look for online (contact information, press releases, fact sheets, company information, and downloadable images)
- ↪ Divisions
- ↪ Product lines
- ↪ Issues

The idea behind offering these different paths is to ensure that a reporter can find what she is looking for regardless of the approach she takes to her search. Figure 6-10 delineates the different paths that can lead reporters to the same information released by the company. Each reporter selects a path based on the nature of the story she is covering. In Figure 6-10, a pharmaceutical company that manufactures drugs for the elderly has announced a new policy to ensure reasonable prices for its senior consumers. One reporter visiting the site might be researching a story on drug pricing. Another is on the senior citizen beat. A third covers health care in general, and a fourth reports on the company for the daily newspaper in the city where the company is headquartered. Each reporter begins at a point that is intuitive for him or her, but the resources listed under each heading direct each reporter to the press release of common interest to them all.

Special or One-Time Media Sites

So far, our discussion has been about permanent media Web sites that provide journalists with information about your company and its activities. You also can establish a short-term Web site for the media, designed to provide resources about events or to focus on a single significant issue. The same guidelines apply to these sites as you would follow when developing a permanent site—you would

FIGURE 6-10. DIFFERENT PATHS LEADING TO SAME
INFORMATION.

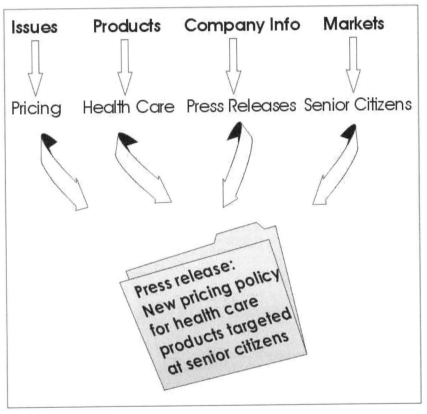

offer the same types of resources. One example is a site developed for Hydro-Quebec, which organized an international conference on electricity. The media site—available in both English and French—featured information about the conference, downloadable copies of speeches delivered, multimedia files (audio and video) for download, the conference schedule, articles from publications covering the conference, and a link to the public conference site. Reporters also had access to media contact information, a list of partners involved in the presentation of the conference, and a form they could use to register to attend.

Figure 6-11 shows Hydro-Quebec's special microsite for the press about a conference.

FIGURE 6-11. HYDRO-QUEBEC'S MICROSITE FOR THE
                          PRESS.

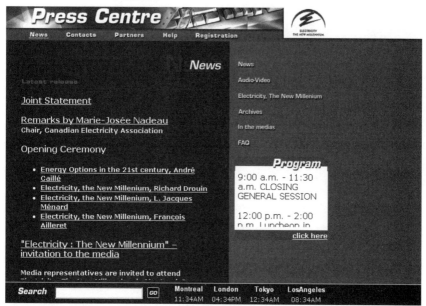

Announcing Your Media Site

Once you have a site available for the media, you need to let them know it is there. You can achieve this in several ways:

- ⇨ Issue a press advisory or release alerting the media to the presence of the site.
- ⇨ Include the address of the site on all press releases and other written material.
- ⇨ Have the address printed on your business card.
- ⇨ Get in touch personally with all your regular media contacts and advise them of the site's availability.
- ⇨ Include the address on your e-mail signature block.
- ⇨ Provide a link from your top-level corporate page to the media site.
- ⇨ Make sure your site is registered in appropriate directories and that business services such as Hoovers and Dun & Brad-

street know the address so they can include it on their Web sites.

Case Study: Media Web Site Announcement Press Release

Smith Bank Opens Web Site for News Media

BOSTON, Massachusetts, May 1, 2001—Smith Bank announced today that it will offer an area with special content on its corporate Web site exclusively for the news media. Smith Bank's media area is designed to provide the media with real-time information about the business.

"At Smith Bank, we understand that the importance of the World Wide Web as an information resource is growing daily," according to John Jones, vice president of public relations. "As a result, our media area will provide real-time information to reporters, as well as serving as an easily accessible source for bios, downloadable photos, and broadcast-quality audio clips quoting our experts on the news of the day. Time is a premium in the news business, so we've made it easy for the media to access the information they're most interested in about Smith Bank."

From the media Web page, reporters can get information about:

⇨ The latest Smith Bank news events, including downloadable sound bites for use by broadcast media on breaking stories

⇨ Advisories about upcoming news events at the Bank and sources to contact for topical stories

⇨ A list of contacts in Smith Bank's media relations unit around the world, with telephone numbers and e-mail addresses

⇨ Current and relevant past Smith Bank news releases, with useful background

In addition, media visitors to the media page will be able to follow links to key recent senior management speeches; bios and photos of Smith Bank senior executives; a photo file with a variety of downloadable print-quality images; a summary and timeline of major events in Smith Bank's history; and a page with links to a variety of banking information sources, including regulators, trade associations, trade publications, and legislative and other government bodies concerned with banking issues. A special search engine allows searches to be targeted to an archive of all the news releases Smith Bank has posted to its Web site or to speeches, as well as to the entire Smith Bank site.

The media page also includes links to a variety of resources publicly available on the Smith Bank Web site that may be of special interest to the media. These include the news release archive, which includes all the releases Smith Bank has

posted on its site since 1994, sorted by topic; financial information about the corporation, including links to earnings releases, stock price history, analyst presentations, and
SEC filings; economic outlooks, data, and reports issued by Smith Bank; a reference
list of the acquisitions Smith Bank has made since 1994; and information on Smith
Bank operations. The media site is exclusively for the news media and is accessible
by password only. A simple application form can be found at *http://www.smithbank.
com/media/register.html.*

Smith Bank is the largest regional bank in the Northeast, with assets exceeding
$1.5 billion. Smith Bank provides commercial, retail, and real estate services.

NOTE TO EDITORS AND REPORTERS: The Smith Bank media site is restricted to
ensure only members of the working press can review this material. The Bank will
not track your activity on the site, which includes proprietary information not available
to the general public.

Online Press Releases

When assembling an online press release, remember that whether it
is listed on a World Wide Web page or is destined for delivery by
e-mail, it is not the same as a paper press release. The medium is
different, and the form of the press release should accommodate and
capitalize on those differences. Consider the three following elements:

1. *Limited opportunity to gain attention.* An editor can quickly
scan a printed press release to see whether the content is intriguing.
If a photograph accompanies the printed release, it takes a mere second for an editor to pull the photograph out of the envelope and give
it a glance to see whether it is worth running; the photograph alone
could motivate the editor to read the release. The online version,
however, offers only the amount of text that appears on the screen.
Anything below the screen requires the deliberate act of scrolling
farther down. If the part of the press release that appears on the
screen is not interesting or compelling, or if it does not contain the
heart of the release, it could motivate the editor to move on to something else. E-mail press releases are even more challenging, since an
editor can dispose of the release with a single tap of the delete key.
The only tool you have at your disposal to capture the editor's attention is the text you type into the subject line. I am *not* suggesting
that you should produce two entirely different versions of your press

releases—one for print and wire services and one for online consumption. In fact, journalists often visit Web sites seeking a copy of a press release they received earlier from a traditional channel, and they want to find *the same* release on the Web that they got over the wire. However, you can incorporate certain elements to enhance the online experience, such as an executive summary that summarizes key information presented in the narrative part of the release, a larger headline font, and a thumbnail of any associated photograph or illustration alongside the release.

2. *Ability to incorporate internal "anchor" links.* One more way to address the previous issue is to build a mini-table of contents for your readers at the top of the release. This also serves to help those who have used search engines to find your release. Reading only the headline may not prompt a visitor to recognize the value of the release; it may even seem that the search engine has found a less-than-pertinent link (they have been known to do that from time to time!). However, a table of contents can list, in order, the elements that appear in the release. An editor can click on any element of interest and jump directly to that element, enhancing the possibility that the release will pique his interest.

3. *Access to other material.* The press release that appears online is not limited to material you can stuff in an envelope. You can make the entire realm of cybermaterial available to a reporter or editor with the click of a mouse. You can offer links to related material (including earlier press releases), full text of background documents, video, animation, and executable programs. One word of caution: Offer these links *at the conclusion* of the release; *do not* build the links into the narrative of the text. Many journalists will be inclined to print the release, rendering links useless. Leave the body of the release free of links so reporters don't feel they are missing something when they use the hard copy.

Some other tips regarding press releases are:

↪ Date the release rather than using the customary, "For Immediate Release." Since reporters using the Web are pulling the release rather than accepting a push of it, it will be important for them to know when it was issued.

↪ Add additional subheads. These do not change the narrative of the release, but do make it easier for journalists to scan the release online. The subheads could match the internal anchor links suggested previously.

➥ Offer links to any coverage the company has received about the subject covered in the release. If the release is about the launch of a new product, link to articles on the Web sites of magazines and other news outlets that covered the launch.

Look at the following mock-up of an online press release to see how one might appear on a Web screen (underlined elements represent hyperlinks):

Press Release
August 18, 2001

Contact:
Shel Holtz
(925) 673-9896
(925) 673-0419 (fax)
Email: shel@holtz.com

Press Release Template Available in Online PR Book

- Use a table of contents
- Add multimedia elements
- Link to related material

CONCORD, CALIFORNIA—*Public Relations on the Net*, in its second edition from AMACOM Books, includes information on how to develop a press release for online use. "It takes less energy to hit the delete key than it does to crumple up a piece of paper and throw it away," according to Shel Holtz, author of the book. "But there are ways to capture an editor's attention online."

One of those ways is to include a contents-like listing at the top of the page, allowing editors to scan quickly the key topics addressed in the release and click to those in which they are interested. Another method is to hyperlink to related materials at the end of the release.

Finally, press releases that appear online can contain multimedia, such as an audio clip from a speech that is being reported, a video from an event you would like covered, even an animation of a new process to make it easier to understand.

Boilerplate information should be kept for the end of the release. The boilerplate is a block of text that tells editors about the company that issued the release.

Related information:
Audio clip of Shel Holtz speaking about online press releases
AMACOM Web site
Shel Holtz's Web site

E-mail press releases can work in virtually the same way, since most current e-mail packages support hyperlinks to Web pages and launch a new e-mail message template when a hyperlinked e-mail address is invoked. However, be sure to use a compelling subject line, as noted earlier. Do not hope that an overworked editor on deadline will open up your e-mail message based on a subject line that reads something like: "New Public Relations Book Offers Tips on How to Get Your Press Releases Read." First, tell the editor that the e-mail is, in fact, a press release. Then be sure to use a compelling subject line that will at least make her want to open the release to see whether anything worthwhile is hidden there. An effective subject line might look like this: "PRESS RELEASE: New book teaches PR people how to keep YOU from ignoring them!" You can bet most editors will at least be curious about what you think companies can do to get their attention!

> #### TIP:
> #### *Make Sure Press Releases Are for the Press*
> I have seen a disturbing trend in the development of press releases. Companies are starting to write press releases for audiences other than the press based on the fact that, on the Web, any number of audiences has access to the releases. The rationale goes something like this: "Since our customers can read the press releases—which are posted to our News directory—we need to make sure the releases are understandable to that audience." I know of one com-

pany that dumbed down its releases based on the fact that consumers were not as sophisticated about the company's issues as the journalists who cover the company. In another instance, a company made its press releases too complex and technical for the average reporters since its customers were generally much more knowledgeable about the technical aspects of the company's products. Another argument favoring this approach is because the press release distribution services (such as PR Newswire and Business Wire) send press releases to independent outlets that post the releases on their sites, it is important that the release be understandable by the audiences that visit those sites (such as investors visiting the Yahoo press release archives). I couldn't disagree more. Producing a single document conveying news that is meant to be meaningful to all audiences is nothing more than laziness. How can you produce a so-called press release for any primary audience other than the press? And considering how important the press remains, why would you want to produce a document that is not optimized for their use? A better solution is to create the press release for the press and a news account for everybody else. On the press release, include a disclaimer that might read something like this: "This press release is for use by members of the print and broadcast media. An account of this information for other audiences is available on the Company News section of our Web site."

TIP:
Use a Database for Press Releases

If you put your press releases into a database, you can create a simple query form for reporters to use to find a given release. Establish separate fields for the date of the release, the headline, the author, the text of the release, and any other pertinent information (such as a plant location, brand name, or key executive). Now the reporter can use the form to conduct a search of your press releases, making it easy, for example, to find a release that was issued six months earlier about the promotion of a particular executive. Talk to your IT staff—the programming required to create such a service is fairly simple.

Integrated Media Campaigns

Although journalists are wise to most of the gimmicks that public relations agencies throw at them, a well-orchestrated campaign can still capture a reporter's or editor's attention and make your message stand out from the rest. That was the case with GroupaXion, a Quebec-based agency engaged to promote a new all-terrain vehicle produced by the company Bombardier. According to Jean-Francois Dumas, GroupaXion's president and CEO, the key objectives of the campaign were to act quickly to short-circuit the competition, raise journalist interest, and personalize the information. At the time the campaign commenced, only a single prototype of the vehicle was available, and rumors about the introduction were circulating throughout the industry.

GroupaXion targeted twenty-one journalists from the United States and Canada who specialized in reporting on all-terrain vehicles. "We sent a personalized e-mail message to each reporter that invited the reporters to visit a special Web page," Dumas explained. The Web page—available only to the reporters on the mailing list—was essentially a tease, advising the reporters that detailed information would be coming in a couple days. A second personalized e-mail directed reporters to a site containing details, including photographs and specifications, along with a complete press release.

As a result of the use of an e-mail–Web tease followed by complete information in an integrated e-mail–Web communiqué, the campaign delivered six front-page articles along with several other articles in other parts of key publications. "One article mentioned the originality of the process used by Bombardier to launch its new all-terrain vehicle," Dumas said.

"Our campaign offered Bombardier, which has been in the ATV business for less than a year, the opportunity to gain substantial notoriety in a very narrow target market," said Christiane Fayad, manager of communications for Bombardier. "It had a real positive influence on our sales."

Vocus offers another example of integrating e-mail and the Web.

The company, which produces automated software for public relations professionals, launched a new wireless tool aimed at journalists. An initial e-mail distributed to public relations agencies (each e-mail appeared to be directed only to one individual and not a list) introduced the concept and invited agency representatives to visit a Web site:

> Subject: Wireless Wave Will Help Reporters
>
> One of the best uses for a wireless application has arrived and it specifically benefits journalists! With the Web, many reporters find they are faced with tighter deadlines in order to keep up with the 24/7 expectations for news. Today, Vocus unveiled the first wireless application that will help journalists by providing public relations professionals tools to immediately respond to their requests for media kits, press releases, product photos, and executive bios anytime, anywhere.
>
> Why is this important? Because public relations is one of the last frontiers not supported by wireless, and this technology is critical for the PR professional in order to meet tight deadlines and have the ability to quickly and appropriately respond to clients or journalists' needs when away from the office.
>
> This technological innovation is a major breakthrough in the PR profession and Rick Rudman, president, CEO, and cofounder of Vocus, would like to tell you more. If you would like to speak with Rick, please call me at (xxx)xxx-xxxx, or mailto:xxx@xxxx.com, or Karen Tran at xxx-xxx-xxxx, ext. xxxx, or mailto:xxx@xxxx.com. To access the complete media kit with an illustration, technical specifications, and features, visit http://www.vocus.com/wireless.

As shown in Figure 6-12, Vocus produced a special page on its Web site to provide information about its new wireless service. Public relations agencies to whom the service was marketed received targeted e-mail messages inviting them to the site, in addition to providing information on whom to contact for more information.

In addition to generating interest in the target market, the program also produced coverage in the media, including articles in on-line publications such as ZDNet's *Tech InfoBase*.

E-Mail and the Press

One-to-one e-mail with reporters can be an effective way to maintain contact, provide information, and pitch story ideas—but only *after* you have established yourself with the reporter and obtained the reporter's consent to do business by e-mail. Of course, you

FIGURE 6-12. PAGE ADDED BY VOCUS TO ITS WEB SITE
TO ANNOUNCE NEW WIRELESS SERVICE
(WEB ILLUSTRATION BY JIM NUTTLE).

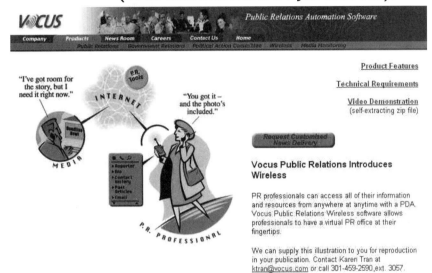

can make that first contact by e-mail, too. "I was reading a family-relationships column in the *Baltimore Sun* by Susan Remer this past September in which Reimer mentioned psychologist-educator Carol Gilligan briefly in the context of her story," recalled Amy Choma, director of communication for Roland Park Country School in Baltimore.

> Carol Gilligan happened to be an upcoming lecturer at our school the following month. I e-mailed Susan Reimer, told her I was a fan of her column and why, and then mentioned that Gilligan would indeed be lecturing at our school. I invited Reimer to the lecture and to an invitation-only reception before, and she ended up interviewing the speaker and several students and dedicating an entire column to the lecture the following week. It all happened very quickly and easily because of the use of e-mail. A simple press release might not have been as effective, since the

connection to Reimer's first story and the timeliness of my e-mail invitation was the key.

Not to mention the fact that the e-mail was *personal*, directed only at that one reporter, rather than a mass distribution of a release to several reporters.

Once a relationship is established, e-mail is an excellent tool for keeping it alive. Again, Roland Park Country School's Choma provides an example:

> I developed a friendly relationship with a *Baltimore Messenger* reporter via e-mail months before ever meeting her. I was able to prove myself as a resource to her by replying to her e-mail messages quickly and thoroughly and taking every request for information quite seriously. I am in the habit of dropping her a quick e-mail every time something interesting comes up at the school, including things I would love to have time to write press releases about but just know I can't get to them. I am constantly surprised by how many of these little tidbits she winds up using. Sometimes things that seem trivial to us are of great interest to particular reports (and vice versa!)

Sending press releases via e-mail and engaging in business with reporters can work well, as it does for Choma, or it can create hazards that could ruin your relationship with a reporter—and any hope of ever getting the kind of coverage from that writer you would like to get. Esther Schindler's "Care and Feeding of the Press"—an online document published on the Web site of the Internet Press Guild (a nonprofit organization promoting excellence in journalism about the Internet, online services, and bulletin board systems)—provides excellent guidelines public relations practitioners would do well to follow. Schindler has graciously given permission to cite from segments of "Care and Feeding of the Press" here. (I could have paraphrased this material, or written a section of this chapter from scratch, but there is something compelling and invaluable about hearing it from the kind of journalist you're trying to reach!) You can get the entire document (and you should—and read it twice) at *http://www.netpress. org/careandfeeding.html*:

From "Care and Feeding of the Press"
By Esther Schindler, site editor, Information Week

Sending Press Releases

Many journalists prefer that you send press releases via e-mail. You will find some die-hard snail-mail folks, and a few who like faxes. If you're about to start working with a new journalist, and you're not sure how they prefer to receive their press information, *ask.* (And, if you do ask, abide by the request.)

That's especially true if you intend to send a fax, since faxes cost us time and money to receive. You'd better be sure I want to get that fax before you tie up my phone lines.

E-mail should be sent as a plain text file: the simpler, the better.

Many writers and editors routinely and automatically delete any mailing that's addressed to more than three people in the subject line, or which has a binary attachment; a virus could put many writers out of commission. Therefore, please do not blindly send binary attachments, such as Microsoft Word files or Acrobat documents or—even worse—huge graphics files.

We don't have a lot of time to spend reading press releases; so the quicker you can get the message through to us, the quicker we can respond. If you have a full press kit with screen shots and four-part harmony, mention in your e-mail message that a full press kit is available; but only send it to those who ask. (Doing so will save you money, anyway.) Better yet, put that press kit on your Web site, and provide the URL in the ASCII news release that you e-mail us.

Let's Make This Clear:
Unsolicited Attachments Merit the Death Penalty

Never, never send an unsolicited file, especially an unsolicited binary file. If you can take away only one message from this article, let this be it. Let me repeat, for emphasis: *Do not send us e-mail attachments, unless you are willing to bet your job that we want that file.*

You may not realize it, but file attachments are really an imposition. You don't know where I am when I receive your message. I could be calling in long distance on my laptop, with barely enough room left on the hard disk to read my text messages. We certainly don't want to take the risk of picking up a virus from you (and yes, this happened to one PR firm). This is one of the major annoyances we journalists complain about among ourselves. In fact, *most of us will delete unsolicited binary files without even reading them.*

Above all, do not send us large graphical files, which may take forever to download. With an average daily e-mail load of several hundred messages, we don't have time to waste with graphic downloads, no matter how cool they look. If you can convince us that your product is worth our time, we'll get in touch with you, and then you can send us all the pretty pictures and information files we need.

If the writer has said, "Sure, send me your information," and the file contents are more than 25K (that's only a few pages in Word), let the journalist know the size first. I may want you to send it to another account, or I may prefer to download it from your site, at my leisure. (Shall I recount the anecdote about the well-meaning PR guy who sent me a 4MB file via my 28.8kbps modem dial-up account? When I was dialing in from a hotel room? And then he sent it five times, by mistake? No, I don't want to see you cringe.)

To Whom Should You Send Your Releases?

The answer sounds self-contradictory: Send it to everybody that might be interested in your message, but don't send it to everybody.

If you really want to find the "right people," your best course of action is to look at the magazines that cover your type of product. Get the e-mail addresses for staffers and contributing editors (regular freelancers) from the masthead or from the magazine's Web site. Often, the publication's Web site also lists the editorial calendar (which means less than you think it does) and gives a clue about which editors handle what topics. This process costs little or nothing, and it's the easiest way to be accurate. If the number of contacts is overwhelming, find the e-mail ID of an editorial assistant; it's the assistant's job to track the journalists' beats.

It's also important for you to figure out—perhaps with the help of that editorial assistant—which writers care about what kind of information. As a technology editor, I don't care about the name of the new CEO or the company's newest business alliance; I only care about products. News editors and feature editors have different perspectives. Sending me the wrong information annoys me, and makes it harder to get my attention the next time you try.

For instance, a well-meaning PR person sent me a message saying, "I thought the attached [product] review, which appears in the current issue of [competing publication] might be of interest to your readers." This PR person actually imagined that I'd reprint a review from another publication? Or was she naive enough to imagine that, since the other magazine had reviewed the software, I'd feel compelled to do so, too?

The answer is no. Even if I was tempted, my first response would be, "Well, we missed that one; someone else covered it already." If a PR person sends me clippings from six other publications, it doesn't make me more likely to write about their client; it has the *precise opposite effect*. It makes me think that the PR person is pitching a story that has been pretty thoroughly chewed over and digested already. Because we're looking for fresh news, I'm likely to move on at that point and throw the PR person's pitch in the trash bin.

If you send a product, e-mail, or press release to one person at a publication, don't assume that it reaches everyone at, or associated with, the publication. That's especially true of the freelance members of the staff. ("Contributing editor" means "a freelancer we like a lot." "Senior contributing editor" generally means "a freelancer we like a heck of a lot, and the editor-in-chief will buy her dinner when they happen to be in the same city.") Even within the on-site staff of big magazines, people barely have time to wave at each other in the hallways. Besides, even journalists who are friends actively compete with one another and tend to hoard certain information.

On the other side of the coin, though, note that writers, freelancers, and editors do talk with (and about!) each other. And yes, we talk about you vendors, both positively and negatively. That's our version of "shop talk." "Gee, you wouldn't believe what happened when I reviewed one of XYZ's products a couple of years ago. They spent twenty minutes on the phone yelling at me for giving them a bad review, when the stupid product didn't even install! They even threatened to sue the magazine." No freelancer who hears such a story will go out of her way to write about XYZ's products; and if they do work with the company, they won't do it with a trusting heart. The lesson here is: Don't screw us. We remember. And there's an old saying about not doing battle with someone who buys ink by the barrel.

(Perhaps that seems harsh, even threatening. It's not meant that way. However, an alarming number of vendors act as though it's okay to screw a writer, and they assume that the word never will get out.)

Don't Call. Really.

You should not call us to find out if we received your press release. We realize that follow-ups are part of many PR organizations' normal operating procedure, but in many cases, it's more likely to create resentment. It is appropriate to follow up on requested information, such as a sent press kit or product, but not on a blind mailing.

If we're interested, you'll hear from us. If we've already established an ongoing relationship because I've covered your products earlier, it's okay to send a follow-up e-mail a few days later to ask if I have any questions; but that's it.

Now, I know this next point goes against a lot of your training, but take our word for it: Nothing sets a writer or editor's teeth on edge more than an eager young voice saying, "I'm calling to see if you got the press release we sent." (It is, alas, common practice to have follow-up calls made by the most junior [read: clueless] members of an agency.) When we're in the middle of a tight deadline, the last thing we want is a phone call that contains no new or useful information whatsoever. Thus, by making such calls, you're harming both clients' and your own reputations. If you actually have something substantive to add, such as pointing out an error in a press release, that's another story; but you're still better off sending us an e-mail about it than calling us.

Possibly the worst phone call is when the PR person just reads from a document, and actually has no idea what he's talking about. If you're going to have someone just read, why not just e-mail me the information? If someone calls, it should be a person whom I can question a little bit about the news.

E-Mail and Telephone Hygiene

Do use meaningful subject headers. Here are a few we recommend against: "Hello Robert," "Press Release," or "Leveling the E-Commerce Playing Field" (the latter about an online comic-book store).

Don't use subject headers that look like spam. Anything with repeated exclamation points, dollar signs, or all caps makes me stab the delete key reflexively—assuming that my e-mail client doesn't automatically route the offending message to the trash first.

Don't use Hotmail, Juno, yahoomail, or AOL, for the same reason. It also looks unprofessional and basically shouts, "Look, we're too poor to afford a real e-mail account."

Do use a signature file with your full contact info.

Don't send a press release to your entire press list, with the entire recipient list visible. (I received one e-mailed press release that consisted of four screens of TO: e-mail addresses, followed by one line of text and an attached Word document. The text read, "Hope to see you there!") When I look at a TO list that's bigger than most people's Christmas card list, I think, "Well, someone else'll be covering this if it's worth attention. I won't bother, because my article won't be unique." We all like to feel special, even if we know otherwise.

Do turn off the option in your mail program that sends a second, HTML copy of the message as an attachment.

Don't attach a vCard. You want me to know how to reach you? Use a signature file. And if you insist on auto-attaching a vCard, please use a filename besides "vcard.vcf."

Don't call to say, "I'm calling to follow-up on the e-mail we sent you announcing that the BelchFire Corp. introduced the ThunderMug 5000." Instead, say, "I'm calling for BelchFire Corp. to announce that we've introduced the ThunderMug 5000." It's a small thing, sure—but the former phrasing focuses attention on the e-mail (who cares about the e-mail anyway?) while the latter phrasing focuses on what's really important: the announcement itself.

Don't start out a phone call by saying, "Is now a good time?" How can I know, if I don't know what you're calling about? It's *always* a good time to call with page one news. However, if I'm struggling to write a story that's already hours late, it's not a good time to call to ask me if I got the e-mail you sent me two weeks ago.

Don't use voice mail as a substitute for e-mail, at least not until we get voice-mail systems with fast-forward buttons. If you can't make your point in less than a short paragraph, hang up, and e-mail me instead. Begin your message with your name and phone number; don't make us listen to the entire five-minute message just to find out how to reply to you.

Don't use the stalker mode of calling. Most of us have Caller ID. We can tell when you're calling three times in fifteen minutes, to try to ambush us at our desks. (Not all of us object to this, but it's a pet peeve for those who do.)

E-mail also can be useful for press releases to key nonmedia audiences. For example, Jim Rink, who directs communications for the Automobile Club of Michigan, added all of the association's branch managers to the media e-mail list. "Media are invited to sign up for a semiweekly e-mail update that links directly to articles and releases on our Web site," Rink said. "By adding branch managers, we keep them up-to-date on recent PR releases and/or corporate issues, which is vital because they often get calls from local media and are often unaware of what's going on. This way, they get the info when everyone else does."

Step-by-Step: Online Media Relations

Before undertaking an online media relations effort, you should follow these steps to ensure that you are delivering the kind of material that will be beneficial to the journalists covering you:

1. Segment the media covering you. Are you covered regularly by trade media? Are you a *Fortune* 1000 company? Are you an industry or profession that receives regular coverage (for example, high tech, health care, or tobacco)? Are you covered as a leader in your market segment?

2. Identify the kinds of information required by reporters working for each major segment you identify.

3. Query the reporters with whom you already have regular contact. Find out whether they want to receive any information by e-mail or would be inclined to avail themselves of a Web site to obtain company information.

4. Establish a media advisory panel to help you identify the nature of the information these journalists would like to receive through each online medium, and the paths they would be likely to follow when accessing that information. Maintain the panel after the site launches to provide ongoing feedback and generate new ideas.

5. Determine which information reporters would want to *pull* and which you may want to be able to *push*. Those that qualify as *pull* items should be on your media relations Web site, while those that are *push* should additionally be available through a customizable subscription service.

Measurement

As always, it is critical that you measure the effectiveness of your online media relations. Use the following questions to guide your assessment:

- How many reporters have given you their e-mail addresses for receipt of press releases, press advisories, and other materials?
- How many reporters have subscribed to any e-mail distribution services you offer?
- How many reporters who have registered to use proprietary parts of your media relations site actually visit the site? Where do they go? What do they download? (If you track this information, you *must* disclose to reporters *before* they register that you will be monitoring activity on the site. However, the goal of such monitoring is not to keep tabs on individual reporters, but rather to aggregate activity so that you can improve the site, making it more useful to journalists.)
- How many reporters contact you after reading material on your site?
- How much content from your site appears in stories written about your company? (Consider your customer case studies, boilerplate materials, press releases, etc.)
- How many reporters participate in online activities such as press conferences?

Conclusion

Your job as a media relations professional is to make a reporter's job easier. In doing so, you best represent your company and make it more likely that reporters will listen to your point of view, your story pitches, and your requests. Use the Internet to facilitate this approach to media relations by making information available, not by invading reporters' e-mail boxes with unwanted e-mail. Reporters are using the Internet at record levels, so it falls to practitioners to understand *what* they use it for. Then build communication efforts that accommodate those trends.

Notes

1. Middleberg Euro RSCG, "Media in Cyberspace" study (2001).
2. Nielsen Norman Group, "Designing Websites to Maximize Press Relations," March 2001.
3. Ibid.
4. Esther Schindler, "Care and Feeding of the Press" (2000–2001), *http://www.netpress.org/careandfeeding.html.*

CHAPTER 7

Investor Relations

INVESTORS AND THE financial community—and all their related subaudiences (for example, mom-and-pop investors, institutional investors, large individual shareholders, brokers, and financial reporters)—constitute one of a public company's most significant audiences. Not only must you convince the kinds of investors you want to attract to view your stock favorably, you must keep them informed about the progress of the company they own—and its response to issues that could affect share value—so they will not sell their stock or seek to take action against the company. Shareholder suits are among the most debilitating actions a company must deal with, and some law firms make their living seeking reasons to file suits on behalf of shareholders. Lawsuits are not the only recourse that shareholders have; they also can engage the company in proxy battles.

The financial community is, in general, heavily wired. Bloomberg helped pave the way to the widespread use of electronically delivered financial information. Everybody from investment analysts to stockbrokers to corporate investor relations managers keep computers on their desks that flash stock prices, earnings reports, and other important financial news. Business Wire, PR Newswire, and First Call have grown their businesses considerably by providing electronic communication systems that satisfy Securities and Exchange Commissions rules (in the United States) that insist financial communities get first notice of any company news that could have an impact on share price.

Yet, the average corporate Web site treats investor relations as an afterthought. Most investor relations sites are dusty corners of the overall corporate homestead, featuring little more than earnings reports, financial-oriented press releases, and annual reports. The annual reports are little more than shovelware—Webified reproductions of the printed report that was distributed by mail to shareholders.

There is so much more that can be done on the Internet to promote the company's brand as a sound investment. But even if you are going to limit your offerings to an annual report, at least make it useful to your audiences so that it brands your company as a worthwhile investment.

Annual Reports on the Web

The argument for making an annual report available on the World Wide Web begins with your definition of an annual report and your understanding of the Web.

Most definitions of an annual report describe a book bound by covers and produced in a traditional linear fashion. Far too may organizations seem to believe they have taken the big step into cyberspace by storing a portable-document version of the annual report on their Web sites. This way (the thinking seems to go), any interested investors, brokers, or analysts will be able to download the file and read the annual report as if they had the hard copy in their hands. Imagine an analyst who needs only one bit of data from the financials who has to download a multimegabyte file and open it on a separate application (the Acrobat reader), then turn the pages until she finds what she was looking for. Talk about frustration! A well-thought-out investor relations Web site would have made such information available with only a few clicks of the mouse.

The problems with using Acrobat as the only means of obtaining an online annual report are too voluminous to list here, but the key disadvantages include:

- ↬ The amount of time required to download a graphic representation of the printed report (generally several megs large)
- ↬ The presumption that people have Adobe Acrobat installed on their system, or that they will take the time to download and install it just so they can read your annual report
- ↬ The fact that the printed report wasn't designed to be read on a computer screen

⮑ A linear presentation of information defeats all of the advantages of making information available online

In addition to these technical issues, also keep in mind that an online annual report can, within the boundaries of regulations, be updated. If your organization restates numbers, the online version of the annual report can be changed to reflect the current, updated numbers. Try doing *that* with a PDF file designed to represent the same printed annual report that was distributed by mail to shareholders.

(Making an Acrobat version available for download *in addition* to a Web version of the report could have advantages, since offering a printable version of any online document is a good idea. However, it still pays to remember that annual reports are often four-color print jobs with high-quality design values, but most offices are equipped with basic black-ink laser-jet printers; the printed copy of the Acrobat file will not look anything like the copies that came off the press, and could serve to diminish readers' perception of the organization.)

Publishing, from the invention of the printing press through the development of hypermediated communication, has hinged upon an economic model. You need to justify the economics of publishing, and those economics drive what you can publish. Annual reports are published based on an available budget that necessarily limits the number of pages and, consequently, the amount of content. A finite number of copies are printed and distributed to people whose names appear on an established mailing list; a small amount is held in reserve for others who may request a copy.

The World Wide Web explodes these historic publishing models. Consider the following two characteristics of the Web:

1. No matter how many people visit your Web site, you only need to produce one copy of the document.
2. There is no cost associated with Web-based publication, beyond the hard-disk space the information occupies—which is minimal.

The information on your Web site is available to everybody, including potential investors who are not on your mailing list. Many of these people may never have discovered your organization without the Web. What if one of them is a just-hired investment analyst working for an investment fund? And what if, based on information she finds in your online annual report, she decides to invest a considerable portion of the fund's assets in your organization's stock?

Some argue that it makes more sense to use the Web as a vehicle for publishing highlights from the annual report. I would suggest that highlights are important, but only if they provide pathways to increasingly more detailed levels of information. Remember, people coming to the investor relations Web site already have an agenda; they *know* what they want. An analyst or broker seeking to know income from continuing operations in 1999 expects to find it, and isn't interested in dialing the 800 number to obtain a copy of the complete annual report.

It is absolutely true that there may be only three people who will ever visit your Web site hoping to learn the three-year history of your organization's earnings from continuing operations. The fact that the Web enables you to store that information where it is easy to find makes the Web the perfect place to retain it. Those who have no interest in the information never need to see it, but it is accessible by those who *are* interested.

If you are going to put your annual report on the Web:

- ➥ Do it in HTML rather than PDF.
- ➥ Start with overview information (with lots of visual representations of data designed for the computer screen) and provide gradually more detailed levels of information.
- ➥ Create the paths to data based on the paths your audiences might take; ignore the old linear format of the annual report.
- ➥ Leave behind all but the most important artwork from your printed report; people come to the Web for information— particularly when they are seeking financial information.
- ➥ Keep your annual report up-to-date—the Web is an immediate medium that screams for currency.

The FedEx Corporation produces both a PDF and HTML version of its annual report through its investor relations Web site. The HTML version provides quick access to the key parts of an annual report an online researcher might need. Clicking on Financial Information, for example, reveals a page with one-click access to all the report's financial detail, from consolidated statements of income to the auditor's report. Financial statements are even available as Microsoft Excel spreadsheets, enabling visitors to load the information into the spreadsheet application to do forecasts, projections, and otherwise use the data interactively.

Figure 7-1 illustrates how extensive financial information is available with a single click from the annual report on FedEx's online annual report, including supplemental material in PDF and Excel spreadsheet format.

Beyond the Annual Report

A well assembled, Web-based annual report can be valuable to an investment analyst, investor, or broker. But why stop there? Look at the range of information your investor relations department addresses, the scope of questions it receives every day. Many in the investment community will view making this information available on the Internet as a service; it also will lighten the load of lightly staffed investor relations departments. Most IR departments focus 90 percent of their efforts on 5 percent of their organizations' shareholders—those institutional investors (and an occasional individual) that own the lion's share of the company's stock. Major pension funds (such as that managed by Calpers, the California state employee union) buy stock in such volume that keeping them happy is a far more consequential task than addressing the questions of individuals who own blocks of shares in the hundreds or thousands. By making information available online, members of the investment and financial communities can retrieve facts and data on their own without encumbering you with the work. For each call you *don't* get asking for this 10Q or that SEC filing, you have that much more time available to focus on the one-to-one conversations with key investors that your job requires.

Investor Conferences

The use of technology to meet virtually with investment analysts is hardly new. Audio teleconferencing has been used for years to conduct meetings with analysts upon the release of quarterly earnings figures. The Internet now provides you with a new tool to add to the mix, allowing investors at their desks (and on the telephone with you,

FIGURE 7-1. FEDEX'S ONLINE ANNUAL REPORT.

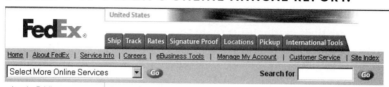

Only FedEx could create an industry, then 28 years later, grow into so much more than an "overnight" success.

Today, only FedEx offers dedicated networks for express, ground, freight, expedited delivery and unique trade services – when customers need greater choice and flexibility in managing their supply chains.

Only FedEx delivers industry–leading, on–time service levels – when time is literally money.

Only FedEx provides the right level of information intensity – when information about the package is still as important as delivery of the package itself.

In FY01, only FedEx had the vision to acquire American Freightways – one of the nation's premier regional, less-than-truckload freight carriers. With the acquisition, we formed FedEx Freight to oversee both American Freightways and Viking Freight.

During a period of challenge and change, only FedEx remains focused on a unique business model – to operate each company independently, focused on the distinct needs of each customer segment, but also to compete collectively, leveraging our greatest strengths, the power of the FedEx brand and information technology. That's why FedEx continues to deliver value for our shareowners, meaningful solutions for our customers and continued opportunity for our employees.

Downloads

- 2001 Annual Report PDF (Adobe Acrobat version, 3.1M)
- 2001 Consolidated Financial Statements (Microsoft Excel, 135K)
- 2000 Annual Report HTML
- 2000 Annual Report PDF (Adobe Acrobat version, 268K)
- 2000 Consolidated Financial Statements (Microsoft Excel, 133K)
- 1999 Annual Report HTML
- 1999 Annual Report PDF (Adobe Acrobat version, 242K)
- 1999 Consolidated Financial Statements (Microsoft Excel, 73K
- 1998 Annual Report PDF (Adobe Acrobat version, 3.8M)
- 1998 Consolidated Financial Statements (Microsoft Excel, 68K)
- Get Acrobat Reader

your CFO, or your CEO) to follow an on-screen slide show, which is actually a series of sequential HTML pages. "You can see by the chart that earnings rose," you can say, then instruct those who are following along to click the arrow at the bottom of the screen to proceed to the next slide. "As for income from continuing operations . . ."

Participants can click the buttons on their own, or you can take advantage of new software, such as Teepee, to control the onscreen tour you give the audience. Each investor participating in the conference would need to install Teepee on his or her computer, but you could supply the software while touting the advantages of the analysts immersing themselves in a multimedia experience without ever leaving their offices.

You also can forsake the telephone altogether and introduce an online conference by using computer-based videoconferencing, such as Microsoft NetMeeting or CU-See-Me. Participants with their own video capabilities would be able to engage in conversation with you face-to-face while those who did not would at least be able to watch the conference even if you could not, at the same time, watch them.

Online Road Shows

Companies invest considerable sums in road shows, which are sophisticated presentations made to groups of analysts and investors in a large meeting environment. The invitation list to these shows is limited, but you can make sure elements of your presentation are available to your larger audience as soon as the show is over by posting them to your Web site. Even if your presentation was produced using a presentation software package, such as PowerPoint, you can convert the presentation to HTML, or make the PowerPoint Web viewer plug-in available for free from your Web site. Microsoft was among the first companies to upload their investor presentations to their Web site immediately following the initial presentation to key members of the financial audience.

Webcasts

Webcasts have grown in popularity among investor relations professionals, driven largely by new U.S. Securities and Exchange Commission rules that require companies to disclose financial information simultaneously to all audiences. Before the rule went into effect, companies routinely conducted conference calls with key analysts. These calls often coincided with the release of quarterly earnings; the analysts were given detailed information about the numbers, along with an opportunity to ask questions.

This practice was questioned by investor activists who claimed that the playing field was far from level, because analysts could make decisions based on information to which they were privy but other investors were not. The SEC agreed and issued the new rule.

Still, there is value in providing a forum to analysts. In order to have their cake and eat it, too, many investor relations professionals continue to hold their quarterly conference calls, but also invited the rest of the investing public to listen in on Webcasts. Several companies record their live conference calls and make them available as recorded Webcasts after the event, often leaving the audio files online until the next conference call, ensuring the information delivered during the call is always available to anyone who wants it.

E-Mail Updates

Companies often have news to share about their finances. Investors often want access to that information. But the audiences often do not know when to visit the company's Web site to pull the news. Some organizations address this issue by enabling stakeholders to subscribe to an e-mail alert on financial matters. Among the kinds of information you can communicate via e-mail are:

- ⮑ Company news that might affect the stock price
- ⮑ Restatement of numbers
- ⮑ The company's spin on issues affecting the organization
- ⮑ Notification of upcoming events, such as conference calls or Webcasts

Edison International, the parent corporation of power utility Southern California Edison, has for years offered a subscription e-mail update. During the California energy crisis, the update served to alert shareholders and others concerned about the company's financial interests about upcoming investor conference call Webcasts meant to address the situation.

Communicate the News Behind the News

The law requires that you use traditional means to communicate information that could have a bearing on the value of your organization, such as a merger, an acquisition, or a divestiture. Provide the details various members of your audience may seek, from complete legal documents to lists of assets of a company you are acquiring. As long as the information is not confidential, there is no reason to keep it secret. An obscure piece of data may be *just* the information an analyst is seeking before making a "buy" recommendation.

If your company is affected by regulatory agencies, you can offer information about any developments taking place in government that could influence your stock price.

Numbers, Please

The financial community can't have too many numbers. Offer performance history, stock charts, comparison charts (top the Standard & Poors 500, for example), trend information, and detailed numbers from your various public filings. Be sure to segment them so each individual visitor to the site can quickly find exactly what he or she is looking for without having to wade through numbers that are not relevant.

Case Study: Diebold's "For Our Investors" Site

Understanding the audience is the key to success for any Web site, and investors are no exception. It is the job of an investor relations department, when engaged in developing a Web site for its constituents, to ensure that the site contains the material the audience is likely to seek online.

Diebold clearly took that approach in developing its investor relations site. The maker of automated teller machines and other integrated delivery systems, primarily for the financial services marketplace, has organized one of the more comprehensive investor sites on the Web.

The company's current stock price is the most dominant element on the page, and includes the latest numbers for the leading market indicators: The Dow Jones Industrial Average, NASDAQ, and the S&P 500. Also available in the same sector of the page, which is titled "Financial Information," investors can find Diebold's stock chart, a well-organized fact sheet covering the fundamentals of the company's financial situation (including such information as market cap, shares outstanding, and price history), earnings estimates (which I have never seen on *any* other investor relations site), Acrobat files of recent financial presentations, and a revenue chart.

Webcasts also are available on the site. These are recorded versions, available through streaming media, of live Webcasts conducted regularly such as quarterly earnings conference calls, analysts meetings, and the company's annual meeting.

Diebold's investor relations site is shown in Figure 7-2.

Other resources populate the site. Easy-to-navigate annual reports are available in HTML as well as downloadable in the original print format as Acrobat PDF files. All company Securities and Exchange Commission filings are accessible, as are financial releases. You can sign up for e-mail alerts notifying you of events, announcements, financial reports, and SEC filings. A financial data book is available in Excel format. The site even includes a list of financial analysts who cover the company, including the company they work for and their telephone number.

Finally (and critically), information on how to reach the investor relations department and other investor-related contacts occupy prime real estate on the home page; nobody has to drill around through the site to uncover these resources.

An Investor-Relations Internet Checklist

Use the following checklist to assess the presence your company should have on the Internet:

1. Is your company public or privately held? If it is privately held, financial information may be limited and the audience too small to make a significant investor relations presence worthwhile.

2. If you are privately held, are you considering an initial public offering (IPO)? If so, it is critical for you to begin branding the quality of your company as an investment as quickly as possible

3. What are your company's most commonly requested investor-related documents?

4. What are your investor relations goals? Are you trying to attract more individual investors? Institutional? Are you trying to retain institutional investors that are seeking to diversify their portfolios?

5. How will your key investment audiences seek information? How can you cross-reference information to make it as easy as possible to find?

FIGURE 7-2. DIEBOLD'S INVESTOR RELATIONS SITE.

for our
investors

about us
solutions
what's news
investors
diebold direct
partners
contact us
search
home

financial data & markets ⊙

DBD	39.68	+0.28
DJIA	9918.890	84.210
NASD	1898.900	23.850
SP500	1146.940	9.910
	11/23/2001 11:33AM	

HIGHLIGHTS

Send Me News
Get news & information by e-mail

Webcast Replay
3rd quarter earnings announcement 2001
Available now.

Stock Quote
Stock Chart
Fundamentals
Earnings Estimates
Financial Presentations
2000 Revenue Chart

Diebold Announces Third Quarter Results

HOW TO HELP
A list of organizations that need your help during this crisis

Diebold Investor Relations
1-800-766-5859 (1-330-490-3790)
stockinfo@diebold.com

National Association of Investors Corporation (NAIC)
Diebold is proud to be a corporate member of the National Association of Investors Corporation (NAIC).

New York Stock Exchange (NYSE)
Diebold is listed on the New York Stock Exchange (NYSE) under the symbol DBD.

Transfer Agent -- The Bank of New York
1-800-432-0140 (1-212-495-1784)
shareowner-svcs@bankofny.com

webcasts ⊙

Analyst Meeting 5/23/01
2001 Annual Meeting
Quarterly Earnings Archive

news & publications ⊙

Diebold Disclosure Policy
Financial/Press Releases
Calendar of Events
Annual Reports
2000 Data Book
SEC Filings

company information ⊙

Investors' Overview
Directors and Officers
Corporate Profile
Analyst Coverage
Dividend Programs
DRIP-Purchase Plan
FAQ
Request Information
E-Mail Alerts

DBD
LISTED
NYSE

DIEBOLD

6. Is your current financial health good or not so good? How do you want to position your company's investment brand in light of current performance? (For instance, if the company has been performing poorly, the focus could be on long-term growth plans.)

7. What issues are you currently facing that could have an impact, either positive or negative, on your company's financial value?

Measurement

How do you know whether your online investor relations efforts are paying off? Try using the following measures:

- Draw a correlation between the number of times your annual reports and other materials are downloaded and the reduced number of requests you get for such materials.

- Track the number of visits to your investor relations Web site, particularly after key announcements and events. If you have developed materials to support or oppose an action, such as a merger, assess the number of visits to the topic-specific page and correlate that information to shifts in public opinion.

- Ask your key investors to rate the value of the Web site. (You can even include a mini-survey directly on the site.)

Conclusion

Investors constitute a distinct and important audience that rates their own strategy for online communication. Use all the tools of the Internet to develop communications that support your objectives for this audience *and* to streamline the operations of your investor relations department (which is typically underfunded and understaffed).

CHAPTER 8

Government Relations

IN MANY ORGANIZATIONS, the government relations department is not part of the company's public relations effort. It should be, at least in a dotted-line relationship. The government—legislative and regulatory branches of federal, state, and local jurisdictions—constitutes an audience no less important than customers, consumers, investors, media, and activists. The same principles are involved when communicating with government (notably negotiation). And it is particularly important that messages sent to various governmental audiences are consistent with those that have been woven into any communications strategies targeted at other strategic publics.

Perhaps the disconnect between government relations and public relations is the perception held by many executives that PR is closer to propaganda than it is to education and negotiation. If that is the case, it is incumbent upon communications professionals to establish the link. The first step is the strategic management of relations between the organization and its other, nongovernment audiences. The exploitation of the Internet for government communications can be a major element in uniting the two functions to the ultimate advantage of the organization.

(In some companies, public relations is a component of a larger department known as public affairs. In these organizations, public relations and government relations often are peer units reporting to the same public affairs executive. Other departments incorporated under this heading include employee communications, community relations, and investor relations.)

Government is quickly catching on to the Internet. Several regulatory agencies are requiring companies to communicate with them via e-mail when sending submissions, filings, and reports. Government servers actively promote activities undertaken by legislatures and agencies. Every state in the United States has a home page (you can access yours by going to *www.state.xx.us* (replacing the "xx" with the two-letter postal code for the state; California, then, would be at *www.state.ca.us*). The White House has a site, as do most of the cabinet offices and the agencies that are part of each cabinet post. You can visit the Internal Revenue Service if you like (all of their forms are available for download) or the Central Intelligence Agency.

Some government sites are better than others. Most states have yet to provide valuable resources configured in a manner that is useful to people visiting the sites. The U.S. Postal Service, on the other hand, has created a lively and informative site that ranks among the best business-oriented sites.

But the bottom line is that government is online. Shouldn't we be communicating the messages targeted at government using the same tools governmental representatives use?

Setting Objectives

Internet-based communication with government can be established in support of any objective in which the government holds the company's future or fate in its hands. Use the following checklist as a starting point to assess the usefulness the Internet can play in communicating key organizational messages to government:

GOVERNMENT COMMUNICATIONS CHECKLIST

1. Is your industry regulated? Do you produce materials, such as pharmaceuticals or construction materials, which are subject to governmental regulations?

2. Do you rely on government funding?

3. Do you work in a controversial industry, one that is subject to attack from activist groups?

4. Do you lobby the government for considerations beneficial to your organization, its customers, or its stakeholders?

5. Do you wish to engage in some activity—such as a merger or acquisition—that requires government approval?

Regulated Businesses

The following two channels of communication can aid in your effort to communicate issues related to regulation of your business or products:

1. Communication to general audiences about your adherence to regulatory requirements
2. Communication directed toward regulatory bodies to reinforce your commitment to compliance and to provide up-to-the-minute information about progress related to efforts to gain regulatory approvals

As much as possible, you should coordinate and leverage the two sets of audiences. For example, you can dedicate a section of your Web site to the processes your company employs in its compliance efforts. A pharmaceutical company provides a good hypothetical example.

Pharmaceutical companies are heavily regulated in every country where they do business. On its Web site, a drug maker will aim much of its content at general audiences including doctors, end users (patients taking prescribed medications), and investors. Government relations professionals in the company, though, can craft a special section that goes into more technical detail about the effort the company makes to comply with—and even exceed—government regulations. This can become a resource to regulators and, in some cases, even to legislators and their aides seeking information about the industry's commitment to meeting guidelines.

The principles can be applied to any regulated organization.

E-Mail

Use traditional communication vehicles to invite regulatory staff personnel to sign up for regular e-mail updates on regulation-related activities. Send brief updates whenever you purchase new equipment, enter new alliances, tighten procedures, or take any other action that will strengthen your ability to comply with regulations. For each product going through the approval process, provide a separate update to the agency representatives who will be involved in the approval process, either administratively or as decision makers.

Discussion Groups

You can develop a password-protected discussion forum using Web technology for ongoing discussions between the company (scientific and administrative) and regulatory representatives. Those involved in the actual testing process can use a similar discussion forum, which is accessible only by authorized individuals. The forum can facilitate communication between company scientists managing the testing and independent researchers contracted to conduct clinical trials.

File Transfer

Archive all test-related documents. Use your Web site to list the documents and provide a brief description, and make them available for download. The multimedia capabilities of the Internet enable you to include not only written documents, but video, as well. My experience at a pharmaceutical company included video of a child who was part of a clinical trial, able to walk for the first time after a few treatments with the drug that was undergoing tests. It was powerful video that could be made available to regulators, giving them a real glimpse of testing in addition to a clinical report. While videos are certainly not required as part of the approval process, they can provide compelling additional evidence of a product's efficacy.

The World Wide Web

Include a section on your public Web site dedicated to regulatory activities. Document the extraordinary steps your company takes to ensure compliance. This site can raise the level of consumer confidence and help build support for the approval of certain products. List the types of products currently in the process, and provide details about the steps through which the products are going (for example, the organizations contracted to conduct the actual studies). For each of your existing products, note the steps that were taken to obtain approval and offer (or link to) the regulatory agency's actual documentation of the approval. This can be particularly valuable should the product come under attack for any reason; having government documentation already available lends credibility to the use of the product for its approved indications.

You also can provide access to all the laws and regulations that govern the approval of your products or services.

Government Funding

Institutions that rely on government funding generally compete with other similar institutions for a piece of a very limited pie. The Internet can serve as a means by which you can make your case for funding. Let legislators and legislative staff members know about the means by which you provide such information by prominently displaying the URL of your related Web site on all printed documentation. On the Web site, you can report on:

- ➷ *The need.* Why the publics you serve are more deserving of funding than those of competing organizations.
- ➷ *Your programs.* Show how the funds you have received to date have been put to use, articulating the fact that your institution makes outstanding use of the funds it receives.
- ➷ *Your plans.* Detail the uses to which you would put future funds, and the publics that those funds would serve.

The fact that this information is readily available to members of your other strategic audiences and to the general public can raise additional support for the disbursement of public funds to your organization.

Case Study: Housing Authority of the City of Los Angeles

Congress represents the target audience for the Housing Authority of the City of Los Angeles's (HACLA) Web site. "Politically, with the climate of Congress wanting to do away with public housing, one of the things we talk about in the Web site is promoting self-sufficiency and creating a sense of family," according to Ozie Gonaque, chairperson of the HACLA Board of Commissioners. "We're not just in the housing business, we're about forming partnerships with our residents and helping them climb the ladder to success. We want our residents to grow out of public housing and into self-sufficiency." This announcement was in a press release announcing the launch of the Web site (at *www.hacla.org*).

Since HACLA's funding comes primary from the federal Department of Housing and Urban Development, the Web site serves as a vehicle for the agency to tell its story to HUD.

What kind of information might be valuable to government agencies scanning the site? One of the main sections features success stories about how people were able to get off public assistance thanks to Housing Authority efforts. The site affords HACLA the opportunity to tell that story to anybody who will listen, about how HACLA can establish programs to divert children from gangs, and other examples that clear up misconceptions about public housing. For example, the site reports that 95 percent of the residents in HACLA public housing are law-abiding citizens.

Other departments include forms and applications on the Web site, along with job listings, lists of new construction projects, and other features—all of which further serve to put the agency's services to its public on display to government-funding decision makers.

Offsetting Activist Attacks

Your organization can experience a full-blown crisis if one of your government-regulated products comes under attack by an activist group opposed to some aspect of the product—how it is marketed, the impact it has on customers, how it is made, or its effect on the environment. The documents showing that the product meets (or exceeds) government standards can be powerful evidence that the company has taken steps to guard against exactly the kind of problem about which the activists have made an issue. Links to related materials can support the company's commitment to the environment, patient safety, and other issues activists might be likely to attack. These links can provide access to:

- ↪ Related policies
- ↪ Testing procedures
- ↪ Special measures the company takes to ensure adherence to policies
- ↪ Documentation of the steps taken to obtain government regulatory approval for the product

↪ Any FAQs you maintain that address environmental safety, product safety, etc.

↪ Customer testimonials, particularly from those whom activist groups claim are at risk from your products

If the government agency that approved your product maintains records on its Web site or elsewhere on the Internet, you can provide links to the site or information about how to retrieve the documents. You can even offer information about how to get documents via U.S. mail.

These measures will be far more effective if they are in place *now*, before an activist group targets your product, than they would be if you build such links and add such documents only as a reaction to an assault.

And, of course, all of the forgoing are valid approaches for protecting your assets *only* if the information is accurate—if your environmental record can stand up to scrutiny, your product safety measures are valid and thorough, and your values are sincerely and fully reflected in your business practices.

Products do not represent the only target of activist attack. In Chapter 10, on issues and cause-related communication, a case study offers insight into a community group working to stymie a company's efforts to ship coal via train through the community. There is no reason to believe your company's efforts may not be similarly thwarted by a motivated group of community leaders, activists, or grassroots groups.

How would an organization like the railroad targeted by Citizens to Stop the Coal Trains use the Internet to offset that effort? Some approaches (none of which, by the way, have been employed by the railroad in question) might include:

↪ Building a microsite that details the benefits of the plan to the community, including any economic and employment benefits. The site could also address each of the objections made by the opposition.

↪ An e-mail update to which individuals may subscribe that offers new information that supports the effort.

↪ A discussion group that invites individuals opposed to the effort to engage in a dialogue with the company and its supporters.

Building Support for Lobbying Efforts

Regulated companies often seek changes in regulatory processes. Pharmaceutical companies, for example, would like approval processes speeded up. Patents, with limited lives, are issued as soon as a compound is formulated. It could take years before the Food and Drug Administration approves the compound for commercial use. Other industries and the businesses within them have similar issues. Some unregulated industries suddenly find themselves facing regulation. Politicians, of course, respond to public pressure. Companies and industries, then, can use the Internet to drum up public support for their positions to exert influence on the politicians who oversee regulatory agencies, as well as the agencies themselves.

Based on solid research and empirical evidence that the change to regulatory practices—or the decision not to impose such practices—would be in the best interest of the public, you should take your case to the public.

Legislative issues could benefit from the same approach. I recall, when working in the late 1970s in the petroleum industry, most of the industry was united in its opposition to the end of the oil depletion allowance. Taking their case public was difficult, since few understood (or cared about) the issues, and those who did were difficult to target. There were no mailing lists of individuals who might be willing to call or write to a legislator to extol the virtues of a special entitlement. By taking the case to the Internet, however, those interested would have been able to find the company's position by following the cognitive links that represented a pathway constructed of their interests.

Individual companies posting their own position pages can be effective, but the power of the medium is diluted when each company buries such a page within the structure of its larger Web site, constructed, perhaps, to address other objectives. Far more forceful would be a single site dedicated to the issue that represents the policies and positions of a coalition of companies within the industry. Each individual company can offer a small but prominent link from the appropriate place on its site to the coalition site. Each company then provides a path to the advocacy site, leading more people to it. Once at the site, visitors see a united front, many entities sharing a common set of ideas and embracing a common position.

Case Study: Caterpillar

In spring 2000, the U.S. Congress passed an historic trade deal that granted China Permanent Normal Trade Relations (PNTR). Caterpillar—along with most businesses—supported the trade legislation. However, equally powerful groups (led by labor unions) opposed it, fearing the loss of U.S. jobs to lower-paid workers on the Chinese mainland. "The business community knew that in order to be successful with the China PNTR vote, members of Congress would have to hear positively from rank and file employees," according to Lisa Young, a legislative communicator in Caterpillar's corporate communications department.

Information designed to heighten employee awareness of the benefits of PNTR status for China appeared on the company's intranet. Employees were driven to the site as the result of an electronic toolkit developed for internal communicators working at the company's various facilities. (The toolkit, offered in print as well as on the intranet, included various resources communicators could use to generate interest in the issue, including sample newsletter articles, Q&A documents, and ready-to-print posters and table-tent cards. Talking points for supervisors also were incorporated into the kit.)

With only one exception, legislators representing districts in which Caterpillar facilities were located voted to approve PNTR status for China. "Caterpillar was second only to Eastman Kodak in the number of employee calls generated to a toll-free number that sent [Capitol] Hill messages in favor of PNTR," Young said. "We processed nearly 500 requests from employees for letters to members of Congress."

Government-Focused Web Sites

Corporations are not the only institutions that can take advantage of the Web to influence government. Nonprofits, associations, and virtually any other organization seeking a legislative or regulatory outcome can muster support via the Internet. In Canada, a lone citizen mobilized a letter-writing campaign through a Web site he established, leading a government agency to reverse itself on the awarding of a television frequency.

Organizations can focus heavily on this aspect of government relations by establishing Web sites dedicated to government-related issues the organization faces. For an example, look at the Web site of the National Rural Electric Cooperative Association (NRECA).

Based near Washington, D.C., the NRECA represents electric cooperatives, which supply power to rural and other customers beyond the reach of larger public utilities. The association's Web site features a link to Legislative Advocacy, which takes visitors to a content-rich site dedicated to power issues under the jurisdiction of various governmental entities.

The site offers details on the potential impact of pending legislation on cooperatives and their customers. A map of the electrical/political matrix on the home page is clickable, leading visitors to summaries of the role each entity plays (such as electrical distribution substations and electric generating plants), along with the issues affecting everyone from these various entities.

An issues focus covers the top issues facing the industry (in mid-2001, those were the California electricity crisis and skyrocketing natural gas prices). Each of these pages provided a wealth of resources on the issues, such as news coverage of the subject; reports on Congressional hearings; transcripts of testimony, charts and graphs; and other reports.

As shown in Figure 8-1, the National Rural Electric Cooperative Association's advocacy site makes it easy for stakeholders to understand issues as well as to take action through various means, including contacting their elected representatives.

A government relations section provides basic information about cooperatives (such as history and models), while the Issues 2001 section offers links to a host of issues the industry faces, including safety, the environment, and the industry in transition. Each link leads to an overview of the issue and links to related content.

At the heart of the section, however, are the Consumer Advocates links, which offer the means for visitors to take action themselves. The Congressional Action Center, for example, lets visitors write to Congress on the National Energy Bill, national energy policy, and electricity utility restructuring. (The site lets you enter your zip code so that you can write directly to your representative, even if you don't know who that is). Several organizations exist solely to provide services to organizations' government relations Web sites, offering legislative databases and letter-writing capabilities. Two such organizations are Capitol Connect (*http://www.capitolconnect.com*) and Capitol Advantage (*http://www.capwiz.com*).

The site also includes briefs on all the key issues Congress is tackling, along with a primer on grassroots advocacy.

Making the Case for Mergers and Acquisitions

If there is any company activity that segregates people into camps of winners and losers, it is the practice of mergers and acquisitions. In

FIGURE 8-1. ADVOCACY SITE AIDING SHAREHOLDERS IN UNDERSTANDING ISSUES.

Electricity and You.

Issue Focus
▶ California Electricity Crisis
▶ Skyrocketing Natural Gas Prices

NRECA Government Relations
- About NRECA
- The Electric Co-op Business Model
- Electric Cooperative Network: A Brief History
- Public Policies [NRECA Member Resolutions]

Issues 2001
- Electric Industry in Transition
- Reliability and Safety
- Cleaner Environment for All
- Consumer's Right to Privacy
- A Wired World: Global Economy
- Meeting the Needs of Rural Americans

Consumer Advocates
- Congressional Action Center
- Youth Programs
- Community Service
- Political Action

NRECA Links
- NRECA Home Page

What's New: Legislative Conference Briefing Book Available Online.

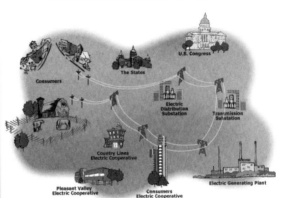

4301 Wilson Boulevard
Arlington, VA 22203-1860

Phone: 703-907-5500

nreca@nreca.org

Site Map | Disclaimer | Privacy Policy

many instances, the government (in the United States, it is the Federal Trade Commission and, in some cases, the Justice Department) must approve mergers, and courts often are called upon to uphold them.

When a company announces a merger or acquisition, invariably those who believe they will be on the losing side take action to block it. Building support for the merger can help influence the ultimate decisions. A merger-related Web site—such as that built as a component of MCI's investor relations site during its acquisition by World Com—can list the various reasons for the merger and the benefits that will be accrued by various publics. Including a press kit about the merger on the media relations site (as Bell Atlantic did during its merger with GTE to become Verizon) can lead to positive media coverage, which also can influence regulators and legislators.

Measurement

Measuring the impact of your online communications with government entities can be a little more difficult than with other audiences, such as the media. However, you can still draw some conclusions using these methods:

- ➷ How many agencies and legislative staffs have opted to communicate with you by e-mail? How many have elected to receive updates you deliver by e-mail?
- ➷ Of the visits to your government-oriented site, how many come from the *gov* domains, signifying the visitor is from the government?
- ➷ Can you draw a correlation between the increased activity on your site and changes in public perception or support?

Conclusion

You can streamline your communications with government agencies and legislative staffs through the Internet, but more important, you can influence government decision-making by building support for your initiatives among the publics that vote.

CHAPTER 9

Community Relations

BUSINESS, IT IS said, function only by the consent of the communities in which they choose to locate. As a result, companies need to include the people who live, work, and raise their families in the geographic areas surrounding their various facilities. This includes not only the headquarters for the company but also remote offices, plants, factories, refineries, sales offices, and any other location where company employees do business.

The community, unlike most of the other constituent audiences with which institutions must communicate, is difficult to pin down. You can slice the community audience in any number of ways:

↪ *The community at large.* Everybody who lives near the company's operations. The impact of the company's operations on the community is largely economic. The company pays taxes to the community. The money it pays local employees is recycled into the local economy. The company and its employees buy goods and services from local vendors. Hard times for the company can translate into hard times for the community (just ask the people who live in Flint, Michigan). A layoff can devastate a community.

↪ *Those who live in immediate proximity.* Specifically, people who would feel the impact of a factory construction, increased factory emissions, or the addition of a new division that would increase vehicular traffic in the immediate area.

↪ *Civic participation.* Local politicians expect organizations to be good corporate neighbors, participating in civic activities and contributing to the community's welfare. Doing so also builds goodwill in the community. Goodwill *can* be banked and used to bolster a company's credibility in times of need or crisis.

↪ *Education.* The academic community seeks to involve companies in teaching children. Involvement ranges from contributing classroom supplies to the active participation of employees in classroom activities. Many companies give employees paid time to teach one day a week; others send employees into the classroom to assist teachers in addressing special subjects. An oil company geologist, for example, might spend time in a classroom while children are studying geology.

↪ *Civic organizations.* Organizations such as the Lions Club, Elks Lodge, Boy Scouts, Girl Scouts, and the Rotary want your company's involvement. At the least, they want financial support and employees to speak at their meetings. Ideally, they would like to use your facilities for group events and direct sponsorship.

↪ *Charitable organizations.* The local Red Cross and United Way, along with charitable organizations that exist only in your community, will look to your company to help pay their expenses and support their causes.

↪ *Special audiences.* If your facility is in an agricultural region, farmers constitute a special audience. Similarly, a facility in a mountain resort area makes merchants and resort operators an audience that rates special consideration.

In a perfect world, it would make sense to subdivide the community into smaller strategic publics. The world is not perfect, however, and most companies commit only a token amount of resources to community involvement. Some organizations cast the entire responsibility for community relations to a nonprofit foundation whose sole task is to distribute money to organizations that seek support. In other organizations, community relations is the orphaned stepchild of a public relations department that is more concerned with bigger issues; only a limited sliver of the total PR budget is earmarked for local community. As a result, these diverse audiences are lumped together under the *community* label.

The Internet can help organizations target specific elements of the community relations audience, if not to actually engage them in direct, two-way symmetrical communications, then at least to target messages to each segment. We'll explore some tactics for achieving this goal, but first, the most important objective of a community relations effort is to garner the support of the community at large.

The Community at Large

The proposition driving communications to the general community is simple: Maintain good relations with the people and institutions with whom you share the space in which you work and your employees live. How you go about that depends on a variety of factors, including the type of community (metropolitan city or small town, for example), the geographic location, the demographics of the community, and the nature of the work you are in (a chemical company has different issues than a consulting firm).

You should mirror your approach to the community on a community portion of your Web site. That is, what you do on your Web site should support the principal strategies of your community relations effort. A company engaged in mining near a community would, for example, want to actively engage the community in a dialogue. (Being visible to the community puts a human face on the organization. Listening and responding to concerns makes your organization a partner in the community and diminishes the potential for future roadblocks, such as opposition to any expansion the company may want to undertake). If active community engagement is a principal strategy, the Web site could support that strategy by:

- Advising the community of upcoming meetings
- Reporting on the results of past meetings, including any agreements reached or actions agreed to
- Providing a community comment form

A large management consulting firm, with no impact on the environment, probably would not consider active community engagement as important as the mining company would. Its community-oriented efforts, then, would focus elsewhere. For this organization, a positive reputation translates into business. (If *you* need a management consultant, wouldn't you be more likely to hire the one with the best reputation?) This organization may want to position its employees as leaders in the community. Employees might participate in a speakers bureau, delivering talks on the areas of their expertise to local civic organizations. The company may encourage employees to run for local office and hold leadership positions in civic organizations (from the Elks to the Boy Scouts) by providing time off. Company employees also may get paid time off to volunteer their time in education (teaching one day a week in community colleges, for example) and other causes. In support of this strategy, a Web site could:

- ↪ Offer a form allowing civic groups to request a company volunteer
- ↪ Use a form to let organizations request speakers from a speakers bureau
- ↪ Include a roster of all employees actively participating in formal company-community programs
- ↪ Spotlight employee volunteers in feature stories

The energy company Sierra Pacific has dedicated space on its Web site for a community-focused subsite. The Nevada-based power company already recognizes the key issues it addresses as a company—*Energy Issues* is one of the prominent links from the home page. Rising prices and fear of power shortages occupy the minds of its customers (who, by the nature of the industry, are also members of the community; the company sells power to the people who live in its service area).

Content on the community relations site focuses on engagement with the community. The company's community-relations mission is "to know our employees, their interests and volunteering preferences, and match them most closely with groups, organizations, events, and projects that provide the best fit for everyone involved."[1] The site offers links to those organizations the company's many employees support, including the United Way. The main links from the home page include:

- ↪ A speakers bureau for schools to find guest lecturers, including a form that allows an educator to select the topic and the age group at which the talk will be directed
- ↪ A special kid-oriented Web site on electrical safety
- ↪ A general safety site that allows organizations to request a presentation on electrical safety

> ➥ Information about the company's programs for low-income families
>
> ➥ Feature stories about Sierra Pacific's community activities, and a form that allows visitors to subscribe to receive features by e-mail
>
> ➥ Information about the Sierra Connectors, a group of company retirees who volunteer for community work through a formal company program

Each of these links ensures that key messages get to the community and that the community sees the company as an active partner, making it more likely that the company would be perceived as having the community's best interests at heart.

Other Community Relations Ideas

Any company activity that builds support for the organization among the local population can be leveraged on the Internet. The simplest use of the Web is to publish your company's community relations report on your Web site. Sierra Pacific produces an annual report covering its community relations activities, and makes the current report—along with two prior years' reports—available on its community relations Web site (at *http://www.sierrapacific.com/comenv/annual_rpt/*). But building an online version of a print publication only scratches the surface of the online potential for community relations.

As shown in Figure 9-1, Sierra Pacific includes downloadable versions of its community annual reports as a part of its community relations Web site.

The following is a laundry list of ideas you might want to apply to your Web site:

➥ *Community mailing list.* On your community relations page, invite local residents to subscribe to a mailing list to receive notices of activities related to the community. Use it to announce construction that might affect traffic, job fairs, sponsorship of a booth or event at community fairs, major grants, and other activities you want residents to know about. The goodwill you build will come in handy in

FIGURE 9-1. SIERRA PACIFIC'S COMMUNITY RELATIONS WEB SITE.

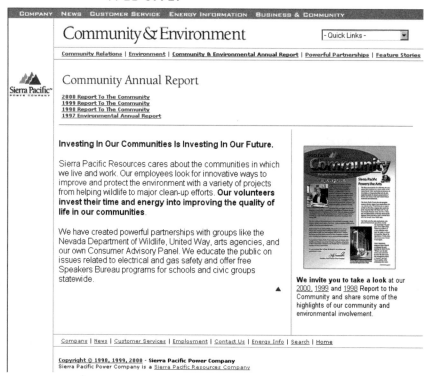

the event of a crisis, since you will be able to use the established mailing list to distribute your point of view to the community, particularly when the crisis hits close to home, such as a toxic gas release or a plant explosion.

↪ *Open house.* Virtual or otherwise. If you host an annual open house at your company, you can promote it on the Web, as well as through e-mail to local residents who subscribe to a community-based mailing list. Whether you host an annual open house or not, you can provide a virtual open house twenty-four hours a day by building a Web-based tour of your local facilities.

↪ *Grant information.* If your company provides grants to the local community, offer information about the criteria for grant distribution. You can even offer advice to those who plan to apply for a grant, as does Quantum, the Silicon Valley manufacturer of computer hard drives. The company suggests that its grant-oriented FAQs will be helpful to those developing a proposal.

↪ *Promote joint projects.* Toys for Tots is a classic example of a community relations activity sponsored by third parties that are no-brainers for companies to join. The Web can be used to publicize the company's involvement as well as to appeal for contributions at company locations. (Even employees—regular visitors to their own company's Web sites—can be the targets of such messages.)

↪ *Arts and culture.* Many organizations contribute their community-oriented profits to local art and cultural resources (often because that is a personal interest of the CEO). If that's the case with your organization, you can do more than note the dollars contributed. You can produce virtual galleries on behalf of the museum to which you donated money, or provide space on your site to promote the local theater production.

Community relations is one aspect of public relations that invites creativity and flexibility based on the needs of the local community, its character, its culture, and the means by which your institution has elected to be involved. Use your imagination!

Neighbors

Many companies already produce newsletters that are distributed to neighboring residents, particularly companies with controversial facilities (such as refineries or plants that handle toxic products). A Web site allows the company to expand the volume of news it makes available and to maintain related archives of information that would be too voluminous for publication in each issue of the bulletin (such as detailed safety information). The site could help calm any niggling fears some of your neighbors may have. For an example, take a look at *NetWorks,* a Web-based newsletter produced by the Sacramento County (California) Public Works Agency. *NetWorks* is aimed at people in the agency's service area, covering issues that could affect customers (for example, a recent issue notified residents that rolling blackouts in the area could have an impact on water pressure, or even cause water shortages). Updates on construction projects also are a regular part of the newsletter.

As shown in Figure 9-2, the Sacramento County Public Works Agency publishes a newsletter advising community residents of various agency-related issues, such as updating construction projects.

Neighbors also could sign up to receive e-mail bulletins on issues that interest them (the Web site could serve as the vehicle they use to subscribe to the bulletins). One might list local employment opportunities, another could keep neighbors informed about upcoming construction or maintenance, a third about activities that might temporarily increase traffic. The more you communicate with local

FIGURE 9-2. ONLINE NEWSLETTER ALERTING LOCAL RESIDENTS ABOUT UPCOMING ISSUES.

NetWorks An Online Publication of Sacramento County's Public Works Agency

| Home | Newsroom | Past Issues | In the News | Departments |

Rotating Blackouts Can Cause Reductions in Water Pressure and/or Water Shortages

Drinking water is distributed through a series of pumps and pumping stations. These pumps rely on electricity to operate. During rotating blackouts the pumps may not operate, causing a depletion of water stored in tanks. This makes it critically important to conserve water as well as energy. Sacramento County is in the process of installing back-up generators at our pump stations but many county residents are served by other water suppliers.

<u>List of county Water Suppliers</u>
<u>Tips for Saving Water</u>

We Want Your Input!
Take Our Web Survey and Tell Us What Information You Need.

FREE Composting Workshops and FREE Composting Bin...

Free composting workshops are being held by Sacramento County Waste Management & Recycling. Workshops begin April 24 and go through Sept. 11. Call **363-9390** for details or go to <u>www.sacgreenteam.com</u> and click on 'What's New'.

Work Continues On the <u>Watt Ave. Bridge Improvement</u>. The Improvements are scheduled to be completed in the summer of 2002.

Looking for a good job with a great future? Sacramento County may be looking for you...

A Publication of
Sacramento County Public Works Agency
827-7th Street, Room 304
Sacramento, CA 95814
916-874-6581

residents, the more likely they are to appreciate your interest in them and their welfare.

When you undertake a major expansion or construction project, providing detailed information can help to secure public support for your efforts. A pharmaceutical company for which I worked could have benefited from the Web (had it existed at the time) when it sought to build a plant that produced a near-miraculous drug from the deadly botulism toxin. The local residents vehemently opposed the effort, and the company was limited in the means at its disposal to reassure them of the process's safety. Local meetings were held, which often degenerated into shouting matches because they were attended, naturally, but those most opposed to the construction. A Web site—promoted through local newspaper advertisements— could have made a strong case for the plant, and offered information on upcoming employment opportunities, as well. A site designed to curry neighbor favor for such a project can include environmental information, details about the benefits to the community, and even a forum through which residents can express their concerns and get answers directly from a company representative.

Civic Participation

Let your community know that you do more than occupy space; you play an active part in the community's affairs by encouraging your employees to participate. When I worked in the communications department at ARCO, we reported regularly on employees who ran for public office and those who served on city councils, boards of education, and even state assemblies. The company's public affairs department supported employees in their efforts by giving them time to run and serve, along with encouragement. A company can celebrate the employees that dedicate their time to such activities by featuring them on Web pages. You could dedicate a site under your community relations label to employees who also are elected officials in the community.

Many companies use their community relations subsites to list all the public policy organizations with which its employees are involved. Ashland Specialty Chemical Company, for example, provides links to details about all organizations where employees volunteer their time, from local chambers of commerce and Junior Achievement to the Public Agenda Foundation and the Pacific Research Institute for Public Policy. Other opportunities for civic involvement include the following:

⤳ Position pages that outline the company's stance on local political issues and the steps the company is taking to support or oppose local government action.

⤳ Candidly list the contributions from your political action committee (PAC) to political candidates. (If your PAC is like the one that ARCO sponsors, its members—the employees who join—determine the recipients of contributions, and a listing can show a balance that contradicts popular public opinion that contributions are heavily weighted toward those candidates who would vote in the company's interests.)

⤳ Offer a regular (for example, monthly) report on local issues of interest to the organization. Cover such items as education decisions, showing your company's support for rational improvements to the schools your employees' children attend (which will furnish your company with its future workforce).

Education

Public schools, always in dire need of funding for academic programs, seek support from the local businesses that ultimately will seek to recruit employees who have matriculated through the local education system. Those who advocate reductions in government spending assert that it is the responsibility of business to provide this kind of support since they are ultimately the beneficiaries of an educated population. Many organizations do, in fact, find innovative ways to contribute to local education efforts. The Internet represents a new vehicle for communicating, for facilitating company activities, and even for providing new educational opportunities.

TIP:
Apple Bites into Education
For an excellent example of an education-oriented corporate site, visit Apple Computer's education page at *www. apple.com/education/.*

Following are some approaches to using the Internet—and primarily the World Wide Web—to enhance your institution's reputation as an patron of education in your community.

Promote Your Efforts

Whatever your activities to support education, be sure to promote them on your company's Web site. Capital Blue Cross, a Pennsylvania health-care company, issued a press release (published on the company's Web site) promoting its involvement in the Take Our Daughters and Sons to Work Day. Capital Blue Cross represents one of several companies that have publicized their involvement in this nationwide program. Other sites tout organizational commitment to United Way and other civic programs.

List Available Employees

Employees who have volunteered to spend time in local schools generally do so in order to share an area of expertise. Many employees enthusiastically give their time in classrooms to generate excitement among students for their chosen line of work. When I worked for ARCO, the natural resources company, employees from all walks of life participated in a program sponsored by the Los Angeles Unified School District in which they spent a half day each week in the classroom, teaching an overview course on their profession (such as engineering, chemistry, or geology). Teachers would be equally delighted to know that your employees are available for a one-time visit to the classroom. The only problem for most schools is the lack of information about the employees available for such a program. Develop a section of your Web site that catalogues the employees who can spend time in the classroom, and promote the listing via other media to your local schools.

Sponsor Contests

Use your Web site to promote competitions to help uncover the talents of students in the community. Apple Computer, for example, sponsors various youth-oriented essay contests focused on themes such as the environment.

Offer Used Equipment

Among the many uses of outdated computer and office equipment is the possibility of donating these supplies to classrooms. Create a page on your Web site that allows teachers or school administrators to list their needs. You can then match the equipment that becomes available to the needs of the local schools, and publicize the dollar value of the equipment you have donated.

Educate Students About Your Business

One function of Web sites that several companies have adopted is information about the business or the underlying profession. Students can access these sites directly, or they can be crafted as teacher's aids. Computer chipmaker Intel dedicates an entire subsite to Innovating in Education, offering online resources (such as a virtual walk through a computer, including a teacher's guide to using the site with students), instructions on how to build a school Web site, a teacher's training program, and a science and engineering fair.

As shown in Figure 9-3 and Figure 9-4, Intel's Web site offers lesson plans on a variety of topics. This feature offers students and teachers the opportunity to learn about computers.

Provide Distance Learning

The next step beyond offering a site to educate students about your business is to actually sponsor a class. Your expert employees can serve as virtual professors for classes that focus on specialty topics. These can be miniclasses appropriate for grade school or full-blown classes for which community colleges offer course credit. Distance learning programs take advantage of a variety of Internet applications, including the Web, e-mail, and discussion groups. Students sign up for the class using an interactive Web form. Reading assignments can be delivered on a Web page, via e-mail, or in books that students purchase at the campus store (or that your company supplies). Lectures can be delivered on the Web, via e-mail, or as articles posted to a discussion group. Discussion groups also are used for asynchronous discussions about the reading and lectures. Testing can be delivered on the Web or in person, with a proctor supervising the process.

FIGURE 9-3. INTEL'S HOME PAGE OFFERS AIDS FOR
TEACHERS.

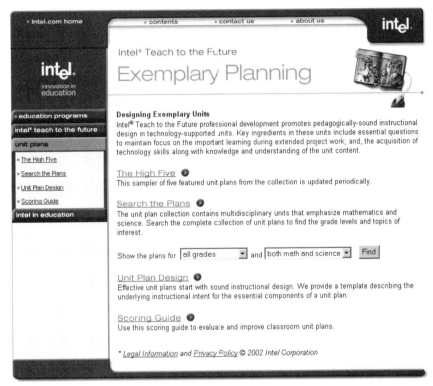

Civic Organizations

Civic organizations gather in every community, catering to interests ranging from social interaction (such as the Elks) and business contacts (like the Rotary) to personal development (Toastmasters helps individuals advance their public speaking skills in a social setting). The simplest forms of communication can be enhanced online. If your organization hosts Toastmasters meetings, for example, you can display meeting times on your Web site and use your online facilities to provide e-mail bulletins to members. If you already maintain listserv software, you can even provide Toastmasters participants with a mailing list they can use to engage in discussions on various speaking-related topics between meetings.

As for other civic organization activities, consider some of the

FIGURE 9-4. INTEL OFFERING LESSON PLANS ON ITS WEB SITE.

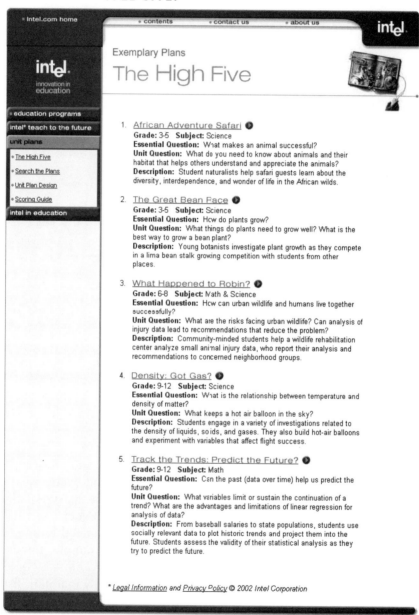

following ideas to enhance your image with the often-influential members of these groups.

Electrify Your Speakers Bureau

One of the best ways to increase your visibility in the community *and* to respond to the needs of organizations is to provide guest speakers. Your organization employs individuals with a wide range of specialties and interests who can represent the company at monthly civic organization meetings. Many companies include speakers bureaus as part of their community relations efforts. Publicizing the availability of specific speakers, however, can be problematic. On the Web, you can easily produce a roster of speakers with information about their topics, and even build a simple interactive form that allows an organization to request a speaker. A smidgen more sophistication would enable you to produce a calendar displaying the availability of your various speakers.

IBM Research offers speakers on a variety of topics via its Web site; subjects include Interactive TV, Smart Networks, and Performance Issues in WWW Servers. Each speaker's name is hyperlinked to the appropriate e-mail address, enabling visitors to make a request directly to the speaker. Berkeley Lab offers speakers on topics such as Fusion, the Genome and its Applications, and on its Thermally Insulated Car Project. An online form allows organizations to request a speaker directly over the Web.

In Figure 9-5, Red Hat, a distributor of the Linux operating system, offers a speaker request form on its site, along with a listing of all upcoming speaking engagements by employees.

Build a Community Forum

Budgets are tight for volunteer organizations, and many cannot afford a Web presence, but you can offer them a page or two of space on your server to promote their local activities. At the bottom of the page, include a small banner ad that reads something like, "This volunteer organization Web site is provided as a community service of Acme, Inc."

FIGURE 9-5. RED HAT'S SPEAKER REQUEST FORM.

Request a Speaker

Want to see Red Hat at your conference, convention, university program or user group meeting? Please complete the following submission form.

Provide as much detail as possible, and we'll work to find you a great speaker.

We'll contact you shortly to discuss your request.

Fields marked with an asterisk (*) are required.

Info on Conference/Event

* Conference/Event Title: [   ]
* Date and Time: [   ]
* Venue and Location: [   ]
  Focus or Theme: [   ]
* Expected Attendance: [   ]
  Event URL: [   ]

Audience Profile:
Please specify job titles and
percentages of audience
make-up, if possible.
[   ]

Charitable Institutions

Your community includes organizations dedicated to helping others in need—and there are many different types of needs, leading to an array of charitable organizations that all compete for your limited contributions.

Giving Money

The fact that you make contributions is worth note on your Web site. If you already produce an online community relations report, be sure to include a review of your corporate giving. Review the amounts contributed to each organization, the process by which the money is collected (for example, as a percentage of after-tax profits or through an employee giving campaign). For those that would solicit your organization, you also can offer a summary of the process by which the company decides which charities will be beneficiaries of its giving program.

While in the midst of an employee campaign (such as United Way or Red Cross), be sure to offer updated information on the campaign's progress. The visibility of the campaign on your Web site serves as a reflection of your organization's commitment to charitable giving.

Include links to the Web sites of organizations to which the company regularly donates money, or craft overviews of each recipient of company monies that focus on the reason those organizations are worthy of your attention.

Giving Time

Although companies are limited in the amount of money they can contribute to charity, there is bountiful time. The focus of many charitable institutions is not on contributions, but on voluntarism, since the amount of time people donate to charity-related efforts has diminished in recent decades.

An online community relations report should chronicle the company's organizing efforts over the past year. Even if an effort was not an official company project, but rather was organized by an employee, you can spotlight the employee and note that the company provided the time and office supplies to bring the project to its completion.

Projects that are in the planning stages should be highlighted as well, and progress reports should be posted to update the public about in-progress efforts. Photo spreads showing your employees at work have special value, since people especially like to look at pictures of other people from their own community. If senior management is represented in the pictures, so much the better. (The kinds of projects that are particularly applicable to photography are characterized by Habitat for Humanity, the corporate volunteer effort to refurbish substandard housing to make homes livable for destitute members of the community. Pictures of employees hammering, sawing, and painting display genuine community-based pride and dedication.)

Special Audiences

Communicating with every member of a special audience can be pro-
hibitively expensive—even impossible, given that many special audiences are not easily defined; there are no mailing lists for many of
the special-needs groups with which you may wish to communicate
(e.g., the visually disabled in your community, residents with children
living at home). But there is little expense involved in developing a
simple Web page (or series of pages) that provides information that
meets the unique needs of these special audiences. The Web can
even be used to help you identify the individual members of these
singular communities so that you can communicate with them using
other media, as well.

Alcan Smelter & Chemicals, a division of Alcan Aluminum,
identified one such community in the agricultural business in Canada's interior, according to Kathleen Bourchier, Alcan's strategic communications consultant. The company maintains the Nechako
Reservoir near Kitimat, the location of its smelting operations. The
reservoir's Skins Lake Water Spillway releases water into the Nechako River. "Depending on how much we're being asked to release or
hold back, the amount of water going into the river tends to fluctu-
ate," Bourchier explains. "The farmers who live downstream need to
be kept informed. Our commitment to community relations includes
providing as much information on water flows as we possibly can."

Even before the company launched its Web site, it made water-
flow information available through a variety of media. A call-in telephone line offered a recording with water-level information, and
farmers could subscribe to a fax service, "But the amount of information you could put on a recording is limited, and not everybody has a
fax machine," Bourchier asserts. The agricultural community, on the
other hand, is one of the most wired, using the Internet to obtain
detailed weather reports, crop reports, and a variety of other data.
(See Chapter 3 for an overview of Agriculture Online, a successful
commercial Web site for farmers.)

Using the Web (at *www.sno.net/alcan/*), the company is able to
provide current reservoir levels and water-flow rates, as well as a
graphical chart that shows the year's historical release information—
data that can be useful to farmers in planning their activities.

Clearly, the water-flow information is of limited use to a small, special-interest audience. However, it is invaluable for those individuals and generates goodwill within the community.

Alcan provides instant updates of water flow and reservoir levels on the Web page shown in Figure 9-6, which is geared toward the special-interest farming community that operates on the Nechako River in the Western Canadian interior.

The Internet can provide any number of special-interest audiences with information that meets their particular needs, enabling your organization to engage in a targeted communication effort with individual members of an audience otherwise difficult—or impossible—to reach.

Measurement

Assess the effectiveness of your online community relations efforts by using the following techniques:

- Build a survey on your site that asks members of the visiting public to rate the online effort and submit ideas for future enhancements.

- Measure the number of visitors to community-specific sites (such as those dedicated to educational programs), and record the number of requests for information, sign-ups, or other actions that denote an individual took advantage of a program or service.

- Determine the savings involved in providing information online that otherwise would have been expensive to produce and distribute. Carrying this notion a step further, you can quantify the audiences your Internet presence allows you to reach who would be impossible to identify without the medium.

Conclusion

Identifying the various subaudiences within the community is an expense most organizations cannot afford. The Internet allows those audiences to be targeted and to pull the information they need, and

Figure 9-6. Alcan's Web page for farming community.

ALCAN

Skins Lake Water Release   *Aluminum, an Element of B.C.*

In an effort to keep Nechako River and Nechako Reservoir residents informed about changes to water releases from the Skins Lake Spillway, Alcan has made the commitment to post the current water release rates, and changes to these release rates (measured in CFS - cubic feet per second), on this page on a weekly basis.

The graph illustrating current releases is updated weekly and the same information appears on a weekly basis in the appropriate area newspapers, entitled FLOW FACTS.

We encourage residents to monitor this page to keep abreast of changes in the level of water releases from the Nechako Reservoir.

Skins Lake Spillway

Click on photo above to see the full view of the reservoir.

Current water release

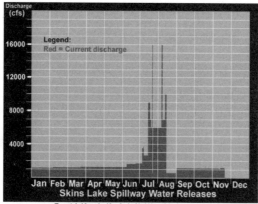

The period of September 07 to October 31 of this graph has been adjusted.

Current discharge = 29.91 cu.m.per/sec.

Current reservoir elevation = 2790.97 feet

Long-term average elevation for this period = 2795.2

Full reservoir elevation = 2800 feet

APM-BC Homepage | Kitimat Works | Kemano Power Generation
Regional Offices | Economic Information | Environment News | News Releases
Community Investment Program | Career Opportunities | Related Links

Email - Alcan Corporate Affairs - B.C. Operations

to take advantages of programs that would have been unwieldy before the Internet provided the company with a means by which to communicate and facilitate those programs.

Notes

1. *www.sierrapacific.com/compnv/comrel/*, Sierra Pacific Web site copyright 1998, 1999, 2000.

CHAPTER 10

Cause and Issue Communication

E VEN COMPANIES CAN take on causes. Some profit-based organizations adopt causes because they are pet projects of the
CEO. Others take on a cause that is linked directly to its line of
business. Some merely want to be good corporate citizens.

Promoting a Cause

First off, let's distinguish between an *issue* and a *cause*. An issue is a
matter for discussion, dispute, or debate. When a company addresses
its plans for something a constituent audience perceives as contrary
to its interests, that becomes an issue. A cause, on the other hand,
can be defined as the interest of a group (or an individual) that attacks that interest with fervor and dedication.

Companies face issues routinely. Do they really get involved
with causes? Most certainly—although not at the same rate with
which they face issues! McDonald's is famous for the cause of seriously ill children, which it champions through its Ronald McDonald
House. The oil company Chevron uses institutional advertising to
tout its concern for the environment. Mattel Toys historically has
supported the U.S. Marine Corps's Toys for Tots campaign. The Body
Shop is environmentally conscious as well as focused on humane
treatment of animals, while the fast-food chain Wendy's has embraced adoption as its cause. The National Football League maintains a close alliance with United Way. Across the United States,
organizations adopt stretches of highway, either paying for or provid-

ing the labor to keep these areas free of litter. Organizations support medical causes, social causes (such as the homeless), and cultural (like the opera).

For purposes of this discussion, we'll segment causes into the following two types:

1. Causes embraced by a corporation, such as those listed previously.

2. Focused causes that are the entire occupation of an organization. The Alzheimer's Association has one cause—Alzheimer's Disease. Baseball manager Tony LaRussa's Animal Rescue Foundation (ARF) has one cause—saving stray animals.

Corporate Causes

Corporations adopt causes for a variety of reasons. In some cases, the cause is directly related to the organization's line of business. Mattel's causes *always* relate to children, while Merck Pharmaceuticals' causes almost always relate to medicine. Other organizations pick causes based on their desire to improve or bolster relations with local communities—Levi Strauss & Company is an excellent example. Some organizations adopt causes that improve their image in an area where their image may be subject to negative perceptions. As an oil company, Chevron is painted with the broad brush of all oil companies that are (in the words of environmental activists) raping the environment. By focusing on the environment as a cause, the company is able to separate itself from the pack and establish a more solid image in regards to the environment. Some companies embrace causes because they are important to somebody in a position of power within the organization.

These organizations should take advantage of existing Web resources to link the company to the cause. However, a page or subsite of the corporate site may prove inadequate; these usually provide little more than an overview of the organization's involvement with the cause. Since the larger site already has a major focus—such as marketing, investor communications, or e-commerce—the resources often are not available to establish a comprehensive site dedicated to audiences interested in the cause instead of the company.

McDonald's presents a better approach with its Ronald McDon-

ald House Charities. The link to the cause is prominent on the Mc-
Donald's home page; it carries weight equal to links to corporate
information, a restaurant locator, a kids' component, and international information. But clicking the link does not take visitors to a
subsection of the McDonald's site—instead, visitors find themselves
on *http://www.rmhc.com*, a site dedicated entirely to Ronald McDonald House Charities. Although the navigation bar provides access to
other elements of the McDonald's site, the key links on this discrete
site provide information that is pertinent to the people looking for
the charity, not the burger joint.

Companies also should employ the market sample of one concept, spreading their message to related sites. For example, the vac-
uum cleaner manufacturer Bissell features a page on its site about
its annual sponsorship of the "Cleaning Spree at Ronald McDonald
Houses Around the World." Visitors to Bissell's site stand a good
chance of learning more about Ronald McDonald House because of
the relationship.

Focused Causes

Focused causes cry out for comprehensive, integrated, strategic
campaigns. These efforts, whether they are global or local, usually
have lofty goals that require more than a cool Web site to achieve
them.

Patagonia, the retail clothing outlet, went beyond its own Web
site's boundaries to address the cause it embraced against genetically
modified agricultural products. (For more on this issue, and how a
leading company in the field addresses activists against its work, read
Chapter 12, "Activism on the Internet.") Patagonia, which embraces
environmentalism as its corporate cause, bought banner advertising
on the Web site of *Mother Jones*, the left-leaning magazine. The advertisements barely mentioned Patagonia; instead, they urged readers
to click through to a letter-writing campaign with mail directed at the
U.S. Food and Drug Administration (FDA). The letters needed to be
sent by a deadline if they were to have any effect on a decision regarding genetically modified foods that the FDA was about to make. Of
course, the letter-writing campaign was housed on the overall Patagonia Web site. It was easy to see that the campaign was part of the
company's site focused on the environment, but the navigation bar
provided one-click access to the product and shopping part of the

site, as well. (Environmentalists would just as soon buy a parka from a company that embraced their own cause than from a company simply out to make a buck, right?)

Let's look at two detailed examples of how the Internet was built into focused causes. The first example is a cause of national scope; the second is local.

Case Study: White House Office of National Drug Control Policy

The National Youth Anti-Drug Media Campaign, launched by the White House Office of National Drug Control Policy (ONDCP), was a multidisciplinary effort. A number of organizations were awarded contracts to produce elements for the campaign that were suited to their expertise. Management of the paid advertising elements of the campaign, for example, were awarded to the advertising agency Ogilvy & Mather. Fleishman-Hillard, one of the world's largest public relations agencies, was selected to manage communication programs and outreach initiatives—in other words, public relations.

The campaign's five-year goal is to educate and enable the youth of America to reject illicit drugs. You've probably seen the campaign's centerpiece "What's Your Anti-Drug?" messages in a variety of media. (The *anti-drug*, as defined by the campaign, is whatever you get hooked on that keeps you off drugs. Books might be your anti-drug, or sports, or volunteer work.)

An Integrated, Strategic Campaign. The communicators at Fleishman-Hillard overseeing the account recognized the need to tap into both traditional and interactive media, and to ensure that the two were tightly integrated. Ensuring that integration would happen meant adopting a strategic approach to the challenge. First, the team established key strategies for affecting the desired outcome, which included:

- ➤ Educating target audiences about the consequences of drug use and the significance of the problem
- ➤ Providing the target audiences with useful ways to act on their knowledge base (for example, demonstrating resistance skills for youth or parenting skills for parents)
- ➤ Delivering the same set of messages in a variety of venues and methods to continually reinforce the ideas in fresh, innovative approaches

Next, the team identified places where the audiences were open to influence, including home, school, and work, and where the audience members worshiped and where they engaged in leisure activities. A matrix determined which locales were appropriate to the five primary audience segments (kids in school, for instance, don't go to work, but parents and grandparents aren't in school). Ultimately, the models and matrixes that emerged from the up-front project work were designed to allow at-risk youths to resist drugs over the long haul.

In assessing the best role for interactive communication, the team considered a behavior change continuum provided by behavioral specialists working on the campaign. The continuum, portrayed as a perpetually reinforcing loop, begins with the target audience (at-risk youths in their "tweens" and early teens, ages 10–14) considering how relevant the issue is to them personally. Once they have determined it is relevant, they contemplate the information they have absorbed, and then commit to avoiding (or stopping) the use of drugs. Finally, that commitment must be sustained. For each of those four steps, the team saw opportunities to incorporate online media (which not coincidentally is heavily used by the target audience). Online advertising leading kids to content-rich Web sites would, for example, work well in creating an awareness of the possibility that drugs could become a very negative part of a tween's life; or to contemplate the positive aspects of not doing drugs. Interactive features on those sites would lead to an active engagement between the tween and the content; that engagement would lead most tweens to give their behavior some thought. To make a commitment to staying drug-free, a youth would share that intention with an online audience. By creating a community of kids committed to resisting drugs, the team would provide a tool making it easier for those kids to stay on the right path.

Campaign Web Sites. Taking the campaign to the Net was not a simple matter of building an anti-drug Web site. In fact, any content had to appeal greatly to the audience—particularly the tweens, who have access to tens of thousands of Web sites that would seem more appealing than an anti-drug site. It was important to generate traffic to the sites, but getting them there wasn't nearly enough. They had to come back and use the site, and they had to talk about it with their friends. Among the elements added to the list for integration into the campaign were the following:

- Rich content
- Games
- Events
- Discussion forums and bulletin boards
- Custom e-mail newsletters
- Downloadable tools
- Chat

It became clear early in the planning that achieving this objective would require that the content spread beyond the boundaries of the sites created specifically for the project. It was equally important to place content on *other* sites where members of the target audience spent time online.

Ultimately, the team created seven discrete sites dedicated directly to the campaign. Two were aimed at parents and caregivers, one at *www.TheAntiDrug.com* on the World Wide Web and a parallel section on America Online's proprietary network. According to these online resources, parents are the anti-drug. The sites are aimed at parents and offer news, opportunities to get more involved, advice, and community. Parents also can sign up for a biweekly e-mail newsletter called "Parenting Tips." Parents began subscribing at a clip of about two hundred each week. The newsletter, built using HTML, adopts the same design of the Web site. The site also offers interactive elements, such as a diagram of a typical home—when you mouse over parts of the home, you learn which inhalants are probably in the room. (In the bedroom, kids can find hair spray, air freshener, and nail polish remover.)

The component of the White House Office of National Drug Control Policy's suite of Web sites shown in Figure 10-1 focuses on the role parents play in keeping their children free of drugs.

Three sites were developed for tweens and other young people. The flagship site of the campaign, Freevibe.com, is among these. Designed in the style that appeals to the demographic, Freevibe has a few distinct sections:

FIGURE 10-1. WEB SITE FOCUSING ON PARENTS' ROLE IN ANTIDRUG EFFORT.

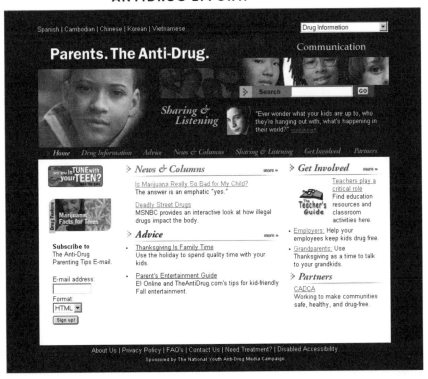

➪ *Heads Up* is the information resource.

➪ *Shout Out* is the site's community. Here kids can post messages to bulletin boards with themes like Your Stories, Peer Support, and Rumors. There is also a poll, and a viral component—the ability to send e-mail to someone you know who is having problems with drugs. The e-mail postcard, sent under the signatures of celebrities like tennis star Venus Williams and pro skater Andy MacDonald, has been sent by some four thousand visitors to Freevibe so far. Visitors also can sign up to become an "I Count Advisor," one of the volunteer youths who provides informal counseling in the online bulletin board-driven communities. As a result, the site facilitates the development of kids who promote the campaign's objectives in their online interactions with their peers.

➪ *Hang Time* offers ideas about what to do instead of drugs. You can find "Five Things to Do This Weekend," for instance, interact with some Hollywood and musical stars, or find something to do with your time that is "(a) more fun, (b) cooler, (c) cheaper, (d) healthier, and (e) generally way better than drugs!" The list provides links to resources if you want to make money, get into sports, become a writer, or spend more time outdoors.

➪ *My Anti-Drug* is devoted to the message behind the slogan, helping kids understand the notion of an anti-drug. Visitors can even add their own anti-drug to the list.

Freevibe is the centerpiece of the White House Office of National Drug Control Policy's online campaign, as shown in Figure 10-2.

The second site, Straight Scoop (*www.straghtscoop.org*), is a news bureau for the youth editors of middle school and high school newspapers, Web sites, radio stations, and television stations.

The content on this site is mirrored in America Online's It's Your Life section.

Another site is for teachers, mirroring the parents' site, suggesting that teachers can be the anti-drug. And a site aimed at the media provides press releases, downloadable advertisements (print and video), and other resources for reporters and editors.

The family of sites had attracted over 36 million page views through January 2002.

In addition to the viral components on the Web sites, the campaign sends e-mail alerts about the campaign to some six thousand subscribers from more than five thousand organizations.

Employing the Market Sample of One. In addition to the content target audiences can find on the sites built by the team, the campaign's message can be discovered on dozens of other Net destinations where the target audience is likely to go. The effort to spread the message across the Net involved building long-term partnerships *and* taking advantage of special events and short-term opportunities.

Father's Day, for example, presented the team with a hook for messages aimed

FIGURE 10-2. *FREEVIBE,* BELOW, AND THE ANTIDRUG.COM ARE CENTERPIECES OF THE U.S. GOVERNMENT'S ANTIDRUG CAMPAIGN.

at parents—how dads can keep their kids drug-free. Partnerships were developed with various organizations that agreed to host the campaign's contents, including articles, logos, and (in every case) links to TheAntiDrug.com. Oprah Winfrey presented another opportunity when she decided to do a show on drugs in schools; the campaign was able to get its messages and links onto Oprah's Web site.

Longer-term sites got plenty of attention, too. Working with NASA, the campaign developed a microsite called "Explore Space . . . Not Drugs." Linked from the part of the NASA site aimed at kids who want to become astronauts, the site includes real astronauts talking about drugs, games, a drug information database, and (of course) a link to Freevibe.com. The site drew thirty thousand visitors the first month of its operation, and ultimately directed ninety thousand visitors to Freevibe.

Figure 10-3 illustrates how the White House Office of National Drug Control Policy reached beyond its own suite of sites to work with the National Aeronautics and Space Administration (NASA) to create an anti-drug message for youths interested in becoming astronauts.

A far stretch from NASA is Barenaked Ladies, a pop band with a hit album and a Web site. The team first approached Reprise, the record label, which in turn brought the band to the table. The band's Web site featured a link to the campaign's Freevibe site, noting that the anti-drug site contained an interview with band member Ed Robertson; the link was the leading nonadvertising driver of traffic to Freevibe for three months.

Other partnerships included the search site Lycos, the women's content com-

FIGURE 10-3. **NASA** SITE JOINING ANTIDRUG EFFORT.

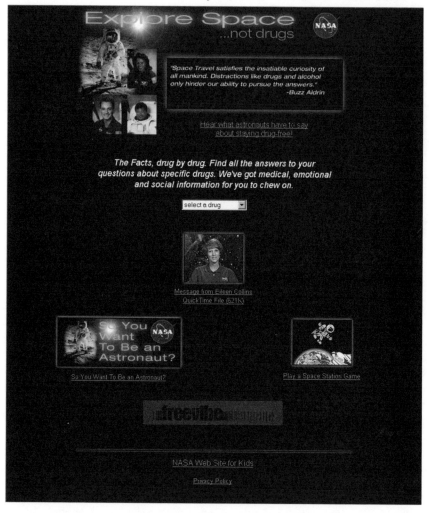

pany Oxygen (the MomsOnline.com site endorsed the campaign and included information and a link in its e-mail newsletter, which is distributed to fifty-three thousand subscribers), and About.com, among others.

The campaign also bought key words at Yahoo. A search for "Ecstasy" for example, would return a content-rich banner ad.

Special events were also part of the online effort. Using chat capabilities on America Online, Lycos, Talk City, and Sun Microsystems's YoungZone.org, the team arranged and promoted anti-drug-themed online events with celebrities including actresses, athletes, comedians, and singers. The campaign even hosted an online concert series.

The campaign also bought banner advertisements, based on the belief that click-through rates on nonprofit, message-oriented banners would be higher than they are for product-oriented advertisements. The actual click-through rate confirmed that belief.

Case Study: Stop the Coal Trains

When Dakota Minnesota & Eastern Railroad proposed a $1.4 billion project to build a coal pipeline that would include a direct run through the city of Rochester, Minnesota, a coalition of civic leaders from all facets of the community launched a campaign against the proposal. To manage the campaign, the coalition contracted with the public relations firm Weber Shandwick Worldwide, which immediately saw the value of incorporating a Web presence.

The cause featured a specific, tangible, measurable goal: convincing the federal Surface Transportation Board (STB) to expand the public comment period following the release of a Draft Environmental Impact Statement (DEIS). The typical comment period is 90 days, but the group wanted an extension to 180 days in order to:

- ➭ Give experts in the legal and environmental fields adequate time to address problematic findings within the DEIS report and submit meaningful analysis to the STB
- ➭ Allow more time for Citizens to Stop the Coal Trains to gather support from local citizens and send personal letters to the STB
- ➭ Slow the railroad's momentum
- ➭ Send a strong message to the railroad that the city of Rochester was intent on—and capable of—stopping the project

Initial research helped crystallize the agency's strategy. For example, the communication team learned that the railroad involved had the worst safety record of any U.S. railroad in its class. Research also helped demonstrate the importance of out-of-towners to Rochester, including the many patients who visit the world-famous Mayo Clinic. Even a slight drop in patient visits to the clinic would affect the entire community, the group determined. Research even established how congestion at railroad crossings would increase response time and increase the potential for accidents.

With research in hand, the campaign established a series of tactics:

- ➭ Position the citizen's group as a leading advocate for Rochester and its citizens.

↝ Educate the people of Rochester about the dangers the coal train presents and how it would affect their everyday lives.

↝ Gain media attention and coverage about the coal train, involving community members representing the sectors that stood to be most affected by the train—business, health care, schools, and seniors.

↝ Bring Rochester's concerns about the project to the attention of politicians at all levels.

↝ Provide citizens with the ability to contact the STB to voice their concerns.

The campaign featured all the traditional elements of solid public relations, including a press conference the day the Environmental Impact Statement was released, a video to attract local attention, a speakers bureau, and a public rally and town hall meeting. The campaign also featured a print and broadcast advertising campaign targeting key audiences; the print advertisements featured a response card readers could fill out and send to the STB. Both the print and broadcast advertisements included the address of the campaign's Web site, *http://www.stopthecoal trains.com*.

The Web site was developed to serve the following three primary objectives:

1. Provide another method for citizens to send letters in support of the letter-writing campaign.

2. Offer comprehensive, detailed information—based on the extensive research that had been conducted—that could not be offered in such complete form through any other media.

3. Provide individuals outside the community—such as Mayo Clinic patients—with information that might compel them to send letters of their own.

"The irony of the situation was that the Surface Transportation Board doesn't accept e-mail communication," according to Cathy Kennedy, vice president at Weber Shandwick's Minnesota offices. Letters generated for the STB from the Web site were directed to the citizen's group, which printed them and sent them on to the agency, which treated them like any other letter delivered by the Post Office.

The Web site made it easier for citizens to contact their elected representatives. A form included a field for zip codes, allowing a database to automatically generate a letter to the appropriate legislators. The process included the option of indicating that the sender of the letter was a citizen of Rochester or an option that read, "I am not a resident of Rochester, but I am concerned." Local businesses were encouraged to notify their out-of-town stakeholders about the site so they could become engaged.

The components of the site—except for the citizen's group logo—were developed exclusively for the online component of the campaign. An interactive map, for example, featured mouseover effects: When you rolled your mouse over various parts of the proposed train route, you saw a detailed view of the nearby facilities that would be affected by the project (such as schools, medical centers, hospitals, nature centers, emergency services, facilities for senior citizens, and parks). The site even included links to independent third-party resources, including a story published in *RailwayAge* magazine online that suggested the project might not be economically feasible. Another link took readers directly to the part of the railroad's site that addressed the proposal.

Ultimately, the site attracted over seventy-five thousand visitors and generated about eight thousand letters. Weber Shandwick's Kennedy credits the online presence with playing a key role in the STB's decision to extend the public comment period by sixty days.

Following the victory, the team decided to leave the site up as an information resource. Visitors can still express their concern to legislators, and the site will be ready to tackle the next phase of the campaign depending on the STB's final decision. (The STB granted the extension.) In the meantime, the public affairs officer for the railroad was quoted in a trade publication: "As the process gets longer and more complex, the market changes, the economy changes and prices change. There could come a point when we're no longer able to afford the project. The billion dollar question remains: How long will that be?"[1]

Communicating an Issue

Organizations seeking to manage public opinion cannot ignore their issues; they must address subjects that are causing debate and discussion among their constituents. A company seeking to build a new facility near a neighborhood will almost certainly come face to face with NIMBY (Not in My Back Yard) sentiment; the issue, then, is growth. A cell phone company may want to address the issue of talking on cell phones while driving. Drilling for oil in a protected wilderness could well be an issue for an oil company.

Taking advantage of a company's existing Web site is a useful first step, particularly if the organization creates content on its site *before* the issue becomes a crisis. For most organizations, adding such content usually happens *after* a crisis has erupted—at which point, the information on the company's page is even more suspect, in the eyes of the constituent audiences the organization is trying to reach, than usual.

The contents of an issues-oriented Web page that exists within a site are of limited value. For an example, let's consider an environmental issue. In this scenario, let's say an oil company is participating in a consortium that has been invited into the rain forest by the government of Peru to look at the potential for natural gas exploration and recovery. You are the public relations counselor for the company, and you think it would be a good idea to say something about the precautions the company is taking to prevent environmental damage. You convince the company to draft a statement about your company's involvement in the project, and add some information about the nature of those precautions.

Sounds pretty good, doesn't it? But how effective will those pages be? Consider the following problems with this approach:

↝ The company Web site on which these pages reside is primarily targeted to investors. Most investors are not overly concerned about environmental issues—at least, not in the context of the information they look for on the company's site. Thus, the site's primary audience won't see the information.

↝ The environmental audience probably won't see it, either. How would they find it? Even if you undertake a campaign to alert environmentally minded people about the site, most wouldn't get past the fact that it is hosted by an oil company, which they already don't trust.

↝ If you're putting this information on your company's site, isn't it safe to assume that your counterparts in the other eighteen companies in the consortium are doing the same? Now you have nineteen separate messages about the project, with no assurance of consistency. Some of the key messages may even be contradictory!

Once again, the idea of "putting something about it on our Web site" proves less than effective. Thinking through the issues, it seems to make better sense for all of the members of the consortium to band together and build a microsite dedicated specifically to this issue, targeting only the environmental activists who could, if uninformed, decide to make the project a cause.

That is precisely what a real consortium did in this situation, as outlined in the following case study.

Case Study: Camisea Project

The Camisea.com Web site was created and managed by Shell Oil, but it's not *about* the multinational oil company per se, so the company name is not prominent. Instead, the site is about the issue: drilling for oil in the region of the Peruvian rain forest known as Camisea. The drilling (which never proceeded, because the project was deemed unworkable by the partners; the site was removed shortly after that decision was made) would have been a multicompany effort partnering Shell with the local Mobil operations and an engineering consortium led by Bechtel that included Peruvian and Brazilian partners.

"We haven't yet made the final investment decision whether to go ahead with the project," noted Andrew Vickers, Shell's external affairs manager in Peru, before the decision not to go forward was made. But Vickers decided to proceed with a site dedicated to the region where the drilling would take place should the company decide to proceed. Why is Shell's logo nowhere on the site? "We're not trying to hide," Vickers said. "The project is more than just Shell. We have our partners, the engineering consortium, but more important, we are guests here in Peru. Many parts of Peruvian society will have a role in the project. The site is dedicated to the project and all that it stands for, not any one participating company."

Still, you might expect the site to be a propaganda piece designed to build support for the project. Vickers vehemently disagreed. "This is not a public relations tool; I'm not a public relations manager," he said. "The site is about providing people with accurate information such that they can form a viewpoint. The data in the site is raw. For example, you can view the environmental impact assessment in its original form." According to Vickers, public relations in its traditional form is outdated. "Today, you need to provide accurate and speedy information."

A consortium of oil companies and engineering firms pooled resources to create a special microsite addressing the issues associated with exploration for natural gas in the Peruvian rain forest.

The site was designed to address the fact that the exploration and production would be taking place in an environmentally sensitive area, characterized by tremendous biodiversity and occupied by indigenous people. According to Vickers:

> These facts create very sensitive issues for us and for many other people. A lot of people have an interest in these issues. It made sense to give people access to the information that we have so they could see for themselves what we're doing. We live in a CNN world where communication has transformed everything. The best way to live in that world is to show everyone what you're doing, and the Web is the best way to do that. You can incorporate words, pictures, and other media in any combination, and people can visit the parts that interest them.

To emphasize the fact that the site is not a public relations ploy, Vickers explained that much of the site was written by noncommunicators. "The environmental section was written by the Smithsonian Institution," he stated. "The history section was prepared by a famous Peruvian historian. The energy section was written by the Peruvian Ministry of Energy and Mines." Even the engineering portion of the site was crafted by company engineers, without any spin from the communicators. "We just asked them to write about what they do." These third-party content areas of the site also serve to heighten credibility among an environmentalist audience already skeptical of anything oil companies would have to say.

The site also included all related news releases, speeches, and other documentation, captured in a library section. The news section was updated with the latest information, and the entire site underwent regular updates as new information became available.

Vickers called the site the flagship communication for the project, and as such, it drew considerable attention. "In the first few days the site was up, we had 300 visitors per day, primarily from Shell. Now, the prime audience is in the U.S., followed by Peru," Vickers explained. The e-mail generated by the site initially came from job seekers; then members of the Rainforest Action Network came to visit. "We had a link to the Rainforest Action Network on the site," Vickers added. "We sent them a note telling them we're linking to them. They've been hypercritical of us in the past. We knew from the outset that we wanted to do this project differently. Transparency and objectivity were our goals from the outset."

Vickers knew all this was a far cry from the communication methods employed by oil companies in the past. "The exploration-and-production business traditionally has not communicated as thoroughly as it could have," Vickers explained. "We make significant contributions to society, but we have failed to communicate that message, and therefore people draw conclusions about the industry that are less accurate than they could be." The site, he said, was designed to play an important role in communicating what the company did, the benefits it would have produced, and its efforts to minimize the environmental impact.

But Vickers insisted the site was not driven by communications: "We're identifying the issues that people are interested in first and putting communication on top of that. The issues underpin the site."

Elements of an Issue Communication

The Camisea project represents one set of solutions designed to address one target audience—stakeholders concerned about the environment. There are other tools at your disposal for addressing an issue using online communications.

Your Own Web Site

There is value in stating your position on an issue, or even creating an entire issues subsite, for your organizational Web site. Any publicity the issue generates that links your organization with the issue will lead some people to visit your site to see what you have to say about it. It is important to keep in mind that audiences visiting corporate Web sites—particularly the media, and especially when the content is issues-oriented—start off skeptical. Your content should do as much as possible to allay that skepticism. Note that many of the materials referenced next rely on third parties. When somebody *outside* the company reinforces a point of view consistent with that promoted *within* the company, credibility is heightened.

Regurgitating your written communications on this site is not sufficient to qualify the effort as an effective online communication. Instead, consider offering a brief summary of the issue and your organization's position on the issue. Then, offer links to the following resources:

- Any written documentation visitors to the site may be interested in.
- Resources from other organizations that support your company's point of view, including testimonials and alliances. If your issue is environmental and your organization has struck up an alliance with the Natural Resources Defense Council, link to its site—the independent, third-party validation will help to improve the credibility of your position.
- Links to other information (on other Web sites) about the issue.
- An offer to receive e-mail updates about the issue.
- List any recognition (honors and awards, for example) you have received for your efforts around the issue.
- Let people know how they can get involved.
- Provide visitors with the opportunity to engage in community. Create a discussion area or establish a discussion-oriented e-mail mailing list.
- Offer case studies to illustrate your organization's commitment or the degree of its involvement in the issue.
- Catalog press releases related to the issue here (in addition to incorporating them into the press release archives that exist elsewhere on your company's site).
- Provide a fact sheet that lists any statistics that help you make your case.

➫ Links to industry association sites that provide more comprehensive coverage of the issue.

Microsites

Microsites—such as the Camisea.com site—are of particular value since they focus on the *issue* and not on the *company*. Because these sites are often built collaboratively—with partners and allies—credibility is somewhat less of an issue, particularly if you have recruited resources to contribute to the site that are beyond reproach.

Much of the content identified previously also applies to microsites, with the exception of any material that focuses on the organization. You can identify the organization and indicate its involvement in the issue, but the site is not about the company. It is also advisable to incorporate more interactive elements in this type of outreach, such as games (if the site is aimed at kids) and database-driven features (one site dealing with the issue of energy costs provided a calculator to assess the savings households could realize if they insulated their homes).

Community

Any opportunity to participate in community will be well received by audiences. Most issues already involve some level of debate, therefore, moving that debate to a public forum has advantages—despite the fact that management often doesn't like to hear what dissident voices have to say. Knowing the issues makes it easier to devise strategies for addressing them. Knowing the influencers within the communities makes it easier to know whom to reach out to.

You can establish your own community, as Shell Oil did to reach out to environmentalists (see Chapter 12, "Activism on the Net"), or you can simply point to places where communities already exist. McDonalds doesn't offer any such links on its Ronald McDonald House site, but easily could direct parents of seriously ill children to discussion forums populated by other such parents.

Expert Panels

Consider assembling a panel of experts who have no direct affiliation to your organization who are willing to answer questions from your audience about the issue.

The Market Sample of One

Your issue is also somebody else's issue; there are people out there who care about the issue you've adopted. How do they find your site, or your content? When employing the market sample of one concept, it is important to place content on other sites. You can do this through banner advertising, but would be better served through content syndication. It's great that the late Dave Thomas of Wendy's fast-food fame developed a page about his support of adoption, but how much better would it have been for getting that message out to write articles that appeared in places where the target audience was likely to read them? The idea of content syndication would have articles authored by Thomas occupying space on adoption-related sites and parenting sites, for example. (In fact, the Wendy's site itself could include Thomas-bylined articles available for reproduction in other media.) From a media relations standpoint, Thomas could have been available for interviews with online journalists.

Measurement

Depending on the goal established for your cause or issue communication, measuring the impact can be unbelievably easy or painfully difficult. The Stop the Coal Trains campaign had a clear and measurable goal: Convince the Surface Transportation Board to extend the public comment period. Based on the campaign's ability to influence the STB, the board extended the comment period. The volume of mail generated by the campaign makes it even easier to assess the impact of the effort on attaining the ultimate goal.

Measuring something like the youth drug program, however, is more complex. "A recent progress report on the campaign, compiled from a large amount of third-party data, found that the campaign is reaching its intended youth and parent audiences and achieving breakthrough antidrug awareness," according to David Wickenden, senior vice president and senior partner with Fleishman Hillard.

The research, which mirrors the behavioral change model that serves as a foundation for the campaign, found that the campaign communications have succeeded at changing drug attitudes, beliefs, and intentions. Research also shows that youth drug use is declining. The impact of the interactive components has been determined in part by measuring the volume of activity on the sites—more than 22 million pages of the dedicated sites had been viewed through August 2001. Clearly, these results are harder to come by. Considerable research is required, and correlations must be drawn between the viewing of Web pages and the impact on the target audience's behavior.

In the case of causes and issues, however, the primary measurement *must* link directly to the goal.

Conclusion

Companies addressing issues or promoting causes can be well served by using the Internet, but they need to avoid the trap of thinking that a Web page about the subject at hand—the online equivalent of an institutional advertisement—will be adequate. The principles of online communication are probably best served in addressing issues and causes, along with activists.

Notes

1. Rick Dougherty, public affairs officer, DM&E, quoted in *Interactive Public Relations,* February 2001.

CHAPTER 11

Employee Communications

YOU WON'T FIND many public relations professionals who agree with me that your employees are your most important public relations audience. They are more important than the media, and even more important than investors and analysts. If your employees are not on board with your key messages and reflecting those messages to the various audiences with which they interact, they can derail even the most carefully conceived and brilliantly executed public relations plan aimed at any other audience set. If they *are* on board, they can make the campaign a reality, converting the words and images into genuine customer experiences.

Don't think so? A couple years ago, Bank of America launched a public relations campaign around a new employee program. Employees—the focus was on tellers and other bank branch workers—would adopt Automatic Teller Machines (ATMs) and diligently keep them clean. They would buy their own paper towels and glass cleaner so that the screen would be free of fingerprints and smudges. They would pick up trash around the ATM and generally ensure that it projected the image the bank wanted its ATMs to project. Employees, according to the campaign, were excited and enthusiastic about the program. Articles that said so appeared on the front page of newspaper business sections across the United States.

So far, so good. Bank of America had succeeded in getting ink about how dedicated its employees were, especially when it came to providing a service that ultimately benefited the customer.

Shortly after the campaign launched, my wife had business in a Bank of America branch. While doing her business with the teller, she casually asked whether the teller had adopted an ATM. The teller's response was laughter. "Oh, you bet," she said. "In my spare time, with the money I make as a teller, I'm going to buy cleaning supplies and take care of an ATM." Then she turned to the teller next to her and said, "Have *you* adopted an ATM?" Her colleague's response mirrored her own sense of ridicule.

That response was evidently echoed in branches across the country. There was no follow-up press about the program. Anybody who had engaged a teller in discussion about the program left with a perception that was diametrically opposed to the perception the public relations effort was designed to create.

In other words, employees who were not on board killed an otherwise solid PR program.

The reverse is equally true. In the mid-1970s, I had my first corporate communications job at the oil company ARCO (now part of British Petroleum). I hadn't been there long when the big oil crunch hit, resulting in skyrocketing gasoline prices (by mid-1970s standards), odd-even days at the gas pump (you could only buy gasoline on days that matched the last number of your license plate—even numbers on even-number days, odd numbers on odd-numbered days), and volumes of negative press about the oil companies. All of the well-thought-out advertisements that Mobil Oil bought—part of a legendary communication program implemented by Herb Schmertz in which Mobil ran educational editorials explaining its position—did nothing to keep consumers from assigning Mobil its share of the blame.

ARCO was another story. Despite record profits, post-crisis consumer research indicated most consumers didn't lump ARCO in with the other oil companies. What was different? From my perspective, it was the company's complete candor with its employees about the reasons for the crisis. Employees who understood what was happening explained it to their friends and neighbors. Employees formed a speaker's bureau, taking the message to the Elks, Kiwanis, and Rotary clubs, along with anybody else who would listen. Employees of other oil companies preferred that their friends not ask them about the crisis—they weren't equipped to answer questions. ARCO employees welcomed the questions. In effect, the company had fifty-five thousand public relations representatives out in the field pushing the company's message.

In other words, under the right circumstances, well-informed employees can accomplish more than a carefully orchestrated media-based public relations campaign.

Now, in the networked era, it is easier than ever—and more important than ever—for employees to serve as "brand ambassadors," carrying the company's messages to the various stakeholder audiences with which they naturally and frequently interact: suppliers, vendors, customers, partners, and consumers, among others.

Communicating the Brand

There is much buzz about *brand* these days, and companies talk extensively about making their employees *brand ambassadors.* Exactly how do they do that? The fact is, most of these companies only *talk* about it. Although they exhort their employees to "live the brand," most employees don't even know what the brand is!

Before employees can evangelize a brand to the various publics they touch, it is important to ensure that they understand exactly what a brand is. Numerous definitions have been thrown out, but the one I like is:

> Brand is defined as the emotional reaction you have to a company or product name. How do you *feel* when you hear Coca Cola? Exxon? Union Carbide? Napster?

The goal for employees, when interacting with members of various stakeholder audiences, is to behave in a manner that reinforces the way the organization *wants* those audiences to feel when they hear or think about the organization or its products and services. Online tools can be used in a variety of ways to promote that goal, as the following example illustrates.

Case Study: Nortel Networks

In the world of the Net, where users determine which message they see, it is more important than ever for companies to associate a message with their image, to become recognizable as the _____ (insert your noun here—leader in its industry, best in its class, most desirable, etc.) on the Web. When a company wants to change its brand, it makes sense that it would turn to the Web as a means of promoting that change. And since employees either reinforce or undermine the brand identity with every action, it makes equal sense that the intranet serves as a change tool inside the organization.

But the communications staff at Nortel Networks was not prepared for exactly how effective a tool the intranet could be.

Nortel, the Canada-based global telecommunications giant (formerly known as Northern Telecom) has had a strong brand for a long time. Nortel is a telephony company. "We're known for providing very robust and reliable backbone networks for telephone companies and, more recently, for Internet service providers," said Sylvia Kowal, senior manager of Employee Communications. "We had also been offering data networks and expertise, but we weren't known for it."

Following its acquisition of Bay Networks, a leading data networking company, Nortel had all the pieces in place to offer integrated networking solutions. Using Nortel's products and services, companies could put all their networking eggs in one basket, so to speak. "Our philosophy is that it should be just as easy to make a data call as it is to make a voice call," said Kowal. Nortel had the equipment and expertise to provide that degree of functionality.

Changing the company's image to reflect that focus, however, was a considerable undertaking. "We had a full suite of programs to address the external market. But with more than seventy-five thousand employees around the world, we needed some intense communication to equip our people with the message and advise them of the direction the company was taking and the implications for them," explained Kowal.

While executives took to the road to deliver the word, Kowal took to the intranet, developing a unified program that included components employees could retool to suit their needs and their audiences. The communication effort included video clips of television advertisements, internally produced videos explaining the new image, and clips of executives discussing the change with customers. All video was available in both Quicktime and RealPlayer format. Employees also could download PowerPoint presentations about the new branding effort, review FAQ lists, submit questions (which were answered publicly on the intranet within twenty-four hours), and even participate in live chats.

"We had up to thirty thousand unique visitors to the site each month," Kowal noted. Product groups and other divisions constructed their own Web sites that explained how their efforts fit into the new scheme.

The most compelling element of the campaign, however, was a bit of interactivity inspired by Kowal's research into audience preferences. That research included a paper on "twitch speed," the speed at which the Nintendo/MTV generation wants to get information.

The article on the twitch factor, which originally appeared in the Conference Board's magazine, *Across the Board*, is available at *www.games2train.com/site/html/article.html*; demonstrations of games similar to the one Kowal launched are also available on the Games2Train site. "Our population is very much like what the author of the twitch speed article was talking about," Kowal said. "I knew I had to reach people in a manner that was fun for them, nonthreatening, educational . . . and would only take about ten minutes. A game came to mind."

Kowal had previous experience in producing games, and the more she thought about it, the better the idea sounded. She contracted an outside company to develop the Web-based game, which was presented in two installments. The game featured a series of questions about the company, and was designed so that everybody could win. "You kept answering the question until you got it right," Kowal said, noting that those with a perfect score were eligible for a small prize, and those who were perfect in rounds one *and* two were eligible for a bigger prize.

Some thirty-five thousand employees from twenty-eight different countries played the game. Even though the game was available only in English, entries came from Brazil, Chile, China, Colombia, India, Israel, Italy, Japan, the Philippines, Portugal, Spain, Holland, and Turkey, among others. "Language evidently isn't a barrier," Kowal concluded.

Employees continue to play the game today, and other groups in the company have contacted Kowal for help in developing similar interactive tools to get their messages across. The result that matters most to Kowal is that employees have embraced the concepts the Web efforts were designed to promote.

There are other ways to get employees involved in the brand by using the company intranet as the means of facilitating that involvement, including:

- Offering employees an opportunity to participate in a speakers bureau organized online
- Publishing articles (or links to articles) that have appeared in the public press about the company's brand, helping employees understand perceptions that exist outside the company
- Allowing employees to submit best practices in which they have engaged that have had an impact on public perception of the brand

Connecting Employees to the Marketplace

Employee communications in general is a large topic—too large to address in one chapter of a book. Internal communication efforts have many goals, but few are as significant as the goal of ensuring employees understand the need for change. Employees who know why changes must occur in the company are rarely surprised by the changes, often support the changes, and sometimes even uncover the need for them. Employees who do not understand the need to change often wonder if the Three Stooges are running the company, do not support the change, and often undermine it with their negative attitudes.

Supporting the understanding of change requires that employees have a deep connection to the marketplace—that is, to the external stakeholders whose perceptions and opinions shape the company's success or failure. Roger D'Aprix, the leading thinker in proactive internal communication, is correct in suggesting that organizations change because of forces in the marketplace, such as customer perceptions, shifting market boundaries, or the introduction of new competitors or products.

D'Aprix wrote in the manual, *Employee Communication: The Comprehensive Manual for People Who Communicate with Today's Employees*, that

> If today's turbulent changes are to be understood and accepted, someone on the communication staff had better prepare a clear strategy to make that communication happen. In the old days, we waited around for someone to inform us so we could tell others. Today we must inform ourselves early and offer proactive strategies to help the organization enhance the understanding employees have of the various customer and other marketplace forces critical to the organization's success.[1]

Strategic employee communication aimed at helping employees to understand, support, and promote change has taken many guises, including "Open Book Leadership," in which employees understand the forces affecting the organization as well as the board of directors. Achieving this level of understanding requires access to information, and intranets can provide that kind of access better than most other tools. Consider the following elements of an intranet in support of (but not as a replacement for) a proactive change-oriented strategic communication strategy:

↝ *Competitor links.* In addition to simply providing links to competitor Web sites, you could make links directly from product-oriented or service-oriented content on the intranet to pages of competitors' competing products or services.

↪ *Competitor intelligence.* Sears, Roebuck and Company has a site on its intranet where employees can contribute information they have learned about competitors; this information is studied by the organization at the highest levels as part of Sears' effort to meet competition head-on. Sears employees learn about the competition (primarily other retail outlets) when they visit a competitor. Other companies can obtain this intelligence through other means. Pharmaceutical company sales representatives, for example, might learn about a competitor's activities while visiting a doctor who met with a competitor's sales rep the day before.

↪ *Customer profiles.* List the organization's primary customers and provide details about them. Profiles can also include interviews with customer representatives who speak about their relationship with the company, including its strengths and weaknesses.

↪ *Marketplace data.* This information can include a variety of information, including demographic material, links to articles published by outside media about the company's marketplace, and reports obtained by the company.

Involving Employees

Besides educating employees, the intranet can be used to mobilize them in support of the organization's efforts to influence an outside stakeholder. Consider the following example from the late 1990s at Aetna, the health insurance provider based in Connecticut.

Case Study: Aetna

Aetna's Employee Communications Director Steve Perelman applied the company's intranet's strengths to an internal petition drive initiated by Richard Huber, Aetna's chairperson.

"He was quite upset about all the HMO-bashing that was going on during the summer and early fall," Perelman recalled. As an outlet for his frustration, Huber drafted letters that he sent to a U.S. senator and selected members of Congress. He shared the letters with employees by posting them on Aetnet, Aetna's company-wide intranet. From the letters he provided a link to the articles that had sparked the

letters. "He got forty or fifty e-mail messages from employees thanking him for sharing," Perelman said.

Huber was energized by the response. Clearly, the subject was close to the
hearts of many employees; many had been as upset by the unbalanced media coverage as Huber had been. "He said he believed we could do more with the intranet,"
Perelman explained, "so we put together a petition drive using an e-mail message
with an embedded hyperlink." The message was sent to the twenty-eight thousand
of Aetna's thirty thousand employees who had access to Aetnet. "If you wanted to
sign the petition, you clicked the URL, which brought you to a simple form, where
you would enter your name, your employee number, and the state in which you
worked," Perelman explained. Huber's e-mail message began:

> Like many of you, I've been very disappointed with all the managed care
> bashing we've heard in the past few months, particularly as the election
> nears . . . Many of you suggested that we speak out forcefully and make
> our voices heard. Therefore, I've decided to offer employees all across
> the country the opportunity to sign a "petition" asking managed care
> critics to stop the uninformed bashing of our industry. I'm going to sign
> it, and I invite you to join me in doing so if you wish.

The petition itself began: "We, the undersigned Connecticut employees of
Aetna, voluntarily call on politicians and others who criticize managed care to adopt
a 'truth-in-campaigning' policy and cease their unjustified and uninformed attacks on
the managed care industry, which is one of Connecticut's largest employers." The
petition noted that, in the past year alone, Aetna U.S. Healthcare paid more than
$23 billion to meet members' health care needs. "During this time, our members
visited their doctors 35,000,000 times, gave birth to 280,000 babies, received
4,600,000 immunizations, and had 1,200,000 mammograms."

The e-mail message went out on a Thursday; by Monday, more than seventy-
eight hundred employees had signed on. "Our technology folks provided frequent
updates, almost like election returns, which I passed along to the senior vice president
of Communications," Perelman said; from there, they were delivered to the chairperson.

The response was so positive that on the Monday following the distribution of
the e-mail, Aetna decided to place advertisements displaying the petition in newspapers the following Sunday. "We ended up in twenty newspapers in thirteen states,"
Perelman said. "We ran a double-truck in the Hartford Courant with over two thousand signatures, a full-pager in the Philadelphia Inquirer with over sixteen hundred
signatures, and smaller ads in eleven other states where we have a major presence."

Based on the success of the effort, Perelman and his team are considering
tapping Aetnet's potential for other targeted grassroots efforts, a move consistent
with a long-standing element of the intranet. Aetna Issues is a site devoted to various
position papers and other documents outlining Aetna's stand on topics that affect the

business. "Aetna Issues is clickable directly from the home page," Perelman said; "that's how we're reinforcing our position on issues and ensuring our employees really understand them.

"From the intranet point of view, this has helped raise the awareness and appreciation of Aetnet within the company," he added.

The intranet as internal activist tool as realized by Aetna is symbolic of the tool's potential. All it takes is management and communicators with the vision to apply it.

Leveraging Supervisors

In most employee surveys, when asked for a preferred source of information within the organization, most employees will point to their immediate supervisors. (The question is a flawed one, since it does not specify the focus of the information. If asked for the preferred source of information about employee benefits, the immediate supervisor probably would not make the top of the list. Nevertheless, even among organizations that ask for the preferred source for a variety of topics, employees select their immediate supervisor most of the time.)

Supervisors are rarely identified, however, as being the *actual* source. Companies make little effort to communicate directly with supervisors in support of broader employee communication goals. Organizations should recognize the value of reinforcing key messages with supervisors so that they have the correct answers when employees come to them.

Before becoming Qwest, US West, the telecommunications company, sent supervisors a weekly e-mail that covered key communication issues. As a result, supervisors were armed with the appropriate information when employees came to them looking for answers or opinions. Several companies have developed intranet sites for supervisors and managers where those with responsibility for staffs can get the information and resources they need when they need it.

Employees Connecting with the External Public

Employees can engage the public through activities such as the petition drive in the example above. But the Internet creates another

venue for employee interaction with the public. Employees can publish articles in discussion groups and engage in conversations on bulletin boards. They can even respond to media inquiries sent by
e-mail.

Organizations should not attempt to tell employees they are for-
bidden from talking about the company in an online discussion. As
the authors of the seminal book, *The Cluetrain Manifesto*, have made
clear, the line has blurred between your employees and your marketplace. For example, employees who work for a toy company may also
have children who play with toys. They may participate in a parent-
oriented discussion group (like the excellent communities at Parent
Soup, at *www.parentsoup.com*). In one of those discussions, the subject of toys may arise, and the employee—based on his experience
working for a toy company—may offer an opinion or cite a fact. In
all likelihood, the employee engages in this discussion from home
using his own computer and his private online access account. It
would be inappropriate for the toy company for which he works to
ban such activity. (In fact, if the employee says the right things, the
discussion could lead to improved perceptions of the company. Remember, people online prefer to hear a human voice rather than a
distilled, filtered, legally approved corporate voice.)

It becomes important, then, to ensure that resources and guidelines are in place—and clearly communicated—to help employees
understand their obligations:

↪ Inform employees of the various types of information they
should never discuss—online or off. This would include financial information that has not been disclosed (which could constitute a violation of Securities and Exchange Commission regulations in the
United States, or other regulatory agency rules in other countries),
proprietary information, and anything else that could damage the
company's reputation.

↪ Advise employees that they should never talk to the media
without first notifying the corporate communications department.

↪ Instruct employees to use their own e-mail accounts, and
not the company account, when engaging in non-work-related discussions. Even if they are participating from the office computer,
they can use a Hotmail (*www.hotmail.com*) or Yahoo mail (*mail.
yahoo.com*) account to disassociate themselves from the company's
domain name.

↪ Provide accurate information on various issues that are under discussion online so that employees can correctly portray company positions and other information.

Measurement

Volumes have been written about how to measure the effectiveness of an internal communication program. (I highly recommend *How to Measure Your Communication Program*, by Angela Sinickas, the leading thinker in employee communication measurement.) However, measuring the impact of internal communications on external outcomes is another matter. Certainly, quantifiable measures would be virtually impossible to identify beyond counting the number of speakers bureau bookings and the number of employees participating in specific efforts (such as letters to legislators or signatures on a petition). Look to qualitative measures, including:

↪ References to employees in media coverage of company-related events and issues

↪ The results of focus groups with external stakeholders that mention employee influences

↪ Linkages that can be drawn by inference between an employee effort (such as the Aetna petition drive) and the desired outcome (in Aetna's case, less reference by political candidates to the HMO issue)

Conclusion

Whenever employees can reinforce or derail an effort to influence other constituent audiences, opt for reinforcement. Take advantage of internal technologies, from the intranet to e-mail, to help employees understand issues, to be aware of the consequences of negative comments, and to support organizational initiatives.

Consequently, an internal communication component—including intranet and e-mail—should be built into virtually every external communication campaign.

Notes

1. *Employee Communication: The Comprehensive Manual for People Who Communicate with Today's Employees* (Chicago: Ragan Communications, 1996), 387.

CHAPTER 12

Activism on the Net

IF THE INTERNET has made it possible for anyone to publish, activists have embraced that capability with more fervor than nearly anybody else. It's not difficult to see why. The nature of the Internet makes it the perfect place for people and organizations with an agenda to drum up support from other like-minded individuals as well as people with only a passing interest in the subject. Existing groups promoting social causes and disgruntled customers—and everybody in between—can apply the potential the Internet affords.

Before the Internet, organizing an effort required activists to follow a fairly well-prescribed sequence of activities that began with an individual or a small core group handing out leaflets on street corners. From among the recipients of these makeshift communications, a few were likely to be sympathetic to the cause and respond to the flier. As the group grew, they were able to begin meeting in auditoriums that attracted more attention. The larger membership was able to pool its resources to buy promotion that was more effective. Eventually, the group would band together with similar organizations in other geographic locations to leverage its influence. The process could take months, even years.

On the Internet, the same process can occur in a matter of days or hours. Three factors unique to the Internet account for the speed with which activist groups can coalesce:

1. *The many-to-many model.* While traditional activist groups needed to use rudimentary publishing tools just to have fliers to distribute, the Internet allows for the distribution of high-quality material that is available to anyone who is interested, anywhere in the

world. There are no editors to assess the usefulness or appropriateness of the material. Good taste is not a prerequisite. Accuracy is not a requirement. All a person needs is a ten-dollar-a-month Internet account, a computer, and a connection to the Net.

2. *The receiver-driven model.* The mass-media process is based on the likelihood that the distribution of information to massive numbers of people will result in the message hitting home to the small percentage of the audience that is either already interested in the subject or finds the issue compelling. On the Internet, there is no need to distribute information to those who are not interested. Web pages with the key words *gun control* will attract those who have an interest in the subject (pro and con); nobody else is likely to go. Several methods exist by which activists can alert prospective colleagues to the existence of such a site, including careful placement of the site in various online indexes and announcements in topic-specific discussion groups.

3. *The Internet's global reach.* There is no need to identify the geographic areas in which interested individuals are likely to live, nor is it necessary to start locally and only later expand to larger geographic reaches. Instead, the Internet can compel attention from anybody, regardless of where an individual might live.

As a result, every activist group imaginable, on every side of an issue, has staked out territory on the Internet, from mainstream causes (for example, reproductive rights, environmentalism, and capital punishment) to the fringe (for example, white supremacy, Holocaust revisionism, and government UFO cover-ups).

Often, society's institutions are the targets of activist groups. Some organizations are obvious targets, like Planned Parenthood (attacked by abortion foes) or Playboy (which incurs the wrath of feminist organizations). But equally as often, organizations that are simply doing business can run afoul of a group with a cause. For example, in only one brief trip through the Internet one sunny Tuesday afternoon, I uncovered the following missives:

➷ A site promoting a boycott of Adobe Systems Inc. Adobe makes software that allows people to read e-text but prevents copying the text file. A software engineer in Russia worked on a product for his company that made it possible to copy the text file (in compliance with Russian law, which requires that programs produce a least one copy of documents). When the engineer visited the United States to speak at a conference, he was arrested by the FBI for copyright violation. Adobe was reportedly behind the arrest. The site calls for a boycott of Adobe and provides links to resources about the case.

↪ Another boycott, this one against Nike, has its own home page. The action is based on reported labor abuses at the company's plant in Vietnam.

↪ A site protesting a toxic waste site near the town of Killmark in the United Kingdom calls on people to "organize, organize, and organize."

↪ An online petition calling for the abolition of all nuclear weapons.

↪ "Five Reasons to Hate Disney," a personal diatribe against The Walt Disney Company.

↪ A "sucks" site (any site that follows an organization's name with the word "sucks," as in *acme_sucks.com*) about an insurance company that focuses on how the company treats its clients and its agents.

↪ A site that included a protest kit to help anybody interested in organizing protests against an individual deemed responsible for freedom-of-speech issues on a radio station. The kit includes ready-to-print flyers, signs, and guides for protests ranging from intensive activities to lunchtime actions.

In each case, the Web-based site was also the subject of some discussion on Usenet discussion groups. The synergy of the two Internet media reinforces key messages and targets new members.

Existing Causes

Causes that have been around for some time—whose existence, in fact, predates the Internet—have found the Net to be a worthwhile place to establish a presence. From their online venues, they can attack the institutions they perceive to be obstacles to the kind of change they seek to affect. From the environmentalist sector, for example, the Sierra Club—one of the oldest and most mainstream of activist groups—maintains a Web site. One section, called "Take Action," offers visitors the ability to send letters to targeted individuals who are in support of—or in opposition to—issues that mirror Sierra Club positions. The Sierra Club also is the focus of a Usenet newsgroup *(alt.org.sierra-club)*. Greenpeace also maintains a Web site, along with dozens of smaller environmental organizations. The National Organization for Women (NOW) and Planned Parenthood have sites, as does the National Right to Life Council. The National Rifle Association is online, as is The Center to Prevent Handgun Violence. In fact, virtually every activist and lobbying organization has established a Web presence. Electronic activism has come of age. Even the Webby Awards, seen as the legitimate recognizer of online excellence (the Oscars of the Web) has a category for Activism. The 2001 winner was Volunteermatch.org, but the People's Choice Webby for Activism went to ActForChange.com, a far less benign site that aggregates protest information on issues ranging from health and science, global affairs, and government to environment, family and education, and work and economy.

If your organization engages in any activity that might attract the attention of an existing, mainstream protest organization, you are likely at some point to become a target.

These organizations have become increasingly sophisticated in their use of the Internet as a vehicle for spreading the word and mobilizing the masses. Consider the Respect at LAX campaign, developed by the Service Employees International Union (SEIU) in an effort to unionize passenger service workers employed at Los Angeles International Airport. The effort had its own Web site called Respect at LAX. To draw visitors to the site, the union undertook an effective campaign of banner-ad placement on Yahoo, the online directory service. For example, a search for an Internet fulfillment company might lead to the listing of Gage Marketing Services, a company owned by AHL Services Inc., which is also the parent company of Argenbright Security, which employs security workers at LAX. Atop that page, a banner advertisement read, "Un-fulfilled," and urged readers to click the ad before doing any business with Gage. The advertisement linked to a microsite on alleged problems with Gage; the site also reinforced the relationship between AHL and Argenbright, and directed visitors to the Respect at LAX site. (When a magazine contacted AHL to learn how they were planning to address the situation, a company spokesperson responded with confusion; the advertisement had not been brought to the company's attention.)

Eventually, Yahoo cancelled its advertising agreement with the union and the company wound up permitting a unionization vote. As of now, entering the "Unfulfilled" address in a Web browser redirects visitors to Fly Safer Now, another union site aimed at Huntleigh USA, another airport security employer.

This example is hardly the only instance of labor unions employing the Web. Hungry for the means by which they can communicate effectively on limited budgets, unions have embraced the Web, as in the following examples:

⇢ *Alliance @ IBM* is the official site of the IBM Employees' Union. However, there is no employees' union; the site is dedicated to union efforts at mobilizing employees to form one, leading to collective bargaining. At one point, the site featured the image of a worker holding a sign reading, "I want a contract." That image appeared to the left of a picture of IBM CEO Lou Gerstner; the caption beneath Gerstner read, "I *have* my contract!" The text linked to information on Gerstner's income pulled directly from IBM's own proxy statement posted to the company Web site. The union used information IBM published against the company.

⇢ *Walmartyrs* represents another effort to unionize, this time focusing on employees of Wal-Mart, the global retail chain. The site features the alleged reports of employees who claim to have suffered sexual and racial discrimination. The site also offers updates on lawsuits against the company and even offers a streaming video clip of a news report on Wal-Mart employees in Cleveland who reportedly were strip-searched when some money turned up missing.

Activists are always seeking new ways to use the Web for their purposes. Take a look at DMOZ, the largest open effort to catalogue all the content on the Web. A noble effort, DMOZ recruits volunteer editors to handle categories in which they are interested to create an index that should, based on the size of the volunteer base, blow away the volume of sites indexed on Yahoo. But the volunteers can have agendas, like the one who listed Monsanto (which will be discussed later in this chapter) under the category "Society: Issues: Business: Allegedly Unethical Firms." How would you like *your* company or client appearing under that heading? (The popular search engine Google is among the search companies that subscribe to DMOZ for their directory listings, meaning you don't have to use DMOZ directly to find Monsanto listed under that controversial heading.)

What You Can Do

Not all existing activist efforts are housed within organizations such as unions and clubs. In many instances, long-standing activist-oriented publications marshal as much support for activist causes as institutions can. The magazine *Mother Jones* has led several liberal causes over the years, and continues its efforts on its Web site. Over a long period of time, the *Mother Jones* site ran article after article critical of Shell International (parent company of Shell Oil) for its environmental policy as well as for human rights issues centered around Nigeria.

Shell did not take the assault lying down. In response, the company bought banner advertising on the *Mother Jones* Web site.

Mother Jones's publisher, Jay Harris, told *Advertising Age* magazine that the Shell advertisements were unusual on the leftist magazine's site, which accepts advertising mostly from "companies that have positioned themselves as being socially responsible," such as the Body Shop and Patagonia. The ads did not merely direct readers to a page of text-based defenses. Instead, the link led to a discussion area on the Shell site; readers of *Mother Jones* were invited to engage in a dialogue with the oil company about the issues the magazine had raised. *Mother Jones* could have rejected the advertising, but elected to accept them with the following explanation (appearing in the MoJo Wire section of the publication's site):

> While we reserve the right to reject advertising that we believe is false, libelous, or hateful, we respect and value the right of free expression. We understand that Shell does not *need* us as a conduit to the public for lack of other opportunities. But we do not censor theirs or any other ads or attempt to shield our readers from points of view with which they (or we) might differ. Our primary goal is to provide readers with the most comprehensive information possible and allow them to make their own informed judgments. With that in mind, we are offering the selections below

from our coverage of Shell in recent years, along with additional information from other organizations.

Shell's Web site includes a forum area where users are invited to discuss the company's record and policies. We encourage MoJo Wire readers to participate and to give feedback on Shell's campaign. We also encourage you to tell us what you think of our decision to run the ads.[1]

Shell's example makes it clear that organizations can address traditional activist organizations through the Internet. Some other techniques to consider employing include:

↪ Monitor the sites of the organizations about which you know. Not only will you discover when your organization has been mentioned, but you will also get a better handle on the issues and agendas of the organizations that can conceivably turn public opinion against you. Armed with the knowledge of what disturbs the organization, you can mount an effort to offset the negative publicity. You may even wind up altering your approach to the issue based on what you learn from your opposition.

(When I worked for a pharmaceutical company, I began monitoring an animal rights newsgroup called talk.politics.animals. Animal rights activists are a natural activist public for a pharmaceutical company, because pharmaceutical organizations are required by the U.S. Food and Drug Administration to submit data from animal testing before they are permitted to begin human clinical trials for new drug treatments. After monitoring the group for several months, I concluded that the composition of the animal rights community was vastly different from the company's perception. That understanding led to a new position statement and a new approach to addressing the concerns of that particular public.)

↪ Provide information on your Web site that reinforces your position. Try not to approach the information defensively. Assume that individuals who visit your site with an interest in the topic stumbled upon the activist group's message and are curious to see your point of view. You're never going to change the minds of those who are active in the cause anyway, so you may as well focus on those who are still willing to be influenced by a candid, credible, accurate presentation of information.

↪ Be a regular lurker in pertinent discussion groups. Make individual determinations about whether to reply to potentially damaging posts, and if you *do* reply, determine whether to respond to the individual or to the entire group.

↪ If appropriate to the situation, invite dialogue about the situation in a discussion forum, preferably one that resides on your own site.

Instant Activists and Individuals with Agendas

Although traditional activist and protest groups have adopted the Internet as a new and important medium, the Net is serving an entirely new community of individuals and groups who have never before had the resources to communicate to a worldwide audience. These individuals and small groups represent a new frontier for organizations seeking to maintain their positive reputations, since anybody—for any reason—can lash out and raise opinion against you.

It doesn't take much for someone with a cause to organize a campaign to attack your products, activities, industry, or market. Start an online protest and you could even find it listed in a meta-protest site, which aggregates protest information from a veriety of sources. Examples include Protest.net, InFact.org, ActionNetwork. org, or CorpWatch.org.

Other sites have cropped up to aggregate protest and activism around a single issue. The site a16.org was originally built to coalesce activism against the World Trade Organization; it was one of the forces leading to the protests at the WTO meetings in Seattle. Now, the site addresses all of the sources of globalization and reports on activism and protest opportunities aimed at a number of organizations.

Case Study: NutraSweet

Activists led by an individual named Betty Martini have taken to the Web in an effort to discredit—and ultimately outlaw—aspartame, the active ingredient in the artificial sweetener NutraSweet. The activist group does not fit the mold of traditional groups; it has no name, no membership roster, and no meeting dates. Instead, online activists play follow-the-leader, taking their cues from others. Their issue is a belief that aspartame represents a health hazard, causing brain cancer, Parkinson's disease, and other illnesses.

These activists post attack Web pages; one flagrantly employed NutraSweet's own logo, changing the words so it read, "FDA Approved Brain Cancer." They lurk in discussion groups, ready to make their point whenever anybody innocently asks whether NutraSweet is a healthful alternative to sugar. In a thirty-day period in 2001, over two hundred messages were posted to Usenet newsgroups featuring the word *NutraSweet*. Since 1995, the number of messages posted (and still accessible) approaches twenty-six thousand. Most of these posts appeared in a newsgroup titled *misc.health.diabetes*, although some messages were cross-posted to other related newsgroups, such as *sci.med.pharmacy, alt.support.diet, misc.health.alternative,* and *sci.med.nutrition.* A variety of other newsgroups were represented, as well, but none so prominently as these. The nature of these groups indicates that people with a specific agenda populate them. A review of the newsgroups indicated a fair representation of activists, but most of the participants were diabetics themselves, or individuals seeking information on behalf of friends or family. And (embracing the market-sample-of-one model) the activists were there, waiting for them. They respond to articles that ask simple questions, such as, "Is Nutrasweet the same as aspartame?".

A typical article reads much like this one from Martini, whose activist-oriented posts make regular appearances on *misc.health.diabetes*, with cross-postings to *rec. food.drink, sci.med.pharmacy*, and *misc.kid.pregnant*.

> I have read in the last few [days'] discussions about aspartame reactions recurring again months after having ceased the toxin, and also with detoxifying and losing weight which you would expect releasing poison. I have mentioned in the past it is common to have a severe reaction should you accident[al]ly get the least little bit of NutraSweet or even another toxin. James Bowen, M.D., has discussed this with me on several occasions, and since he called tonight, I asked if he would dictate some information on the issue so it could be put on the list for all who have had questions. Also, please keep in mind that aspartame is not an additive; it is a chemical poison. The best way to understand NutraSweet is to think of it as a minute dose of nerve gas that eradicates brain and nerve functions.

Martini's single-mindedness is an example of how Usenet can be used by a single individual to generate an activist movement in a manner that simply was not possible prior to the development of Internet-based many-to-many communication.

Given the many-to-many nature of the Internet, those who disagree with the activists have an equal opportunity to convey their message. There are a number of posts that dispute the facts as presented by those who disparage NutraSweet, such as the following article:

Sorry, Betty, but you need to brush-up on your artificial sweetener metabolism and toxicology before you spread your hysteria around NutraSweet.

Aspartame (NutraSweet) is a dipeptide ester, which is metabolized in the gut and absorbed as its constituent amino acids, aspartate and phenylalanine, as well as methanol. MOST of the methanol (which you seem quite concerned about) is effortlessly and seamlessly excreted UNCHANGED because it's already very polar. There's no need for glucuronidation or sulfonation although some small amount of these metabolites might be formed, too. Oxidation to formaldehyde is also possible, but this is a reactive compound, existing briefly, the excreted metabolite being formic acid. Again, however, I'm quite sure most methanol absorbed from aspartame is excreted unchanged for the reasons stated above.

Now, does this mean anything to you? I doubt it. You (Betty Martini) probably produce more ENDOGENOUS methanol than that produced by aspartame use. Do you think that there is any relationship between the amount of pure methanol ingested and potential toxicities? How much methanol absorbed acutely causes blindness and how much will kill you? Do you imagine that several packets of NutraSweet taken over a day could provide this quantity of methanol? NOW, do you think your concern is realistic?

The problem is that the activists have an agenda and promote it proactively, while those who take issue with the activist point of view are merely reacting, responding to the messages that incite them to say something. Many people who disagree with activists will simply shrug and not take the time to reply, thinking that there is little point in doing so. For every article that takes issue with the activists, there are several that support the point of view. After all, people who have no issue with a product, or believe in a product, rarely have a reason to post messages in a discussion forum! In general, the majority of posts are clearly based in the opposition camp. As true believers, they will not be dissuaded by rational discussions undertaken by the company.

The company's best defense is to use its Web page (at *www.nutrasweet.com*) to promote the healthful nature of the product. The section of the site that offers the health-related information is not reactive. Instead, it is a simple presentation of facts, ranging from physician testimonials to official FDA records from the process the product underwent to get government approval. Although the activists will not be convinced, the consumer who stumbles upon the activist point of view is likely to want to visit the NutraSweet page to see what the company has to say. Their authoritative information stands a good chance of negating the malicious information that led them to check out the home page in the first place.

As shown in Figure 12-1, NutraSweet's site is loaded with information designed to instill confidence in its product and deflect criticisms levied by online activists.

Nike and Unocal are examples of other companies that have made their case on the Net, establishing special microsites within

FIGURE 12-1. NUTRASWEET'S WEB SITE ADDRESSING ASPARTAME CONCERNS.

their organization Web sites to address the human rights issues the activists have raised.

Rogue Web Sites

In the broadest sense, "rogue" Web sites (a term coined by New York public relations agency head Don Middleberg) are unofficial sites that address a company, a product, or other entity that is owned by another organization. Rogue sites break down into essentially two categories: those that attack something and those that merely appropriate intellectual property (such as sites established by fans of a television show or movie).

Fan Sites

Both categories of rogue sites have generated concern among organizations that make major investments in establishing a brand image, only to see them affected by a site that an individual with an agenda can build in an afternoon.

The sites built by fans and enthusiasts present organizations with a troubling conundrum. These sites are the online equivalent of fan clubs, and constitute a new form of free publicity. A search of the Yahoo! online directory revealed more than one hundred sites that fans have constructed dedicated to the *Simpsons* television show, with names like "100% Unofficial *Simpsons* Site," "Brian's Tribute to the *Simpsons*," "Homer Land," and "The *Simpsons* Simp-A-Rama." There are 860 *X-Files* sites, more than 1,270 *Star Wars* sites, and some 1,760 sites dedicated to *Star Trek*.

Although these sites are reflections of enthusiasm for the shows, they also incorporate trademarked and copyrighted images, and even sound and film clips. As a result, the Fox Network, Paramount Studios (which launched a campaign in 1996 aimed at some forty unofficial *Star Trek* fan sites), and Lucasfilm have been among the most aggressive at trying to shut the sites down, sending cease-and-desist letters from attorneys to the site owners, threatening them with legal action unless they remove the sites they so lovingly built. Mattel has taken similar action against builders of Barbie fan sites, claiming it needs to protect the trademark it has so carefully nurtured.

There is a legitimate reason to protect these trademarks and copyrights. Under the law, a company that does *not* enforce its trademark for a sufficiently long period of time can lose those rights altogether.

The risk involved in taking such action goes beyond alienating a core base of customer support. Not only will disenchanted fans turn against the organization seeking to shut them down, they will do so online, where their rants can be read by countless other fans, coloring their perception of the organization, as well. The online discussions of the actions will run the gamut from disparaging the poor treatment of loyal fans to claims of outright censorship.

Depending on the general popularity of the subject, forcing the removal of fan-oriented sites could be enough work to keep a full-scale law firm busy for years; for each site removed, another two or three could spring up overnight.

Lucasfilm is among the companies that have begun backing off the effort to eradicate fan sites from the Web. Consider the case of a Web site called TheForce.net, which draws as many as fifty thousand fans daily and features more than nine thousand pages of content assembled by some fifty-two staffers working in the United States, Canada, and Australia. The site is a volunteer site with no affiliation with Lucasfilm. Yet, Lucasfilm has not only allowed the site to continue but it has also established a relationship with the site. "The Force.Net is an example of our core fan base expressing itself. They're the foundation that has sustained this franchise for twenty-three years," said Lucasfilm's marketing vice president Jim Ward in an interview with the magazine *Business 2.0* (May 15, 2001 issue). "Star Wars has always been about a collective experience—people coming together to share what they love about the films."

"While there is cooperation, there's still conflict too," according to Joshua Griffin with TheForce.net. "They're still protective of their property. The guidelines are modified almost daily as we post news and information. But there's good understanding between us and the communication is open."

Figure 12-2 shows how Lucasfilm has established a relationship with TheForce.net rather than trying to shut it down.

Lucasfilm isn't alone. A number of companies are recognizing the value in their online user communities to help them enhance brand identity and generate buzz, not to mention strengthening the

FIGURE 12-2. LUCASFILM ENTERING INTO RELATIONSHIP WITH THEFORCE.NET.

relationship with this core group of fans (or, in some cases, customers) who serve as evangelists of the brand name—with or without the company's help or consent.

Guidelines for Dealing with Fan Sites

If your organization owns the trademark or copyright for an entity that is likely to encourage the creation of fan sites, avoid using a scorched-earth policy that treats all sites the same. Instead, evaluate each site. Do *nothing* if the site does not:

- ⮑ Use copyrighted materials
- ⮑ Misrepresent the entity
- ⮑ Potentially damage the organization's ability to earn profits from the entity

Except for the use of copyrighted materials, the situations listed previously do not necessarily represent violations of trademark or copyright law. Except for instances of copyright violation, assess the site to determine the degree to which it could damage your organization's investment. Only if it meets the threshold criteria you establish should you proceed to take other actions. Resist the temptation to immediately send letters threatening legal action. Ultimately, those threats can do your brand more harm than good. Try the following steps:

1. If a certain type of site seems to be gaining momentum, try to co-opt the effort and make it part of the company's official approach to branding the entity. Fan fiction, for example, has been a part of *Star Trek* fandom for more than thirty years. Since it would be impossible to stop the practice, the owner of the trademark can turn the fan fiction to its advantage, publishing the best efforts, holding contests, and promoting careers of promising talent. In this way, the company does not lose its hold on its brand, but rather brings the rogue efforts into the official fold.

2. Develop an official site from which fans can extract authorized images for use on fan-oriented sites. Use the official site to list acceptable uses of trademarks and copyrights, and to

explain why the company pursues efforts against unacceptable uses. Provide access to company authorities for questions. These are your best customers; they provide public relations that you cannot buy. Rather than alienate them, work with them so that their efforts satisfy their desire to promote their favorite entity while also meeting your need to protect the way your brand is presented to the public.

3. Use e-mail to contact individuals who built sites to lead them to the official site and to explain what your organization finds objectionable about their efforts. (When The Force.Net published a link to storyboards from the second entry in the latest *Star Wars* trilogy, Lucasfilm lawyers contacted the staffers, who removed the link; it was the relationship established between the company and the fan site that made it easy for the company to make the request.) Make it clear that you do not wish to inhibit the free expression of ideas, but that you wish to ensure that the brand remains as appealing for others as it did for the fans who built Web sites dedicated to it. Provide your telephone number (or that of the appropriate company representative) so the fan can discuss specific issues with the organization.

4. If these steps do not lead the fan to revise the site, send e-mail that expresses regret that the individual is putting the company in the position of having to take less agreeable action.

5. Only if the site threatens the brand and the owner of the site is completely intractable should you resort to legal action.

Attack Sites

Attack sites present companies with a different type of dilemma. The whole point of such sites is to turn the general public against an organization or its brand based on the disenchantment an individual feels. Such sites are much quicker to gain notoriety than fan sites. They can be built by:

➥ *Disgruntled customers.* The site Cigna Sucks was built by a Cigna insurance policy holder who had trouble getting claims paid. Whether she was right or wrong, she was able to use the Web to air her grievances. A similar site was aimed at Wells Fargo Bank, which was constructed by a customer who had trouble with a single check.

↪ *Ex-employees.* An ex-employee of First Boston Bank published proprietary salary figures on the Web.

Now, a consumer with a bad experience has a new recourse: create a Web site to tell her tale to the world. Figure 12-3 shows the Web site of a CIGNA policyholder, which was created to complain about the insurance company allegedly failing to pay a claim.

In addition, competitors can build anticompany or antiproduct sites. Even those looking to profit from your misfortune can take to the Web. When Firestone tires were implicated in a series of deaths and injuries, a Web site opened at *www.firestonerecall-legal.com.* Far from being a government site, or one launched by the tire company, the site was the product of a law firm looking for victims on whose

FIGURE 12-3. DISGRUNTLED POLICYHOLDER'S WEB SITE CREATED TO COMPLAIN ABOUT CIGNA.

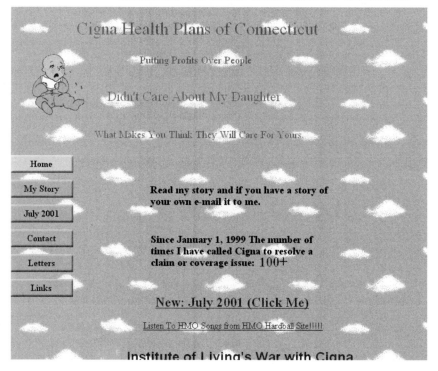

behalf it could file lawsuits. (You can find many similar sites—
www.tireaccidents.com is a site from a law firm looking for *any* tire-
related accidents that might make a good lawsuit; this site dedicated
a special section to the Firestone crisis.)

Virtually anybody with an axe to grind can produce a quick Web
page designed to denigrate your brand. And for those who don't want
to take the time or trouble to craft a Web page (or don't know how),
there is always the *Sucks500.com* Web site, which lists nearly every
company in the United States. Click on the name of a company and
contribute your own post about what is wrong with that particular
organization.

Many companies approach rogue sites by bringing the attorneys
to bear. The approach can be effective in removing the site. Despite
the fact that the Web provides a level playing field, allowing the "little
guy" to publish a manifesto, few of the little guys can afford the fees
associated with fending off a legal attack funded by a corporate entity. However, companies need to be aware that often it is only the
money that produces the desired results; the force of the law itself is
questionable. Companies cannot win a case in court simply because
somebody has made derogatory comments about them; the First
Amendment guarantee of free speech protects such comments. Instead, the law requires a company to prove it has suffered damages.
(Individuals are held to a lower standard in a libel case; they need to
show only that their reputations have been damaged.) Making the
case that the company has suffered damages specifically as a result
of an attack Web site can be difficult, considering organizations are
still struggling to figure out how to measure the effectiveness of their
own Web sites!

Furthermore, sending lawyers after purveyors of attack Web
sites can add fuel to the fire. In fact, the Web can add fuel to the fire
when the issue originates *off* the Web. That was certainly the case
with artist Tom Forsythe, whose sexually suggestive images involving
Mattel's Barbie doll led Mattel to file suit against the artist for trademark violation. The company spent two years waging its battle, which
led free speech and civil rights organizations to adopt Fosythe's
cause. One Web site, Creative Freedom Defense, went so far as to
publish some of the images in question, giving them far wider distribution than they ever would have seen had Mattel ignored the art, or
sought some other way to address it. (The artist, claiming his work

was parody and thus protected, won from a federal judge in Los Angeles the right to continue selling the art—at least for now.)

Many attack sites are the product of an existing relationship gone sour between the site author and the target of the attack. One insurance company, for example, was the focus of an attack site built by an individual whose claim was denied. In these cases, the customer often has tried a number of other avenues before resorting to the construction of an attack site. Building the site is a last resort, a means by which the customer can vent frustration and anger. More often than not, the source of the original dispute is a misunderstanding. Therefore, a site that appears to have been built based on a customer grievance can usually be addressed by solving the original problem.

Again, taking the legal approach does not always result in satisfactory publicity for the company, even if it results in the elimination of the site. For example, let's look at the case of a customer upset that his car, still under warranty, was not repaired. He received no satisfaction from the manufacturer or the dealer, and vented his frustration on a Web page. As a result, the dealer nullified his warranty and threatened him with a libel suit. He wrote to the *alt.consumer. experiences* Usenet newsgroup seeking help. In addition to presenting the situation in a new venue, he obtained advice about how to proceed from some knowledgeable newsgroup participants—advice that covered everything from ignoring the threat because the suit was not winnable to filing a class action lawsuit of his own. This is certainly not going to improve the public perception of the dealer that sought only to remove the negative site in the first place.

The best approach is to e-mail the site's author. The following templates can serve as a model for constructing your e-mail to the author of an attack site borne of a bad experience with your organization:

Templates: E-Mail to Attack-Site Author

↪ *Use this template when the Web site focuses on a case of perceived mistreatment:*

Dear [*insert person's name*]:
    I was recently directed to the World Wide Web site you have built, and was quite distressed to learn of your grievance with our company. The

circumstances you cite contradict the core values of our organization, and the approach we insist our representatives take with customers.

I hope you will give me the opportunity to rectify the situation. Please call me at *[insert your telephone number]* so I can get the details of your situation and take action to make sure we appropriately and adequately address your concerns and rectify any misunderstandings for which we may have been responsible.

[Insert your company's name] certainly respects your right to use the World Wide Web—and any other legal means—to express your feelings. However, we feel it would benefit both of us if we can achieve our ultimate goal of meeting your needs and returning you to our community of satisfied customers. I am looking forward to hearing from you.

☞ *Use this template when the Web author is not satisfied with a company decision:*

Dear *[insert person's name]*:

I was recently directed to the World Wide Web site you have built and was quite distressed to see that you have chosen to take your dispute with our organization public. I have researched the case your site addresses, and believe we can come to an amicable understanding if we have the opportunity to speak with each other directly. Please call me at *[insert your telephone number]* so we can discuss the situation. If the information you present in the course of our discussion warrants it, I will see to it that your case is reviewed.

Our goal always is to serve the interests of our customers and to adhere to the guidelines and rules by which our business is governed. I believe a candid conversation between us can resolve any differences we may have.

I am sincerely looking forward to hearing from you.

Activist Groups

Any group opposed to your organization's activities can take its complaints directly to the public by establishing a Web site. Those sites can simply protest your actions, or they can call readers to actions ranging from letter-writing and telephone campaigns to product boycotts.

In general, companies that find themselves in such straits have not undertaken two-way, symmetrical communications to begin with. The Web site is a symptom of a larger issue that needs to be addressed through the proactive, ethical practice of public relations techniques. Using legal tactics to remove a Web site will not suspend the group's activities or cool its desire to have your company stop the behavior the group finds offensive. It would be far more effective to move beyond the realm of the Internet and engage in a negotiation-based communication effort that results in victory for both the activist group and your organization, in the end turning the group into an organizational ally.

Sound far-fetched? Edelman Public Relations pulled off just such a victory on behalf of its client, StarKist Seafood Company (owned by H.J. Heinz). StarKist—the world's largest tuna canner—was among the tuna companies targeted by environmentalists based on the practices of tuna fishermen that resulted in the inadvertent death of dolphins. Environmentalist publicity had increased public awareness of the needless suffering of the intelligent dolphins, and a boycott loomed. Consumer opposition to the incidental dolphin catch soared, although research left it uncertain how the tuna-buying public would respond to price increases associated with changes in fishing practices. StarKist also would face potential opposition from fishing fleets to any change in policy.

The company finally agreed with Edelman that it should be the first tuna canning company to announce a dolphin-safe policy—that it would buy tuna only from fishermen who adhered to standards that minimized the risk to dolphins. Edelman and StarKist met with representatives of key environmental groups, as well as government leaders, before making the announcement. The actual press conference featured not only StarKist but also environmental group representatives who lauded StarKist's announcement.

Edelman claims the resulting publicity generated nearly a billion (that's not a typo—it is billion with the letter *b*) impressions in a one-week period. (An "impression" is public relations jargon that describes one member of an audience seeing and/or hearing a message.) Sales increased proportionate to the outpouring of customer support. The company was able to leverage its leadership on the issue through a variety of efforts, including the development of an in-school educational program. According to Edelman sources, the two-way, symmetrical approach helped StarKist turn a controversial issue threatening sales and image into a positive demonstration of corporate responsibility and leadership that led to improved business and overwhelming customer support.

Of course, not every negotiation will result in a complete reversal of your company's position on an issue. However, you usually *can* achieve positive results through direct negotiations with the activist public that is attacking your organization. At one time, I worked for a pharmaceutical company which, by its nature, was a target of animal rights activists. Most animal-rights organizations draw scant distinction between those companies that conduct animal tests because they are required to do so by federal regulatory agencies and those that test merely as a means of conducting research. The U.S. Food and Drug Administration *requires* pharmaceutical companies to submit data from animal studies before it allows a company to proceed with human clinical trials (which are required before a company can obtain approval from the FDA to market the drug). As a means of reducing the risk of boycott and other activist actions that could be aimed at our company, I suggested organizing a committee comprising company scientific personnel and representatives of mainstream animal rights organizations. The goal of the committee would be to research alternate testing methods that would satisfy the FDA's requirement for data that would prompt them to permit human clinical trials. Presenting a united front, the committee could submit alternatives to animal testing to the FDA. In the meantime, the activist group would recognize that the industry had no choice but to continue conducting its tests to develop treatments for debilitating human illnesses and conditions. Through its close contact with the company, the activist group would see that our approach to animal testing was humane, and that we engaged in such tests only when absolutely required by the letter of the law. (The company, sadly, did not agree with the approach I recommended.)

Any activist group that believes its concerns are being addressed in good faith will not take a grievance to the Web (or to any other public communication vehicle). Those that already exist on the Web are subject to removal at best, and revision at the least.

Case Study: Monsanto

Monsanto is the company most readily identified with the manufacture and distribution of agricultural products that manipulate the genetics of foods, such as grains, to grow products that are stronger, larger, or have greater yields. As the focus of violent protests, genetically enhanced foods have obtained the derogatory moniker "Frankenfoods."

Addressing the highly emotional antigenetic activism meant treating the Web not as a platform for building a single, static Web site, but rather as an "opportunity to create a dynamic network of multiple information resources, interested audiences, and third-party allies that can be leveraged to influence real world decisions and activities at the local level," according to Jay Byrne, who as the director of Monsanto's Internet Outreach Programs orchestrated the company's response. "The goal has been to redefine Monsanto as a 'life sciences' entity (versus chemical industry) on the Web and gain support for our biotechnology and agriculture products."

As part of its ongoing outreach and marketing to attract new and repeat visitors to Monsanto.com, Byrne and his colleagues undertook the following initiatives:

➪ The company established several Web sites targeting different stakeholders, including a Biotech Knowledge Center, which is a site aimed at teachers, another targeting farmers, and several country-specific sites. The company also established partnerships with owners of sites that embrace biotechnology.

➪ Updates on key biotech-related issues are posted daily on all Monsanto sites, ensuring that visitors get new information.

➪ The sites provide links to more than three hundred other Web sites that support biotechnology.

➪ Daily content updates are sent to Web content partners at more than three hundred sites on a daily basis. These include articles, background papers, and speeches, in addition to other content. These partners often post selected elements of these updates to their sites and redistribute key information to their e-mail lists.

➪ Subscribers receive biweekly e-mail updates with news related to the issue. These updates include news that both supports Monsanto's point of view as well as items that support activists' positions. Delivering a balanced update is critical, according to Byrne, to heighten the company's credibility. If the update (which goes to nearly twenty thousand subscribers) only included news items that supported Monsanto, only Monsanto supporters would be likely to subscribe to it, since Monsanto would be singing to the choir. Because the update presents unbiased reporting, the subscribers include the activists protesting the company's products and research.

➪ Monsanto's family of sites has chat rooms for issues where online discussions take place. In 2000, over twenty-seven thousand posts were contributed to those discussion boards in five different languages.

➪ The "Contact Us" e-mail is replied to within eight hours, generating nearly forty thousand messages in 2000.

Byrne noted that focus groups conducted to assess the impact of the online efforts reported that the company is viewed as "trusted," that it "respects" visitors to the site (regardless of their opinion on the issues), and that Monsanto was a "leading edge" company with "nothing to hide." The effort has been recognized with a Netty Award (sponsored by *Interactive Marketing and PR News*) for best public affairs Web site, best corporate Web site by the Creativity in Public Relations Awards (presented by *Inside PR Magazine* and *Reputation Management Magazine*), along with a variety of other awards and recognition.

Monsanto's Biotech Knowledge Center, shown in Figure 12-4, is only one of the many Web sites assembled to help address the issue of genetically enhanced agricultural products.

Cases of Mistakes and Misunderstandings

Some activist attack sites find their way onto the Web based on misinformation or misunderstandings. Shortly after the inaccurate Usenet post about Tommy Hilfiger (see Chapter 5), several sites promoting a boycott of Hilfiger products appeared on the Web. In these cases, it would be a simple matter to contact the site owners directly and inform them of the truth, resulting in the removal of the offensive sites.

Other Rogue Sites

Not every site fits neatly into one of the categories described in this section. I heard about a site that misrepresented the facts about a business. The company in question sent a letter from its lawyers to

FIGURE 12-4. MONSANTO'S WEB SITE ADDRESSING CONCERNS ABOUT GENETICALLY ALTERED FOOD.

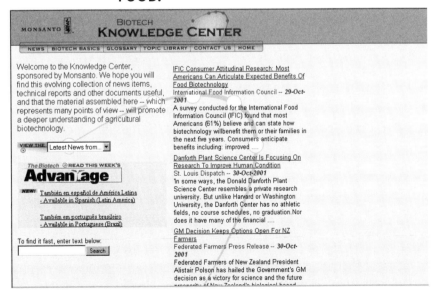

the owners of the site, who turned out to be local schoolchildren who had built the site as a class project; the information was based on their recollection of what their parents—employees of the organization—had said. Imagine the public relations disaster *that* might have caused! Organizations need to think before they unleash the lawyers. You have the following three courses of action open to you:

1. *Ignore it.* Consider whether the site is actually costing the company much business. Ignoring the site sends a message that the charges have no merit and are not worth the company's time and effort.

2. *Address the issues.* Use the company Web site to put a positive face on the topics with which the attack site takes issue. If the attack site disparages the quality of a company's merchandise, make information about the high quality of merchandise a prominent feature of your site.

3. *Take legal action*—But only as a last resort.

Then there is the case of overly enthusiastic employees, licensees, franchisees, or others with a relationship to your organization who build sites. I did consulting work for one company where I found an employee's personal Web site with two prominent features: One was his dedication to his job, featuring pictures of himself and his colleagues at the workplace; the other targeted his fondness for sadomasochistic sexual behavior. Nobody would deny this individual his right to discuss his sexual preferences online—sex, after all, accounts for about 7 percent of the pages on the World Wide Web. But it does not help the company to have its brand associated with behavior that a significant part of the consumer public might find offensive. In another instance, an independently owned gasoline station owner had developed a site that addressed the policies of the company whose name the station bore. There was nothing untoward about the remarks other than the fact that they were not official and did not accurately represent the brand image the company had spent considerable time and effort crafting.

In these cases, the solution is simple: Advise the individual who built the site of the problems it could pose for the organization. In the case of the employee, asking that either the company information or the sexually explicit material be removed should be sufficient. (If not, it becomes a matter for human resources to address as a violation of the employer-employee agreement). The latter case could be dealt with by providing the gas station owner with verbiage that *does* conform to the branding of the company's image.

General Guidelines for Rogue Web Sites

Regardless of the type of rogue site you encounter, consider the following alternatives to risking the fallout that could result from sending legal threats:

1. Assess the potential damage of the site as a means of measuring your response.
2. Contact the author of the site to determine the core reason for attacking your organization.
3. Offer to find a way to resolve the differences.
4. Make sure your Web site offers your company's point of view on any issues of substance addressed on the rogue site.
5. Provide material the site author can use that more accurately reflects your company's position or activities.
6. Use legal muscle *only* after all other avenues have been exhausted. (That way, you can always say that the organization tried to reason with the site author before resorting to more draconian means.) Make absolutely certain that the site violates a law that can be upheld in court. Do not use the threat of a lawsuit as a means of getting somebody to back down who is not violating the law but cannot afford to fight against the resources your organization brings to bear.

Discussion Forum Attacks

I was at a speaking engagement in Minnesota talking about the implications of the Internet as a communication tool to a group of electric utility managers. During a break, a member of the audience told me a story. He had bought a product, he said, that never worked properly. When he contacted the customer service department of the company that made the item, he was put through voice-prompt hell, and ultimately disconnected—not once, not twice, but three times. After the third time, he took his frustration to a consumer newsgroup on Usenet, not unlike the consumer mentioned earlier who took his complaint about his vehicle warranty to a newsgroup. Later that day, he found an e-mail message in his in-box from the company's vice president of customer relations. The message informed him that his experience was an aberration, a complete contradiction of the company's commitment to customer service. The vice president couldn't understand what happened, but was determined to find out what went wrong. He included his work *and* home telephone numbers, and urged the disgruntled consumer to call him.

As it turned out, the problem was traced to a snafu in the company's telephone system that was corrected within a matter of hours. The defective product was replaced, and the consumer received profuse apologies. He returned to the newsgroup, where he posted a retraction of his earlier message and applauded the company's sincere, dedicated, one-to-one customer relations effort. That kind of publicity is invaluable.

Of course, the vice president in question did not visit the newsgroup only by chance, see the article, and decide on his own to reply. It was, instead, part of an orchestrated effort to ensure that the company was not misrepresented or damaged by what people say in online discussions. Your organization can develop a plan, as well, that protects the institution's image and ensures that accurate information is presented in the global discussion of Usenet newsgroups.

Assuming you are using the monitoring techniques discussed in Chapter 5, you will know when somebody has posted an article to a discussion group that warrants your attention. At that point, use the following sequence of activities to determine if, and how, to respond:

1. *Assess the potential damage the post can cause.* During a demonstration of DejaNews as a tool for finding newsgroup references to a company, an audience member asked if her company—a major airline—appeared anywhere in the hundreds of thousands of articles available for searching. I entered her company's name, and found several messages dealing with the airline, including one that called for a boycott. Color drained from her face as she leapt from her seat, about to dash for the telephone. But a quick read of the article revealed there was no cause for alarm. The author was recently divorced, and his ex-wife had called the airline and instructed them to

transfer his frequent-flier miles to her account. His anger was the reason he was calling for a boycott. The few responses the article generated said basically, "You think you can start a boycott of one of the biggest business-travel airlines over this? Get a life!"

Clearly, this article does not warrant any form of response; the airline's interests are best served by simply ignoring it. You should evaluate each message based on:

↝ Its content

↝ The number of responses the article generates

↝ The tone of the responses

2. *Determine to whom will you respond.* If the article warrants a reply, determine how you will reply—either to the individual who submitted the article or to the newsgroup itself. Often (as in the case of the disgruntled consumer mentioned previously), individual contact can result in a swift resolution of the situation, leading to a converted customer who will sing your praises instead of damning your inadequacies.

TIP:
Keep Your Contact Virtual

NEVER make direct contact with an individual who has posted something to a discussion group or mailing list. (For instance, don't find the individual's telephone number and call to make contact by telephone.) People who post articles to discussion groups online perceive themselves as participating in a virtual environment. They expect all subsequent communications to come by the same means. Making voice contact can create a sense of disconnect that can alienate the individual, making it much more difficult to engage her than if you keep the discussion where it started—in cyberspace.

If the reference to your organization has become a general topic of discussion in a newsgroup, it may be more appropriate to make your statement to the entire group.

3. *Read the FAQs and lurk before posting.* Find the FAQs associated with that newsgroup before you say anything you may later regret. The FAQs contain all the pertinent information about a newsgroup, including the group's charter and commonly asked questions that already have been addressed in discussions that have gone before. (You can find a list of Usenet newsgroup FAQs on the World Wide Web at *www.cis.ohio-state.edu/hypertext/faq/usenet/*.)

Even after you have read the FAQs you should lurk for a while before submitting your own article. Lurking gives you the opportunity to make an assessment of the newsgroup. Is it a valid discussion area, or is it mostly teenagers sounding off? How seriously does anybody take anything posted here? How do people react to responses that disagree with what they have said?

4. *Don't preach; participate!* Newsgroups are virtual communities. They were well established before your organization was mentioned, and will continue to exist after the furor over the reference to your organization has faded from memory. Members of the community expect new contributors to behave like a member of the community. If you storm into the newsgroup like some sort of authority figure, you will earn the community's disrespect and possibly do more harm than good, even if you do manage to set the record straight.

Using a fictitious situation, let's take two different approaches to a response to a Usenet article. The situation: A hospital patient has been discharged after only twenty-four hours because (he claims) his insurance company would not authorize a longer stay. The early discharge led to medical complications. The article has led to a continuing discussion of the company's practices, none of them charitable.

Response #1

I'm a representative of Acme Insurance Company, and your contention that we don't care about the health of the people we insure is absurd. Your health is our primary concern. If you were discharged after twenty-four hours, it is because the considered opinion of our on-staff medical experts determined that additional hospital time was unnecessary and would be wasteful. It is not uncommon for complications to follow a hospital stay regardless of the length of the stay. To blame your insurance company for your unfortunate turn of ill health is to shift the blame away from the real reasons your health deteriorated, which may be less pleasant to face.

Response #2

I have been reading the posts that have been contributed to this group with some distress. I joined this group because I work for an HMO—the one everybody's discussing, in fact—and as part of the health care community, I wanted to get involved in discussions that could help me do my job better. I was, frankly, surprised to find my own company under discussion! Because I work here at Acme Insurance, I know that our first and greatest concern is for the patient, above all else, including profits. You can imagine how I felt when I read about your experience. I'd like to do something about it. If I can get more information about the specifics of the case—what hospital you were in, the dates, etc.—I can follow up and find out exactly what happened. If anybody else in the group has had similar experiences, I'd like to look into those, as well. I can report back what I find, and let you know what kind of action the organization is willing to take.

Which of these two responses is most likely to result in constructive discussion that ultimately could influence the online audience to change its perception of the organization? Of course, in the second response, the organization must, in fact, be willing to look into the allegations and take action, if appropriate (which is consistent with a public relations philosophy that embraces engagement of the audience and negotiation to achieve win-win results).

Using the Net to Address Offline Activism

Organizations can use the Internet as a channel for communicating information to individuals who are the recipients of misinformation. One company has embraced the Internet, e-mail, and other technology to help clients bypass media and attack groups and provide information directly to stakeholders.

Relations with the government and corporate audiences are often hampered by misinformation campaigns aimed at confusing and alarming the local citizenry, according to Michael Logue, CEO for E-Power PR in Vicksburg, Mississippi. "Corporate and government communications staffs are often limited in delivering their messages by media outlets that are not receptive to their message," said Logue. "The impact is continuing mistrust with local communities around plants and facilities."

Grassroots and national organizations undertake campaigns to attack government and corporate programs and projects. Responding to these campaigns, Logue asserted, can cost up to half a million dollars each in operational response costs, programs delays, and fallout associated with lost credibility, recruiting problems, and troop morale. In many cases, the entire program or project dies. "The attack may come from the media, a local individual, national groups, or politicians," he said.

The indirect communication techniques employed by most corporate and government communications teams have often met with mixed results.

"The strategic use of current technology re-empowers the communications officer to gain control of the information process using simple Web page templates and software already on hand—like Microsoft Outlook (an email program)—to provide information directly to a public that is already looking on the Internet for that information," explained Logue.

Other key benefits of using the Net include increased community credibility, relation building with key community leaders, and a closer bond between the communications and technical team members.

Logue has presented the concept to many corporate and government regional and national forums. The presentation covers the use of the Net to turn the tide on issues ranging from base and facility expansions to solid waste and pollution issues, how to use existing software and resources to combat misinformation campaigns, and how to use business processes (e.g., auto letter to the editor, address the press, auto signatures and auto-responders) to accurately deliver corporate messages and bypass the media.

"The excitement level for the new process is extremely high

across many corporate venues," Logue said. "Companies are finding they no longer have to lose the Information War."

Measurement

Use the principles of monitoring to assess the impact of online activism on your organization. You can assess the savings you have produced by communicating directly with these activists, or by ensuring that your company's answer to criticism is readily available and easily found. Undertaking this kind of monitoring often allows you to forestall crises. A solid method of measuring the impact of communication is to determine the money the organization did *not* spend on a crisis because it was prevented. Even as the Internet presents you with the challenge of an old West–like environment with few rules, it also affords you the opportunity to uncover crises before they emerge and save the company the cost of dealing with the crises after they become fodder for traditional media.

Conclusion

The Internet has opened the door to a new form of communication. As the many-to-many model predicts, individuals and organizations now have the power of the press readily available—all it takes is a computer, a ten-dollar-a-month Internet account, and a little time. Organizations need to understand how to address the material these individuals and groups can present to avoid the damage that can be done by responding as though the old one-to-many model still was dominant. Diplomacy can serve your cause far better than legal action.

Notes

1. Mother Jones Web site, *www.motherjones.com/shellednote.html.*

CHAPTER 13

Crisis Management in the Wired World

THE SPEED OF the Internet has changed virtually all aspects of public relations, but none more dramatically than how an organization deals with a crisis. Whether the crisis was spawned online or is the type of crisis that could have befallen any company in the days before the Internet existed, the Net has complicated the job of the public relations practitioner given the task of minimizing the damage.

Let's look at some of the characteristics of the Net that have taken crisis management into an entirely new realm:

- Anybody can create a Web site about the crisis, ranging from the company's traditional critics to previously unknown parties outraged by the situation or the company's conduct during the crisis.
- Anybody can participate in discussions about the crisis, ranging from employees (who could either defend or attack the company) and investors (including those who want to take advantage of the circumstances to short their holdings and profit from a downturn in the stock) to activists seeking to leverage the crisis for their own purposes and customers who speculate about what the crisis means for the company's ability to support its products and services.
- The media can publish articles about the crisis instantly. Rather than wait until the 6 P.M. newscast or tomorrow's edition of the daily paper, publishers (as we have already noted) are frequently opting to publish to their Web sites *first*. In other words, the story is available for readers as soon as the reporter finishes writing it.

↪ Upon hearing about the crisis, interested parties make a bee-line to the Web, often starting with the company's Web site. They look for the company's response. From there, they check the news sites, then the forums (which can often provide links to hastily constructed third-party crisis-oriented Web sites).

Managing a crisis was never easy, or fun. The Net has only exacerbated the situation. The first step in understanding how to plan for a crisis and how to act when a crisis is in full swing in this new online environment is setting the baseline. What is a crisis, why do they escalate, and what are the key elements in addressing them?

Understanding Crises

Before we begin, let me state candidly that this is *not* a comprehensive exploration of crisis management. That would require a full book, and several good ones already exist. (Some of my favorites are listed in Appendix E.) Instead, this section is designed simply to help readers understand the basics that will drive the strategies to employ online.

Also, it is important to add this caveat: Good communication will not save a company that behaves badly. Companies in a crisis brought about by circumstances beyond their control still need to behave in a manner that shows concern for the perceptions of their audiences. Those companies in a crisis they have brought upon themselves need to *change* their behavior if they are to have a prayer of regaining audience confidence. Effective communication will help companies adhering to these fundamental principles to get their message out, but even the best communication cannot salvage a company that is making bad decisions and doing bad things. A company raping the environment, for example, cannot use public relations to enhance its reputation. A contractor using cheap building materials resulting in a high-rise collapse cannot put a positive spin on the situation by employing communication tactics in order to wind up with a positive brand.

The Types of Crises

There are two ways to look at the different types of crises that can beset a company: One is based on *why* the crisis occurred; the other is based on *where* it occurred. In the second category, it matters whether the crisis began in the real world or online. In the first category, there are four types of crises:

Meteor Crisis

A meteor crisis is, as its name suggests, one that falls unexpectedly from the sky and causes significant damage. You cannot anticipate a meteor crisis, but when one hits, it can seem senseless, random, and terrible. Most often, the company suffering a meteor crisis is a victim; nothing the organization did invited this disaster. Nevertheless, the company stands to suffer a loss of confidence among its key audiences if it does not respond quickly and capably to the situation. The organization's ability to deal with the crisis determines how its audiences perceive the company—as responsive, caring, and decisive or as hesitant, heartless, and guilty.

Johnson & Johnson was the victim of a meteor crisis when an individual tampered with bottles of Tylenol pain medicine on store shelves. When an employee at a manufacturing plant ignores safety rules and causes an explosion, the company experiences a meteor crisis. An earthquake that shuts down operations is a meteor crisis, as is the often tragic scenario of a disgruntled ex-employee bringing a gun into the company's building to shoot those who he believes are responsible for his woes.

Predator Crisis

In a predator crisis, somebody is out to harm the company. Yet, even though the company is subjected to the schemes of this third party, the company is usually *not* a victim. More often than not, this kind of crisis occurs when somebody leaks information about something the company did that it knew was wrong. Anybody who has seen the movie *The Insider* knows what a predator crisis is—it's when Brown & Williamson Vice President Jeffrey Wiegand, distressed at the tobacco company's internal machinations, leaked damning company documents to the press.

An employee airing the company's dirty laundry is by no means the only kind of predator crisis. A company can find itself in these straits when a dispute goes public, such as secret planning to take an action to which certain audiences might object or when labor negotiations are going sour. When a company is caught failing to comply with a new government regulation, it is a predator crisis. When a law firm files a class-action lawsuit against the company, it is also a predator crisis.

Most crises are seen as short-term, but some—particularly those pushed along by a predator—can last for years. A labor union that strikes an organization will relentlessly continue to attack the organization, seek to build sympathy among the company's key constituents, and keep the company in a defensive, responsive posture.

The damage from a predator crisis can be dramatic. Your reputation and credibility can be tainted or even ruined beyond repair. After Wiegand leaked those damaging tobacco company documents to the press, nobody looked at the tobacco industry the same way.

Breakdown Crisis

A breakdown crisis occurs when a company fails to perform. This can often be the most difficult type of crisis to address, since the company caused the crisis entirely by itself, with no helping hand from fate or a predator. Consider a company that puts a newly hired employee into a dangerous job before the employee receives adequate training. If that employee fails to monitor a particular gauge because she never received the required training, and that failure results in a devastating explosion, the employee is not to blame—it is the company's fault.

Other examples of breakdown crises are less exciting to imagine than a plant explosion. Financial malfeasance is a breakdown crisis, because somebody in the organization failed to follow financial rules. It is a breakdown crisis when an employee circumvents the company's guidelines and breaks the law. A company that dumps toxic chemicals at night is setting itself up for a breakdown crisis, as is a company that takes manufacturing shortcuts that result in a product failure.

Most of the crises companies face are breakdown crises. Open the business section of any newspaper and you will probably find a company suffering through one. The dot-com world was shaken by a succession of companies that had to restate earnings because of a less-than-ethical approach to reporting sales. Any company that gets caught doing something it shouldn't suffers a breakdown of the policies and processes that are designed to prevent these situations from occurring.

Morphing Crises

Of course, a crisis that begins one way does not always end up as the same type of crisis. A predator crisis can easily become a breakdown crisis as the public's attention shifts away from the predator and toward the company's perceived wrongdoing. Even a meteor crisis can quickly become a breakdown crisis. An airplane crash usually starts out as a meteor crisis. ("Oh, my God, one of our planes went down!") If the postcrash investigation turns up that a mechanic falsified an inspection report and the airline was aware of the problem, then *wham!* The company is smack in the middle of a breakdown crisis.

One of my good friends and colleagues—a specialist in helping companies through crises—once worked with a beverage company that had to contend with an employee who was drinking the company's alcoholic beverages while driving a delivery truck. He wound up driving the truck into a crowd of pedestrians on a sidewalk, killing one and injuring dozens. Certainly, the company had a clearly articulated policy against such behavior. The company only hired drivers it believed were responsible. Who could anticipate one driver would break the rules? Although the company was definitely a victim in this scenario, it stood to suffer reputational damage as the public, media, investors, and other constituent audiences perceived a failure of the company in addition to the individual driver. Even though this situation is a genuine meteor crisis, the *public* perceives it as a breakdown crisis, and thus the company must deal with it as if it were, in fact, a breakdown crisis.

Why Crises Escalate

If every decision a company makes during a crisis is based on sound goals, strategies, and objectives, most organizations would come out of a crisis in reasonably good shape. Unfortunately, most organizations either don't consider these objectives or abandon them in the heat of the moment.

In fact, the management of most organizations tends to go through seven clearly delineated stages during a crisis:

1. *Surprise*. Management was caught unaware.

2. *Insufficient or inaccurate information*. Early reports are usually sketchy, delivered by excited, agitated individuals. They rarely offer a comprehensive picture of the situation, and are often riddled with errors. Yet it is to this information that management begins to react and make decisions.

3. *Loss of control*. Now information is coming in hot and heavy. The stock price is plummeting. Everybody wants to know what is going on. This escalation of events leads invariably to public scrutiny.

4. *Public scrutiny*. Now the media are pounding at the door. Customers are calling their sales or support reps to find out what the crisis means to them. The general public—as risk-averse a group as ever existed—wants information to find out how worried they should be.

5. *Siege mentality*. Feeling assaulted, executives circle the wagons, barricading themselves in their offices and conference rooms. The natural consequence of behaving as though one is under siege is to become defensive and perceive the audiences demanding information as the enemy.

6. *Panic*. In the old Western movies, circling the wagons was often the prelude to a massacre. Arrows flew between the wagons; some of them were burning, and soon settlers were either dead or dying inside the circle while the wagons burned. Executives under siege may well feel like those clichéd movie characters, and begin to panic. Panic leads to bad decisions.

7. *Short-term focus*. Panicking executives find it difficult to act in a manner consistent with the goal (survival) and objectives of a crisis management plan. Instead, they seek to put out the biggest fires burning closest to them.

Because so many companies find themselves going through these stages, they make decisions and take actions that do not serve their long-term interests or those of their stakeholders. These mistakes are compounded by some of the factors with which companies must contend that are inherent in any crisis:

↪ *Lack of credibility*. There is a natural inclination to automatically assume the worst about the organization at the center of a crisis.

Thus, everyone from the general public to news reporters tends to cast a cynical and untrusting eye at official company representatives.

↪ *Risk aversion.* The public is risk-averse. That is, most people will oppose any action that may put them at risk. Risk can be physical (fumes from a toxic spill), economic (as when a stock's value nosedives or when a breadwinner's job is threatened), or emotional (a loyal customer made to feel like a fool for standing by the organization). (A great recent example is the widespread abandonment of Democratic support for former President Bill Clinton following his last-minute pardon of a convicted financier that appeared to be financially motivated. For many Clinton Democrats, this was just too much.) Nobody likes to look like an idiot. Consequently, the public is inclined to believe any message that suggests an organization is creating or perpetuating a risk.

↪ *The media's role.* Traditionally, an organization relied on the media to convey its messages. Press releases were issued, press conferences conducted, questions answered, and statements made. Then, the company crossed its fingers and hoped the media portrayed the messages favorably to the public. However, the media's role is not to advocate on behalf of the company. In fact, more people watch the news or buy newspapers if conflict is at the heart of the story. As a result, a company's best efforts to reassure its publics can be dashed by a reporter adopting a "he says, she says" approach, weighing the company's efforts against the criticism of a third party, such as an activist group.

↪ *Advocacy groups.* Advocacy groups (another label for activist groups) will almost always exploit a company's crisis for their own purposes. Many executives may feel like these groups are kicking them while they're down. However, from the groups' perspective, the crisis is damning evidence of what they've been saying all along. Environmental groups, for instance, will be merciless in their attack of an oil company whose tanker broke up on the rocks of a shoreline and spilled oil into an environmentally precarious part of the ocean. Consumer groups will lash out at a company that has distributed a hazardous product. In many cases, these groups are not wrong (even if they are sometimes unreasonable, inaccurate, hostile, and even devious). But their view of the crisis is something public relations practitioners should assume.

↪ *Emotion, not logic, is at issue.* Far too many organizations engaged in a crisis try to deal with it by reciting facts and engaging in rational, logical debate. The executives at these companies are confounded and disappointed when these arguments fail to resonate with the public. But the public will *never* respond to logic during a crisis because a crisis is, at its core, an emotional beast. Crises are, in the minds of observers, characterized primarily by symbols, or visual images they can conjure in their imaginations that represent the core of the situation:

CRISIS	SYMBOL
The Exxon *Valdez* oil spill	Dying oil-covered birds
The Rodney King incident	Video footage of four policemen savagely beating an unarmed man on the ground
Tylenol tampering	Poisonous capsules on store shelves or, worse, in bathroom medicine chests
Dow Corning silicon breast implants	Women suffering incredible pain and medical conditions

Managing Crises

Following is an overview of the considerations for addressing an organizational crisis:

Objectives

In any crisis, all decisions, statements, and actions should be based on a set of objectives designed ultimately to achieve the overarching goal of surviving the crisis. These objectives include the following:

- Present and maintain a positive image of the organization.
- Deliver timely, accurate, and current information to interested parties.
- Remain accessible to key constituents.
- Monitor all the channels of communication to identify and address messages that are inaccurate or misleading.
- Maintain the support of the company's key constituent audiences.

The Basics of Responding to a Crisis

Some fundamental rules of crisis management, to which organizations should closely adhere to meet the objectives listed previously, include the following:

⮑ *Respond.* "No comment" is never an option. Always respond quickly, accurately, professionally, and with care.

⮑ *Never engage in debate or confrontation.* You'll lose. Publicly arguing with anybody during a crisis makes the organization look hostile, defensive, argumentative, and *guilty*. This does not mean an organization cannot present its facts and evidence. But this should be a simple, objective presentation—and not points to score—during a confrontation with the union, government regulators, local authorities, reporters, or (in the worst-cast scenario) victims of the crisis.

⮑ *Address the perceptions.* In previous pages, I have used the long-standing term *crisis management*. In fact, the use of this term is probably responsible for more crisis efforts gone wrong than any other factor, because it leads companies and public relations practitioners to believe that they can actually manage a crisis. The truth is that you cannot manage a crisis, because too many elements are beyond your control. What you *can* manage is the perceptions created by the crisis. To succeed, you must begin with an understanding of the symbols already embedded in the heads of your audiences and their natural responses to the crisis. Perception is reality, as any public relations professional already knows.

⮑ *Admit mistakes.* Once you know for a fact that your crisis is of the breakdown variety, you should quickly admit the mistake, and then note what actions are being taken to ensure that the situation can never happen again.

⮑ *Reinforce your values.* Every company has a set of values; many companies post these values as plaques on conference room walls. We've all heard them, and can probably even recite them: "We conform to the highest standards of ethical and moral behavior . . . Our customers always come first . . . Employees are our most important asset. . . . " When management finds itself mired in the seven stages of a crisis, however, these values often find their way into the trash heap. Consequently, the company's behavior during the crisis seems to directly contradict the values it has so carefully espoused all those years, making the situation even worse. In a crisis, your values count. Make sure that every action the organization takes and every word its spokespersons speak reflect those values.

↝ *Set your key messages.* After the Democratic National Convention in 1999, Democratic presidential candidate Al Gore had a commanding lead in the polls over Republican contender George W. Bush. In the months leading up to the election, Gore's lead gradually slipped until he finally found himself behind Bush and the loser of the contest. One important reason for Gore's failure to hold on to his lead was that he did not reiterate a key message, while his opponent did. Anybody asked what Bush's key message was would be likely to respond, "I don't trust government; I trust the people." What was Gore's key message? Nobody knew. He was all over the map, and nobody could pin a single idea to him. (You would think Gore would have learned from his boss of the previous eight years, Bill Clinton, who knew the value of a dominant message. Clinton won the 1992 election on the strength of one catchphrase: "It's the economy, stupid.") The same is true for an organization in crisis. Select a key message and make sure that it comes through loud and clear in every statement, press release, and interview.

↝ *Tailor your messages to address the "angry" party.* The angry party—the victims of an accident, the employees who have lost their jobs, the labor union, the customers injured using your product, the activists outraged by your behavior—is the reason the crisis stays in the public view. If the angry party can be satisfied, its concerns addressed, there will be little value in continuing to intensify the situation. Thus, your key messages should focus on the issues and perceptions of that group—which automatically means that you will acknowledge the angry party's concerns, rather than dismiss or ignore them (which, again, will make your company look arrogant, heartless, and insensitive).

↝ *Define your symbols.* Okay, the public has symbols of the crisis in its head. What symbols would you like the public to replace those symbols with? As noted earlier, the symbol of the Exxon *Valdez* disaster was (and continues to this day to be) dying birds covered in oil. Exxon's chairperson noted during the crisis that there was no point in his going to Alaska; he could do more to coordinate the company's response from his office at the company's headquarters in Manhattan. No doubt, this was true; it was also *logical* and *rational*.

The *emotional* response of the audiences watching events unfold was that Exxon's chairperson was cold and unfeeling; he didn't care about those dying birds. If, however, he had flown to Alaska and had his picture taken on the bow of the *Valdez*, flanked by two uniformed Coast Guard officers, gazing out at the damage, he would have appeared more sympathetic. And how much more important would it have been if he could be seen on his knees on the shore, cradling one of those dying birds in his arms? These images would have become the *new* symbols of the crisis, and Exxon's reputation would have suffered considerably less damage.

↪ *Set specific objectives.* General objectives have been noted previously, but each crisis will lead to additional objectives that are specific to the circumstances. If a worker has engaged in an act of violence in the workplace, one objective would be to portray the company as a safe and desirable place to work. In an environmental crisis, the company would want to protect the company's reputation as an environmentally conscious organization.

↪ *Establish metrics.* You won't know whether your crisis management efforts have succeeded if you are unable to measure their impact. You must know what success looks like. Some results are easy to measure: the strike ends, protestors vacate your property, or sales return to precrisis levels. Others require a bit more work: newspaper coverage of the crisis begins to take on a less negative tone, for example, or the company records a reduced number of hostile customer calls.

↪ *Leverage existing relationships.* Organizations that have established solid relationships with third-party groups can call in their chits during a crisis. Take, for example, a company that has worked hard to develop a relationship with a large, mainstream environmental advocacy group. The company has changed some of its practices based on input from the group. They meet regularly to review the company's progress. They negotiate in good faith. In the event of an environmental accident, the advocacy group will be less inclined to pounce on the company than if the relationship had been hostile, or nonexistent. A call to the group's leader would remind him of the company's good-faith efforts ("We're one of the good guys") and its intention to continue the relationship, explain the facts of the crisis, and explore ways the advocacy group could help the company get through the crisis.

The Company's Priorities in a Crisis

When the wagons are circled and management is focused on putting out short-term fires, companies are inclined to serve the wrong audiences, or to serve them in the wrong order. Too often, the rallying cry in the boardroom is, "Protect the stock price!" leading to efforts aimed at investment analysts and financial markets. Sadly, making shareholders the top priority almost always results in a devaluation of the stock price. Companies that want to protect their value should focus on their audiences in the following order:

1. The affected party or parties (the victims, if there are any)
2. The customer
3. Employees
4. Local communities in which the company operates
5. Shareholders

Johnson & Johnson followed these priorities during the Tylenol tampering incident. The company's first concern was for the individuals who had taken the tainted medicine. Its actions reflected that priority. Next, to protect customers and consumers, the company pulled the product from store shelves, eliminating further risk to the public. (Further risk was eliminated when the company promised not to return the product to shelves until a way could be found to make the bottles tamper-proof.) The company also issued advisories and warnings through multiple channels to those customers who may have purchased Tylenol. Interestingly—but not surprisingly—taking care of these audiences first is precisely how Johnson & Johnson addressed shareholder concerns about the value of the company's stock. In other words, take care of the top priorities first and the others will take care of themselves.

Crises Go Online

All of the principles outlined above are valid in the Internet age. However, the Internet has thrown two monkey wrenches into the works. Thanks to the Internet, the word of a crisis spreads faster than ever and rumors are easier than ever to start and perpetuate. The number of channels through which information (and misinformation) is communicated has exploded. Managing a crisis has become exponentially harder than it was before the Net hit the scene. But, also thanks to the Internet, organizations have new tools they can use—and, in many cases, they *must* use—to address the crisis, meet the overarching goals of survival, and return to normalcy.

Let's look at some of the new crisis factors the Internet is responsible for:

Publishing Is Instantaneous

In the early days of the World Wide Web, as traditional news organizations began developing their own Web sites, publishers adopted a position that the Web—this new medium used mainly by computer geeks and schoolkids—would *never* scoop the good old-fashioned newspaper. Most newspaper Web sites carried stories that had already appeared in the printed version.

As the Web becomes more pervasive—and is used by nearly everybody, representing no particular demographic group or groups—publishers have begun rethinking that position. In fact, some publishers are going so far as to redefine the business they are in. Are they printers of paper documents that contain the news? Or are they distributors of news through whatever channel gets it into the hands of the public as quickly as possible? In the 1999 "Media in Cyberspace" study, about 20 percent of news organizations indicated their Web sites regularly scoop their publications; roughly another 20 percent noted they sometimes allow a story to appear online before it appears in print.[1] Among the news organizations surveyed were the *New York Times* and the *Wall Street Journal*.

Previously, a company could count on a little breathing room before the public learned of a crisis (unless it was a really *big* crisis, the kind of disaster that prompts television networks and radio stations to interrupt regular broadcasting). Not so any longer. As soon as a reporter can get the facts and crank out the copy, the story can appear on the Web, in discussion forums, and in postings to e-mail mailing lists.

In fact, it is not impossible that the story of a crisis could find its way online *even if there is no crisis.* Some reporters will publish a rumor found online if they can get somebody to verify it; some (especially if they are under deadline pressure) may even go to press with an unsubstantiated rumor gleaned from somewhere on the Internet.

Everybody Is a Publisher

Trained professional reporters are not the only ones who can publish reports of a crisis in a heartbeat. Anybody with an Internet connection can spread the word, whether it is accurate or not.

Consider the nontraditional publisher we discussed back in Chapter 2. This is an enterprising, entrepreneurial individual publishing a one-person Web site that serves as the watchdog of an industry. When a company within that industry experiences a crisis, it takes the crusader a matter of minutes to publish information. Without the safeguards that are in place at mainstream news organizations, the information appearing on the site may be inaccurate, even deliberately false. Yet, the publisher of that site may have a loyal following of readers who, upon reading the reports, post messages to discussion forums, including a link to the watchdog site.

Audience Attention Is Fragmented

We've addressed audience attention in earlier parts of this book, but it is an important issue to revisit from the perspective of crisis communication. Before the Internet, it was not difficult to disseminate a company's messages. After all, how many channels were there for audiences to pay attention to? Three television networks, a couple local TV stations, local radio stations, a couple newspapers, a handful of trade publications, and you were covered.

Those comfortable days are long gone. The number of television networks has expanded, and cable TV has thrown another monkey wrench into the works. But the expansion of traditional media is nothing compared to the Internet. In addition to all the traditional news sites on the Net (CNN.com, NYTimes.com, MSNBC.com, etc.), there are countless new channels, and they continue to expand, it seems, almost hourly.

> ↝ *Nontraditional news sites.* It wasn't CBS or the *Washington Post* that broke the story of President Clinton's dalliance with Monica Lewinsky. It was the Web site of one man— Matt Drudge—who had no journalism training and who es-

chewed conventional journalistic practices. Drudge published every rumor that crossed his desk based on the philosophy that some of them were bound to be true. Drudge was not characteristic of *every* nontraditional site. Some are more responsible, like C|NET. All of them, however, are potential vehicles for communicating about your crisis—and for your critics to communicate about it, too.

➯ *Discussion forums and mailing lists.* If your company is publicly traded, I can guarantee that any crisis you experience will instantly become fodder for conversation on Yahoo!'s financial bulletin boards. And Yahoo! is only one of the homes for such conversations. Tens of thousands of discussion groups exist across the Internet, running the gamut from Web-based forums to the Usenet news communities that flourished long before the Web was launched. As if that is not enough, there are even more mailing lists than there are discussion forums. (See in Chapter 3 for more information about mailing lists and discussion forums.)

➯ *Activist sites.* Don't assume that activist groups opposed to your practices won't use their own sites to communicate your messages (spun to accommodate the group's point of view, of course). Every allegation of unfair labor practices in third-world countries by apparel companies quickly finds its way to the sites of groups working to put an end to such practices.

➯ *Individual sites.* Anybody with something to say about your situation may feel free to publish his or her opinions on a personal site—and state them as fact!

➯ *Search engines and portals.* Many Web users don't automatically turn to a particular site for news and information. Instead, they launch a search using key words, hoping to be able to select the best resource from among the many available. Complicating matters is the fact that many of these portals, such as Yahoo!, offer their own news feeds, often through a contractual relationship with a wire service such as Associated Press or Reuters.

➯ *Blogs.* It sounds like an alien species on *Star Trek*, but *blog* is a relatively new term, a hybrid of "Web log." Individuals by the scores are maintaining daily logs, which include sites and online articles of value they've seen. It is becoming increasingly common for people to find a blog they like to serve as their guide to useful online content—just one more obstacle to getting your content in front of the audiences that matter.

With thousands of sites carrying information about your crisis—not to mention the online channels of traditional media—the audiences you need to communicate with are harder than ever to reach. Nobody is reading *all* of these messages—nobody has the time! Individuals pick and choose the channels they will pay attention to, based on how credible they find the channels to be (which is, in turn, based on an individual's point of view—a twenty-year-old vegetarian will pay more attention to news posted on the site of People for the Ethical Treatment of Animals than he will to the coverage offered on CNN or the site of a group of scientists engaged in animal testing).

Traditional Channels Still Exist

All of the attention you must pay to the Internet is additive—that is, you have to handle the Internet side of crisis communication *in addition* to the traditional channels. While a significant portion of the population is out there forming their own opinions based on their online activities, the people who still count on old-fashioned journalists and opinion-makers are still out there.

Your Credibility Isn't What It Used to Be

It's worth repeating: In the wired world, credibility is earned based on what you say, not who you are. Organizations once had some built-in credibility based on the fact that they were, well, organizations. If General Motors or Chase Manhattan Bank *said* it, there was a good chance at least some of it was true. Besides, what did people do when they read something questionable released by a reputable company? What they *didn't* do was rush to the library and hit the *Reader's Guide to Periodical Literature!* Today, however, it is easy to key a few words into a search engine and find plenty of material to contradict a company's point of view. Even journalists, according to the Middleberg/Ross "Media in Cyberspace" study, are more likely to accept the credibility of an objective third-party site (such as that of an established advocacy group) than that of a corporation.

Since, in a crisis, audiences already view corporate representatives with heightened skepticism, this general decline in the wired public's inclination to believe what a company has to say is worth keeping in mind.

The Public Has Grown More Cynical

For a variety of reasons, the public—including audiences vital to a company's survival of a crisis—has become increasingly cynical about what business has to say. Frankly, business has only itself to blame for this situation. Between an ever-decreasing emphasis on individuals, the maddening focus on quarterly earnings (about as short term as it gets), and companies that have simply done a lousy job of earning public confidence—along with all the verbiage that has characterized an organization's face to the public (satisfaction guaranteed, etc.)—the publics that matter have adopted a healthy "prove it" attitude.

Certainly, not every company is engaged in questionable business practices. Most businesses are run ethically by people who are working to do the right thing. But the few companies that misbehave are the ones that get attention. The media cover their foibles and consumers take to the Net to rail against their policies. It is definitely unfair, but business-at-large has been painted with the same brush.

Precrisis Planning

Even without the Internet, companies should plan and rehearse how they will deal with a crisis when (not if) one inevitably strikes. Most of the elements of precrisis planning are covered in books dedicated to the subject. But, because the vast majority of companies have no crisis plan, let's review the basics anyway, along with the implications the Net has added to the mix:

Be Aware of the Crises That Can Happen

Every company should know the issues that could result in a crisis. No company can know *every* crisis that can befall it. By definition, crises are surprises. Still, companies can anticipate many things that can go awry. There are two basic categories to consider are:

1. *Situations inherent in the company's operations.* If the company operates a manufacturing facility, it should be obvious that employees can be injured and equipment can malfunction. Airlines prepare for horrifying and rare—but inevitable—crashes. What kinds of situations are possible because of the type of business you are in?

2. *Situations that arise from issues associated with your business.* Because pharmaceutical companies engage in animal testing, animal rights activists will find them. Because oil companies have an impact on the environment, environmentalists will take issue with them. Health Maintenance Organizations need to control health-care costs, but consumer groups will object. Unpleasant as they may be to think about, you need to understand the issues inherent in your organization's operations.

These days, knowing the issues isn't enough. You also need to know where the people who matter will be discussing those issues. Find the mailing lists and discussion forums so that you can monitor the tone of the discussion and track the response to your messages— and where you may need to engage in some interaction with participants on behalf of your organization. You also need to know which Web sites will cover your crisis.

To be truly prepared, you should already be monitoring these forums. You could try to conduct such monitoring in-house, but that would be time-consuming beyond anything you've ever experienced. Instead, you should monitor the key influential discussion groups and mailing lists, but outsource monitoring of all online discussion to an outside company that specializes in this activity and has the resources to make it happen. (Monitoring is discussed in more detail in Chapter 5.)

Develop a Crisis Plan and Rehearse It

Knowing what can go wrong will provide you with all the fodder you need to craft a plan to address audience concerns when a crisis happens. Who says what? To whom? When? Who makes decisions about the messages? What happens if key people are out-of-pocket—if, say, an earthquake takes out corporate headquarters—who makes decisions and speaks for the organization in that case?

Once a plan has been developed, don't let it sit on a shelf. Rehearse it at least once a quarter, involving all key participants. Most airlines take such rehearsals for granted.

Thanks to the Internet, part of your planning should include identifying and monitoring discussion of the crisis and response to your actions. In your drills, make sure one or two comments are posted to a fictitious discussion group that requires a reply from the company to test how quickly a useful answer can be posted.

Finally, make sure you have your own Web strategy in place. Prepare templates that are ready for you to populate with content when a crisis hits; call it your Crisis Page. Don't link to it from anywhere until the crisis hits; then, add a simple link to your home page to allow visitors to get the information they need with one click.

Case Study: Templates and Dark Pages

U.S. Forest Service. "We have a Web template that we take with us on national incidents which are of a size and complexity to warrant calling out a national inter-agency incident management team," according to Sheela McLean, who works in communication services for the U.S. Forest Service in Juneau, Alaska. "That means big forest fires, floods, earthquakes, hurricanes, etc." McLean noted that the incident-specific Web site has worked wonders for Pacific Northwest's national team, helping to centralize accurate, detailed up-to-the-minute information. "It also allows us to speak in a consistent voice to hundreds of thousands of sometimes frightened or worried people at one time, not to mention giving consistent background information to our friends, families and the media."

Because the template is prepared in advance to have content plugged into it, a site can be up and running in only a couple of hours, McLean said. Once the incident is over, the site is archived.

Case Studies: Linking to Crisis Content

UPS. When faced with a pilot's union strike following a lengthy labor dispute with the Teamsters Union, UPS knew it had to restore customer confidence. On its home page, it added a link to a page where visitors could find regularly updated information about the negotiations, including the first date that deliveries could be affected (sending the message that customers could safely continue to send packages through that date), the types of services that would (and would not) be affected, and other useful information.

BankOne. On its home page, BankOne maintains a space for major news and announcements. If there is no major news, the space remains blank; text appears only when the company has something important that it needs to make prominent.

Southern California Edison. During the California power crisis of 2001, Southern California Edison incorporated code onto its home page so that a separate, smaller window launched whenever the home page was opened. This window directed visitors to a wealth of information about the situation and Edison's response to it without requiring any changes to the home page itself.

Figure 13-1 shows how visitors to Southern California Edison's Web site saw

FIGURE 13-1. WEB SITE PROVIDING LINKS TO INFORMATION ABOUT CALIFORNIA'S ENERGY CRISIS.

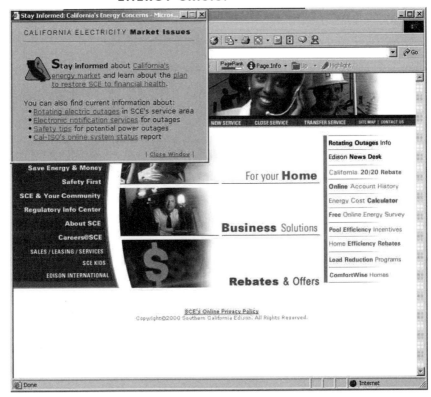

a special window open providing links to information pertaining to the California energy crisis.

There is no limit to the number of Web sites that do not address the crises their companies are experiencing. Usually, these sites are managed by the company's marketing department, which doesn't want a bad word spoken on their upbeat, profit-motivated sites. Although this approach may seem sensible (who would buy a product from a company that has a huge recall notice smack-dab in the middle of its home page?), it is actually counterproductive. Upon hearing about a crisis, many members of your audience will turn to your Web site to see what you are doing about it. If they see nothing, they could think you are doing nothing, not acknowledging the situation, or even covering up aspects of the crisis. If the site is your company's online presence, ensure that you are ready to post information immediately.

Your templates should make it possible to quickly add all manner of material that may emerge from the crisis. We'll talk about it in detail later in this chapter, but some examples include legal documents that have been filed, the text (or even audio/video files) of speeches and press conferences, and official government documents.

Don't limit your templates to the World Wide Web. Remembering that employees are among your key audiences, you should ensure that similar templates exist on your intranet, and that the crisis plan includes updating the intranet at least as quickly as you update your Web site.

One of the best approaches to addressing a crisis on an intranet is to include a list of links to all relevant content. On the intranet, companies maintain a great deal of content that employees can use during a crisis. By way of example, let's look at a product recall. You can create links to policy information, pertinent passages from customer service materials, even instructions posted to show mechanics how to remove and replace a defective part. Imagine a reporter calling you and asking, "What happens to the defective part once it has been removed?" Under pre-intranet guidelines, you probably would have responded, "What's your deadline; I'll have to get back to you," after which you would have started making telephone calls to find out the answer. If a page of crisis-related links is available, however, you can click to that information and provide the reporter with an answer in a matter of minutes.

If you provide opt-in communication tools (see chapter 3 for more information on permission-based communications), you have a built-in audience already receiving your messages. Include your key crisis messages in these e-mails.

Case Studies: Opt-In Communications

Edison International. Edison International, the parent company of Southern California Edison, invites investors and investment analysts to subscribe to its e-mail update, which offered updates about the California energy crisis.

Verizon. Verizon, the telephone company, allows reporters and editors who subscribe to receive only those e-mail press releases related to their areas of interest. Those reporters that cover an aspect of Verizon's business facing a crisis would automatically receive the company's messages in related releases, speeches, and other communiqués to which the reporter/editor has opted in. (See details in Chapter 6.)

Educate and Involve Your Key Partners

In most companies, company lawyers must bless every word uttered to constituent audiences during a crisis. Doesn't it make sense, then, to bring the legal staff into the crisis planning process? They need to understand that the consequences of remaining silent may well outweigh the risks of speaking out. They should become partners in the process rather than obstacles.

The same is true of other internal functions, depending on the nature of the organization. Identify those partners and ensure that they participate fully in the planning and drills.

Address Your Issues Before They Become Crises

If you know what issues could blow up in your face, your Web site provides you with an opportunity to establish a record and a position well in advance of any problems that may arise. Use your Web site—at the very least use the media relations component of your Web site—to make your positions clear.

Case Studies: Establishing Positions on Issues

Hewlett-Packard. The high-tech manufacturing company Hewlett-Packard (HP) covers a variety of key issues in its online newsroom, including its trade policies. Since the company manufactures the type of high-tech equipment the U.S. Government wants to keep out of the hands of its enemies, real or perceived news of a breach of security could send reporters to HP to assess the risk of the company's sensitive equipment falling into the wrong hands—especially since reporters covering HP already know that the company maintains operations in the People's Republic of China. In its online newsroom, HP goes to great lengths to explain its relationship with China, the role of the World Trade Organization, the company's history in China, and the types of products it sells there.

Verizon. In its Web-based pressroom, Verizon maintains a public policy section. Reporters covering the dangers of talking on a cell phone while driving can find the company's position and a wealth of other information there, from white papers to research results.

Build Special Crisis Microsites

When a crisis is in full bloom, it could serve you well to build a microsite dedicated to the crisis. If you have a crisis template, the page you developed from the template in the early stages of the crisis will serve as a springboard to a fuller, more detailed site.

One of the benefits of a dedicated microsite is the ability to create sections that target specific stakeholders. For example, when Alaska Airlines lost an airplane in a crash off the coast of California, the airline's microsite created a special section dedicated specifically to victims' family members; that section took an approach that was considerably different in its tone and presentation than the section of the site aimed at media. The media component of the site included information on the hours that media representatives were available.

The microsite established during the Kosovo crisis by the International Red Cross presents another example of how a site can target different audiences and meet specific objectives for each.

Case Study: International Red Cross Crisis-Specific Microsite

When war broke out in Kosovo in March 1999, the International Red Cross and Red Crescent Movement launched a major humanitarian operation. Hundreds of staff and volunteers were mobilized from around the world to deliver food to the displaced, trace missing persons, and provide medical aid for the wounded.

However, the Web site of the International Committee of the Red Cross (ICRC), the leading Red Cross agency in the operation, was not prepared to support the new action.

"We had the information on Kosovo spread throughout our site and five clicks from the home page," said Glenn O'Neil, communication advisor at the ICRC. "Our first action was to make the information accessible and relevant."

The number of visitors to the ICRC Web site increased suddenly by about 300 percent as the crisis escalated—a clear sign that the ICRC had to adjust its Web site to match the level of interest and to support the humanitarian operations that had been launched.

"We had journalists calling for interviews, relatives looking for family members and local Red Cross branches calling asking how they could help," said O'Neil. "We had to act quickly to use the Web to alleviate the heavy demand for information."

Within the space of several days, a new microsite was assembled, accessible directly from the ICRC home page via a special banner. The strategy focused on the following three objectives:

1. Providing real-time information
2. Supporting people and organizations wanting to help
3. Providing an online service for people affected by the war

A major challenge for the Red Cross was ensuring that information fresh from field operations was available and posted online. There was great interest in what the Red Cross was doing, where it was active and the challenges it was facing. So the ICRC, together with its sister organizations, the International Federation and local Red Crosses, put together a daily report on its activities, which was posted on the microsite. This update provided key stakeholders with current information, communicating that the Red Cross was actively aiding the victims of the fighting.

For people and organizations wanting to help, the Web site made it possible to donate directly from the site and designate the donation to go to the Kosovo operations. In addition, for those wanting to provide goods or food, guidelines were published, detailing what was needed and how it should be delivered.

In any major crisis situation, the Red Cross traces missing persons to reunite those separated during fighting. An Internet service, Family News Network, was launched for the Kosovo crisis. Family members could search a database online to locate relatives, send messages to them, or register their details on the database. The network was coordinated through Red Cross staff working in refugee camps and various *ad hoc* accommodation centers where displaced persons were staying.

As the crisis continued, the Red Cross worked on constantly improving the microsite by adding new features such as human interest stories, FAQs, maps detailing Red Cross actions, and a photo gallery of current activities.

"Our site was often mentioned in media coverage on the Internet and the war, from the *Financial Times* to *Yahoo Internet Life*," said O'Neil. "More importantly, thousands of people used the site to locate family members. The two sides involved in the war—NATO and Yugoslavia—were both consulting our site based on the feedback we got from our field staff. We felt our voice was heard through the Internet."

With the war officially over in July 1999, the ICRC scaled back the microsite and incorporated the content into its main site. However, the experience was not forgotten—a similar model was used for the next crisis awaiting the Red Cross in East Timor.

The Tools of Online Crisis Communication

When a crisis occurs, companies need to apply their precrisis planning to the details of the existing circumstances. The precrisis work ensures that the company knows what to do in the broad sense. The specifics, of course, will vary depending on the nature of the crisis. But in every crisis, the same tools are available and should be applied.

The World Wide Web

Consider the following three types of Web sites when communicating about your crisis:

1. Your company site
2. A special site you create dedicated to the crisis
3. The sites of your supporters, advocates, and allies

Your Company Site. Because the Web is a so-called pull medium— one in which people extract the information they want when they want it—it is likely that interested parties will flock to your site as soon as they learn your organization is at the center of a crisis. Responding quickly by making information available is critical. Ensuring that the information is complete, detailed, and accurate should be a given.

Of course, you should never provide information that hasn't been verified. If, in the early stages of a crisis, you only know a few things, then those few things are all you should post—along with a clear promise that you will update information as soon as it becomes available.

Case Study: Using Your Web Site

Napster. Everyone has heard of Napster, the file-sharing service that incurred the wrath of the Recording Industry Association of America (RIAA). As the company struggled to retain the loyalty of its users (in the face of emerging sites that offered the same capability without the threat of a court-imposed shutdown) and the interest of investors, it used its site to plead its case.

Napster was using its home page to convey the latest information about its legal struggles. In addition to a summary of the most recent legal doings, the home page offered a quote voicing support from an industry insider (with links to more in a section of the site called "Speak Out," where quotes from artists and other industry representatives provide additional support).

The Press Room is where reporters can find Adobe Acrobat (PDF) files of legal documents related to the case, along with press releases and links to coverage about the case from other media, including daily newspapers and industry magazines.

A Special Crisis Site. A simple link on the home page can link to a special site dedicated to the crisis. This is different than a home-page link to a single page. Instead, this is a comprehensive site that includes a wealth of resources about the crisis.

You can gain several advantages using this approach, not the least of which is that other organizations will be inclined to provide a link from their content to your crisis page—leading visitors to the site where you have worked so diligently to ensure that your organization's message is clear.

One of the challenges of maintaining such a site is the need for objectivity. Although you need to ensure that your company's point of view is well represented, you must also offer the other side's information.

Case Studies: Crisis-Specific Sites

Microsoft. When the U.S. Justice Department filed antitrust charges against the giant software company, Microsoft's response included building a side as part of its Web presence dedicated to the antitrust issue. Because of the comprehensive nature of the site, it became a resource for journalists working the story—a rare thing for a company-sponsored site, and especially for a company perceived to be as biased as Microsoft. But the site is so rich in resources—both favorable and unfavorable to the company's point of view—that reporters came to view it as an unbiased source of information.

The information resides in the company's PressPass section, under "Legal News." In addition to the latest news about the situation, a DOJ Antitrust Trial box links to comprehensive archives, including a chronology, key court decisions, appeals, final judgments, findings of fact, conclusions of law, trial transcripts, defense exhibits, Microsoft witnesses, deposition transcripts, an index of legal filings, and background information. Reporters would be hard-pressed to find such complete resources anywhere else.

Microsoft isn't entirely unbiased, of course. That is why the company also has produced a separate subsite, called the Freedom to Innovate Network, to promote its point of view. Even this site includes links to the resources in the PressPass. But it is the content that supports the company that makes the site stand out as a special site dedicated to a crisis.

From the home page, visitors link to the Freedom to Innovate Network by clicking on the words *DOJ Versus Innovation*. Once at the dedicated subsite, visitors learn that "a non-partisan, grassroots network of citizens and businesses who have a stake in the success of Microsoft and the high-tech industry" maintain the site. Here, visitors can get answers to frequently asked questions, learn about Microsoft's relationship with other companies around the world, obtain summaries of key policy issues (such as privacy and copyright protection), and read comments from elected representatives, legal experts, opinion leaders and think-tank scholars, economic and industry experts, editorialists and commentators, and businesspeople and consumers.

A highlight of the site is the ability to sign up to send e-mail to your elected officials directly from the site. The site also features a newsletter and links to the PressPass archive of trial documents.

Pacific Gas & Electric (PG&E). Linked directly from PG&E's home page, consumers in Northern California—the market PG&E serves—can find a plethora of information and resources designed to create greater understanding of the issues and help consumers deal with the fallout of the crisis. In addition to FAQs, this portal includes the following categories:

- What is going on and how did we get here?
- What is PG&E doing?
- News from around the state.
- What can you do?
- Keeping track of the latest news (links to other related sites).
- More information (listing of key players, etc.).

Third-Party Sites. Approach your allies, partners, supporters, and others who agree with your point of view about getting the word out through their sites. This "market sample of one" approach ensures your message is seen where audiences look for information, even if they don't find your site.

Measurement

The cost of a crisis to a company goes far beyond dollars and cents. The cost in reputation, future goodwill, and other intangibles translates ultimately into bottom-line values. You can use the Internet to mitigate these costs—and measurement is not difficult. You can survey your publics to determine how well your Net efforts contributed to the dissipation of the crisis.

Other measures to employ include the following:

- ➷ Monitor media access to your crisis site.
- ➷ Categorize and analyze the public responses you receive at your crisis-dedicated e-mail address.
- ➷ Determine how much of your crisis material was adopted by the media.
- ➷ Monitor the tone of other material online and try to draw a correlation between that response and the material you have made available.
- ➷ Watch the symbols that others use to portray the crisis and see how they match those you have communicated online.
- ➷ As you display sympathy for victims, for example, determine how much of that reaction is accepted in discussions in forums and in reporting by media.

Conclusion

In a crisis, the online public will turn to your Internet presence to learn what you have to say, to try to understand your point of view, to hear your response, to assess your morals, and to judge you as an organization. The results can be powerful, or devastating, depending on the approach you take. Plan beforehand how you will use the Internet during a crisis. Make sure your crisis plan integrates the Internet with other media and communication channels. Have the pieces in place and ready to swing into action when a crisis hits. For it is never a matter of *if* . . . it is only a matter of *when*.

Notes

1. "Media in Cyberspace" is conducted annually by Middleberg Associates Public Relations and Dr. Steven Ross of the Columbia School of Journalism. For information about the study, see *www.middleberg.com*.

CHAPTER 14

Going Directly to the Public

For each of the audiences that have preceded this chapter—and for audiences that cross over or combine the specific publics we have discussed—the Internet provides your organization with a unique opportunity to take its message directly to the public without the filters that other media can apply. This chapter offers a brief review of ideas about how to ensure that your online message is crafted in such a way that you get the maximum benefit of the medium.

Filters

Before the Internet, few media have been available that allowed you to get your message to your audience precisely the way you wanted it presented. Marketing and advertising, of course, were always within your control, subject to limitations imposed by law (such as truth in advertising and regulatory restrictions imposed by agencies like the Food and Drug Administration on such organizations as pharmaceutical companies). However, in matters of public relations (not including those marketing communications messages aimed ultimately at selling products or services), you had to rely on third-party organizations to deliver your message on your behalf. Rarely do those organizations find that it serves their own interests to simply pass your messages along unedited to their publics.

Paramount among these third-party institutions are the news media. Your efforts to build a new factory in the heart of a small community, for example, often are explained in news releases and press conferences. Although your company has gone to great pains to include all pertinent information and address all issues that may arise, the news outlets that receive the releases and cover the press conference will not present your information for you. Their interests are different, and they are dedicated to serving their audiences' information needs based on their charter, the feedback they get from their audiences, and any other agenda they may be carrying (for example, selling more newspapers or increasing viewership by being deliberately provocative or controversial).

The media limits the amount and nature of the coverage you receive in a number of ways:

↬ Time constraints induce editors and reporters—particularly the electronic (television and radio) media—to shorten anything you say into "sound bites," the two or three sentences that make the biggest impression on a listening or viewing audience. In many instances, these sound bites are taken out of context (sometimes deliberately, sometimes due to simple misunderstanding), resulting in an impression that is the complete opposite of what you had in mind. In any case, the report the public receives focuses on only a few issues, and not necessarily those that you consider important.

↬ Reporters already have a sense of the issues that will be important or controversial, and focus on those. These could be minor issues from your point of view, and limiting coverage to them keeps the public from hearing those things you consider to be most important and influential.

↬ If time or space is limited and your news doesn't fit into the editorial needs of the media outlet, you will receive no coverage at all. Newspapers, magazines, radio stations, and television stations are under no obligation to do your communications for you just because you produced the materials to assist them in their reporting.

Without the Internet, bypassing the media requires substantial investment, and then can be effective only if you have the means to reach your target audience. If your target audience is hard to define, ensuring the public understands what you believe to be important becomes an even more onerous task.

It is not impossible, of course. In Chapter 9, for example, I noted that oil and chemical companies often distribute newsletters to homeowners living in neighborhoods that surround refineries. The audience is easy to identify and the cost is negligible. It is far more expensive to blanket the general public with information that supports your position.

To varying degrees, companies can try to get their messages directly to their respective publics. Institutional advertising can contain 1-800 telephone numbers or offers to sign up for fax service, for example. But the Internet provides you with your first real means of delivering to a specific audience the information you want them to get about any issue that involves or affects them.

Opportunities for Direct Communication

The brief history of the Internet makes it clear that people will find the information they want online, particularly when an issue heats up. As noted in Chapter 13, which focuses on crisis communication, you can offer information to the public about your response to a crisis that the media would never cover in the kind of detail your Web site can offer. Alaska Airlines's presentation of in-depth information about its crash, with different content aimed at different audiences (for instance, families of victims were referred to pages that presented information differently than it was positioned for the media), is a classic example of a company taking its message directly to the people most interested in the crisis. The media helped by reporting on the availability of the site.

But you are not limited to crisis communication when making your case or presenting your messages. In fact, any activity, event, issue, opinion, or position that generates a press release or an effort to pitch an item to the press is a likely candidate for communication on the Internet. You also can present information to audiences that you had no means of reaching before.

Principles of Direct Communication

Since the Internet is a relatively new medium, no tradition has yet been established about how to ensure that direct communication with the public will satisfy the needs of the organization. Use the following guidelines to improve the delivery of your Web-based public relations communications:

Don't Use the Web as a Panacea

Always remember that there is more to the Internet than the World Wide Web. As I have noted several times, the Web is a medium that works best when information is available for those who go looking for it, using the pull model of communication. It is far less effective as a means of pushing a message to various audiences. Remember the lessons of e-mail and newsgroup campaigns as a means of communicating with an audience. Consider, for example, daily one-paragraph updates on the status of labor negotiations in newsgroups populated by customers who depend on your ability to continue producing a product that they use. You could distribute the same updates via e-mail to those who subscribe, either from your Web site or by sending e-mail to an address listed in the newsgroup-based updates. The updates could easily contain links to additional information that resides on your Web site, luring those individuals who genuinely desire more detail.

Offer Alternate Paths to Web-Based Information

Remember that on the Web, readers come at the information they want based on their perspective, not the way you have laid it out. For example, consider a hypothetical situation in which a company wants to offer information on the environmental soundness of a particular product. That information might be obtainable by following any of these paths:

- ➫ Each product description contains a link to an environmental statement.
- ➫ The information is contained as part of an overall environmental component of the site.
- ➫ A public affairs site includes a listing of issues, including the environment.

Build a Dedicated Site

If the issue is important enough, dedicate a site (or a clearly delineated portion of your corporate site) to it. Crisis-oriented sites are classic examples of the wisdom of this approach, but you don't need a crisis to set aside a special-topic area. Many companies already have designated a part of their Web sites for environmental issues. You could do the same for any issue you deem to be important or that you believe an audience cares about.

Common Sites for Common Issues

If, as a company, you support or oppose pending legislation or regulation, you *could* build your own page outlining your rationale and eliciting support for your cause. However, when everybody in your industry who shares your viewpoint does the same, the message becomes diluted and confused. How many people interested in the issue will take the time to read every company's statement? How many would even be able to *find* them all? Even if they did, odds are that each statement will be different from the others to some degree, thereby creating inconsistencies.

The Camisea Web site discussed earlier in this book is an example of how a consortium of companies built a single Web site to express their aggregated position on oil exploration in the Peruvian rain forest. Each company could easily have created a link from its Web site to the consortium's specialty site rather than attempting to position the issue independently on separate pages.

The Internet community at large undertook a similar campaign in opposition to the Communications Decency Act (CDA). A blue ribbon icon was available for Web site owners to add to their Web pages; clicking on the ribbon linked visitors to a central CDA opposition page. For a brief period, the page instructed all Web-site owners to turn their sites black as a show of solidarity—tens of thousands complied. Although Congress eventually approved, and the president signed, the CDA, the effort received considerable attention as a sign of the Internet community's ability to join together in pursuit of common interests. (The U.S. Supreme Court ultimately struck down the CDA as unconstitutional.)

Business and industry should take a lesson from the individual inhabitants of the Internet. If trade associations will not take up the call to centralize positions shared by the majority of their members in a manner that allows each member company to capitalize on the effort, companies should band together on their own. Your company could even lead the effort, inviting your competitors to join the endeavor for the common good.

Point to Additional Resources

Since interested individuals will search for information on the subject you are communicating, you may as well point them to those
resources. Offer a list of additional Web sites that contain pertinent
data, along with newsgroups and discussion forums where the subject is under discussion. Although you should highlight those that
support your point of view, don't ignore those that do not. You need
to make it clear that you are cognizant of the material. By providing
links, you have the opportunity to address inaccuracies or other problems with questionable sites and discussions; that is an opportunity
you will not have if a reader finds the information on her own and
never discovers your site.

Be Candid

It should go without saying: Do not lie or twist facts. What many
brand as *public relations* is actually propaganda. As I explained at the
outset of this book, *real* public relations is the process of engaging
your constituent publics in a process of two-way symmetrical communication, designed to result in both sides achieving their objectives. In that way, your organization obtains public sanction to
continue its operations and engage in new enterprises.

But, in cyberspace, the requirement to be candid and forthright
is doubly important. The online world is nothing like the world in
which traditional public relations is practiced. Here, audiences have
a wealth of alternative information sources. They can talk with each
other and point one another to facts that contradict your assertions.

Let Audiences Talk Back

The Internet is interactive, so you should give your audience the opportunity to offer feedback. Letting members of your publics know
that you are listening—in fact, that you *want* to hear what they have
to say—enhances the credibility of your statements. Include a button
on your Web page that invites people to submit their comments, or
add your e-mail address to other forms of communication and invite
readers to submit their thoughts. Be sure to respond to every message
you receive, even if an automated program generates the response.
And don't ignore the feedback that you receive. Categorize the com-

ments, analyze them, and then use them to refine your approach, your position, or the way you couch your comments.

Monitor Reactions

Using the techniques described in Chapter 5, monitor newsgroups, discussion forums, and the World Wide Web as part of your effort to assess audience response to the messages you are communicating. Incorporate analyses of the feedback into your overall evaluation and use it to tweak the message or the means by which you are delivering it.

Measurement

Content analysis of material appearing in the media will give you a benchmark against which to measure. If the media is spinning a story, or focusing on one particular aspect of the story, your online communications can be targeted more toward the messages you believe are most important. Now you can assess public opinion to determine whether your focused message is having an impact or helping the public to understand your position in spite of the media spotlight shining elsewhere.

You can count the visits to your site, and determine as best you can how many came from members of your target audience. Traffic-monitoring software, for example, can note the domain associated with a visitor. This can help identify the region or country from which somebody came.

Other means of assessing the value of going straight to the public can be entirely anecdotal. For instance, media coverage of your efforts, positive responses from members of the public, and forum discussions about your site can be used to show that your efforts are paying off.

Conclusion

If everybody is a publisher on the Internet, your company is, too. The Net gives you the means to communicate directly to the public. Your candid, useful presentations to your many publics will buy you goodwill in times of trouble.

CHAPTER 15

Measuring the Effectiveness of Your Online Efforts

EACH CHAPTER IN this section of "Public Relations on the Net" has concluded with a review of how to measure the effectiveness of the effort. Of course, most measurements should be focused on the initial objectives that you establish. Setting solid objectives must be at the core of every communication effort's initial planning stage.

Why? Because a public relations effort is considered to be successful only when it meets its objectives—and ultimately helps to achieve the overarching goal. Objectives must be measurable. It is not enough to set a measure that says, "Increase support for our plans to build a plant in the Willow Pass neighborhood." How will you know that support has increased if you cannot measure it? A more useful objective would be, "Record a 30 percent increase in the support among residents of the Willow Pass neighborhood for our plans to build a new plant." You would determine the current level of support, and then establish a public relations effort that allows you to assess the increased support. The measure you use depends on a variety of factors, including the audience, the media, and the outcome. For example, if you held a meeting, you could begin by asking how many members of the audience supported the project. At the end of the meeting, ask again. Did 30 percent more people raise their hands? If so, you met a measurable goal, and can report to your management that you achieved the objective established for the meeting.

The principle of measurement applies equally to communication efforts that take place on the Internet. In fact, proof that you are achieving a return on the investment made in the Internet may be even more critical. Many CEOs acknowledge the need for traditional public relations, but remain skeptical of the new computer-mediated communication tools. You need to demonstrate that your online communications are serving the company's bottom line or helping the company to achieve its goals.

Unfortunately, most efforts to assess the effectiveness of Internet communication campaigns focus on the tool rather than on the results. For example, many communicators brag about the number of hits their Web sites receive. "We got ten thousand hits last week!" is a common boast. It is also empty, meaningless. Hits (as explained previously) are a means of measuring the number of files downloaded from your server; each hit represents a request for a single file. Server administrators monitor hits to assess the load on the server. Once a server starts recording a threshold number of hits, it might mean the time has come to upgrade the server's capacity or to increase the bandwidth coming in and going out of the building. As a means of determining how many people visited a site, however, it means nothing:

> ⇨ Since a hit records each file retrieved, a Web page with three graphics, a Java applet, and a sound file represents six hits. Another page with only text will record only one hit. Which pages were visited? How many people actually came to your site and saw what you wanted them to see? Hits won't tell you.

> ⇨ Hits also won't tell you whether the individuals who visited your site were part of your target audience.

> ⇨ You won't be able to determine from hits whether your site influenced the behavior, attitudes, or opinions of those who visited.

To avoid the false measurement results generated by hits, software companies have developed programs that do a better job of monitoring the number of unique visits to a site and the behaviors of the visitors. (WebTrends is the most popular server-based software installed for this purpose.) These programs provide a more valid number, since they help you to determine precisely how many people visited your site. Depending on the sophistication of the software, these tracking programs can also tell you:

➥ Where the visitor is from (based on her e-mail domain)

➥ On what page the visitor started

➥ What pages were visited, in what order

➥ How long the visitor spent on each page

➥ What the visitor did on each page (for example, complete a form, download a file, or play a game)

Although this is useful information, it still does not assess the site's effectiveness at exercising influence over targeted visitors. To stop your evaluation effort at recording information about visitors is the online equivalent of assessing a print campaign based on the demographics of the people who received it!

Genuine measurement requires that you build the assessment process into the communication effort—which, subsequently, requires that you begin with objectives that can be measured. The following are sound methods for measuring the effectiveness of an online public relations effort.

Measure the Web's Impact on an Integrated Campaign

If you are doing your public relations professionally, the efforts are integrated across a variety of media designed to achieve common results. If that is the case, you can establish criteria to determine the type of impact your Internet efforts are having on the total campaign. For example, if your efforts are aimed at the defeat of a particularly onerous piece of legislation, your Web site may include the means by which visitors who share your opinion of the legislation can send e-mail, faxes, or letters to their elected representatives. You can easily measure how many citizens send missives to their representatives, and assess the impact of that action on the ultimate disposition of the legislation.

You can even record meaningful statistics simply by heightening awareness of your cause or position on an issue. These numbers become more significant, however, if you can link the individuals who visit the page with a particular audience segment or demographic. I would be willing to bet good money that your Web site has an address like the one I have been using throughout this book: *www.acme.com*. Everybody who visits comes to the same URL. You could, however, employ the same technique that telemarketing professionals use when they advertise on television. Have you ever seen a television advertisement for the Popeil Pocket Fisherman or a Ronco product? When the telephone number appears on the screen, you are nearly always instructed to "Ask for Operator 24."

Of course, there *is* no Operator 24. When you comply with the requirement, the telemarketer on the other end of the line makes a notation that helps the organization determine which television show you were watching when you saw the advertisement. Operator 24 is the number associated with, for example, the *Tonight Show*; Operator 31, on the other hand, is the number assigned to one of the local late-night newscasts.

You can adopt the same technique by listing unique URLs that all go to the same page. You will know, however, that someone who went to *www.reply1.acme.com* saw the advertisement in *Popular Mechanics,* while the visitors who came to *www.reply2.acme.com* are responding to the listing they saw in newspapers that ran your press release. Now, you can begin to determine which media are attracting the greatest numbers of visitors to the site, and assign demographic information to the volume of visits.

Case Study: Humongous Bank

There actually is no bank with such a name, although residents of Vancouver, British Columbia, came to recognize the name and even to associate it with *any* large, bureaucratic bank. That suited Richmond Savings just fine, according to former Corporate Communications Manager Paul Mlodzik, who said that was the goal behind the invention of the fictitious bank (a campaign which finally wound down after running several years beyond its projected lifespan due to its popularity).

The campaign dates back about two years before the site was launched, when Mlodzik said Richmond Savings—the nation's third-largest credit union—learned that 15 to 20 percent of bank customers at any given time were unsatisfied with their bank and willing to make a switch. "Unfortunately for us, they usually just switched to another bank," he said. "We wanted them to consider switching to the credit union as an alternative."

The way to achieve that objective was to develop Humongous Bank. The bank's motto was "Your money is our money." The campaign began with radio commercials portraying beleaguered customers receiving outrageously bad service.

The commercials won some awards, but also raised questions about Richmond's unfriendly portrayal of bank employees. "Employees are trying their best, but it's the system that's the problem," Mlodzik explains, so the campaign shifted gears to focus its attack on the overwhelming bureaucracy associated with large banking institutions.

That focus led to the launch of a print advertising campaign, which also generated interest and increased awareness of Humongous Bank. The most recent print advertisements have taken a new approach, giving Humongous its own persona. "It was mock advertising, as if it's coming from them instead of us," Mlodzik said. "We developed a logo for them, and a jingle." One advertisement shows a couple of smiling bankers with the text, "We built this bank one service charge at a time." Another offers: "Maximum return on our investment: That's what we expect from our customers."

The development of the direct-from-Humongous ads led to the notion that the ersatz bank should have its own Web site. "The ideas started flowing very quickly at that point," Mlodzik recalled. Mlodzik interviewed several Web development companies, but as he neared a decision, the advertising agency that had developed the Humongous campaign started its own Internet division. "We worked very closely with them on the development of the site," Mlodzik said. "We were very concerned that the site be an extension of the brand, not a standalone entity that didn't relate to all our other efforts."

The work was hard, but also fun. "The banking industry is not noted for its willingness to take risks," Mlodzik said; "On this assignment, no idea was too wild."

Launching the site was pinned entirely on the media. Three days before the site went public, the local press received an invitation with a big *H* on it that informed them that an imminent event would stun them. Two days prior to launch, the fictitious CEO of Humongous sent a personal letter that noted, "I have seen the future, and it is humongous." With one day left, reporters received a press release—on Humongous Bank letterhead. The only reference to Richmond Savings was the contact telephone number, although, Mlodzik asserted, most Vancouver media knew by now that Humongous was the invention of Richmond Savings.

The strategy was a success: The largest television station in town used its news program to take viewers on a three-and-a-half-minute virtual tour of the site, and the newspapers were generous in their coverage. With that coverage, and coverage that has continued since the launch, activity on the site has skyrocketed with hundreds of thousands of visits.

The real proof, however, has been in the hard-core measures that Mlodzik used to assess the effectiveness of the campaign. For example, in 1998, unaided recall of Humongous Bank leapt from 3 percent to 17 percent, and aided recall rose to 83 percent. "It became part of the lexicon," Mlodzik said. "People don't even use bank names, they just call them all Humongous, which is great, because grouping them all together is just what we were trying to do." As for the bottom line, the credit union's membership grew 40 percent during the early stages of the campaign, well above pre-Humongous growth.

The site itself is based on the notion of entering the Humongous Bank building. "It's a good navigation metaphor," Mlodzik said, "and we can keep it fresh easily by adding different departments, changing what's on the various floors, and even adding more floors if we need them."

When visitors enter Humongous Bank, they see a row of teller windows, but as soon as you click on any window, it instantly closes. Visitors are forced to go to the elevator, where they see their various options. For example, customer service is on the first floor, where your feedback options are limited to only those things the bank wants to hear. On the second floor, you can apply for a loan by completing an online application. The form asks questions like, "Have you ever cheated on your golf score? Do you occasionally lie to telemarketers? Have you ever removed the tag on a mattress? Can you be trusted? Can you prove it?" Once the form is completed, the visitor submits the form and is presented instantly with the "Loan-O-Matic" machine—a Shockwave file that looks like a slot machine. Pulling the handle down causes the wheels to spin, and the answer comes up with results like, "Fat Chance, Pal" or "Try Another Bank."

The investments department is on the third floor, where a visitor's personal profile is submitted to draw him into investing in a Humongous portfolio. The fourth floor is the mail room, where visitors can submit their comments. Floors five through twelve are still under development, Mlodzik said, but that doesn't keep him from having fun with them. JavaScript messages appear on the screen when you click on these floors. Try the fifth floor, the vault, and you are told, "Sorry, we're busy counting our money right now." The thirteenth floor is where CEO Markus Stroiber keeps his offices. Visitors can click on his head to learn what he is thinking. His thoughts include such musings as, "They say you can never be too rich or too thin. Frankly, I've always thought being thin was overrated."

So how, exactly, does a visitor find out about Richmond Savings? The elevator button panel includes an emergency exit, which leads to a screen that asks, "Had enough of big bank attitude?" and invites visitors to click through to the Richmond Savings home page. (The Richmond Savings home page features a graphic of a dead brontosaurus, feet in the air, and the invitation to "Find out what's happening at Humongous Bank.")

The integration of the Web with the rest of the campaign worked both ways. Radio and print advertisements were a send-up of a Bank of Montreal campaign inviting customers to visit the bank's Web site. "Everyone knew instantly when they hear[d] it that it's a satire of the Bank of Montreal ad," according to Mlodzik.

Record New Customers or Clients

An Internet presence coordinated with a larger campaign can produce new customers even if the Web site does not facilitate purchase transactions. You don't even need an interactive component on the site—any kind of tool that visitors use to acknowledge they stopped by—to produce these kinds of results.

Let's say you work for a hypothetical company that manufactures digital cameras and sells them wholesale to camera retail dealers, who in turn sell them to consumers. You produce a magazine advertisement that touts the benefits of your product, and invites visitors to your site to see actual digital images and to obtain additional detailed information. Upon visiting your site, the customer explores the three different models you produce, and decides she wants to buy one. Your company, however, does not sell directly to the consumer. But you allow the visitor to enter her zip code into a field, generating a list of nearby retailers who have the camera in stock.

As part of your relationship with your retailers, you have asked them to ask each customer who buys one of your company's cameras to indicate where they found out the dealer had the camera in stock. The dealer tallies up the number of people who replied, "The Acme Web site," and sends a monthly report to the company (no doubt by logging into the company's extranet and entering the number on a special Web page).

Now, you can take concrete numbers to management, showing that the Web was an integral part of the communication chain.

Measure Internet Impact on Audience Behavior

Influencing behavior is, after all, the Holy Grail of public relations. Why not measure how well the Internet helps your company to achieve that goal?

A friend of mine once worked for the visitor and convention bureau of a well-known city. Her efforts focused on convention planners, the target of her Web site. Although the site might attract individual vacationers interested in the city's potential as a vacation spot, they were not the audience whose behavior she wished to influence. The site included information that convention planners would need to make decisions. For example, a section of the site dispelled myths about the city, thereby enhancing its desirability as a convention destination. She also included information about hotels (including capacity, room availability, and conference facilities), convention center details (including available dates), and the city's recreational facilities.

My friend had many different goals for the site. She hoped it would attract people to the city who may otherwise not even consider it for their conventions. She hoped it would put a better face on the city's reputation. But her measurable objective was to reduce the amount of time a convention planner would spend on the telephone with a convention bureau sales representative. A convention planner visiting the site could answer many of his own questions by looking at floor plans of various facilities, checking hotel availabilities, reviewing the ease of access to the city from hub airports. In fact, she achieved this goal beyond her wildest expectations. A caller who had not been to the Web site could take up to two hours of a planner's time (not including the gaps between conversations while the planner obtained information and sent literature to the prospect via overnight courier). The average amount of time a planner spent on the telephone with a caller who *had* visited the site was less than twenty minutes. These individuals already knew what they wanted; the call was a formality to get the gears moving.

Measure How the Internet Affects Media Coverage

You can measure the impact of your online efforts by determining how much of your Internet-based materials find their way into editorial content. Look for exact wording from your online materials that appear in the media. You can also keep a running tally of how many contacts were made through your media site that led to interviews resulting in positive coverage.

Identify New Audience Members to Target

The one-to-one nature of the Internet makes it possible for you to obtain detailed information about members of your target audience that you may not have been reaching through conventional means. Ragan Communications, a Chicago-based company that produces newsletters, manuals, and conferences for public relations professionals, invites visitors to subscribe to risk-free, short-term subscriptions of its newsletters. To receive the free subscription, visitors provide Ragan with all the information they need to add the individual to its marketing database and possibly convert the person into a customer by using the company's traditional marketing methods (which are heavily rooted in direct mail).

Executive recruiting companies (better known as *headhunters*) are starting to use their Web sites to identify new contacts. Traditionally, each search begins with calls to a few people the recruiter already knows may be well connected in the desired profession. When visitors to a recruiter's Web site enter their personal information in hopes of being matched for a job, they wind up in the recruiter's database. Now, if a recruiter needs a chief financial officer for a manufacturing company, she can query the database for all related fields, generating a list of contacts, each one of whom may know the ideal candidate. Each new name in the database is a new avenue for identifying potential candidates; each legitimate addition to the database is a solid measurement.

Conclusion

Your Internet site can be far more than a mere presence in cyberspace, yet you do not need to record a dollar received for a good sold to assess the bottom-line impact of the Internet on your communication efforts. Set measurable objectives at the outset, and then record the impact of the Internet against those objectives. Use any of the categories of measurement described previously—or any others that are pertinent to your organization—as a starting point for setting and meeting measurable objectives.

Working with IT Staff

W HO CONTROLS THE intranet or the Web site in your organization? Surprisingly, in a number of organizations, ownership of online media continues to be a cause of disagreement. Communicators (regardless of the department in which they work—public affairs, corporate communications, marketing communications, or advertising) naturally believe they should be in charge, since the Web is a vehicle for the delivery of news and information, and ultimately has a significant impact on audience perceptions of the organization and its brand. However, in many organizations, information technology (IT) professionals think online communication tools should be in their jurisdiction, because, at their core, they are part of the company's computer network.

Who owns the intranet or the Web site? There are actually two ways to answer this question correctly:

1. *The audience does.* If the site is designed to accommodate the media, then the media own the site. If it is geared toward customers, then *customers* own the site. (The concept of audience ownership is addressed at length in Chapter 3.)

2. *The company does.* Online communication tools are a resource to be leveraged to the organization's greatest possible benefit.

It is a conceit that communicators view these systems as strictly communication tools. Many Web sites, intranets, and other online tools also serve as an infrastructure. Intranets facilitate everything from expense reporting and performance evaluations to supply purchases and benefits enrollments. And the Web manages transactions, e-commerce, customer service functionality, and a host of other activities that cannot be considered as communications. Although communicators can play a role in these areas, it is highly unusual to expect *traditional, non-Web* performance evaluation processes and sales transactions to be housed within the communications department. And prior to the introduction of the Internet, the IT department did not control these functions, either.

Several factors can be blamed for the turf war over the Net that is waged in many organizations. In some companies, management simply fulfilled its obligation to deal with the Web as an integral part of the organization; it is seen as something extra that is managed by whomever is interested. However, in many organizations, the real problem rests with the relationship between the communications department and IT. It is a relationship that needs to improve if the two departments are going to work together to produce and maintain a top-flight system. And work together they must. Neither department can do it alone, and neither should be subservient to the other.

Resolving the conflict begins with understanding how the problem emerged in the first place. After all, it wasn't all that long ago that the relationship between the communications department and IT was limited to getting new computers installed and configured.

At fault, fundamentally, is the unprecedented speed with which the World Wide Web has become a computing standard. Previous technologies took years to roll out, according to Brad Whitworth, communications manager at Hewlett-Packard in Palo Alto, California. "But the Web wasn't developed because companies determined they needed it," says Whitworth. "It was already there, and people started [to] bring it in." The more people began using it, the greater the demand for it to solve problems that no other technology could address. "It came upon people so quickly because it answered so many concerns," explained Whitworth.

Who Are These Guys?

The importance of the IT department has grown in tandem with business's expanded reliance on computer systems. Overall, investment in IT has grown from 3 to 5 percent of a company's capital budget in the mid-1980s to about 17 to 25 percent today. With so many millions of dollars at stake, it is not surprising that management has sharpened its focus on the IT department's role.

In general, IT's charter in the company includes the following elements:

↝ *Establish standards.* It is easier for a company to get work done as a team when everybody is using the same system, the same software, and the same file types. If you have ever worked for a company with multiple incompatible e-mail systems, you know how frustrating a lack of standards can be.

↝ *Manage company-wide systems.* Given the increasing reliance on systems, there is more work for the IT department to do. They have to keep the existing systems working, back them up, keep them upgraded, analyze prospective enhancements and replacements, and maintain a digital operation that works smoothly.

↝ *Address systems integration.* In an environment characterized by mergers and acquisitions, there always seem to be divergent systems that need to be incorporated into the workplace.

↝ *Watch the horizon.* An effective network comprising the most appropriate tools for the organization can represent one of the company's most significant competitive advantages. Companies cannot afford to be caught off-guard while competitors embrace a new technology that erodes their advantage. The IT department is responsible for ensuring that the company is prepared to acquire and assimilate the latest offerings, and functions within the standards of an increasingly networked marketplace.

↝ *Budget constraints.* The IT department must work within a budget, no differently from any other department.

Learn the Lingo

One source of conflict between IT and communications is the jargon IT professionals seem to bandy about with arrogant supremacy. Much of the language they speak seems contrived to confound outsiders. In fact, the jargon is simply the language of computers and networking. It is no different, in terms of how difficult it is to learn, than the jargon associated with printing. Most communicators would have no difficulty understanding the following sentence: "I'm going four-up on a sheet-fed, two-over-four with spot varnish, a die cut, and the whole thing's gonna be perfect bound." Yet, few communicators are qualified offset press operators. As professionals, we communicators simply learned enough of the technical side of printing needed to work with our printers and get the results we require.

The IT professionals are the printers of the digital, networked world. Just as we did with printers, we need to learn enough about computers and networks to be able to work with the IT staff to get the same results. (See the Glossary.)

What Is Content?

Often, the friction between IT and communications arises over who will manage content. Just as frequently, there would be no disagreement at all if the two departments defined what they meant by *content*. As communicators, we define *content* as "subject matter." It is the material we craft to achieve communication objectives. It is the key message, the approach taken to the message, and the message's positioning within the communication vehicle.

When IT talks about content, on the other hand, they are usually talking about file types. An AVI animation file, for example, is *content* from the IT perspective. So is a WAV sound file, or a Java applet. These are a concern to IT, which may be nursing a network along that is bursting at its limited-bandwidth seams. Sometimes, a content provider may want to use a file type that is incompatible with the existing system. Do all employees in the company have an Adobe Acrobat reader on their computers? If not, it doesn't make sense to load Acrobat PDF files onto the server.

Of course, you could make the case that Acrobat files would increase the value of the network and provide a substantial return on investment to the organization. Making that business case could lead IT to agree to install the reader on every desktop. It is that kind of discussion that helps the two departments move beyond the discord stage. Engaging in such discussions begins with making a mutual commitment to work together in the best interests of the organization.

Mutual Commitment

Sit down with your IT counterpart and discuss your objectives. The IT department needs to understand what you are trying to accomplish on the company's behalf, and how the intranet and/or the Web figure into the equation. Listen to IT's objectives. With all your cards on the table, take that next big step by agreeing to work together to provide the solutions that the organization needs to be successful and competitive.

Now, you can build a cross-functional team with mutual responsibility for the success of the Web or the intranet. (You don't have to call it a team. It can be a task force, a steering committee—a couple companies have named their groups the *guild*.) The team should take responsibility for the intranet or Web site, since teams work better than a situation in which one department retains control while others are merely subservient to the demands of the controlling group. Teams establish their own set of objectives, separate from those on which the team members are evaluated within the context of their departmental jobs. Once the team has established its objectives, each member works toward those common goals.

Further, teams identify the strengths each member brings to the table. Ownership ceases to be such an important issue; instead, the focus is on results. Few communicators would want to be responsible for wiring routers, writing interactive programs in C++ or Perl, physically increasing network bandwidth, selecting operating platforms, or installing software on every desktop in the entire organization. Conversely, few IT professionals would claim expertise in setting communication objectives, identifying target audiences, or measuring the effectiveness of communication efforts.

But when the team is committed to the best organizational results, the objectives come first, followed by a discussion on how best to achieve them. Then, IT can propose technical solutions to problems that might never have surfaced in a different, more confrontational environment.

Promoting Your Online Efforts

THE BEST ONLINE communication programs imaginable are of little value if nobody knows they exist. Many of the current promotional methods are limited to registering Web sites with search engines. Although this is a valid tactic, it is far too confined by itself, and will reach only a fragment of the total audience for whom your messages were assembled.

As in promoting any other public relations message, you should plan to use a variety of media and methods to reach the widest possible audience. Here is a review of the most common means of promoting online communications.

Online Promotion

Although it is important to incorporate other media and methods into your plans to draw audiences to the Internet-based elements of your communication campaign, you must account for those people who are already online pulling information suited to their particular interests. Before we explore the means by which you can incorporate your other communications into your Internet promotion plans, let's examine the ways you can draw those who are already on the Net invoking the pull model.

Search Engines or Indexes and Meta Tags

Three categories of search utilities exist on the Internet. One, the meta-search utility, is simply a means by which you submit a query simultaneously to multiple search sites. The next type of utility is a search *engine or index,* characterized by Google (at *www.google.com*), HotBot (at *www.hotbot.com*), and AltaVista (at *www.altavista.digital.com*). Engines send automated agents, also known as *bots* or *spiders,* onto the World Wide Web, Usenet newsgroups, and other portions of the Internet, collecting every scrap of information they can find. A Web page is added to the engine by dividing the words it contains into an index; each word is attached to the location of the page from which it came. When you enter a query, the engine searches the index and returns every page that satisfies the query. As a result, the more detailed your query, the more likely that you will retrieve a listing of sites that meet your needs. (Google, in addition, caches a version of every page it retrieves; even if the page is moved or removed, you can still view the cached version through Google.)

Among the ways search engines rank sites in response to a query is through the multiple occurrences of the key words submitted for the search. Google uses a relevance model, which ranks sites based on the number of other sites that link to it based on the query word. Another method is examining the page title, and a fourth is by cataloguing the site's meta tags.

Meta tags are a component of HTML that appears in the head (not the body) portion of the code. Meta tags exist solely to assist search engines in their cataloguing of Web sites. The two types of meta tags most commonly used are *description* and *keywords.* The description tag is a place to write a one-line boilerplate-like description of the site. A description meta tag would look like this:

⟨meta NAME = "description" CONTENT = "Acme's media relations Web site offers press releases, transcripts, print-ready photos, and other resources for working journalists."⟩

The keyword meta tag allows you to introduce every word you can think of that might be entered in a search engine query field by someone you hope would find your site. This is what a keyword tag looks like:

⟨meta NAME = "keywords" CONTENT = "media, media relations, journalist, reporter, editor, newspaper, news, press, press release, press conference, transcripts, speeches, filings"⟩

> *TIP:*
> *Don't Overdo It*
> You can earn the wrath of many Web surfers if you throw
> too many words into the meta tag, leading people to find
> your site even if it doesn't contain a thing that matches
> their needs. Far too many meta tags are littered with doz-
> ens, even hundreds of words in an effort to ensure that the
> site appears near the top of every search that may have
> even the most tangential relation to the topic. Limit your
> meta-tag keywords to those that are genuinely relevant to
> the site. You also need to stay within the bounds of ethical
> behavior when using meta tags. Incorporating your com-
> petitors' names or stock exchange ticker symbols into a
> meta tag may increase the number of visits to your site, but
> that doesn't mean those visitors will appreciate you for it.

Search Directories and Site Registration Services

Search engines are fully automated. Search directories, on the
other hand, are managed through human intervention. Just as the
Dewey Decimal System was devised to help categorize book types
in libraries, search indexes try to catalogue the contents of the
World Wide Web, placing sites into categories, subcategories, sub-
subcategories, and so on. If you know exactly what you are looking
for, you can begin to drill with relative ease through a well-planned
search index. Yahoo! (at *www.yahoo.com*) is the best-known search
directory; others include Infoseek (at *www.infoseek.com*) and Lycos
(at *www.lycos.com*). A typical category set might look like this (taken
from the Yahoo! site):

Computers and Internet: Internet: World Wide Web:
Searching the Web: Search Engines.

Most of the directories include a feature for site owners and
managers to submit their sites for inclusion on the index. There are
literally hundreds of directories of various kinds that permit you to
add your site to their list. You might know about submitting your site
to Yahoo!, but would you know that you can also submit it to the

Online Marketers Resource Locator? If you are a public relations consultant, would you know to add your site to the International Consultants Yellow Pages?

To ensure that you gain the greatest possible exposure on the plethora of directories, services have been created that handle submission for you (for a fee, of course). It can be well worth the modest cost to ensure that your site is listed with every pertinent directory. Check into Submit It! (at *www.submit-it.com*). There are free submission utilities as well, which get your name to some of the larger directors. Try Add It! (at *www.liquidimaging.com/submit/*) or 123Add It (at *www.123add-it.com*).

> ### TIP:
> #### *When to Pay*
> The free utilities are great for being listed in the top search engines in a few simple steps. The fee-based services tend to offer greater flexibility in addition to access to less well-known directories, such as business specific directories. You should assess the audience that you are seeking for your site to determine whether the top directories will suffice, or if you need exposure in the more targeted directories. Services like Submit It! provide lists of the directories included in its service, so be sure to see whether there are directories to which you would want to be added, and whether it is worth your while to have Submit It! do it all at once (as opposed to visiting each directory yourself to submit the URL).

Cross-Linking Agreements

The many-to-many nature of the Internet has led to the practice of cross-linking agreements, in which you agree to include a link to my site if I build a link to yours. Find sites that are related to your business or issue, and e-mail the site owner suggesting the relationship. Don't limit your e-mail to a request (for example, "I saw your site today. If I create a link to it on my site, will you do the same on yours? What'd ya say?") Instead, articulate why the relationship would be beneficial, and where the synergies lie.

For example, if your organization is offering a series of new education-oriented grants, you might contact managers of sites that attract local teachers and school administrators. Adding your link adds value to the content of the site, since many of the visitors to the site may want to submit grant requests. You benefit through the teachers and administrators who might otherwise have never found your information about the new grants.

Sponsorship

As addressed in the "market sample of one" discussion in Chapter 2, sponsorship is one of the best ways to attract visits to your site. Exactly what the term *sponsorship* means can vary. The site you target can sponsor your content in exchange for a link to your site, which is the approach Hobart Industries took when it offered information on the Dorothy Lane Markets site. You can also sponsor an entire site, paying to develop and host the content, which was Hobart's approach with Peter Good Seminars. In both cases, the approach generated an impressive number of click-throughs to Hobart's site.

Banner Advertisements

When given an adequate budget, you may want to develop a banner advertisement and buy space on sites that are likely to attract your core audiences. Banner advertisements have gotten a bad rap over the last couple years—and justifiably so, given their pathetic click-through performance (currently hovering under one percent). Still, a well-executed banner advertisement in the right place can attract the kind of attention you need.

The banner advertisements that people are ignoring are product and service pitches. Two banner ad campaigns at the Web site of *Mother Jones* magazine (both reviewed in earlier chapters of this book), however, drew plenty of clicks. These advertisements did not pitch products. One invited ecology-minded individuals to send a letter to the U.S. Food and Drug Administration opposing genetically modified agricultural products. The other, from Shell Oil, invited discussion on the Shell Web site about issues for which *Mother Jones* had taken the oil company to task. The message seems to be that a banner advertisement with a compelling message that doesn't seem to be selling anything can still work.

This approach is true even for commercial endeavors. When Yoyodyne (a permission marketing agency later acquired by Yahoo!) wanted to attract high-income taxpayers to sign up to participate in a contest promoting a new premium tax service, the company positioned banner advertisements on sites trafficked by high-income individuals. The advertisement simply noted that Yoyodyne's client would pay the winner's federal taxes the following year. The promise that you might win a tax-free year was enough to lead tens of thousands not only to click the advertisement but also to enroll in the contest.

E-Mail and Discussion Groups

Use existing mailing lists of individuals who have asked to be notified of relevant information to announce that your site exists, or that new content in which they may be interested has been added. Do the same for mailing lists or discussion forums you have established. You can make brief announcements in relevant Usenet newsgroups, listserv mailing lists to which you subscribe, Web-based bulletin boards, and other discussion forums, politely alerting group participants that your online material is available. Be sure to address (in one or two sentences) why the participants in that particular virtual community should care—that is, how they could benefit from your offering.

Integration with Other Media

So far, we have reviewed ways to get information across about your Internet communications using the Internet itself. These techniques are fine for those members of your target publics who are already online seeking information consistent with what you have to offer. What about those who are not online, or who are not looking for anything related to your message—even though they would be interested in your message if only they knew it was there? The following approaches can be applied to non-Internet communications as a means of luring your audiences to your online materials.

Company Materials

Your organization or client produces reams of print materials as a matter of routine. Pertinent online information should become a standard part of everything from business cards and letterhead to institutional brochures and press kit folders. Include the company's top-level URL on general materials. Department-specific materials should feature both the general URL *and* any targeted URLs. For example, the vice president of investor relations should have a business card with the company's Web site *and* the investor relations' site URLs. Business cards also should include e-mail addresses.

I have seen URLs on a variety of other promotional items, including pencils and pens that have traditionally been imprinted with company names, logos, and telephone numbers; t-shirts; notepads; and pocket calculators.

Related Campaign Elements

When creating an integrated communication effort, each media component must be evaluated and used to its best advantage. The Web, for example, is an ideal storage device, allowing you to categorize vast quantities of information, making it easy for people to find details in which they are interested even though most other people would find the information tedious and irrelevant.

The following examples are ways to mesh traditional and Internet media into a complete public relations endeavor:

➭ In print materials that form the crux of your communication, point readers to your Web site where they can get additional information on any element of the print material in which they may have more interest. The Web can also offer interactive features (such as calculators or configurators that allow users to configure a product or service to meet their requirements, usually by completing a form) that aren't possible to include in print. This allows you to go into greater detail on each of several topics, affording the opportunity to exercise influence over individuals who have highly targeted interests.

➭ Offer the full text of materials that appear in print. For example, if your bulletin or newsletter includes quotes from an executive speech, you can refer interested readers to the Web site for the complete text (and even an audio file) of the speech. If a mailing seeking support for the construction of a new facility includes segments of an Environmental Impact Report, you can archive the entire report on your Web site.

➥ Include a list of e-mail addresses, each of which is managed by an autoresponder. Those who wish more information on a particular aspect of your subject can send e-mail to one address to receive a response that provides details on that issue. E-mail autoresponders do not provide material that is as graphically appealing as a Web site, but far more people have access to e-mail than to the Web, making it a resource that can be accessed by larger portions of your target audience.

➥ Note that updates to the material you have produced in print will be available on your Web site as soon as they become available, enticing audience members to visit the site to see whether new information has been posted.

➥ Offer access to interactive materials associated with the information you provide in print. If you are promoting your company's stock as a sound investment, for example, you can incorporate an investment calculator into your Investor Relations Web site. Current shareholders can calculate the increase in value of their stock since purchasing it. You can promote the site in your annual and quarterly reports.

➥ Invite readers to submit questions through the Web site.

➥ Host special events on the Web site that are promoted in print. These can include everything from Webcasts (don't scoff at the Victoria's Secret fashion show Webcast; it may have been a technical disaster but it was a public relations coup). Host experts or celebrities in live chats or limited-time asynchronous discussion forums.

Advertising

All of your advertising efforts should refer to your Web site URL. Everything from display advertisements in magazines and newspapers to television commercials and billboards can include a reference to your Web site (and, even better, to specific sections of your site that relate directly to the focus of the advertisement).

I remember reading *Time* magazine and seeing a display advertisement for Pentel pens. At the bottom of the advertisement, the URL for the company's Web site was listed. Now why, I wondered, would I want to visit the Web to look at pens? Since I was curious, I visited the site, and found a wealth of information that simply isn't available anywhere else (as far as I know). What kind of information?

For example, there was an illustrated, step-by-step instruction guide to unjamming a mechanical pencil. I don't know whether I'll ever need to retrieve that information (I don't use mechanical pencils), but if I do, I know where it resides on the Internet. And my opinion of Pentel was elevated based on the value-added information they have posted to their Web site.

Announcements

Be sure to make a big fuss when you launch a Web site, a new feature on a Web site, a discussion group, or any other Internet-based service. Distribute press releases and press kits (including printable screen shots), invite reporters to call in for a guided tour (they're online while you walk them through the site), and pitch unique elements of the launch to targeted media. Get as much press coverage as you can for your site. If the site is part of a larger campaign, be sure to use the same logos, letterheads, and other identifiers to link the site to the brand you are communicating through other means.

Writing for the Web

W**RITING IS** at the core of good public relations. The other skills—such as strategic planning, negotiation, and research—that comprise a well-rounded communications professional are all but worthless if good writing skills are not evident. Any new hire in a communications job is assessed initially on the quality of his or her portfolio, and many are given writing tests as part of the hiring process.

When it comes to the Internet, many communicators believe that good writing is good writing; the medium is not a factor. Evidence supports the contrary. One study showed that material rewritten to incorporate the principles of good *online* writing made a document nearly 125 percent more usable to the reader.

In Chapter 3, we reviewed several characteristics of reading computer screens that make it a dramatically different medium than anything printed on paper. These characteristics include:

- *Physical characteristics*. Online material is not linear or three-dimensional; however, it is interactive and multimedia.
- *Physiological impact*. Eyestrain is induced by reading light (which reduces the blink rate) and by having to adjust to font size that is beyond producer control. Scrolling induces nausea.

The consequence of these factors is that people do not read written material on computer screens. Research conducted by Sun

Microsystems suggests instead that people *scan* the material they retrieve; their eyes bounce around a screen in random patterns, seeking out key words that will signify that the page contains the information the reader was seeking. (Be sure to go back and read Chapter 3 for details about each of these characteristics.)

In a world where people are not inclined to read what you have written, even though they rely on the contents of the Internet to find information they need, writers face a variety of challenges to get readers to pay attention to their copy. In fact, *attention* is the currency of the information economy. Some argue that *information* is the information economy's currency, but any economist will tell you that currency is derived from that which has value *and is scarce* within the economy. Information is far from scarce. If anything, now that everybody has the ability to produce information, we are drowning in information. Attention, on the other hand, is scarce. People can pay attention to only one thing at a time. The fact that you are reading this book right now means that you are not listening to an advertisement on the radio, catching a public service announcement on television, or paying attention to what somebody might be saying in the next office. You're certainly not reading another book or magazine. The trick, then, is getting people to pay attention to what *your organization* has to say. And when they will not read your carefully crafted prose, you need to adopt different writing strategies to capture your share of the available attention that exists in your targeted marketplace.

Your Role as a Writer

As the writer whose job is to ensure that your audience gets the message you have to deliver, your role in the online world is considerably more expanded than it is in the paper world. Although you still have the power of words to use, you also have the following to take into consideration:

- ⇨ *The context.* You need to consider the context of each chunk or page or file of information to ensure that the reader understands what you are trying to say regardless of where they start in your online document.

➪ *The design.* In print, the writer generally hands finished text to a designer, who makes it look good and enhances its meaning. Online, the design of the page needs to happen simultaneously, and is *part* of the writing process.

➪ *The audience.* In print, all audiences get your written work in the same format. The special needs of subaudiences are irrelevant; each must extract what is relevant to them from the same document that other subaudiences are using. Online, however, different audiences can view your work in different ways; they can approach the information from different paths. Thus, special attention needs to be paid to who the readers are.

➪ *Related information.* In print, you can include a bibliography at the back of the work. Online, you need to be aware of related information available at the click of a mouse button. Will readers be able to find contradictory documents? Are there documents online that already cover what you want to cover to which you can link? Are there sites on the intranet or Internet to which you can guide your readers to support or enhance your words?

➪ *Multimedia.* Will an audio or video clip, an animation, an interactive tutorial, or some other multimedia tool be beneficial?

➪ *Interactivity.* Are you accommodating the expectation of interactivity?

➪ *Navigation.* Are you making it easy for your readers to move effortlessly through your document, and to find what they are looking for?

TIP:
Understand What Readers Want and Need
Readers *want* control, but they *need* direction!

Your job, as the writer of the online document, is to help the reader identify what she is seeing so that she can quickly determine its value to her, and then be able to move quickly and effortlessly to the next element in your document (or to some other realm of the Internet—should that be her choice).

The New Models and Their Implications for Writing

Chapter 2 explored the four new models of communication that have evolved from the electronic communication revolution: many to many, receiver driven, access driven, and the market sample of one. Each of these models has implications for the approach you take to writing a document for online presentation.

Many-to-Many

↝ *Think beyond the page.* A written work is self-contained between its covers. An online work is, by its very nature, connected to other online elements. You need to consider what those elements are that relate to your work.

↝ *Writing is ongoing.* In print, your work is complete once it comes off the press. Online, you need to continuously revise, update, and correct your work in response to feedback from the online community of readers.

↝ *Incorporate links.* The material posted by others, along with the discussion groups related to your subject, may enhance your document. Consider linking to them. You may even want to develop a dedicated discussion capability as *part* of the material you are producing. For example, if you are writing about benefits enrollment, an online forum where employees can discuss among themselves the various options gives you some control over the many-to-many nature of the Web.

Receiver-Driven

↝ *Nonlinear writing.* Your writing must, in most instances, be produced in a nonlinear fashion. That is, although you will use an outline or structure for your work, each component part must make sense in its own right and be both findable and usable for the reader.

↝ *Write in chunks.* Rather than write in a steady flow, you must write in chunks, each one containing a contextual element of the whole. When repurposing material for the Web, you need to identify the elements that contain a single unit of information—a single notion, concept, or thought—and recast it as a standalone element of information that works in its own context in addition to the context of the larger piece.

↝ *Learn to use hyperlinks.* Hyperlinks are the cognitive language of the Web that allows people to find the information they want. They are not an afterthought, but a fundamental, integral part of the writing process.

↝ *Select the right media for key messages.* If every reader must see certain parts of your information, how do you overcome the receiver-driven nature of the Web? When people pull only the information they want, and customize their environments to screen out material of no interest, how can you ensure that your material will be absorbed? You need to consider using more push-oriented tools—such as e-mail—and procuring space on the top-level home page that everybody sees for such messages. You may even need to decide whether the online environment is the appropriate one for this information.

Access-Driven

↝ *Understand your audience(s).* You need to know the audience you are targeting with your information and how they are most likely to be able to receive it.

↝ *Prepare text in multiple formats.* Of course, not *every* audience will have access to the Web environment—at least, not for a while. As a result, communicators may be in a position that requires them to produce multiple versions of their material to accommodate *different* preferred access points.

↝ *Use primary medium as the foundation.* If most of your readers are online, the online document becomes the primary document and is used as the source for producing secondary (for example, print) documents.

Market Sample of One

↝ *Link from related sites.* Part of the writing process involves identifying related sites and knowing how to establish links from them to the information that you are producing. You should also explore the use of banner advertisements as a means of advertising the presence of your information on the system.

↪ *Develop FAQs.* Frequently asked questions (FAQs) are lists of questions and answers that people may have about your subject. By establishing a FAQ, you accomplish several things. First, you provide material that is easily captured in a search engine's index, making it easy to find. Second, you can provide links to related information. Third, you can have the content owners of other sites create simple links from their site to your FAQ.

Guidelines for On-Screen Copy

General Guidelines

Length

↪ The shorter the better—generally you want to fill only one screen.

↪ No more than two "page-downs."

↪ Offer links to related information.

↪ Don't become carried away with hyperlinks—using too many of them disrupts the flow of the document.

Style

↪ The writer's so-called voice is important—regardless of the document's nature. A conversational style is preferred by online readers.

↪ Use lists and bullet points.

↪ Where you choose to use a narrative approach, use short sentences. Use emphasis (italics and bold face) sparingly and only to help the reader in her efforts to scan the page.

Navigation

Writing a document for the screen *must* incorporate navigation tools. The primary goal of navigation is to make it as easy, intuitive, and seamless as possible for a reader to find what he is looking for. Navigation (buttons, icons, or text) needs to guide readers to the following:

- The beginning of the document
- The previous chunk of information (remember, chunks need to be context-independent—a reader should not be forced to read other pages to understand the information that is on the page he is currently viewing)
- The next chunk of information
- Any indexes or tables of contents
- Search engines that will help the reader to find information for which he is looking within the document
- The home page of which the document is a part

Writing Electronic Newsletters

E-mail newsletters are those that are distributed to your audience via e-mail. Most e-mail newsletters are distributed as actual e-mail messages, generally limited in scope to ASCII text; however, there are some e-mail newsletters that have more capabilities. But they all share the following traits:

- Readers must retrieve them as e-mail, so the larger they are, the longer they take to download.
- Readers must read the entire newsletter to find what is important to them, along with the all messages in the rest of their e-mail.

When writing e-mail newsletters, stick to only the facts. You should avoid feature-like elements and adopt a newspaper-lead approach as the style for the entire article. If additional information or levels of detail are available, point readers to where this information can be found. Don't assume that every reader will be interested in every detail.

Use short, spartan sentences. If you are producing your newsletter in ASCII—that is, it uses only the characters you can see on your

keyboard, ensuring its compatibility with absolutely *any* e-mail software application—you should abide by the following guidelines:

- Put a listing of all headlines or subject lines at the top of
  your message. That way, readers can browse quickly through
  the list to see whether any of the articles are of interest.
- Limit articles to one or two paragraphs.
- Separate articles with a line of nonletter characters, like
  these:

$$= = = = = = = = = = = = = = = = = =$$

$$* * * * * * * * * * * * * * * * * * *$$

$$\% \% \% \% \% \% \% \% \% \%$$

Of course, you are not constrained to delivering newsletters produced only in ASCII. There are numerous ways to distribute newsletters that incorporate graphics and design elements. You can use an
application file such as Word (if all members of your audience have
Word), a dedicated e-mail newsletter application such as E*News, or
portable document programs such as Acrobat, Envoy, or Common
Ground.

Here, it is important to limit each article to a single screen. The
formats allow you to use hyperlinks, and you should take advantage
of them so that a reader can move easily between and among articles.
You also should avoid redesigning your publication each issue, or
overdesigning it. Instead, develop a template and stick with it.

Writing for the World Wide Web

Overall Structure

Just as you would with a document for paper, it is important to
begin with the *structure* of your document when writing for the Web.
In fact, it is even *more* important, because that structure will become
the basis for hyperlinks, chunking of text, navigation, and other elements that the reader will use to take advantage of the document you
have produced.

When preparing an online document, think in terms of an information *tree*, in which your main information is on the trunk, key levels of information are on branches, secondary levels of information are on branches sprouting from the key-level branches, and so forth.

Once the tree is developed, in addition to using it as the intuitive guide for your writing, adapt it as an outline of links for your reader, like this:

Health and Welfare Plans
    Introduction to Plans
Medical Plans
    HMOs
    PPO
    EPO
    Indemnity Plan
Dental Plans
    Indemnity Plan
    Dental HMO
Vision Plans
    Vision Service Plan (VSP)

Of course, you can provide even deeper levels of links. For example, under each of the medical plans, you can include links to the categories of coverage, the claims-filing process, eligibility, and other categories of detail. These links do not need to appear all on one page. For example, clicking on HMOs can take you to a list of more links.

Be sure to consider your audiences as you map out (develop a storyboard that shows every page of your document and how they link to one another) and then write your document (that is, write copy to fill the boxes on your storyboard). You could conceivably have more than one type of audience viewing the same document. Consider, for example, a document designed to provide information on a 401(k) investment plan. Part of your audience may comprise individuals who have never before invested in a 401(k), or never been part of a company that offered one. These novices require information that walks them through the particulars of a 401(k). On the other hand, many of your employees have been investors for years, and do not need to be held by the hand to understand the material. Instead, they only want to know specific information, like the five-year history of the high-risk/high-yield foreign stock fund. Ultimately, the document contains the same information for both groups. The only question is how each audience gets to the information. The tree in Figure C-1 offers a simplified explanation of how different audiences use the same chunks. It shows the parallel paths different audiences would use to get to the same information.

Here, the novice is able to move logically and linearly through the document, learning what he needs to know about 401(k) plans, ultimately getting to the section in which he learns about investment options. The experienced user, on the other hand, is able to select either an alphabetical or functional listing to quickly find the specific plan in which he is interested.

Another example might be a medical plan. Consider information on hospitalization. One employee may wonder what the hospitaliza-

FIGURE C-1. PARALLEL PATHS LEADING TO SAME INFORMATION.

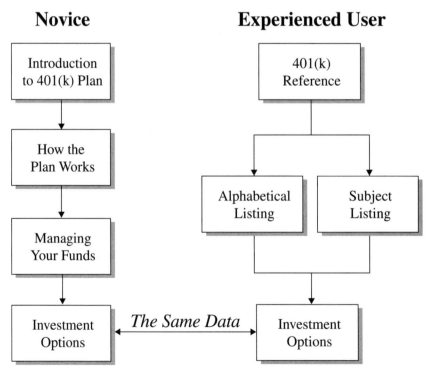

tion benefits are under various plans to help make an enrollment decision. In this case, it makes sense to offer links to the various benefits available under each plan for comparison purposes. Another employee, however, has a child that just broke his arm. This employee wants to know what coverage applies. He might begin on a chronological life events listing, first clicking on "Dependent Accidents," and then clicking on "HMO," because that is the plan he is in, before clicking on "Hospitalization." Ultimately, the information on HMO hospitalization is the same—it is even the *same file*—but two different employees took two different paths to get to it.

The Written Word

The actual writing of text for the computer screen encompasses a variety of elements that require thinking that differs from what is required for paper and print. This section reviews each of the key elements of writing for online consumption.

Use Chunks

In many cases, the best approach to writing for the screen is to reduce your text to the smallest component chunk. The best instance in which to do this is when there is so much information that producing it in a linear, one-document fashion will overwhelm readers with information and make it difficult to find only the information for which the reader is looking.

A chunk of information should contain a well-defined concept that stands on its own—that is, it makes sense in its own context. The idea contained in the chunk should be clear, and should flow smoothly.

The size of the chunk itself should be determined based on the following:

➥ How much text is required to convey the full message, idea, or concept?

➥ How long does it take to download the file that contains the chunk?

➥ How difficult is it to scroll or page-down through the document?

↪ What is the trade-off between scrolling/page-down and click-ing and waiting for hyperlinked pages to appear?

A reasonable rule of thumb is to avoid exceeding two page-downs (or three screens) in order to read through the entire page.

One of the advantages of chunking information is that you can avoid re-keying information. For example, you may have disclaimer language or other legalese that appears throughout a printed docu-ment. In a hypertext online document, that disclaimer needs to exist only once on the server. At the end of the document, you can provide a link to the disclaimer rather than type it into different HTML pages over and over again.

Write About Your Subject

When writing for the Web, because it is so new a medium, many writers tend to become distracted by the medium itself. You should concentrate on the subject matter and avoid references to the Web, which will distract readers from the message you are trying to send. Besides, most readers are savvy enough about the Web that they don't need you telling them to "click" or "point your cursor" or take any other action that is about the medium. After all, on paper, you wouldn't say, "Put the corner of the page between your thumb and forefinger and flip it so it turns to the next page." "Click here" proba-bly appears more than any other two-word combination on the Web. Don't let it appear on *your* site.

Avoid Mechanics in Your Writing

In addition to refraining from references to on-screen actions, try not to mention the environment in which you are writing unless it is specifically relevant. Don't talk about the intranet, the Internet, or the Web if you can avoid it. Also, avoid references to archives, files, directories, and other terms that refer to the medium instead of to your message's key subject.

Don't Write About Writing

Your readers are interested in your subject, not the tools you are using to write about it. Avoid references to the mechanics of your writing.

Also, it doesn't pay to be flowery or overly expressive on-screen. Just offer the information and keep it as short as possible. Avoid language like, "Following is a list of . . ." Your reader *knows* it's a list when she sees it. Writers don't write this way for paper; online, it's almost a point of pride to show that you have figured out how to use HTML to make a list. But such writing is extra text that distracts the reader's eye away from key messages during the process of scanning.

Listen to Your Links and Your Document

Listening to the elements of your document means listening to the signals they send and the reactions they create.

Listen first to your links. Are there so many that they distract the reader from the main message? Will too many links invite the reader to leave the document and go elsewhere? Each link is an invitation to a choice for your reader; readers are forced to decide whether to click on the link and go where it takes them or stay with the document they are reading.

Next, listen to the document itself. Based on the paths you created to get there, does the document make sense? Does it provide the proper context? Are the links offering information consistent with what the reader is expecting from the page?

Limit Distracting Elements

Bold face and italic text, used in print to create emphasis, have a different effect on the screen. When a reader scans a screen, anything that jumps out as different will draw the eye. If the bold face or italic text does not contain the key element of your message, it serves as a distraction, making it more difficult for the reader to absorb that key point. Try to establish rules for the use of bold face or italic type.

The same principles apply to horizontal lines, an HTML element that serves to divide one part of a Web page from another. Having too many lines makes it difficult to scan, and can frustrate the reader. Guidelines that help you use horizontal lines according to a scheme will make it easier for the reader to understand how they help him use the information on the page.

Redundancy

Although the Web is growing at an unprecedented pace, there are still many individuals without access to the Internet—even in companies with extensive intranets. There are blue-collar and factory workers, field representatives, drivers, agents, and a host of other individuals who still need to receive material in print.

That doesn't mean that you, as a communicator, need to handle that distribution. You can make a hard copy available *online* and shift the responsibility to the supervisor to take advantage of having access to the hard-copy version. If they have employees without access, supervisors can print out a hard copy, photocopy it, and distribute it. The same method works for employees who need to take hard copies of material home to spouses or domestic partners.

Use the online document as the basis for the single-file hard copy. This approach argues even more against referencing Web actions or online mechanics in the text. "Click here" won't mean anything to an individual reading a hard-copy printout of the document.

Make sure that the hard-copy version is available as a link at the top of the first page of the online version of the document, just as MCI did with its annual report. You could use the Web and its hyperlinking capabilities to review the online version of the report, or one click would lead you to a download of a Microsoft Word version that you could print out and read the old-fashioned way.

Document Elements

When you write a Web document, you need to include the following elements:

↪ *The title.* This is the text that appears at the top of the screen, in the band of color that begins with the name of the application (for example, Netscape Navigator or Internet Explorer). Your title should not address the specific context of the material on the page, but rather should be a brief description of the topic.

↪ *Main headline.* In HTML parlance, this is called Head Level 1. This is the headline that tells the reader what this particular page is about. Keep it short.

↪ *Subheads.* You may not like the way Head Level 2 looks under Head Level 1, or how Head Level 3 looks under Head Level 2.

But the text was designed to make it easy for readers to distinguish between levels, so resist any temptation to use the head-level settings for design purposes. Stick with the approach as it is written. Sub-heads should summarize the topic of the material under them.

Each document (one long page or a collection of chunked pages) should contain a table of contents, and a link back to the table of contents, so readers can quickly get to the information they need. You might want to include an index as well, particularly if there is a great deal of material with numerous key words. The table of contents should appear *at the beginning* of the document; the index, on the other hand, should be accessible only if a reader clicks on the link to see it.

Credibility

When your words go out into the world between the pages of a magazine, the fact that the magazine is recognizable as a product of an organization (along with the obvious implication that the organization had sufficient money to print and distribute it) inherently lends credibility to the publication.

There is so much online that just about anybody can put there, that such credibility is called into question far more quickly than it is presumed.

There are several steps you can take in the preparation of your document to ensure that the audience views it as credible, including the following:

- ↪ The name of the sponsor (the department, division, unit, or team under whose authority the information was produced)
- ↪ The name of the subject matter expert who is accountable for the accuracy and timeliness of the information on the page
- ↪ An e-mail link to the author, such as:
  <A HREF = "mailto:john@doe.com">John Smith</A>
- ↪ The date the document was distributed
- ↪ The date(s) the document was revised
- ↪ Any other information you can provide to reflect how current the document is

Hyperlinks

From a writing perspective, there are several types of hyperlinks, such as the following:

- ➯ Links within the same document
- ➯ All headlines at the top, linking down to the text to which they refer
- ➯ Links within text to glossary definitions, footnotes, and other descriptive text
- ➯ Links to other documents on different Web pages

When linking to another document, it is best to *not* set your links within the body of your text. However, this is not a hard-and-fast rule, and many Web page writers don't follow it. But many readers are surprised when they click on a word in the middle of a paragraph and find themselves suddenly transported to another Web site. The flow of the text they were reading has been lost. It is better to set your off-site links at the bottom of the page, by using buttons, icons, or textual links. In any case, ensure that the links you provide are relevant, and don't overdo it. A page loaded with outside links (other than a page that is *designated* as an index of links) can be frustrating and difficult to read.

Your hyperlinks should be treated as annotations that clearly indicate what the reader will find when she clicks on it. Vague links, links that tease, and links that are meant to raise curiosity are not effective on business sites. At a base level, ensure that your link covers the nature of the content that will be found (for example, "a foot-and-mouth disease update"). What else you need to include depends on your audience. In the case of this example, a professional audience may need to know that the material is aimed at them and not at a lay audience (for example, "a foot-and-mouth disease update for doctors.") It may also be important that they know how timely the information is (for example, "a weekly foot-and-mouth disease update for doctors.") Finally, they may need to know the source of the information to determine its credibility and relevance (for example, "a weekly foot-and-mouth disease update for doctors from the Centers for Disease Control").

Be careful how much text is actually part of the link. You can treat a link (particularly one that is not embedded in the copy, but rather part of a list of links in a box or at the end of the document) as a headline and subhead, by hyperlinking only the first line:

Foot-and-mouth disease update
A weekly bulletin for doctors from the Centers for Disease Control

When linking within the text, make sure that you are only using the links from headlines to text and back to the table of contents, or to brief footnotes or glossary definitions. You should avoid using in-text links to take readers to a new thread of narrative.

Online Resources

IF THE INTERNET offers an abundance of information to your audiences, it provides an equally plentiful wealth of resources for you in your efforts to communicate with your various constituent audiences. One bit of warning: Web sites come and go! Most of the resources listed here are likely to be around for some time, but you can never be certain. This list of resources is maintained in a version that is routinely updated on the author's Web site at *www.holtz.com*.

Public Relations Tools

ProfNet

www.profnet.com
Journalists often need sources they can quote. Public relations professionals frequently want their clients to be quoted. ProfNet is a clearinghouse owned by PR Newswire that puts the two together. Reporters submit queries about the type of source or information for which they are looking. Several daily e-mails are sent to subscribers (mostly public relations practitioners) listing the queries. (The subscription is fee-based.) ProfNet offers a variety of categories to subscribers, from Energy/Environmental/Agriculture to Law/Crime/Justice (a total of thirteen lists).

Communication Arts Magazine

www.commarts.com
The Web site of the best print magazine on graphic design includes

exhibits, contest winners, and other sources of ideas for your own foray into print presentation.

The PR Network

www.theprnetwork.com
A site dedicated to providing information on what is happening in the world of Internet public relations, advertising, marketing communication, and new media. The site offers a directory of companies and services, as well as a weekly e-zine and mailing list.

The Professional Practice Center

www.prsa.org/ppc/index.html
The Public Relations Society of America's customer service and information resources site includes an online mailing list where peers post questions, ideas, and best practices. The site also includes studies, reports, surveys, and other resources.

Customizable News Sources

CRAYON (CReAte Your Own Newspaper)

www.crayon.net
A clever use of the Web that allows you to create your own customized listing of news, columns, and features, which you store on your hard drive. Whenever you load it, it automatically pulls in the latest updated information via e-mail, a Web page, or both.

Professional Public Relations and Communications Associations

International Association of Business Communicators (IABC)

www.iabc.com
IABC is one of the two leading communications associations (the other is PRSA). IABC tends to attract communicators who work in-

side corporations or for agencies that handle corporate (or institutional) public relations. The IABC Web site includes a discussion forum where various communications issues are discussed. It is worth noting that IABC also maintains a discussion group on CompuServe's Public Relations & Marketing Forum, which is available via the Web at *www.csi.com/forums.*

Council of Public Relations Firms (CPRF)

www.prfirms.org
An industry group for public relations agencies.

Public Relations Society of America (PRSA)

www.prsa.org
PRSA, the other major communications association, is focused more on marketing-oriented public relations, although the organization certainly addresses corporate PR, investor relations, and a host of other topics. Members tend to be agency employees (or PR counselors) engaged in account management. PRSA also maintains a discussion group on the CompuServe Public Relations & Marketing Forum at *www.csi.com/forums.*

National Investor Relations Institute

www.niri.org
NIRI is a United States–based organization that is tightly focused on investor relations and financial communications. The site includes a treasure trove of links to investor relations sites elsewhere on the Web.

Society for Technical Communication

www.stc.org
Membership includes writers, editors, illustrators, printers, publishers, educators, students, engineers, and scientists employed in a variety of technological fields.

British Association of Communicators in Business

www.bacb.org
Representing European business communicators.

National Association of Government Communicators

www.nagc.com
Membership covers writers, graphic and video artists, editors, broadcasters, photographers, and public information officers—anyone involved in any field that has anything to do with disseminating information within and outside of government.

Canadian Public Relations Society

www.cprs.ca
CPRS is the Canadian equivalent of PRSA.

Communicators Roundtable

www.roundtable.org
An organization representing twenty-four communications, public relations, marketing, graphics, advertising, and information technology organizations, with nearly seven thousand members.

Council of Communication Management

www.ccmconnection.com
The site of another communication association, this is a small group of employee communication managers.

Public Relations Resources

Holtz Communication + Technology

www.holtz.com
The author's Web site includes links to other resources, a collection of essays on the application of technology to strategic communication, a knowledge base of online public relations tools, and a variety of other resources.

Investor Relations Information Network

www.irin.com
Billing itself as the "World-Wide Data Bank of Annual Reports," this

site features outstanding examples of online annual reports and other investor relations–oriented material.

National PR Network

www.usprnet.com
An attempt at a virtual community of public relations counselors and suppliers, the National PR Network features regular industry updates, employment news, and additional resources.

Business Wire

www.businesswire.com
The online home of one of the premiere news distribution services.

PR Newswire

www.prnewswire.com
A leading international electronic distributor of news releases, photographs, and other material destined for the media and financial markets.

NewsPlace

www.niu.edu/newsplace
A collection of resources for journalists and other writers conducting research.

Marketing 1 to 1

www.marketing1to1.com
A consulting firm that offers numerous free resources to help develop a greater understanding of the 1:1 marketing concept. Sign up to receive a weekly newsletter or to participate in discussions online.

Public Relations Agency Web Listing

www.impulse-research.com/prlist.html
A comprehensive listing of public relations agencies in the United States and abroad that maintain Web sites.

American Demographics Magazine

www.demographics.com
Because demographics are such an important part of traditional communications, this magazine can be useful—particularly since you can search its archives for information related to your current communications undertaking. Typing *environment* into the search page, for example, brought up a number of references, including an article on the declining interest of U.S. citizens in the environment.

Public Relations Discussion Forums

PRFORUM

About one thousand public relations practitioners, academics, and students participate in this discussion group. Quality of content varies, but there are enough nuggets to make it worthwhile. To subscribe, send the words *SUBSCRIBE YOUR_FULL_NAMEPRFORUM* to the e-mail address: listserv@listserv.iupui.edu.

Public Relations Mailing Lists

ACR-L

ACR-L is a list to discuss the topic of consumer research. This list serves as a bulletin board for researchers, practitioners, and graduate students working in the interdisciplinary field of consumer research. To subscribe, send the words *SUBSCRIBE ACR-L YOUR_FULL_NAME* to the e-mail address: listserv@listserv.okstate.edu.

Direct Marketing Digest

An unmoderated mailing list focused on direct marketing and relationship marketing. For information, send e-mail to dm-intro @argo-navis.com. For subscription information, send e-mail to dm-info@argo-navis.com.

Electronic Marketing Digest

A place for marketers and communicators to trade war stories about their online experiences. Subscribing can be accomplished on the World Wide Web at *www.webbers.com/emark/*

EventWeb

Interactive marketing guidance for those who produce meetings, conferences, and trade shows. Subscribe on the Web site at *www.eventweb.com.*

Crisis Communications

A Blueprint for Crisis Communication

www.niu.edu/newsplace/crisis.html
No charge for this document that runs through the basics of a good crisis communication plan.

Crisis Communication

www.colorado.edu/conflict/peace/problem/crisiscom.htm
An academic overview of crisis communication with good resource links and case studies.

Pier System

www.piersystem.com
An intriguing concept: Host your crisis response center on the servers of a service that includes media databases and press release distribution mechanisms.

Crisis Manager Newsletter

www.bernsteincom.com/newsletter.html
Case histories and articles from a crisis management expert.

Resources on Writing and Designing for the Web

Good Documents

www.gooddocuments.com
A good, concise overview of the rules for writing Web-based documents.

PRSA Technology Section

www.tech.prsa.org
The Public Relations Society of America divides its activities into sections, and the technology section has assembled a vast array of resources on its Web site.

Journal of Electronic Publishing

www.press.umich.edu/jep/index.html
The quarterly from the University of Michigan offers useful insights, research results, and other proprietary information.

Journal of Computer Mediated Communications

www.ascusc.org/jcmc/
From the University of Southern California's Annenberg School of Communication, the journal offers an academic take on the impact and influence of online communication, including but not limited to the World Wide Web.

What is Good Hypertext Writing?

kbs.cs.tu-berlin.de/~jutta/ht/writing.html
Jutta Degener writes and teaches in Germany, but uses outstanding English to promote notions of what makes for good online copy. The associated list of so-called dangerous words is a winner, too, warning writers of onscreen text to avoid using everything from *click* to *hot*.

Tim Berners-Lee's Style Guide for Online Hypertext

www.w3.org/Provider/Style/Overview.html
Berners-Lee invented the World Wide Web and currently chairs the World Wide Web Consortium, so he would know! The site advises on hypertext structure and elements to include in each document.

Applying Writing Guidelines to Web Pages

www.useit.com/papers/webwriting/rewriting.html
Jakob Nielsen is the coauthor of this site, which presents research results used in a study the senior scientist at Sun Microsystems conducted on Web readability. An earlier document, still of tremendous value, is at *www.useit.com/papers/webwriting/writing.html*.

General Internet Information

All About the Internet

www.isoc.org/internet-history/
A brief history of the Internet, including an Internet timeline, from the official Internet Society.

Cyberatlas

www.cyberatlas.com
A compendium of Internet statistics and research focusing on demographics and use of the Internet and its various components. Well maintained and up-to-date.

Internet Index

www.openmarket.com/intindex/
Interesting facts about the Internet, updated regularly. For instance, 40 percent of people watch PC and television screens simultaneously. (You needed to know that, right?)

Google Groups

groups.google.com
A utility that allows you to find Usenet newsgroup postings containing words that match your query.

HTML Information and Tutorials

A Beginner's Guide to HTML

www.ncsa.uiuc.edu/General/Internet/WWW/HTMLPrimer.html
Widely acclaimed as the best beginner's guide to HTML, this tutorial from the National Center for Supercomputing Applications walks you through the various stages and elements of Web page and site development.

Yale Web Style Guide

info.med.yale.edu/caim/manual/contents.html
Covers interface design, site design, page design, Web graphics, multimedia, and animation.

Web Pages That Suck

www.webpagesthatsuck.com
Learn good design by looking at bad design.

Webmaster Reference Library

www.webreference.com
An electronic magazine coupled with a variety of resources.

Spinster's Guide to Writing for the Web

www.bc.edu/bc_org/avp/ulib/sys/html/spin.html
From Boston College's library, this guide offers ideas for improving Web-site readability and design.

Search Engines and Directories

Google

www.google.com
The author's favorite search engine.

HotBot

www.hotbot.com
Another gem.

AltaVista

www.altavista.digital.com
One of the early search engines, from Digital Equipment Corporation.

Yahoo!

www.yahoo.com
The best of the search indexes, Yahoo! features a variety of other elements, including news, weather, maps, and more.

Lycos

www.lycos.com
A combination index and engine.

Go

www.go.com
Another combination index and engine, this one also allows you to scour Usenet newsgroups, the news, and companies.

Search.Com

www.search.com
An all-in-one index of search engines and indexes.

General Writing Resources

Strunk & White's Elements of Style

www.columbia.edu/acis/bartleby/strunk/
The generally accepted bible of writing style is online for quick reference.

Bartlett's Familiar Quotations

www.bartleby.com/100/
Need a quote quickly? Visit this site, type in a search term, and you'll have plenty of options from which to choose. (Samuel Johnson wrote, "Knowledge is of two kinds: we know a subject ourselves, or we know where we can find information upon it.")

Grammar and Style Notes

andromeda.rutgers.edu/~jlynch/Writing/
Another good resource for style, and grammar is thrown in, as well. List owner Jack Lynch will even respond to queries about grammar and style.

Copyright, Trademark, and Other Online Legal Issues

Cyberspace Law for Non-Lawyers

www.ssrn.com/update/lsn/cyberspace/csl_lessons.html
Lectures from a mailing list that provides a compendium of legal issues related to the Internet and the online world, from copyright and privacy to libel and contract law. Fascinating and easy to digest. The site includes a discussion area where you can raise a question and get a genuine legal opinion. I used this site to help a client make a decision about fair use of materials from another publisher. It's an invaluable resource.

Recommended Reading

A WEALTH OF literature exists that can help you to conduct public relations and communications campaigns, understand the Internet and the World Wide Web, and use the Internet and the Web for your marketing-oriented communications efforts. The following list of recommended reading is by no means comprehensive. I recommend these books based on having read them or knowing the authors. Most of these books are available for purchase via the Internet. You can search for them individually at Amazon.com or any of the other online booksellers; I have also compiled a direct link to all these books via my Web site at *http://www.holtz.com.*

You can find another good public relations reading list at the Web site of the Council of Public Relations Firms at *http://www.prfirms.org/bookstore/default.asp.*

The Internet

Evans, Phillip, and Thomas Wurster. *Blown to Bits: How the New Economics of Information Transforms Strategy.* Boston: Harvard Business School Press, 1999.

Hafner, Katie. *Where Wizards Stay Up Late: The Origins of the Internet.* Minneapolis: Econo-Clad Books, 1999.

Locke, Christopher, et al. *The Cluetrain Manifesto: The End of Business As Usual.* Boulder: Perseus Books, 2001.

Nielsen, Jakob, *Designing Web Usability: The Practice of Simplicity.* Indianapolis: New Riders, 1999.

Rheingold, Howard. *The Virtual Community: Homesteading on the Electronic Frontier,* rev. ed. Boston: MIT Press, 2000.

Fundamentals of Public Relations

Caywood, Clarke, ed. *The Handbook of Strategic Public Relations and Integrated Communications.* New York: McGraw-Hill, 1997.

Cutlip, Scott. *Effective Public Relations.* Upper Saddle River, New Jersey: Prentice Hall, 1999.

Dozier, David M. *Managers Guide to Excellence in Public Relations and Communication Management.* Mahwah, New Jersey: Lawrence Erlbaum Associates, 1995.

Fonbrum, Charles. *Reputation: Realizing Value from the Corporate Image.* Boston: Harvard Business School Press, 1996.

Grunig, James E, ed. *Excellence in Public Relations and Communications Management.* Mahwah, New Jersey: Lawrence Erlbaum Associates, 1992.

Seitel, Fraser. *Practice of Public Relations.* Upper Saddle River, New Jersey: Prentice Hall, 2000.

Wann, Al, ed. *Inside Organizational Communication.* San Francisco: IABC, 1999.

Crisis Management

Barton, Lawrence. *Crisis in Organizations.* Boston: South-Western Publishers, 2000.

Caponigro, Jeffrey. *The Crisis Counselor: A Step-by-Step Guide to Managing a Business Crisis.* New York: McGraw-Hill, 2000.

Cohn, Robert. *PR Crisis Bible: How to Take Charge of the Media When All Hell Breaks Loose.* New York: St. Martins Press, 2000.

Coombs, Timothy. *Ongoing Crisis Communication: Planning, Managing and Responding.* Thousand Oaks, California: Corwin PR, 1999.

Fink, Steven. *Crisis Management: Planning for the Inevitable.* Campbell, California: iUniverse.com, 2000.

Janal, Daniel. *Risky Business: Protect Your Company from Being Stalked, Conned or Blackmailed on the Web.* New York: John Wiley, 1998.

Jones, Clarence. *Winning with the News Media: A Self-Defense Manual When You're the Story.* Tampa: Video Consultants, 2001.

Media Relations

Matthews, Wilma, and Carole Howard. *On Deadline.* Prospect Heights, Illinois: Waveland Press, 2000.

Marketing and Marketing Communications

Godin, Seth. *Permission Marketing.* New York: Simon and Shuster, 1999.

———. *Unleashing the Idea Virus.* New York: Do You Zoom, 2000.

Janal, Dan. *Dan Janal's Guide to Internet Marketing.* New York: John Wiley, 2000.

Middleberg, Don. *Winning PR in the Wired World.* New York: McGraw-Hill, 2000.

Writing for the Web

Holtz, Shel. *Writing for the Wired World: The Communicator's Guide to On-line Content.* San Francisco: IABC, 1999.

Sammons, Martha C. *The Internet Writer's Handbook.* Boston: Allyn and Bacon, 1999.

Internet Fundamentals

IN THE FIRST edition of this book, Chapter 3 included considerable text that introduced public relations professionals to the work-
ings of the Internet. I scrapped that material from this edition based
on my observation that, even if they don't know how to apply these
tools strategically, most people working in public relations know what
they are. Still, for those who need only the simplest explanations, I'm
including it in this new Appendix section.

The Internet

The Internet is, at its core, a network comprising smaller computer
networks. Each of the networks—and each of the computers on
those networks—can retrieve information that is made available on
any of the other networks and their computers. In other words, when
you are on the Internet, the information available to you expands
beyond what is on your hard drive or local network. You have access
to all the information that others make available from their systems
throughout the Internet.

This sharing of information is made possible by a series of *protocols,* which are rules that govern how computers handle certain types
of information. The family of protocols that governs the Internet is
called Transmission Control Protocol/Internet Protocol (TCP/IP).
The Internet is non-platform specific; that is, it works on any type of
computer—PCs running DOS, PCs running Windows, Macintoshes,
UNIX, anything. As long as the network and its computers are con-

figured to address TCP/IP protocols, they can function as a component part of the Internet.

TCP/IP tells computers how to locate the source of information,
and how to manage the delivery and receipt of information. Specifically, the Transmission Control Protocol manages the packaging of
data into small packets. Each packet is sent over the Internet via the
fastest route at the instant it leaves its point of origin. When all the
packets arrive at their destination, they are reassembled so that the
recipient can see the data in its original form. The Internet Protocol
handles the address that is associated with each packet to ensure that
it goes where it was intended. Every node on the Internet is assigned
an IP "address," a series of numbers separated by dots (or periods).
For example, IBM's IP address looks like this:

129.34.139.30

Of course, while numbers are easy for computers to deal with,
nobody could remember such a string of numbers, no less memorize
dozens or even hundreds of them! To make it easier on us mere mor-
tals, the Internet makes it possible to assign a name to each IP address. When you type *www.ibm.com* in your Web browser, your
request is routed to a piece of hardware called a *name server*. The
name server checks whether ibm.com is a legitimate name. Once
the name is found, the server sends your request to the related IP
address.

Client-server is another term you probably will hear bandied
about as you work with network specialists to implement Internet
communication plans. Client-server refers to a type of computing
activity in which information resides on a computer known as a
server. Servers are configured with appropriate software that incorporates the correct set of TCP/IP protocols to do what they are supposed to do. Your computer is the *client*—that is, it is the individual
workstation that is going to make a request of the server. When you
retrieve your e-mail, for example, your client computer sends a request to the e-mail server, which makes sure that you are authorized
to receive your e-mail (that is, you enter the appropriate password),
and responds to your request by delivering the messages it has collected to your desktop. (The terms *clients* and *servers* can become
confusing, since a client computer can also be a server, and vice
versa. For example, you can use your computer as a client when you

retrieve your e-mail, but it also can be configured as a Web server, distributing Web pages to other client computers that request them.)

Although TCP/IP comprises these two protocols, it also includes a suite of secondary protocols that rely on TCP/IP to work, which include:

- Hypertext Transfer Protocol (HTTP), which manages information configured for the World Wide Web
- File Transfer Protocol (FTP), which manages the transfer of entire files (such as word processor documents) from somewhere on the network to your computer
- Simple Mail Transfer Protocol (SMTP), which manages the sending of e-mail
- Network News Transfer Protocol (NNTP), which manages Usenet discussion groups

There are many other protocols, as well, that are more technical in nature and are not important to the understanding of the Internet as a public relations tool. For the record, some of these have names like Serial Line Internet Protocol (SLIP), Interior Gateway Protocol (IGP), and Internet Control Message Protocol (ICMP). These are the types of protocols your systems or network administrator should handle; you should never need to worry about them.

It is the protocols that function as a part of TCP/IP—e-mail, the Web, newsgroups, and file transfer—that make the Internet useful and provide organizations with new tools for delivering messages and engaging audiences in dynamic multidirectional communication. We'll explore each of these four sets of tools and how they can be employed in organizational communication efforts.

E-Mail

E-mail takes many forms, but at its core it is a message that one individual sends to an individual or a group of people at a particular address (associated, of course, with the IP address of the recipient). In general, you create an e-mail message using an e-mail client—that is, a software application designed to manage your e-mail needs. These include:

⇝ Creating and sending messages.

⇝ Retrieving messages waiting for you on your server (usually known as a POP3 server).

⇝ Automating actions to messages, such as automatically forwarding all messages from a designated address to a list of other people who should see all correspondence from that individual.

⇝ Managing messages, including establishing categories of incoming mail, such as products, legal, personal, and media. Messages that meet the criteria you select are automatically routed into the appropriate category. For example, if you get mail from *Los Angeles Times* reporters and you know the *Times*'s e-mail domain is lat.com, you can set up your e-mail client to automatically store all mail from lat.com in the media folder.

E-mail clients are available in a variety of configurations. You can spend a lot of money on one, a little bit of money, or none at all. Some e-mail clients can be downloaded for free, including Eudora (from *www.eudora.com*) and Pegasus Mail (from *www.pmail.com*). Microsoft Outlook Express comes with the Internet Explorer program, and Microsoft Outlook, the more robust version, comes bundled with the Microsoft Office package. Netscape Navigator—another free browser available for download from *www.netscape. com*—comes with an e-mail program, as well.

Each e-mail message you receive (or send, for that matter) contains a *header*. The header comprises all the information the Internet needs to route the message to the correct place, and contains a wealth of information you may need. A typical header looks something like this one, which was part of an e-mail message I received from a public relations–oriented Web site (the National PR Network) the morning I wrote this explanation:

```
Received: from julia.siinternet.com [208.225.225.13]
From: swynkoop@usprnet.com (National PR Network Community)
To: ⟨shel@holtz.com⟩
Date: Sat, 24 Jan 1998 14:44:44
Reply-To: swynkoop@usprnet.com
Errors-To: swynkoop@diac.com
X-URL: http://www.usprnet.com
```

X-Mailer: NetMailer v1.04B [D.R-D2F27392415261104]
Subject: National PR Network—New, Free InfoExchange

Let's look at each line of the header to see what we can learn:

➥ *Line One.* This line lists the server from which the mail was sent. This generally refers to the Internet Service Provider (ISP) somebody is using to provide e-mail services to them.

➥ *Line Two.* This line tells us who sent the mail. In this case, it was Steve Wynkoop, one of the founders of the National PR Network.

➥ *Line Three.* This line specifies the recipient of the message.

➥ *Line Four.* This line shows the date and time the message was sent.

➥ *Line Five.* This line shows the e-mail address you should use to reply to the message. If you simply click the "reply" button on your e-mail client, this is the address to which your reply will be sent.

➥ *Line Six.* This line contains the e-mail address that will be notified if the message can't get through for some reason (say, if your mail server is down or the recipient's address was incorrectly entered).

➥ *Line Seven.* This line has the address of the Web site associated with the sender of the message.

➥ *Line Eight.* This line lists what type of software was used to send the message.

➥ *Line Nine.* This is the subject line Steve entered so that I would know what the message was about.

Additional lines can appear on an e-mail header, many of which are highly technical in nature.

Most e-mail is limited to ASCII characters. (ASCII stands for American Standard Code for Information Exchange. These are, basically, the characters you can see on your keyboard.) Newer e-mail clients also allow you to incorporate World Wide Web markup, so that you can add bold face, italics, text sizes, background images, and other elements to your e-mail. You also can attach files to your e-mail, allowing you to send along a word processor file or a graphic image with your basic text.

The World Wide Web

If e-mail remains the most pervasive application on the Internet, the World Wide Web is the feature that opened the Internet to the rest of the world. It also represents the most influential and useful new tool in many years to become available to organizations trying to manage their constituent relationships.

Before the Web (as we know it today) hit the scene late in 1993, all access to the Internet was made through the following methods:

- ➾ Using archaic and nonintuitive text commands.
- ➾ Over remote systems. That is, your computer linked up to another computer that was connected to the Internet. Your computer became a dumb terminal, showing you the results found by the remote computer, and allowing you to tell the remote computer what commands to send next.

Even the World Wide Web (which was first introduced to the Internet community in 1989) was at first a text-driven vehicle. As noted in Chapter 1, the Web was introduced as a new method for navigating the Internet. The author of a document destined for the Internet attached a special text code that associated it with another document somewhere else on the Net. You would use the tab key of your computer to jump to any highlighted text that intrigued you. Once your cursor was over the highlighted text, you pressed the enter key to activate the hyperlink, which would automatically retrieve the new document, regardless of where on the Internet it was housed.

In late 1993, however, a team of students from the National Center for Supercomputing Applications (NCSA) at the University of Illinois introduced Mosaic, a utility for using the World Wide Web that was dubbed a *browser.* The browser retrieved a Web page and then "parsed" it—that is, it interpreted various bits of script embedded in the page, then displayed the text accordingly. Because Mosaic was a graphical interface— affecting type, colors, and other graphical elements—it also could display images, such as photographs and illustrations. And rather than tab over to a hyperlink and press enter to activate it, you could simply point your mouse at the hyperlink (which now appeared as a blue underlined word or phrase) and click on it. The process worked on exactly the same Hypertext Transfer Protocol (HTTP) as the original text-based Web.

This graphical, point-and-click approach to navigating the Internet was so simple that, suddenly, the Internet became accessible to the average computer user. At the same time, other developments allowed users to install TCP/IP software directly on their own computers; they could now establish a direct connection to the Internet. As an increasing number of people signed up and installed Mosaic on their computers, more and more individuals and institutions created sites and pages to which people could navigate. Commercial versions of the Mosaic browser cropped up. Internet Service Providers, the boom business of the mid-1990s, began giving browsers away for free to anybody who signed up for their service.

WHEN DEALING WITH a printer, public relations practitioners need a working knowledge of printing lingo. If you've ever had something printed, you can probably handle discussions that include phrases like "two-up," "saddle-stitch," "touch plates," "spot varnish," and "halftone." Working with video production leads you to understand the technical meanings of "speed," "dub," "boom," and "ADO."

Working with the professionals who produce your online efforts requires the same degree of competence in the lingo. The following glossary defines key terms that you are likely to encounter when you manage the production of online communication efforts. If the term you're seeking is not here, try one of the following excellent online resources:

- Webopedia: *www.webopedia.com*
- What Is: *www.whatis.com*

access Getting what you need, usually with permission, from whoever holds it. Access to the Web or the Internet generally refers to a connection through an access provider (also known as an Internet service provider) or to a commercial online service (such as CompuServe).

access provider (*See* Internet service provider)

Acrobat Adobe Systems Incorporated produces this software, which allows you to capture a document with all of its original formatting—regardless of the software application used to produce it—and let others view it on their computers, regardless of the platform they use. The file Acrobat produces is known as a portable document format (PDF). You need an Acrobat reader to view the document, which is available free from Adobe as well as anybody with the software to produce a PDF file. PDF has become a *de facto* format on the Internet, and is built into most current Web browsers. Thus, if you create a Web page with a link to a PDF file, the file automatically will appear with all original formatting directly on the Web page.

ActiveX A Microsoft standard for programs that can run in Windows, Macintosh, or Web environments. These programs give you the ability to build interactivity into Web pages that goes beyond the limits of HTML. ActiveX components can do many of the same things Java can do, and it also can work in tandem with Java.

address

1. Internet address, the domain, or associated name that you use to get to a host computer.

2. Home page address, or URL, of a particular Web site.

3. E-mail address, which you use to send e-mail to an individual.

agent (*also* intelligent agent)   A program that gathers information or performs a service based on parameters you establish, but on a schedule and without your direct involvement.

algorithm   A formula or a procedure that solves a problem.

American Standard Code for Information Exchange (ASCII)   These are the characters, in general, that you can see on your keyboard. ASCII is the most common format for text files in computers and on the Internet.

animated GIF   A graphic image made up of independent graphic files that combine to create movement on a Web page.

applet   Small application programs, generally associated with the Java programming language. Java applications that run on Web pages are known as applets.

application   Short for *application program*. Microsoft Word, Corel Draw, and FileMaker Pro are applications.

article   In the online world, an article is a message that is posted to a Usenet discussion group.

asynchronous   From the Greek, meaning "not at the same time." Discussion forums are asynchronous because participants don't need to participate at the same time. Rather, one can post a message and leave; others can log on later, read the message, and respond. The original contributor comes back at his leisure to view responses.

autoresponder   Software used to generate a prepared message and send it as e-mail in response to e-mail you received. Any message delivered to a specific address will automatically generate the response from the software. Many organizations establish an e-mail address with the name "info" (as in *info@acme.com*) and invite people to send e-mail to the address to receive more information about the company or its products or services.

avatar   A digital representation of an individual to be used in an online environment. In some 3D worlds, for example, you can pick a fish, a chess piece, or some other character to represent you to other avatars, each of which stands in for the real, live individual sitting at his computer.

back end   An application or program that supports an application or program an individual is using. This application or program usually resides close to where the required resource resides. (*See also* front end)

backbone   A larger transmission path into and from which smaller lines feed. On the Internet, local and regional telecommunication networks connect to a backbone to send traffic generated locally over long distances.

bandwidth   How much stuff you can send at once. A system with low bandwidth cannot handle the transmission of too much information at any given time. This type of network would be an unlikely candidate for audio and video streams, for example. High bandwidth, on the other hand, means that there is plenty of room for many people to grab big files at the same time. Bandwidth is proportional to digital speed. A modem that connects at 28,800 bits per second (bps) has only half the bandwidth of one that connects at 57,600 bps.

banner   A graphic image on a Web site. Banners, generally horizontal strips, are used as a graphic identity for a Web site or as an advertisement (as in "banner ads").

baud   Still used but not accurately, baud is a unit of measure for data transmission capacity. It has been replaced by bits per second (bps), which is frequently mistakenly referred to as bauds per second.

Because It's Time Network (BitNet)   A network of educational sites separate from the Internet, but from which e-mail is freely exchanged on the Internet.

beta   Software in the second phase of testing. In this phase, software is generally distributed to a group of volunteer testers from outside the developing organization. These beta testers provide feedback that is used to correct bugs and improve the software before releasing it for sale to the public.

bit   From a combination of *binary* and *digit*. In digital terms, the smallest unit of information. Bits have only one binary value—either a zero (0) or a one (1). Combinations of bits, which are stored in memory and used to execute instructions, are called *bytes*. Generally, there are eight bits in a byte.

bluetooth   A computing and telecommunications industry specification that describes how mobile telephones, computers, and handheld devices can interconnect with each other and with home and business telephones and computers using a short-range wireless connection.

bookmark   Most World Wide Web browsers allow you to store links to your favorite sites. These stored links are called *bookmarks.* Some browsers give them other names; Microsoft's Internet Explorer, for instance, refers to them as *favorites.* Microsoft uses the term *bookmark* in its FrontPage Web authoring program as a synonym for internal page anchors (hyperlinks within a single page).

As a verb, *bookmark* refers to the act of storing a site's URL in the browser's bookmark section (as in, "I visited a really great site yesterday, so I bookmarked it").

Boolean   Searching for information on the Web and in other online archives (such as the Lexis-Nexis database) requires the use of Boolean search terminology, named for the English mathematician George Boole. Boolean searching employs *operators,* words such as *and* and *or* that connect to words and provide the instructions used to complete a search.

boot   Start your computer, or, more technically, to load an operating system into your computer (an automatic function on most workstations that occurs when you turn your computer on). Comes from the nontechnical term, "Pull yourself up by your bootstraps."

broadband   A telecommunication method that transmits more information in a given amount of time. That is, it's fast! From using a wide band of frequencies.

browser   A program that serves as a graphical interface to the World Wide Web. Mosaic was the original browser; the two most commonly used browsers today are Netscape's Navigator and Microsoft's Internet Explorer. Browsers "parse" HTML files, converting the instructions contained in the code into the text, formatting, images, interactivity, and multimedia the page author intended you to see.

Bulletin Board System or Service (BBS)   A computer that can be reached by telephone or telnet for the purpose of sharing information, exchanging messages, and uploading and downloading files. Computers that are configured to function as a BBS must contain BBS software. Most BBSs are focused on special interests, such as political discussion, local communities, or games. There are more than forty thousand BBSs active worldwide, each run by a *sysop,* or system operator, many of whom run their own BBSs from their bedrooms or garages.

business-to-business (B2B)   Generally referring to a Web site that provides products or services to businesses.

business-to-consumer (B2C)   Generally referring to a Web site that provides products or services to consumers.

byte   An eight-bit long string that represents a character, letter, or symbol on the computer.

C and C++ Programming languages that are widely used in the programming community.

cascading style sheet (CSS) A means of instructing a Web browser how to display certain graphical elements of a Web page. Cascading style sheets were introduced in 1997, and provide desktop-publishing-like control over type in Web pages. Cascading style sheets will be critical in coming years as Web developers embrace XML, since the tags will be used to define data rather than appearance. (*See* XML)

certificate (or security certificate) A file sent to you identifying the source of a program or other item you are about to receive on your computer. Used to assure you that you are receiving the information or file from a valid source.

certificate authority An issuer of security certificates.

cgi-bin The most common name of a directory on a Web server in which CGI scripts are stored. The "bin" part of the directory name is short for *binary*.

chat Typing back and forth with other people on the Internet (or another online service) in real time. The biggest venue for chat is on an Internet service called Internet Relay Chat (IRC).

click Pressing a mouse button, usually over a hyperlink, to initiate an action on a Web page.

click stream The sequence a Web site visitor uses to navigate through a site, or from site to site. You start on a given page, then follow a link to another page, then another link to a different page, and so on. The total route you took is your click stream.

clickthrough rate The frequency with which visitors to a Web site click on an advertisement (such as a banner ad) that is displayed on the page.

client The requesting program or user in a client/server relationship. When you type a URL into a Web browser, you and your browser are the client, making a request of the server that contains the information you wish to retrieve.

co-location A server that belongs to one person or group that is physically located on an Internet-connected network that belongs to another person or group. Many companies make a living by providing a network on which you can co-locate your server, saving you from the expense of acquiring your own Internet connection.

common gateway interface (CGI) The usual method for a Web server to pass control to an application program and receive data back when it is finished. For example, if you complete a form online, the data you submit is passed by CGI to an application that resides on the server, where it is processed, and the results returned to you on your computer screen. Most of the code that is written for CGI "scripts" is completed in either the PERL or TCL programming languages.

compression The reduction of the size of data to save space or transmission time. Most audio and video that you retrieve over the Web was compressed to allow you to retrieve it in a reasonable amount of time.

content management system A system used to manage the content on a Web site.

cookie A file that is placed on your computer hard drive by a Web site that you have visited. The next time you visit that particular site, it will look for the cookie, which helps the site remember who you are, what you've done before on the site, and any other information you may have stored. Contrary to popular misconceptions, cookies cannot read your hard drive, gather files from your computer, damage your data, or provide anybody with access to your system.

counter A program on a Web site that counts the number of people who have visited the site. Many counters look like speedometers.

customer relationship management (CRM) Incorporates methodologies, software, and online functionality so that an enterprise can manage customer relationships in an organized way.

cyber A prefix that can be attached to nearly any noun to couch something as part of the computer or online age. Thus, *cyberspace* is the online world, *cyberfiction* is fiction published online, and *cyberculture* is the culture adopted by people who inhabit cyberspace.

cybercash Digital money that exists on your computer. The total value of the cybercash you have is reduced each time you use it to buy something. There are no standards yet for cybercash, although several companies offer competing methods.

data Information that exists in digital form, usually on a computer.

data mining The analysis of data to uncover information or relationships that may not have been evident before.

database A collection of data—usually by a program designed to facilitate the collection—making it easy to access, manage, update, change, and query the information. Most database applications on the market are relational databases, which allow you to reorganize information in a variety of ways.

denial of service Denial of service occurs when a source (often a hacker) attacks the network, leading to the inability of the organization to use the services of a resource they normally expect to be able to use, such as the World Wide Web or e-mail.

desktop   A computer display that provides you with graphical metaphors for the same tools you might use in an office, such as documents, writing tools, or project folders.

DHTML   Dynamic HTML incorporates programming elements into HTML for increased animation or responsiveness. (*See* hypertext markup language)

digital   Electronic technology that identifies and deals with data in two states: positive and nonpositive. Positive is represented by the number one (1) and nonpositive by the number zero (0). Data transmitted or stored with digital technology is expressed in its most basic format as a string of 0s and 1s.

digital camera   A camera that records and stores the images it has photographed in digital format so they can be displayed or transmitted by a computer. No film is used in a digital camera.

digital subscriber line (DSL)   This is a high-speed Internet access tool that uses existing copper telephone wire to deliver data at speeds as high as fifty times faster than modem dialup. DSL competes mostly with cable access, which uses existing television cable lines.

digizine   A magazine delivered in digital form, such as on CD-ROM or a Web page. (*See also* e-zine)

directory   Sometimes mistakenly called a search engine, a directory is a Web site that attempts to catalogue the contents of the World Wide Web. Unlike search engines, directories apply human decision making in the process of placing sites into categories. Yahoo! is a search directory.

discussion group   A catchall phrase for any bulletin board where you can leave messages to which others can respond asynchronously. Discussion groups exist on the Internet in a system called Usenet, on commercial online services, and on Web pages, as well as on privately run BBSs.

disintermediation   Giving an individual direct access to information or resources that usually would require a mediator, filter, or third party.

display   The visual interface through which you interact with a computer, usually the monitor. Display modes are the levels of clarity with which you view information on the monitor. There are four general display modes: CGA (Color Graphics Adapter—the earliest of the color display systems introduced by IBM), EGA (Enhanced Graphics Adapter, which allowed viewing of up to sixteen colors), VGA (Video Graphics Array, the accepted minimum standard for current computers, which allows you to see between 16 and 256 colors), and SVGA (Super Video Graphics Array, which can display up to 16 million colors).

distributed   Information that is spread out over a network is said to be *distributed.*

dithering   A computer program's attempt to approximate a color from a mixture of available colors that is undertaken when the original color is not available. Netscape Navigator, for example, offers a palette of colors. If a color you present on a Web page is not one of the palette colors, Navigator dithers a color from those colors that are available in an attempt to come as close as possible to the color you wanted.

domain   Generally, a set of network addresses organized by hierarchy. The top-level hierarchy specifies the purpose of the domain (for example, *com* is a commercial domain); the next level identifies a unique place within the top-level domain (equivalent to an IP address). On the Internet, it is a name with which a name server can associate a record. A domain name locates an organization on the Internet. For example, *www.amacombooks.com* locates an Internet address for AMACOM Books publishing. The domain name system (DNS) takes the name you entered into a Web browser and translates it into a numeric IP address that the Internet understands.

download   Transmission of a file from one computer (usually a server) to another (usually an individual workstation). On the Internet, you usually download a file when you request it from a Web site.

dynamic HTML   New hypertext markup language tags, options, style sheets, and programming that allow you to create Web pages that are more animated and responsive to user interaction than was available with the last iteration of HTML (version 3.2).

electronic data interchange (EDI)   A standard format for the exchange of business data, including online financial transactions.

e-mail   The exchange of messages by computer.

encryption   The conversion of data into a format that cannot be deciphered by anyone other than the individual(s) for whom the data was intended. The format into which data is converted is known as a *cipher.*

end user   The individual at a workstation who uses the information, software, or hardware you have produced, or the individual for whom the information, software, or hardware is designed.

engine   A program that performs an essential function. On the Internet, a *search engine* is a program that uses an algorithm to search an index of words from Web sites, newsgroups, or FTP archives based on a specific query or search argument.

enterprise   An organization or institution that uses computers as an integral part of its business.

enterprise resource planning (ERP) The set of activities supported by various application software programs that helps businesses manage the important elements of their processes, including product planning, parts purchasing, inventory management, interacting with suppliers, providing customer service, and tracking orders.

environment The combination of hardware and software in a computer (as in an *operating system environment*) or on a computer network (as in the *intranet environment*).

ethernet A protocol that makes it possible to run a local area network (LAN).

extranet A collaborative network based on Internet technology (that is, TCP/IP protocols) that links an organization with key audiences. Extranets are different from Web sites because audiences (including customers, suppliers, and strategic partners) have access to proprietary information, such as inventory and account status. Audiences also can submit information that can be sent directly into proprietary company databases. Often, an extranet is conditional access to selected portions of a company's intranet.

e-zine A magazine that exists online. Short for electronic magazine, e-zines can be independent online publications or the digital versions of print publications.

file A single unit of data saved under a name. These can be executable files (those that launch a program), data files (something you created and saved in an application), or support files (those that interact with a program to make it work).

file formats Usually a three-letter extension appended to the name of a file. That extension determines its format. For example, *exe* is an executable file, *doc* is a Microsoft Word file, *wp*5 is a WordPerfect file, *bak* is a backup file, and so on.

file sharing The process of making files available to others on a computer network. Networks allow you to establish various levels of access, so some may have the ability to work with your files, some may only be able to view them, and others may not be able to see them at all.

file transfer protocol (FTP) The TCP/IP protocol that enables the transfer of files from a server to a user's computer.

finger A program you can use through your Internet service provider to get information on another user (such as the user's name, the Internet service provider he uses, the last time he was logged on, and other information he may choose to make available).

firewall   A combination of hardware and software that is used to isolate a computer network from intrusion by the outside world, usually users of other networks.

flame   An e-mail or newsgroup message that is the online equivalent of hysterical yelling and screaming. Flames often attack individuals for their ideas, the way they expressed themselves, or their online behavior.

flame war   An online discussion that has degenerated into a series of personal attacks.

flamebait   A message posted to a newsgroup that is deliberately provocative, designed to elicit strong responses, or flames.

flash   A program developed by Macromedia that allows animation and other multimedia elements to be displayed on a Web page. Requires users to download and install a plug-in; however, more than 96 percent of all Web users have Flash installed on their computers.

forum   A virtual discussion venue hosted by a non-Usenet service. (*See* newsgroup)

frame   A separate section of a Web page that you can control independently of other sections. Frames are created in HTML, resulting in an effect that establishes separate windows within the Web browser. For example, an index of a site could exist in a narrow frame on the left side of the browser; clicking on each entry opens up a new page in the larger frame that occupies most of the browser to the right of the index frame.

frequently asked questions (FAQ)   These are lists of questions and answers that provide people with basic information on a given topic or site. FAQs originated in Usenet newsgroups, where newcomers would pepper the existing community with questions that already had been repeatedly addressed. FAQs evolved so newcomers could get those answers without bothering those who have been a part of the community, keeping the online discussions more focused on new and emerging issues. FAQs now exist on Web sites and mailing lists, as well.

front end   An application or interface with which the user interacts directly. (*See also* back end)

gateway   The entrance to a network.

gigabyte   One hundred megabytes, or about a billion bytes.

gopher   An Internet-based system for storing files in a hierarchical format. Gopher (developed at the University of Minnesota; hence the name) predates the World Wide Web as a means of finding information made available for public retrieval. Most of the material on Gopher servers is becoming outdated as the Internet migrates to the Web; however, many academic institutions still rely on it.

gopherspace   All of the information contained on all the Gopher servers across the entire Internet.

graphical user interface (GUI)   The graphical, visual metaphors on a computer screen that a user uses to work with the information the computer contains. Windows 95 and the Mac OS are GUIs. DOS, which is text-based, is *not*.

graphics interchanges format (GIF)   Developed originally by CompuServe, GIF is a standard graphical file format and is the predominant format used on the World Wide Web. (*See also* joint photographic experts group)

groupware   Software designed to run on a network and allow groups of people to work together in a collaborative fashion regardless of their physical proximity to one another. Lotus Notes is groupware.

helper application   Small programs that work in tandem with a Web browser to complete an action or an effect. When a link on a Web page is associated with a file that runs on a helper application, the browser automatically launches that application and the file runs in the application's separate window. This is different from plug-ins, which run as part of the browser window. (*See also* plug-in)

hit   A means of measuring the number of files requested from your server. Each hit represents a request for a single file. If your Web page has two graphics and a Java applet, four hits will be recorded each time that page is accessed: one for the page itself, one for each of the graphics, and one for the applet.

home page   The entryway or starting point for a World Wide Web (or intranet) site. The first page someone sees when visiting your site is generally named *index.html,* and is almost always the home page.

host   A computer that has full two-way access to other computers on the Internet. Hosts are assigned Internet Protocol (IP) addresses made up of a local number and the network number.

hyperlink   Text produced in HTML that is tagged to be presented as a link to another element. Hyperlinks (shortened from the original *hypertext link*) can take you to another part of the same page, another page on the same site, another page on another Web site, a non-Web document (such as a word processor file), or a multimedia element. Links that go to a multimedia element are often referred to as *hypermedia.*

hypertext markup language (HTML)   The scripting code used to create Web pages. HTML is supposed to be a standard code—that is, the script produced for any Web page will produce similar results in any browser. That standardization is controlled by the World Wide Web Consortium. However, in their competitive efforts, Microsoft and Netscape continually add new features as elements of new browser versions; they hope to have the features incorporated into the next official standard iteration of HTML. The current HTML version is 3.2; the next version probably will be 4.0.

hypertext transfer protocol (HTTP)   The TCP/IP protocol that makes the World Wide Web work on the Internet. HTTP governs the treatment of files—including graphics, text, sound, and video—between Web servers and browsers.

imagemap   Hot spots on a Web page that allow you to click on a part of a graphic that is hyperlinked to another destination are enabled by imagemaps. Imagemaps designate the coordinates of the hot spots and incorporate the links themselves. There are two types of imagemaps: Client-side imagemaps are built into the HTML code and are enacted directly by the browser. Server-side imagemaps are more complex, requiring a separate file with hot-spot coordinates to be stored on the server.

impression   Each time an HTML page is requested from a server. Different from hits, which records only individual files requested from a server, impressions are more valuable to communicators who need to know how many times a page has been viewed.

information technology (IT)   A common acronym for the departments within organizations that are responsible for computer-related activities. The term also relates to any technology used to create, store, exchange, and use information.

integrated services digital network (ISDN)   A means of sending data over regular telephone lines at speeds higher than possible using a modem. If you have an ISDN line, you also need a terminal adapter or a router to convert the data to information you can view on your computer screen.

intelligent agent   (*See* agent)

interactive voice response (IVR)   Computerized system that walks callers through a series of prompts to obtain information from recordings over the telephone.

interactivity   The exchange between a computer and the individual using it. Various programs and applications have varying degrees of interactivity, with games at the high end and productivity tools like word processors at the low end. The World Wide Web is popular in large part because it provides tremendous levels of interactivity to users.

interface   The various elements on the computer screen (including text, buttons, and other tools) that allow you to interact with the program or application you are using. The verb version of the word *interface* generally means to interact or communicate with someone or something.

Internet   The global network of computer networks that are interconnected using the TCP/IP suite of protocols.

Internet protocol (IP)   This is the set of rules that is responsible for the address of each packet of information sent from one computer to another on the Internet.

Internet relay chat (IRC)   The system for real-time dialogue between people on the Internet. IRC allows individuals to establish chat rooms, with names that identify the topic under discussion. Individuals "enter" the room and engage in real-time chat by typing back and forth to one another.

Internet service provider (ISP)   A business that provides access to the Internet for individuals and businesses. (You would use an ISP if your organization does not have its own point of presence on the Internet.) When you dial a number to connect to the Internet, you are dialing one of your ISP's modem numbers. ISPs provide a range of services, including hosting Web sites.

Internet telephony   The use of the Internet for voice telephone calls, faxes, and other activities generally associated with the telephone. Since a connection to the Internet is almost always a local call, long-distance charges evaporate when you use the Internet; however, you do sacrifice sound clarity and usually experience a short delay when the party at the other end speaks.

intranet   The principles and protocols of the Internet applied to a private network within your organization for the exclusive use of employees (and, in some cases, other select audiences, such as suppliers and strategic partners).

IP address   A 32-bit number that identifies each sender and/or receiver of information that is sent in packets across the Internet.

Java   A programming language developed by Sun Microsystems that can be executed on a Web browser by any computer regardless of the platform it uses. The programs developed in Java are called *applets,* and run directly in the browser window. Java applets can produce animation, interactivity, and a number of other Web programs.

Java development kit (JDK)   A software development package from Sun Microsystems that implements the basic set of tools needed to write, test, and debug Java applications and applets.

Javascript   Not to be confused with Java, Javascript is a scripting language developed by Netscape that can be incorporated into Web pages. Javascript is used to create functionality on Web pages that range from images that change when you roll a cursor over them to automatically changing pages (such as changing to the current date).

joint photographic experts group (JPEG)   JPEG is a format for displaying graphic images on Web pages. JPEG files (which have the extension *jpg*) are better for photographs than GIF, which is better for clip art.

Jughead   A tool used for searching gopherspace. This search utility is similar to Veronica, another search facility. Both are named after characters from the Archie comic book series.

junk e-mail   Also known as *spam,* this is unsolicited e-mail that comes to your in-box, usually trying to sell you something. (*See also* spam)

K–12   Kindergarten through twelfth grade. A designation used to identify the purpose of a Web page or other online resource (for example, "This site is an ideal K–12 resource.")

killer application (killer app)   An application or program that becomes so popular, useful, or necessary that it induces people to buy computers and install networks in order to use it. Many people have bought computers to exchange e-mail, making e-mail the killer app of the Internet.

kilobit   A thousand bits.

kilobits (kbps)   Thousands of bits per second. A measure of bandwidth. A 28.8 modem transmits data from the Internet to your computer at 28,800 kbps.

kilobyte (KB)   About a thousand bytes.

kiosk   A common location for a computer, keyboard, and monitor where people can access information. Kiosks are generally perceived as high-tech structures, such as those found at entrances to malls, hospitals, and high-rise buildings. However, a kiosk can also be a table or a cubicle containing a computer. The only requirement to qualify as a kiosk is that the system be available to groups of people who are in physical proximity to the kiosk.

kludge   A patchwork solution to a technology problem.

leased line   A telephone line that is rented for exclusive use, twenty-four hours a day, seven days a week, from your location to another location. Required for the highest-speed data connections.

legacy   Applications and data that was produced for the last technology but still exists within the enterprise. Information technology departments are routinely challenged to keep legacy data useful even though the technology used to store and use the data has changed.

lightweight directory access protocol (LDAP)   A software rule enabling anyone to locate organizations, individuals, and other resources (for example, files and devices in a network) whether on the public Internet or on a corporate intranet. The "lightweight" designation means that it contains less code than DAP, which is the more complex directory access protocol.

Linux   An open-source operating system that has been installed on many Internet servers and a variety of other devices. (*See* open source)

Listserv   As a proper noun, Listserv is a program that is used to manage e-mail mailing lists. As a common noun, it is a generic name for all programs that manage e-mail mailing lists. In both cases, users subscribe to the list by sending an e-mail message to the listserv. Subsequently, any messages sent to the mailing list are distributed by the listserv to all subscribers.

livecam   A computer attached directly to a computer and linked (usually) to a Web site to display a current image. Also known as Webcams, these cameras are used to show progress on a construction project or how a particular landmark (like the Wailing Wall in Jerusalem) looks at any given moment.

local area network (LAN)   A network of computers connected to a single server that exists within a small geographic space. Individuals on the same floor or in the same building might be on a LAN.

log   A file that records each individual request for a file that a server has received. Also known as an *access log*.

login   Noun: The account name used to gain access to a computer system. Verb: The act of logging in to a computer system.

lurk   To read posts in a discussion group (such as a Usenet newsgroup) without posting an article of your own. Lurking gives you the opportunity to get the lay of the land, learn the culture of the group, and find out who the influential participants are. As long as you don't post a message, nobody will know you visited.

mail bomb   The practice of sending huge amounts of e-mail to a person or address with the sole intent of punishing somebody, usually for sending spam (unsolicited e-mail) or breeching netiquette. Mail bombs can cause entire servers to crash, affecting everybody who uses the server, not only the offending party.

mailing list   A list of people who subscribe to a listserv. (*See* Listserv)

mainframe   A large computer that handles the heavy-duty computing activities of businesses.

markup Characters inserted into text files that will be interpreted by a program to determine how the text (and other elements) should be displayed. The characters that constitute the markup are called *tags*. In HTML, the markup language that gives World Wide Web pages their appearance, <b> is a tag that designates type should appear in bold face. Thus, the following line would appear in bold face on a Web browser: <b>This is bold-face type.</b>

Mbone A portion of the Internet that has been reserved for the distribution of audio or video files to multiple users at the same time. The technical term for the distribution is *IP multicasting*.

megabit A million bits.

megabyte About a million bytes.

megabytes (Mbps) Millions of bits per second. A measure of bandwidth.

megahertz (MHz or Mhz) The clock speeds of computer microprocessors are designated by their megahertz rating.

meme Taken from the biological notion introduced by Richard Dawkins, a meme is an adaptive mechanism that permits humans to pass ideas from one generation to the next. On the Internet, a meme is a statement that becomes accepted as fact and takes on a life of its own despite dedicated efforts to correct inaccuracies. For example, the urban myth of the Good Times virus, which is a hoax, has become a meme; it keeps cropping up despite the fact that the hoax has been soundly discredited.

Microsoft Internet Explorer (MSIE) Microsoft's Web browser.

mirror site A Web site that has been copied and placed on another server to reduce traffic to the original server and make files available from a server located geographically closer to the individuals who might want to access them.

modem A device that interprets analog data transmitted over a regular telephone line into information that can be viewed on the computer. The word comes from *modulator demodulator,* since the modem demodulates the analog signal and converts it to a digital signal the computer can understand; and modulates a digital signal from the computer, converting it into an analog signal to send it to somebody else via modem.

MOO An object-oriented MUD. (*See* multiuser dungeon)

Moore's law Posited by Gordon Moore, founder of Intel, Moore's law suggests that the amount of storage possible on a microchip will double every eighteen months. Moore's law is the basis for the speed with which state-of-the-art computer technology becomes obsolete.

Mosaic   The first World Wide Web browser, distributed in late 1993 by a graduate student team at the National Center for Supercomputing Applications at the University of Illinois. The team was led by Mark Andreesen, who later became a senior executive at Netscape.

mouseover   The act of rolling your mouse over an object on the computer screen resulting in the image changing. You can create the mouseover effect using Javascript. (*See* Javascript)

moving picture experts group (MPEG)   The format for compressing video for transmission over the Internet.

multicast   Data that is transmitted from one point to many points simultaneously. Used for video and audio transmissions, as well as for routine updates, such as a sales staff's database. (*See* Mbone)

multimedia   Multiple media employed in a single presentation. A Web site that uses graphic images, text, and sound is a multimedia Web site.

multitasking   Doing more than one thing at a time. In computing terms, multitasking is a function of a computer that can be engaged simultaneously in multiple tasks. For example, you can receive a fax and work on a spreadsheet at the same time.

multiuser dungeon (MUD)   A text-based virtual environment that provides a social environment on the Internet. The structure of a MUD can allow those who build it to create multiple rooms with objects in them that can be occupied by people who visit the MUD. The metaphors employed can be as widely varied as a conference facility or a medieval castle. Those who visit the MUD can interact with each other as well as with the objects that have been created and placed in the MUD's various rooms.

multiuser simulated environment (MUSE)   Another version of a MUD. (*See also* multiuser dungeon)

native   Original.

Netcaster   The so-called push technology adopted by Netscape for its Navigator Web browser.

netiquette   Standards of behavior established for the Internet, applied generally to newsgroup communities and e-mail. A combination of *network* and *etiquette*.

netizen   A member of the Internet community, notably one who participates in general discussions about the Internet and its governance. Also refers to people on the Internet who use the network as a means of engaging in political debate and decision making. A combination of *network* and *citizen*.

Netscape   Netscape Communications Corporation, the company that makes and sells the Navigator browser. Navigator is often called Netscape, but the word specifically refers to the company, not the browser. Netscape also makes server software and other related products.

network   Computers or other networks connected to one another, or combinations of computers and networks connected to one another.

network computer (NC)   A computer designed to be linked to a network. The NC contains few elements of its own, such as a hard disk, a CD-ROM, or a disk drive. Instead, it would be managed from the server to which it is connected, and any applications that run are downloaded from the server. Designed to be inexpensive (under $500), NCs were initially introduced by Oracle and Sun as an alternative to Microsoft's Windows operating system.

network news transfer protocol (NNTP)   The protocol that governs Usenet newsgroups on the Internet.

newbie   Somebody who is new to the Internet. Also refers to any new user of any technology. Experienced users often grow impatient with newbies and their seemingly endless flow of questions, and refer to them as "clueless" newbies.

newsgroup   A virtual community facilitated by the Usenet system, comprising individuals who share an interest in a specific topic. The Usenet hierarchy starts with a broad description of the kinds of topics included, such as *rec* (recreational), *soc* (societal), and *sci* (scientific). Descending levels of the hierarchy are used to identify the specific topic under discussion (such as *soc.culture.pakistan.history*, where interested participants can discuss the cultural history of Pakistan).

node   A connection point on the Internet.

object-oriented   A form of computer programming that focuses on data "objects" and their relationships rather than on the procedures operating on the data.

online service   Also known as a proprietary service. Online services provide access to the Internet through their own proprietary interface, and often offer their own content. Examples of online services are CompuServe, America Online, and the Microsoft Network.

open source   A system where the underlying code has been made publicly available. Anybody can develop applications for the system, and (in many cases) it is standardized. The Internet is an open system. Lotus Notes is not an open system; it is proprietary, because IBM (which owns Lotus) retains the source code and only authorized institutions can develop Notes applications.

operating system (OS)   The program that makes a computer work. DOS, Windows, UNIX, Linux, and Mac OS are examples of operating systems. The OS manages the operations of all other programs on a computer.

packet   A unit of data that is sent from a computer to another point. Generally, when a file is sent over a packet-switching-based network, the file is deconstructed into small (32-bit) units of data, each of which is an individual packet. Each packet takes the fastest route at the instant it is sent. When the packets arrive at their destination, they are reassembled with other packets so the recipient can view the entire file.

page   A single HTML file on the Web. A Web site is made up of multiple pages.

palette   The colors that a Web browser is designed to display. Colors included in images that do not match these colors are dithered to approximate the desired color as closely as possible.

password   A code used to gain access to a secure system.

peer-to-peer (P2P)   A transient Internet network that allows a group of computer users with the same networking program to connect with each other and directly access files from one another's hard drives without benefit of a central server. Napster is a form of P2P, as is the new groupware application Groove (*www.groove.net*).

PERL   A scripting language used by programmers primarily to allow a Web page to include programming elements, such as calculations and retrieval of information from databases.

pixel   The unit of measure for computer screens. Screen resolution is defined as the number of pixels that appear horizontally and vertically on the screen. The standard resolution of 640 by 480 means that 640 pixels will fit on the screen horizontally, and 480 will fit vertically. The pixel is the smallest unit or image on the screen. Color images are made up of pixels, each of which contains only one color.

plain old telephone service (POTS)   The standard telephone service, as opposed to newer technologies, such as ISDN.

platform   The system that makes the computer work. Platforms include an operating system (such as Windows 95) and a microprocessor (such as the Intel Pentium II). The Mac OS will not work on the Intel Pentium II, just as Windows 95 will not work on the Motorola chip that powers Macintosh computers. The Windows/Intel platform has come to be known as *Wintel*.

plug-in (or plugin)   A small program that is executed as part of a Web browser (as opposed to a *helper application,* which runs in a separate window).

point of presence (**POP**)   A point of access to the Internet. Each POP has a unique IP address.

port 80   The default port (the place on a computer that is connected to another device) on a Web server that receives requests from browsers.

portal   A starting point, such as an opening Web page that serves as the gateway to other content. On intranets, portal now means a customizable gateway that uses an employee's profile to configure a page that provides access to the online resources that employee is most likely to need.

post office protocol 3 (**POP3**)   Not to be confused with POP, POP3 is post office protocol 3, the standard protocol for receiving e-mail. (Simple mail transfer protocol (SMTP) is the protocol for *sending* e-mail.)

posting (or post)   A single message added to a discussion group.

presence   When you have a Web site dedicated to your organization, a product, an issue, or any other particular topic, you have a *presence* on the Internet.

pretty good privacy (**PGP**)   A tool for encrypting messages that can only be decrypted by the individual for whom it was intended.

protocol   Rules that govern the means by which data is transmitted across a network. TCP/IP is the suite of protocols that governs the Internet. Protocols that are part of this suite govern e-mail, network news, the Web, and other elements of the Net.

proxy   A device that resides on a firewall or gateway that handles requests for information. The proxy server operates based on customized instructions that determine what type of information will be allowed in and out of the network. Companies use proxy servers to restrict access to objectionable or non-work-related Web sites, for example.

push   Technology that allows Web-based information to be delivered to you without you initiating a request for the information. In general, *push* is the model that characterizes e-mail, while the Web encourages you to *pull* information. However, technologies continue to be introduced that help information providers push their Web-based information, often after users have signified their interest in having the information pushed to them.

Quicktime   Apple Computer developed this process for viewing audio/video/animation on a computer screen. Quicktime has been incorporated into the Web as a means of integrating video clips into a Web page.

RealAudio   Streaming audio and video technology developed by Progressive Networks, RealAudio is the *de facto* streaming technology on the Web. (*See also* streaming)

robust   Refers to either a system that is strong or one that is designed with a full complement of capabilities.

router   A combination of hardware and software on the Internet that determines where a packet should be sent next.

scalability   The ability of a computer system to function well when it grows or shrinks.

search engines   A utility that allows you to search the contents of the World Wide Web, Usenet newsgroups, and other Internet data, based on a query you construct. There are two types of search engines. One is a directory, in which people intervene to categorize Web sites. If you want information on how to get a passport, you would start with the "government" category and drill down. The other is an engine, which scours the Web, gathering all the pages it can find and indexing the words on each page. When you search an engine, the utility searches for all pages that contain the word or words you request. Finding information on how to get a passport on an engine would involve conducting a search based on a string of words like, "passport obtain new."

secure sockets layer (SSL)   Netscape Communications designed this protocol that enables encrypted, authenticated communications to move across the Internet.

server   A combination of hardware and software that responds to requests from clients. Servers are configured to serve up Web pages, e-mail, newsgroups, and other elements.

shareware   Software that is available for downloading to allow you to try it before you buy it. Most shareware works on the honor system; if you continue to use it, you are expected to pay for it, but if you don't, you can still continue to use it. Recently, some shareware programs have been equipped with time-out functions that render them useless after a specified trial period (usually thirty days).

Shockwave   A Web plug-in that allows you to view multimedia files developed in Macromedia Director. Shockwave is commonly used for combinations of animation and sound, but also allows the user to manipulate the image. Thus, Shockwave is popular for games that can be played directly from a Web page.

shovelware   Content that is converted to HTML without any change to its structure or substance, and simply "shoveled" onto the Web.

simple mail transfer protocol (SMTP)   The protocol for sending e-mail.

site   Any self-contained collection of Web pages, comprising the total "book" on a given topic. A collection of pages that addresses a company's line of business is a company Web site.

smiley   Any ASCII text character used to convey an emotion. Used in e-mail and in newsgroups as a substitute for facial expressions. Smileys are viewed sideways. The most common smiley is a smiling face used to connote happiness or joy: :-)

   If you tilt your head to the left, you see that the colon is the eyes, the dash is the nose, and the close parenthesis is the smiling mouth. Smileys were popular as the Internet grew, but have been used less and less as people have learned to express themselves in e-mail. Smileys also are known as *emoticons*.

spam   Unsolicited e-mail sent in bulk to many e-mail addresses, usually for advertising purposes. (The name comes from a Monty Python routine, in which a waiter describing the restaurant's offerings increasingly adds the word *spam* to the listing until the entire description is nothing but spam.)

splash screen   The first Web page you see when you go to a site when the page is designed to capture your attention. These often introduce the site, before automatically loading the actual home page. In other instances, you see the splash page that contains a link to the home page.

streaming   A format for sending video and audio files over the Internet in real time. When you retrieve a video or audio stream, you can see or hear the file as it reaches your computer, without having to wait for the entire file to download first.

streaming media   Also, streaming audio and streaming video. A stream is a multimedia file (audio or video) that "streams" from the server to the desktop in real time. Media that does not stream must be fully downloaded before it can be viewed or heard, but streaming media begins playing almost immediately.

structured query language (SQL)   A standard language for using a database in a network environment.

style sheet   Inserted into HTML code, a style sheet defines the characteristics of type that appears on the page. (*See also* cascading style sheet)

surf   The act of following hyperlinks from one Web page to another. Adapted from the term *channel surfing*, which is the act of clicking through television stations with a remote control device. Surfing suggests a random approach to viewing pages as opposed to a structured search for specific information.

system A collection of computer elements (for example, hardware, software, or connectivity tools) that combine to serve a common purpose.

system operator (Sysop) An individual who runs a computer server, although the term is generally associated with the individual responsible for a privately operated BBS. Additionally, individuals who manage discussion forums on CompuServe are known as sysops.

T1, T3 A telephone company–provided line that delivers Internet data directly to your building, eliminating the need for an Internet service provider and requiring you to obtain and configure the hardware and software to essentially become an ISP for your own employees. T-1 lines transmit data at 1.544 Mbps and T-3 lines at 44.736 Mbps.

tag Text that is used in markup to define how text should be treated. (*See also* hyperlink, hypertext markup language)

telnet A method by which you gain entry into another (host) computer on the Internet.

terabyte About a thousand gigabytes.

thin In terms of a client, a low-cost, centrally managed computer with no accessories such as hard drives or CD-ROM drives. These computers get and store data from a central server. A thin server is a computer with just enough hardware and software to support a single specific function that users can share on a network.

thread The elements of an online discussion (in a newsgroup or forum), in the order in which they were added. Threaded discussion outlines show each post along with the responses, usually by indenting responses. In this way, you can determine the levels of the discussion.

TIF (or TIFF) A graphics file format, common for high-resolution graphic images but not viewable on a standard Web browser.

transmission control protocol (TCP) TCP tracks the packets of data that move across the Internet.

transmission control protocol/Internet protocol (TCP/IP) Used to designate the family of protocols that define the various functions of the Internet.

uniform resource locator (URL) The address you type into a Web browser to retrieve a page from a server.

Unix A computer operating system with the TCP/IP protocols built in. Many servers running on the Internet use Unix as their operating system.

Usenet The system of asynchronous discussion groups on the Internet. (*See also* network news transfer protocol) vaporware   Software that a company has described and promised, but that has not yet been produced. Many software companies float the idea of a software package to assess its viability in the marketplace. Vaporware also is used to describe software that has not been released by the official release date.

Veronica   A utility for searching gopherspace. (*See also* gopherspace, gopher, Jughead)

videoconference   A conference in which parties in different cities interact with one another by viewing each other on a television or computer screen. Videoconferences can involve groups or individuals (for example, one-on-one) conferencing. Previously an expensive television-based system, the Internet has led to the development of computer-based videoconferencing that is comparatively inexpensive.

virtual   Of the computer instead of "real." A virtual meeting would be one that took place over the computer (such as a videoconference) instead of person-to-person in a conference room.

virtual private network (VPN)   A private network that runs using public systems, including the Internet. If you run a VPN, you save your organization the cost of having to install a "real" private network.

virtual reality modeling language (VRML)   A scripting language that allows you to create three-dimensional environments that can run on the World Wide Web.

virus   A program that "infects" your computer. Viruses are generally attached to other programs that you might download or obtain from an infected disk. When they are activated, they launch activities that range from the harmless (such as displaying a message) to the devastating (like wiping out your hard drive). You can prevent most viruses from infecting your computer by installing an antivirus program, and keeping it updated with current virus definitions.

Web site   A collection of Web pages that combine to form a complete entity. As the pages of a book form the entire book, so the pages of a Web site comprise the entire site.

Webcast   The delivery of a broadcast (live or delayed) over the World Wide Web.

Webcasting   The scheduled updating of news or information accomplished by pushing the information to your desktop via the World Wide Web. (*See also* push)

Webmaster   A nebulous term that has little meaning, but generally describes the individual with responsibility for a Web site or server. The meaning of the term varies, including the individual responsible for content, infrastructure, or both.

Wide Area Information System (WAIS) A commercial software package that allows indexing of vast quantities of information, and then making the package searchable across networks like the Internet.

wide area network (WAN) A collection of local area networks that are interconnected, providing each LAN with access to the others. A WAN also can be a collection of private networks that are linked together.

wireless Access to online or telecommunication services through signals carried over the air, rather than through wires.

wireless application protocol (WAP) The protocol for delivering online content over wireless devices such as handheld computers and digital cell phones.

wireless markup language The scripting language used to create content to be distributed over wireless devices, such as handheld computers and digital cell phones.

workstation A computer for individual use.

World Wide Web (WWW) The universe of resources on the Internet available by using the HTTP protocol. (*See also* hypertext transfer protocol)

XHTML Extensible hypertext markup language, which is a reformulation of HTML 4.0 as an application of the extensible markup language. (*See* XML)

XML Extensible markup language, the successor to HTML. The tags in XML define the nature of data instead of how it should be displayed. XML will increase the Web's capability of handling data.

zine (*See* e-zine)

zip A format for compressing data to reduce its size before transmitting it over a network. Reducing the size of a file means it can be transmitted more quickly, and the recipient can download it faster. When you retrieve a file that has been zipped, you need to unzip it by using software designed for that purpose.